Emphasis Art

A Qualitative Art Program for Elementary and Middle Schools

SEVENTH EDITION

Frank Wachowiak

Late of University of Georgia

Robert D. Clements

University of Georgia

Longman

New York   San Francisco   Boston
London   Toronto   Sydney   Tokyo   Singapore   Madrid
Mexico City   Munich   Paris   Cape Town   Hong Kong   Montreal

Publisher: Priscilla McGeehon
Acquisitions Editor: Virginia L. Blanford
Development Editor: Barbara A. Conover
Senior Production Manager: Valerie Zaborski
Project Coordination, Text Design, and Electronic Page Makeup:
    Elm Street Publishing Services, Inc.
Cover Designer/Manager: Nancy Danahy
Cover Illustration: Courtesy of Baiba Kuntz, Glencoe, IL.
    Kay Solomon, Grade 5.
Senior Manufacturing Buyer: Dennis J. Para
Printer and Binder: R. R. Donnelley and Sons Company
Cover Printer: The Lehigh Press, Inc.

Library of Congress Cataloging-in-Publication Data

Wachowiak, Frank.
    Emphasis art : a qualitative art program for elementary and middle
schools / Frank Wachowiak, Robert D. Clements.—7th ed.
        p. cm.
    Includes bibliographical references and index.
    ISBN 0-321-02351-X
    1. Art—Study and teaching (Elementary) 2. Art—Study and teaching
(Middle school) I. Clements, Robert D. II. Title.

N350.W26 2001
372.5'2044—dc21

                                    00-026666

Please visit our website at http://www.awl.com

ISBN 0-321-02351-X

1 2 3 4 5 6 7 8 9 10—DOW—03 02 01 00

Contents

Chapter 17

Chapter 18

PART 5

Chapter 19

Chapter 20

Chapter 21

PART 6

Chapter 22

To children everywhere who make the teaching of art a never-ending, forever-rewarding adventure, and to their teachers, in both elementary and middle schools, who share in the wonder and discovery. With special thanks to teachers of art around the world and to former students, now teachers and professors of art, who have been so generous in sharing the results of their teaching to help make this book a colorful treasury of child art.

 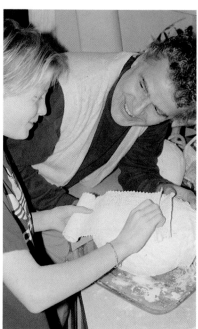

FRANK WACHOWIAK   ROBERT CLEMENTS

Preface

The seventh edition of *Emphasis Art* has its origin in Frank Wachowiak's teaching of art to children, beginning with his first elementary-school art classes in rural Minnesota and continuing for the next 50 years. His passion for a life in art was shown as he said, "I was born in 1913, the year of the Armory Show." After receiving his M.A. degree, he did his first art teaching, but service in the Navy interrupted his teaching career until after the war and after he had received his M.F.A. degree. In the happy, charged environment of children's searching, discovering, and creating as he taught and studied children's art all over the world (especially at the University of Iowa Lab School and the University of Georgia Children's Art Classes), he found that it was easy to stay young at heart. Frank passed away in August 1998, just two weeks after we signed the contract for this seventh edition of *Emphasis Art*. His inspiring words, the beautiful examples of children's art, and his clear technical directions, of course, continue in this new edition.

As in the last previous editions for which I have been responsible, Frank Wachowiak's belief in the intrinsic worth of the art-studio experience remains central; however, I have added considerably more material on current approaches to art education. The emphasis is on art—art as an adventure, a flowering, a celebration, and a discipline with its own singular demands, unique core of learning, and incomparable rewards.

The reader familiar with the sixth edition of the book will notice nine major areas of change in this seventh edition.

1. The chapters on teaching in general have been moved near the book's beginning, since these chapters usually are read near the beginning of a course.
2. This edition brings an expanded coverage of evaluation and assessment. Evaluation of Objectives, as a topic, is covered in expanded Chapter 32, and examples of evaluation instruments are given. The

material on instructional objectives has been revised and integrated into this chapter.

3. A new Chapter 6, Educational Psychology Considerations on Children's Development, precedes and sets the stage for the chapters on sequential curriculum for specific grade levels. It especially focuses on the theories of the constructivists.

4. Because states are increasingly funding kindergarten programs and teachers are teaching art at this level, a new Chapter 7 discusses art for kindergarten.

5. Chapter 12 on Art for Students Experiencing Significant Mental or Physical Disabilities has been expanded, with additional coverage of strategies for helping students with disabilities. Chapter 13 on giftedness has been revised to include new findings on creativity.

6. One major thrust of education in our day is the increased attention to how general elementary classroom teachers can integrate art with other subjects. The two chapters added in the last edition gave recommendations for integrating art learning and learning in science and social studies. Now, suggestions for integrating art with other subjects have been expanded in a new Part 4, Art's Content: Integration with Other Subjects. A section on mathematics integration is included in Chapter 15: Science, Math, and Art. The integration of the arts (art, drama, and music) is now a separate Chapter 18, as are reading and visual literacy, now Chapter 17. Chapter 16 on social studies includes multicultural issues.

7. A few decades ago art centered on art issues such as abstraction, modernism, and formalism. In recent years, both art and art education have turned increasingly to an examination of social, cultural, historical, and political issues. While this new emphasis occurs throughout the book, it is mainly put forward in Chapter 16, Social Studies, Multicultural Inquiry, and Art Integration. Of course, in truth, these two approaches—art as art and art in context—really do interconnect. One cannot stand without the other.

8. Art educators have identified art criticism, art history, and aesthetics as the formal disciplines that can best aid students in art education. These three areas, along with studio production, comprise the elements of discipline-based art education (DBAE), and many state education department policies mandate that art education treat the four areas of art criticism, art history, aesthetics, and art production. In recent times DBAE has wrestled with how to incorporate multiculturalism; these incorporations appear in Chapters 16 and 21. Additional coverage of non-Western cultures and art also has been included.

9. In Part 6, Teaching Art, a new section on markers has been added to Chapter 22 on Drawing. The section Computer Art has been expanded and includes numerous Websites for the study of art and art history.

10. A new companion Website to the text provides a wealth of resources for both students and instructors.

The response of educators at all levels to the sixth edition of *Emphasis Art* has been gratifyingly positive. The book's clarity, structure, and wealth of colorful illustrations have found enthusiastic endorsement. The art teaching strategies, motivations, techniques, and evaluative procedures described in the text are based on actual experiences and observations of outstanding elementary- and middle-school art practices both in this country and abroad. This new edition again concerns itself with the adventures, joys, responsibilities, problems, and rewards of teaching art to children; with the strategic, guiding role of the teacher; and with the ongoing evaluation of lesson objectives in design and composition, art history, art criticism, and aesthetics. In many chapters, new illustrations have been added showing the work of students in today's schools.

Emphasis Art is designed first and foremost for elementary- and middle-school teachers of art who want to augment and enrich their art programs. It also is proposed as a text for the college or university student in search of high-caliber elementary- and middle-school art practices. It offers a lucid description of a proven, dynamic program for those veteran teachers who seek continuing challenges, new techniques, and classroom-tested art projects for their instructional repertoire.

Acknowledgments

I wish to particularly acknowledge the contributions of three teachers who have been especially helpful in this seventh edition: new contributor Beverly Mallon, Chase Street Elementary School, Athens, GA, and continuing contributors Joyce Vroon, Trinity School, Atlanta, and Baiba Kuntz, Glencoe, IL, for many new and continuing illustrations.

I wish to acknowledge the contributions of two professors who coauthored earlier editions. Without the shared efforts of these authors and Frank Wachowiak, the earlier book(s) would not have come into being: Theodore K. Ramsay, Professor of Art, University of Michigan, Ann Arbor, coauthor of the first and second editions of *Emphasis Art;* and David Hodge, Emeritus Professor of Art, University of Wisconsin, Oshkosh, coauthor of the now out-of-print *Art in Depth.*

Other new contributors include: Jenni Horne, Flat Rock Middle School, Tyrone, GA; Katrina Bonds, Austell, GA; and Gwenda Malnati and Eric Hamilton, Athens Montessori School, have shared slides for the new edition. Also, my appreciation goes to the Crayola® Dream-Makers® program.

For continuing permission to use illustrations, many thanks also go to Dr. Melody Milbrandt, West Georgia State University, Carrollton, GA;

Barbara Thomas, Gainesville, GA; Jackie Ellett, Rockbridge Elementary School, Gwinnett County Schools, GA; Debby Lackey, Fulton County Schools, Atlanta; Donna Cummins, Rockview Elementary School, Atlanta; Carol Case, Cobb County Schools, GA; Alisa Hyde, Savannah, GA; Julie Phlegar, East St. Tammany Parish School District, Slidell, LA; and Sharon Burns-Knutson, Iowa City Schools, IA. Thanks to ongoing contributions from Faye Brassie, Nancy Elliott, David Harvell, and Mary Lazzari—all from the Athens, GA, schools. Thanks to those who taught with Frank Wachowiak in his University of Georgia children's art classes and who have continued to give permission to use artworks: Dr. Mary Hammond, Athens, GA; and Dr. Patrick Taylor, Kennesaw, GA. Other teachers throughout the nation have works reproduced: Shirley Lucas, Oshkosh, WI; Alice Ballard Munn, Anchorage, AK; Ted Oliver, Marietta, GA; Carolyn Shapiro, Brookline, MA; Mary E. Swanson, Nashua, NH; and Dr. Lawrence Stueck, Watkinsville, GA. For assistance with 77 child art pictures, thanks to Dr. Barry Moore, Curator of the International Collection of Child Art and Professor of Art Emeritus, Illinois State University, Normal, IL. The USSEA Art Collection of Dr. Anne Gregory, Los Angeles Public Schools, is represented by works of students of Barbara Bluhm, Maine, and Susan Whipple, Oregon Christian School. My colleagues at the University of Georgia who are involved in art education also have helped: Dr. W. Robert Nix, Dr. Carole Henry, Dr. Andra Johnson, and Dr. Diane Rives. My wife, Dr. Claire Clements, has contributed student artworks, as well as constant encouragement.

The beauty of this book has also been made possible through the contributions of art teachers from around the world: Chen Huei-Tung, Tainan, Taiwan; Jean Grant, coordinator, arts and humanities, Department of Defense Dependents' Schools (DODDS), Atlantic Region; Eric Ma Presado, Manila, Philippines; James McGrath, coordinator, arts and humanities, DODDS, Pacific Region; George Mitchell, Atlanta; Federico Moroni, Santarcangelo, Italy; Michihisa Kosugi, Saga, Japan; Norihisa Nakase, art education liaison, Tokyo, Japan; Michael F. O'Brien, American High School, Seoul, Korea; and Linda Riddle, Heidelberg, West Germany. For permission to use published material, thanks to Masachi Shimono, editor, *Nihon Bunkyo Suppan,* Osaka, Japan; and Professor Osamu Muro, Executive Director, *Art Education Magazine,* Tokyo, Japan. Nostell Priory, Yorkshire, England; the Boston Museum of Fine Art; and the National Gallery of Art and the Hirshhorn Museum in Washington, DC, among others, have given permission to reproduce artworks in their collections.

I would also like to thank the following reviewers for their comments and suggestions during the revision process: George Geahigan, *Purdue University;* Gaye Green, *Western Washington University;* Cheryl Grossman, *University of Missouri-Kansas City;* Julia Marshall, *San Francisco State University;* Ruth McBride, *Colorado State University;* Michael Smith, *University of North Florida;* Dennis Taylor, *Southern Illinois University at Carbondale;* and Leo Twiggs, *South Carolina State University.* To the members of the editorial and production staffs at Addison Wesley Longman, and Elm Street Publishing Services my grateful acknowledgment for their contributions—especially those of Acquisitions Editor Ginny Blanford, Developmental Editor Barbara Conover, and Production Editor Ingrid Mount.

Robert D. Clements
rclements@home.com

PART 1

INTRODUCTION TO ART

Previous page: *Third- and fourth-grade students are proud of their class-painted mural showing them playing ball, jumping rope, flying kites, and skating together. Notice the space created by overlapping and diminishing sizes of figures and objects in the foreground, middle ground, and background.*

Chapter 1

THE ROLE OF ART IN SOCIETY AND IN THE SCHOOLS

Art education fulfills many important functions of schooling. Ten rationales for art education in the schools and in society are discussed briefly. They are not mutually exclusive, but instead overlap each other. Also, other writers might refer to these rationales by different names.

Cultural Understanding

On the one hand, art is an international language; it is universally accessible even to those with little knowledge of how it was used in a culture. Through its organization and content, it communicates meaning without words. On the other hand, because it comes from a specific culture, art is relative to the time, place, and circumstances of its creation. For the members of any cultural group, art provides a mirror, reflecting the group's unique sense of cultural identity. Indeed, art is one of the main ways cultural identity is transmitted, maintained, and analyzed.

Culture is more than a people's artistic, musical, food, holiday, and historical heritage, however. It also is the shared values, attitudes, belief systems, and cognitive styles that affect and direct a society's behavior and give meaning to life. Art is both intentionally and unintentionally a carrier of such cultural value and meaning, encoded in a sensuous medium. The symbolic relationships shown define religions and social structures.

Although art communicates some of its meaning across eras and cultures, its creation is relative to its culture. It helps to create a sense of cultural community and identity. **Top:** *Dropped Bowl with Scattered Slices and Peels, 1989, Claes Oldenburg and Coosje van Bruggen, Art in Public Places Program, Miami, FL.* **Middle:** *Native-American kachina.* **Bottom:** *Mola (reverse appliqué) by San Blas Indians.*

3

The shared aspirations of many are shown in the mural which artist Eddie Edwards and students at Martin Luther King Elementary School, San Diego, created about Reverend King's dream, "We shall overcome." It is described in Kay Wagner's article, "A Mural Worth a Million Words," School Arts Magazine, *January 1991.*

In summary, art helps students understand that there is a connection between an artwork's content and form and the culture and time in which it was created. It helps students see culture as an interpretive social scheme that people project upon existence in order to create their own identity.

National Needs

Our nation needs citizens who can think for themselves, communicate effectively, and appreciate our nation's cultural diversity. As our nation's culture becomes more and more media-based, citizens capable of responding intelligently are increasingly important. Art education serves to develop such skills, broadening understanding and enhancing acceptance of fellow human beings.

Giving Importance and Making Special

The arts are important to a nation's people and to their culture. Consider, for example, that more Americans go to museums than to sporting events, and over one million Americans from all communities and cultures call themselves artists. Communities and cultures make art because art makes events special. When art celebrates ordinary experiences, these experiences take on new significance. By making events and things stand out from the commonplace, art transforms and reorganizes our conceptions of the world.

Personal Communication and Expression

At the heart of arts learning is the process of giving form to and making meaning from personal experience. The idea that a person can make an individual statement through art—one that brings meaning and pleasure to self and others and that communicates to others—is a powerful rationale. This rationale is all the more poignant in a technologically advanced society in which so much of what we use is made by unseen others in remote parts of the world.

General Creativity and Artistic Creativity

Art education promotes higher thought processes, such as a willingness to imagine possibilities, juxtaposing disparate elements in creative and bold ways, a desire to explore ambiguity, and an ability to recognize multiple perspectives. Students should acquire a feel for what it means to transform their ideas, images, and feelings into an art form.

Vocations

Developing beyond the rationale for creative expression is the prevocational rationale that art in the schools is the breeding ground for the nascent development of interest in many careers involving visual creativity, such as film-making, publishing, photography, architecture, computer graphics, interior design, product design, fashion design, landscape design, architecture, and advertising art. In this regard, it is good to keep in mind that among America's leading exports are its intellectual and artistic products, its software, and its films.

Aesthetic Awareness

Art education heightens a student's awareness of the aesthetic qualities in nature, in art, and in life. Dewdrop-laden spider webs, Van Gogh's sunflower paintings, and beautiful moments of daily living are experienced more vividly through the individual's being sensitized in art classes to such phenomena.

An appreciation of Native-American culture is brought to these second-grade children through examining the myths and art of the northwest and southwest Native-American cultures. Each second-grade class selected its own power animal. **Top left:** Wolf kachina with exciting patterns. **Bottom left:** Blue bird kachina based on southwest Native-American stories. **Top middle:** Boy with symbolic collar and headpiece. **Top right:** Black-and-white-striped doll based on Hopi clown kachina. **Bottom right:** A girl in white costume enacts the northwest Native-American myth of how the loon lost her voice.

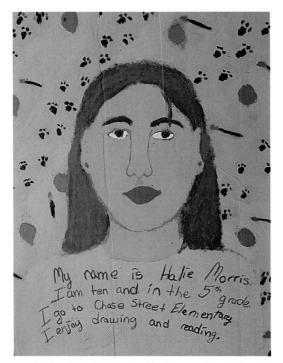

Courtesy of Beverly Mallon, Chase Street Elementary School, Athens, GA.

Fifth-grader Halie Morris's self-portrait on cardboard was motivated by portraits in Benny Andrews's paintings and Howard Finster's folk art replete with explanatory captions. Mirrors were used to assist the students.

Courtesy of Joyce Vroon, Trinity School, Atlanta, GA.

Sports advertising is one of our nation's largest businesses. Testimony to advertising's power is fourth-grader Ross Baird's memory drawing, which recalls the details of the advertising as clearly as the sports action.

Courtesy of Beverly Mallon, Chase Street Elementary School, Athens, GA.

An integration of art, ecological awareness, writing, lettering, and advertising occurred when this fifth-grader won first place in the state of Georgia for her conservation poster. The art teacher emphasized the design principle KISS ("keep it simple, silly"). Students role-played that they were graphic designers at an advertising agency charged with creating an ad for an ecological cause.

Literacy and Cognition

Literacy refers to more than just reading and writing; it also deals with understanding visual phenomena in the broadest sense. Cognition refers to ways of processing information and becoming aware of self and the environment through sight, sound, taste, and movement. Education should develop a young child's literacy in all symbol systems, all modes of thought, and all means of inquiry. This goal is especially applicable in early childhood, when perception more than logic governs children's early views of reality. Children relate to the arts as media for expression and communication at a time when their verbal skills are not fully developed or refined. The arts provide experiences that will later coalesce into sophisticated reasoning and problem solving.

A Core Participant in Learning in School

The arts are great partners and participants in academic learning. Integration with social studies, science, math, related arts, and reading and writing adds richness, new meaning, insight, and excitement to learning in many academic fields. The value of visual art is highlighted when we consider the general role of representation in how we learn and how we express our understanding.

A Different Way of Learning and Communicating in School

In a curriculum crowded with academic subjects and factual learning, art is a welcome means of learning about oneself and the world. The language of art uses a different symbol system—one that fuses into a single entity the cognitive, affective, and psychomotor modes of learning. Replete with billions of images, it gives students the unique opportunity to communicate in a language that is neither verbal nor mathematical, the languages that dominate the curricula.

Americans do believe in arts education. In one national survey, almost all respondents expressed that it is important for children to be exposed to the arts. A large survey of American schools by John Goodlad found that parents do not want, and never have wanted, a "back to basics" curriculum. Instead, they want a curriculum based in four areas: academic, vocational, social-civic-cultural, and personal. In the social-civic-cultural area, the art goal is to apply basic concepts in the fine arts and humanities to the appreciation of the aesthetic contributions by other cultures. In the vocational area, arts are at the core of our nation's artistic products, such as films, Web page design, and advertising. In the personal area of curriculum, which also includes the arts, one goal is to expand a student's ability to use leisure time effectively. When surveyed, students consistently rated the arts as more interesting and enjoyable than academic subjects. However, arts classes, themselves, have been criticized. Goodlad (1984) wrote:

> I am disappointed with the degree to which the arts classes appear to be dominated by the ambiance of English, mathematics and other academic subjects. Arts classes, too, appear to be governed by characteristics which are best described as "school"—following the rules, finding the one right answer, practicing the lower cognitive processes. [The arts] did not convey the picture of individual expression and artistic creativity toward which one is led by the rhetoric of forward-looking practice in the field.

In contrast, this book advocates a qualitative approach for teaching art that brings with it an attitude of rigor and the need for artistic creativity. Art requires a high level of abstract reasoning. Further, the new curriculum in art criticism and aesthetics requires analysis and interpretation—another way to include higher-order cognitive processes in art.

In summary, in the art classroom all of the rationales for education can be addressed: promoting cultural understanding, meeting national needs, giving significance to the commonplace, offering an outlet for expression and creativity, introducing creative vocations, enhancing aesthetic awareness, developing literacy, integrating learning, and providing a different language in which to learn. The goal of education is to help students develop both their intellectual capabilities and their capacity to express their thoughts and feelings. The art classroom is an environment that is uniquely suited to help students meet both aspects of this goal, accounting in large part for the power of art.

A Qualitative Approach to Teaching Art

Frank Wachowiak explains his qualitative approach to teaching art: What is a quality work of art?

"Enriched and stimulated in art classes by a teacher's varied and challenging motivations, children learn to see more, sense more, and recall more. They become more aware of their changing and expanding environment, and they realize that making art is not something special done by special people. While everyone can put [his or her] imprint on a piece of paper, children who express their ideas, responses, and reactions with honesty, sensitivity, and perceptiveness within a framework of compositional principles and design create art. For most students, this sense of design and art structure must grow from the many planned art–life experiences and happenings that are provided by the resourceful teacher. Everyone can engage in art-making behavior. Some people, however, think that anything a child draws, paints, or constructs is art. It may be called art, but the question remains as to whether it is a work of good or bad art. It may indeed be a child's visual statement, but it is not necessarily a quality work of art. To have quality, it must, as much as possible, be expressed in the language, structure, and form of art.

What some observers call "art" in a child's drawing very often is not art at all, but simply a visual report that relates to factual writing. Art, on the other hand, is more akin to poetry, which, like all fine art, comes to life when it distills the essence of an experience in highly expressive and discriminative choices. This is how the qualitative method of teaching art differs from other methods. In poetry, one discovers that the quality of the verse often depends on the choice use of an expressive word, phrase, or couplet, and on effective alliteration, meter, rhythm, and sometimes rhyme. Likewise, in the most evocative, colorful art creations of children, one sees how artworks that employ art principles result in a unity and a rich design that distinguishes these works from ordinary, relatively impoverished expressions.

Qualitative teaching differs from other methods in that it requires the teacher to go beyond initial stimulation. More time, more thought is

The child's knowledge of science, nature, and art comes together as the child represents the natural world, which can be as near as the schoolyard. Teachers should take advantage of the immediate environment—the school playground, the cafeteria kitchen, the band room with musical instruments—as a visual motivational resource. Here, the children are employing 18- × 24-inch sections of hardboard as sketching pads for drawing.

Second-grade children learned about poisonous and nonpoisonous snakes through creating this stitchery mural.

needed. In general, all art methods emphasize the teacher's responsibility for keeping students engaged in worthwhile experiences in order that they have something meaningful to express, draw, paint, print, model, or construct. Often, art methods help the children to recall a past event or provide new visual enrichments through a field trip, model brought to class, dramatization, film, dance, musical recording, story, or poem. For qualitative teaching in art, however, this initial stimulation is not enough. From a preliminary drawing through to the finished product, the teacher also must guide the students as they express their responses. (see also Chapter 8).

Every time children create a work of art—painting, collage, print, sculpture—they should be encouraged to evaluate their efforts in terms of the lesson's instructional objectives, beginning with the initial sketch. If nothing is said about design, structure, composition, line, value, color, contrast, pattern, and other aspects of the artwork, it is presumptuous to assume that students will develop their aesthetic awareness and artistic potential.

Students who persevere when they make art create more fulfilling, rewarding, and exciting art if they are guided to become more fully aware of their environment. If their contact with the world, the people in it, and nature is superficial, and if their identification with and response to visual stimuli is minimal, they are apt to be content with a hasty, casual, lazy, noncommittal, shorthand statement of an event. Stereotyped interpretations such as stick figures, lollipop trees, box houses, and two curved lines for a bird are seldom based on children's richly observed experiences of distinguishing identifying characteristics and noting differences in things. Indeed, without the teacher's help, the average child's art production, limited by abbreviated time schedules, tends to be cursory and sterile.

Teachers who see examples of children's art like those in this text often inquire how long it takes the children to complete projects of such quality. No doubt, they sense that the artworks enriching this text are not the result of a single 45-minute lesson. In most instances, the motivation and preliminary drawing alone take one art period. A completed project may take three to four periods, depending on the age or grade of the

A qualitative artwork, such as this "pet in a garden" oil pastel, takes time to create. On 12- × 18-inch violet-colored construction paper, it took three 50-minute class periods. The preliminary drawing was made in school chalk, then reinforced with a large-sized, black felt-nib pen. Color then was applied up to, but not covering, the black lines. Instructional objectives for color were to use color imaginatively and repeat colors for unity. The animal (pet) was drawn first and the garden environment added afterward. See the child at work on this painting in the circle illustration at the right.

child. When art class is scheduled only once per week, some classroom teachers are concerned that should a project extend over a period of several weeks, they could not hold the children's interest. One way to deal with time constraints and still produce qualitative art is to limit the size of the paper—for example, use 9- × 12-inch instead of 12- × 18-inch surfaces for detailed compositions and 12- × 18-inch instead of 18- × 24-inch paper for expressively free tempera paintings.

Qualitative art experiences should have a regularly scheduled and undisputed place in the curriculum of elementary and middle schools. When art is not allotted sufficient time in the school week, when it plays a subordinate role to every other subject, and when it consists mainly of peripheral activities and stereotyped holiday decorations, expecting it to perform a vital role in children's creative growth is unrealistic.

Likewise, when taught effectively, purposefully, and qualitatively, art has a body of knowledge and skills to be mastered. It has unquestionable merit as a unique avenue to mental, social, and individual growth. Thus, artistic creativity should be recognized, lauded, and embraced as a living and learning experience in its own right. Indeed, if taught imaginatively and qualitatively so that every lesson augments and enhances the students' skills in basic learning as well as in perceiving, reading, analyzing, and building a vocabulary, then art is education."

Courtesy of the International Collection of Child Art, Illinois State University, Normal, IL.

When art is taught both purposefully and qualitatively and the instructional objectives to be mastered are made clear, beautiful work results. A St. Petersburg, Russia, scene of children skiing in the snow uses the figures of many children to fill the page, age 6.

Chapter 2

ART AS ART:
THE DESIGN FUNDAMENTALS

Art is made for many reasons. Usually, its creators want to express something. In children's art, for example, they want to say something about their lives or pets or gardens. Perhaps they want to say something about the activities they do with friends or about nature, or they may simply want to say something about decoration and design. They may want to meet some real, immediate need, as in creating a poster for a play. Their feelings come out as they make the art.

As they strive to express their feelings and ideas, however, they must wrestle with the *elements and principles* of art: its colors, shapes, and variety. It is difficult to talk about art without making recurring references to the basic elements of art—line, shape or form, value, color, space, and texture and pattern—as well as to many of art's fundamental principles, such as balance and symmetry, variety, emphasis, and domination-subordination.

We teach this language of art as if elements and principles have clear distinctions. However, in actuality, the design elements and principles are not written in stone; rather, they merge and blend together. And, obviously, any one element or principle may or may not be applicable to a specific work. For example, an Impressionistic painting may have little to do with line; a Navajo rug may have little to do with space or asymmetry.

Line

Line in art is a human invention—a unique method of perceiving and documenting the visible world. Expressive, sensitively drawn lines vary in weight, width, and emphasis. They may be delicate, bold, static, flowing, rhythmic, ponderous, hesitant, violent, or dynamic. They are achieved through freedom and spontaneity, or through thoughtful and deliberate action. They may converge, radiate, run parallel, meander, twist, skip, and criss-cross to create confusion, rhythm, order, or chaos.

Lines can be thin, thick, or heavy; they can be wavy, fish-scale, jagged, or zigzag; and they can be bold, careful, or tentative. Lines of differing weights and characteristics can create outlines, inner edges, paths of motion, and sheer decorative delight in patterns. While much Western art relies on outlines, this is not true of the art of some other cultures. Teachers and students should turn to nature and select objects for limitless sources of line variety: frost, roots, spider webs, water ripples, lightning, veins in leaves, feathers, seashells, grain in wood, insect wings, shopping carts, birdcages, wicker furniture, and tree bark and branches.

Shape

A study of pictorial design—of composition in painting, prints, and posters—eventually centers on the *shape* of things. The shapes created by lines merging, touching, and intersecting one another take many forms. They may be square, rectangular, round, elliptical, oval, triangular, or amorphous. They may emerge as nonobjective, figurative, or free-form. Often, shapes are flat and two-dimensional, such as squares, but also they can have or suggest volume and three-dimensions, such as rectangular solids, cubes, cones, and pyramids. Often teachers use the term *form* rather than *shape* in describing three-dimensional volumetric objects.

Nature is by far the richest source of inspiration for the study of variety in shapes. Indeed, many artists turn to aging, dilapidated buildings for their drawing inspiration instead of the coldly geometric shapes of much contemporary architecture. There is too much reliance on formulas and rules of perspective in the rendition of tabletops, doors, windows, fences, roofs, and sidewalks. Teachers should encourage students to use artistic license to give vitality to static imagery through meaningful distortion, omission, exaggeration, and free-form interpretation.

Lines depict a variety of types of fish. The lines of the seaweed create interlocking shapes of various sizes that tie the design together.

The shapes of objects or figures in a composition, such as trees, houses, people, animals, furniture, and vehicles, generally are called *positive shapes.* The empty area around them is referred to as *negative space,* even though this space may include ground, water, and sky. Many artists keep the negative shapes in mind as much as the positive shapes to achieve a strong figure/ground relationship. When the positive shapes are varied in size and shape, in many instances the negative spaces or shapes consequently will be just as varied and interesting.

The curvilinear shapes of fish and crescents were paired up in the spiraling, radiating design of this upper-elementary-grade class mural.

The dark-and-light values contrast boldly in this scratchboard. Linear patterns and textures drawn from a still life form other values.

Value

Simply stated, *value* refers to a composition's light and dark elements. Every shade (dark value) and tint (light value) of every color or hue can be thought of as having a place on a value scale. An attractive disposition of values in a picture is even more important than color. When repeated throughout a painting or design, values create movement in the artwork, leading the viewer from one part of the composition to another. Value analyses of master paintings and prints can help students to understand and appreciate the principles employed in achieving successful light-and-dark orchestration. Compositions with sharply contrasting values generally are more dramatic and dynamic in their visual impact.

When famous American artist Georgia O'Keeffe was studying to be an art teacher, her professor at Teacher's College of Columbia University, Arthur Wesley Dow, stressed both in his lectures and in his writings the importance of value. In short, he emphasized that the pattern created by the different values was interesting. Many people acknowledge that the value patterns seen in O'Keeffe's paintings are one of their strongest features.

Color

Can you imagine a world without color? How dull it would be. *Color* has three properties or components: *hue*, the name of the color; *value*, the lightness or darkness of the color; and *intensity* (saturation), the brightness or dullness of the color. Unfortunately, its most amazing property—its magic—often is ignored.

Courtesy of Shirley Lucas, Oshkosh, WI.

Think about color limitation. One color dominates each of these paintings and provides unity. Notice the mixtures of blue and violet and blue and green in the top painting and the mixed yellow-brown color in the bottom painting. Many tints and shades were blended. Small areas of other colors provide brilliant contrast. The theme "If I ran the circus" was the motivational catalyst that prompted these two action-filled tempera paintings by fourth-grade children.

Limitation definitely plays an important role in mastering color orchestration. Students sometimes may be advised to limit their palettes to black, white, and one color in all of its various tints and shades, a system that is very effective. Another suggestion is to use analogous or related colors—those adjacent to one another on the color wheel, for example, such as blue, blue-green, green, and yellow-green. Two or three colors usually are enough; likewise, five colors are too many. Ideally, one color should dominate and set the tone for the whole color scheme.

To avoid pitfalls of clashing color or strident chromatic relationships, students should be counseled to minimize the intensity (or brightness) of colors in a composition. This process, sometimes referred to as *neutralization* or *dulling* of a color, involves mixing or combining a color with its complementary hue, which can be found opposite to it on the color wheel. Red and green are complementary colors, as are blue and orange. Many colors now available in crayon, oil pastel, and tempera already are neutralized—for example, sienna, brown, umber, ochre, and chrome green.

A fraction of bright, intense color will hold its own against a more generous employment of neutralized colors. Surrounded by duller colors, brighter colors in the middle of the picture give it a sense of glowing light. Colors can be repeated to create movement and unity, but remind students to vary the size and shape of the repeated color. Dark, cool colors generally recede; bright, warm colors usually advance. Complementary colors such as red and green in their fullest intensities

Courtesy of Baiba Kuntz, Glencoe, IL.

Limiting colors to greys and tans gives a unifying sense of serenity to this fifth-grade student's collage of an imaginary house.

Chapter 2: Art as Art: The Design Fundamentals **15**

The teacher's strength in teaching about color is evident in this picture. The peacock is crayoned mainly in green and its variations, along with strong, pure accents of blue, red, and yellow. White crayon is especially effective with the dark grey crayon resist.

The color spectrum forms the surreal background, the nose, and the spiraling eyes for this eighth-grade student's black, heart-shaped abstract face done in acrylics.

create vibrant contrasts when juxtaposed. Black, grey, and white can be combined with any color scheme without creating harmonic conflicts. Often, as in the case of black outlining, the dark linear accent gives a contrasting sharpness and sparkle to the composition. The character, identity, and impact of a color depend a great deal on the colors that are adjacent to or surrounding it. For example, a green shape on a turquoise background may be relatively unnoticed, but intense orange against an intense blue (a complementary relationship) will vibrate and arrest the eye.

Ironically, to make colors beautiful, we must consider first not hue but value, because it is the main pattern of values or shades that gives a picture its overall effect and strength. It is more important to vary the shades than to vary the hues. Contrasts of light and dark colors will make a picture bold.

The painters of the postimpressionist era, including Franz Marc, Marc Chagall, and Odilon Redon, as well as contemporary colorists such as Karel Appel, Helen Frankenthaler, Richard Anuskiewicz, and Victor Vasarely, have provided the art world with eye-opening creations in color, resulting in surprises such as blue horses and multihued people. Teachers and students also should turn for inspiration in color usage to the luminous stained-glass windows of Gothic cathedrals, the jewel-like miniatures of India and Persia, the shimmering mosaics of Byzantium, and the fascinating *ukiyo-e* color woodcuts of Japan.

Space

Space is an element both in pictorial composition and in abstract design that often confuses the student. In two-dimensional art expression, *space* sometimes is designated as the negative area between positive objects.

This kind of space often is referred to as *decorative* or *surface space*. Another category of space to be considered is space-in-depth; this is often studied as if comprised of three sections: foreground, middle ground, and background. The following are common pictorial devices for achieving the illusion of space-in-depth on a two-dimensional plane, as in a painting:

- Using vertical placement to suggest depth
- Diminishing sizes of objects as they recede in the distance
- Drawing sharp, clear details in the foreground and blurred, indistinct elements in the background
- Overlapping shapes or forms
- Drawing objects that are farther away from the observer higher on the picture plane
- Using bright, intense colors in the foreground and dulled colors in the background
- Employing perspective-creating techniques such as converging lines and horizon lines

Applying the rules of perspective doesn't guarantee the success of a composition, however. Rules of perspective should not be imposed on children unless they indicate a need for them. Most children must be guided in mastering the intricacies of space-in-depth, which include perspective and foreshortening.

Vertical placement gives this picture depth. Although the shoppers' heights remain constant, this market scene from Turkey shows depth through more distant figures being placed higher in the picture.

Diminishing sizes of farther objects gives depth. In the fifth-grader's Antarctic scene, the biggest penguin is four times as large as the distant penguin. This creates an effect of space, as does their being at different levels.

Overlapping and diminishing the sizes of the dancers' heads creates an illusion of space. This gives an effect of hundreds of dancers in the community folk-dance celebration. The painting is by an 11-year-old from Kastamonu, Turkey.

A related concept about objects in space is *point of view.* Is the art depicted from above (a bird's eye view) or below (an ant's eye view)? Does the art offer a closeup view (a microscopic view) or a distant view (a telescopic view)?

Texture and Pattern

Texture and pattern usually are considered as adorning or secondary elements that add richness and variety. However, they also can become the main feature of a design, as, for instance, in the design of floor tiles or in the repetitions of windows and columns in a work of architecture. Some names for textures are rough, smooth, actual, implied, bumpy, and jagged. Artists such as Rembrandt, Rubens, and Velasquez were virtuosos in painting the textures of hair, silk, velvet, and fur.

Some types of patterns are regular, irregular, stripes (bands), zigzag (chevron), scallop (fish scale), plaid (crossband), notched (crenellated), and checkerboard (counterchange). Patterns can be created by setting up a series of parallel lines or lines that criss-cross, often at right angles. These lines can be straight, curved, wavy, or jagged.

Patterns in nature usually have a mathematical basis. For example, the arrangement of seeds in the head of a sunflower and the bumpy divisions on a pineapple are two of the many natural occurrences of the mathematical series called a *Fibonacci series.* Such seemingly random patterns as those formed by cloud formations, tree branches, or a coastline's indentations are in fact governed by the same geometric phenomenon, *fractal geometry.*

Both pattern and texture can be created by the repetition of individual elements—for example, lines to make grass or circles to make apples on a tree. Patterns usually are made up of the repetition of one or more clearly discernible shapes. In textures, however, individual elements are merged into the whole and are difficult to distinguish. It sometimes is hard

Patterns of bands go across the spectrum in opposite directions on the background and fish.

Imaginative patterns of circles, checkerboards, stripes, and diamonds grace this upper elementary child's oil pastel on pink paper. It was drawn with white chalk and inspired by a stuffed bird and photos of birds.

Clay is the supreme material for creating textures. Buttons, wire mesh, bottle caps, and kitchen tools can be helpful.

A feast of carefully planned patterns and textures enrich this beautifully detailed colored marker drawing of a still life arrangement.

to make a clear distinction between pattern and texture. For example, seen from a distance, apples on a tree would create a texture, but seen from up close, apples on a tree would create a pattern. Microscopes and telescopes can further determine whether something—for example, a view of the galaxy—is seen as a texture, a pattern, or a shape.

Both pattern and texture can be used overall to create a rich, busy effect. However, they may take on even more importance when they are used judiciously and separated by empty, plain areas of a solid, unvaried color. When a texture changes in a progressive way, such as from distinct in the foreground to blended in the distance, it is called a *textural gradient*. This phenomenon can be seen in views of the ocean's waves, clouds, and fields of trees and crops.

Balance and Symmetry

Having considered the *elements* of design—line, shape, value, color, space, texture, and pattern—we now turn our attention to the *principles* of design, such as balance, symmetry, and variety. Students should become familiar with the two types of compositional balance: symmetrical or formal balance, and asymmetrical or informal balance. Although formal balance has

Patterns and textures abound in nature. Teachers can help students to see the series of patterns and shapes in nature's leaves and seeds. These exquisite sunflower oil pastels on black paper have compositions that fill the page. Each seed, petal, leaf, and leaf vein are carefully drawn. Arranged alternately on the stem, the leaves run off the edges of the picture to create dramatic black background shapes. In the picture on the left, wonderful variety is shown in the leaves.

In the middle picture, a flower is drawn side view, and exciting negative shapes remain in the background. In the far right picture, subtle blending of colors on the leaves and petals contrast with the bold, black-patterned head of seeds. It would be wonderful if children everywhere could have the experience of studying with an art teacher who brings out the best in them, as was the case with these students.

gone in and out of favor as styles have changed, a symmetrical arrangement in which objects or figures on the right balance similarly weighted components on the left generally makes a more rigid, static composition. *Bilateral symmetry* is an arrangement in which two sides are similar. *Quadrilateral symmetry*, likewise, has four similar quarters.

A common misconception about art composition is that emphasis can be achieved by drawing something very large at the center of the picture. Size and placement by themselves do not ensure domination, however. The object to be noticed must be emphasized using other attributes as well, such as contrasting value, color, and detail. While there are no hard-and-fast rules, a pictorial creation often is much more interesting and

attractive when the principal subject is not placed exactly in the center of the composition.

Variety, Repetition, Emphasis, and Domination-Subordination

Variety in composition and design is perhaps the most important fundamental principle. Analyses of past and present art masterpieces have revealed the artists' reliance on a variety of shapes and forms in their com-

Saturday Children's Classes. Courtesy of Frank Wachowiak, Athens, GA, and
Mary Sayer Hammond, Fairfax, VA. Student Megan Clements.

*Variety makes an interesting picture. Here, cats' faces are blue, yellow, striped, and banded in
the exciting variety of this animal in the garden scene.*

Courtesy of Timothy Road Elementary School, Athens, GA.

*What riotous variety is shown in this primary-grade child's wonderful marker-pen harbor
scene! No two cabin cruisers are alike. The beach house architecture, the intensely colored
empty spaces, and the windswept trees and hairstyles are delightful.*

positions. Seldom does one discover two shapes that are alike. Look at a
score of multifigure paintings by recognized artists throughout the centuries and you will discover endless variety. No two heads are on the
same level. No two figures are in the same position. No two figures stand
on the same levels in the foreground.

• In nature, examples of variety are evident in the wings of a butterfly,
the stripes on a zebra, the spots on a leopard, the feathers on a bird, the
scales on a fish, the web of a spider, the cracks in an ice floe, and the flakes
of frost on a windowpane. No two wings or stripes or spots are alike, as no
two of us are alike. Despite our uniqueness, however, we must be taught to
employ variety in our graphic imagery. Variety can be employed in every
aspect of pictorial design—line, shape, value, color, pattern, texture—to
give excitement and interest to a work of art. Yet, variety must be coun-
terbalanced by a *repetition* of those art elements if the desired unity is to be
achieved. Just as in living, variety is most effective when combined with
structure and organization.

Yet, too much variety can result in a hodge podge. There must be
some repetition to give structure and strength, some constancy in a sea of
flux. Both differences and similarities are needed.

Related to variety are the concepts of *emphasis* (that one object or
motif should stand out above others) and *domination-subordination* (that

equality is to be avoided in favor of a dominant object or motif). The following techniques are helpful for varying the placement of objects in a
composition:

• Change in size and shape of objects
• Begin objects on different planes
• Terminate objects at different heights
• Touch the edges of the picture plane at different points, introducing
  lines into the composition
• Strategically overlap objects to create even more varied shapes and neg-
  ative spaces.

Formalism and Other Concepts

Certainly, one way to teach art is to revisit, time and again, over the course
of many art assignments, the elements and principles introduced in this
chapter. The basic elements and principles discussed here can provide a
practical design foundation on which to build a qualitative art program
over the years. Indeed, in many art classrooms, the curriculum is based
upon the formal elements and principles—a *formalistic approach* to art.

Sometimes contrasted to the *formalistic* and *media approaches* to art is a *contextualist approach* to art. A *contexturalist approach* to art deals with art's content, expression, and especially the context in which it is made. This approach will be discussed in later chapters. Likewise, in another approach to teaching art, the numerous media by which art is made can be explored. This *media approach* is addressed in the last third of this book. But before exploring these other approaches to the nature of art, let us first discuss in the next chapters teachers and teaching and *how* children make art.

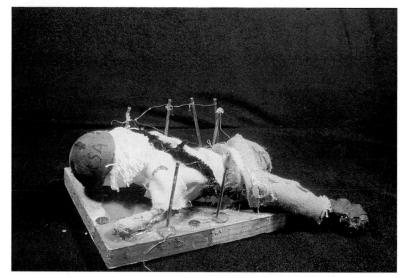

Courtesy of Joyce Vroon, Trinity School, Atlanta, GA.

A contextualist orientation to art is one that focuses more on the story or context shown, rather than on the arrangement of the formal elements. It is shown here in fifth-grader Michael Owens's expressive plaster of paris strip sculpture depicting the horrors of war.

PART 2

TEACHERS AND TEACHING

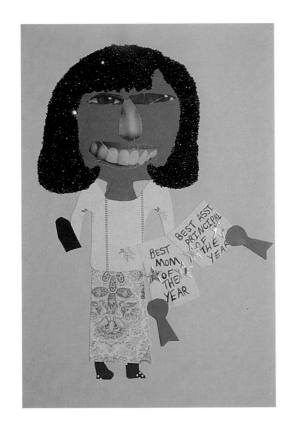

Left and *right*, courtesy of Beverly Mallon, Chase Street Elementary School, Athens, GA. *Center*, courtesy of Joyce Vroon, Trinity School, Atlanta, GA.

Previous page: *Many students admire their teachers, who serve as role models. Teacher portraits can be combined with a study of Romare Bearden's collage paintings. The art teacher preselected magazine pictures suitable for the fifth-grade students to use in depicting their favorite teacher. On the left, a student depicted the assistant principal both as an award-winning administrator and as a mother. On the right, another student captured the assistant principal's organized schedule and beautifully patterned dress. Center, the popular and respected P.E. teacher is caricatured by sixth-grader Robbie Brown.*

Chapter 3

THE ROLE OF THE DEDICATED TEACHER

Wherever an art program of quality and promise exists, whether in elementary or middle schools, in crowded cities or quiet farm communities, in the United States or abroad, there is an enthusiastic, resourceful, knowledgeable, imaginative, and gifted teacher. The teacher of the successful, productive art class invariably is a planner, an organizer, an expediter, a counselor, a dreamer, a goal setter, and most of all, a lover of children, life, and especially art.

Without a well-prepared, creative, and dedicated teacher at the helm, an art program can founder in a sea of hasty, last-minute decisions, in trite, stereotyped activities, or in chaotic, pseudotherapeutic play sessions. The school that boasts a modern physical plant, generous budget, and administration sympathetic to art is fortunate, but if it does not attract teachers who are prepared to teach art confidently, enthusiastically, developmentally, and qualitatively, it has little chance of establishing and implementing an art program of excellence and stature.

Dedication is, and always will be, a vital teaching strength in a democratic society. It transcends teaching expertise. Nothing is written in a teaching contract about dedication, nor is there anything explicit about the requisites of love, patience, and sympathetic support that go hand-in-hand with good teaching. Unselfish dedication and enthusiastic involvement are freewill gifts of a devoted teacher, and they cannot be measured except in terms of the inner fulfillment and satisfaction that they bring.

The best teachers of art, whether classroom teachers or specialized art instructors, believe wholeheartedly in art's unique, spirit-enhancing, and rejuvenating power. In every project, they seek to perfect the critically important motivations, the technical intricacies, and the evaluative strategies. They organize materials, tools, space, and time schedules to produce exemplary working conditions. They search for inspirational art stimuli to renew children's interest in a project whenever the initial excitement wanes. In their enthusiasm, which they display openly and generously, teachers encourage students to open their eyes to the design, color, form, rhythm, texture, and pattern in the world around them, and they believe in art's power to give students a language with which to communicate and express their feelings. They identify with their students and are elated when one makes a discovery or masters a skill.

The St. Petersburg, Russia teacher of this student was well rewarded for the planning and motivation done when this 10-year-old's story illustration showed such a sophisticated use of analogous colors and spatial divisions.

Top left: Stuffed owl and chair, begun by drawing one bird; *Top center:* Drawing of brown owl; *Top right:* Drawing of owl and patterned bird, Mairen Foley, Grade 5; *Bottom left:* Unfinished owl drawing, Grades 5 and 6, colored markers; *Bottom center:* Still life with student, stuffed peacock, African vulture, two owls; *Bottom right:* Owl and green plant, Emily Marsh, Grade 5.

A teacher's influence goes on forever. Artworks by students of Baiba Kuntz of Glencoe, Illinois are on this page and works by students of her teacher Frank Wachowiak are on the opposite page. Master art teacher Baiba Kuntz had her fifth- and sixth-grade students make these carefully observed drawings from a still life of birds. The 19- × 25-inch colored marker drawings were made with no preliminary pencil sketch. When in college, Baiba had studied in several courses with Frank Wachowiak. She later attended his sessions at art edu-cation conventions, and many of her students' works have graced editions of this book. When Frank retired, he passed on to her his taxidermic specimen of an owl (pictured here). Note the wonderful use to which the owl continues to be put. Baiba subsequently added to the collec-tion an African vulture and a peacock in full tail display. She also borrows taxidermic birds from the Field Museum of Natural History.

Conversely, they are genuinely concerned when students encounter difficulties that defy resolution.

A creative, confident, and enthusiastic teacher with a love for children and an understanding of art fundamentals is the catalyst in a productive and qualitative art program. The teacher's own immediate enjoyment of the teaching experience helps students enjoy the intrinsic rewards of learning. The successful teacher must constantly plan, organize, experiment, motivate, evaluate, and build resources, yet the privilege of sharing the contagious, exuberant, magical world of students as they explore, discover, and invent compensates beyond measure for the extra effort that is required.

Who Teaches Art?

Most teaching of art is done by elementary classroom teachers. Some of these teachers feel handicapped by their limited backgrounds in art fundamentals. One reason for this inadequacy is the minimal art experiences that these teachers had during their own elementary, middle, and secondary school years. Another may be the lack of an art education course during their college preparation and in-service work. Nonetheless, three-quarters of these elementary classroom teachers teach either all or part of the art that their students receive in school. The classroom teacher has

Qualitative art learning is evident in the seriousness, deliberation, and confidence shown in this sixth-grade girl's oil pastel on red paper done in Frank Wachowiak's class. Notice how well the hues of blue, red, and yellow-orange are carried throughout the composition.

flexibility in scheduling and can have small groups of students work on certain phases of art projects while others engage in different subjects. Because only one group of students is involved, storage of materials is not a major problem, and there is little chance that elaborate still-life materials will be stolen.

In some schools, art is taught by an itinerant art teacher. The nickname *á la carte,* misappropriated from the restaurant industry, often is used by those who do this mobile type of teaching. Usually, such teachers see 500 to 800 students per week, in 20 different classrooms, in two to five different schools. Supplies—and what passes for an office—are in a closet.

While the classroom teachers may or may not remain in the room, the art teacher in practice usually is left alone to handle discipline. Unfortunately, the art teacher often has little opportunity to observe how the classroom teacher handles disruptive incidents.

In a third type of arrangement, art is taught by an art teacher in a school equipped with an art room. More elaborate equipment, such as hot plates, looms, and sinks, are possible in the specialized art room. An elaborate still life can be constructed. Although this situation prevails in middle schools, it is the case in only a fraction of elementary schools. The middle school teacher usually sees 125 students a day. The elementary art teacher with an art room sees 500 to 800 students each week. This teacher has one 45-minute art period in which to motivate the students, distribute supplies, monitor the lesson, clean up, evaluate the lesson, and store artwork if the project is to go on for a second week.

Guiding Students to Create and to Appreciate

To appreciate their students' developmental possibilities and limitations, teachers must have a basic understanding of the kinds of art that children do naturally. The qualitative art program espoused by this book, however, demands more of students than what they do naturally. Some students do perceive, draw, and compose sensitively, but most require guidance and motivation. Because the teacher is the catalyst, it is the teacher's responsibility to establish a positive learning climate in which inquiry, creativity, and individuality thrive. Teachers of art may ask their students to set higher standards of performance for themselves or demand greater effort than the children have been accustomed to making. In most instances, the best art is the result of perseverance—of purposeful, consistent, and time-consuming effort. The results are not accidental, nor is the product one of undemanding, trivial, or thoughtless activity. Indeed, to teach that art is undemanding is to create a false impression. Teachers can maintain an effective, positive, and productive atmosphere in their classes when they can alert the students to an awareness of the project's objectives and the satisfaction to be achieved in a purposeful art endeavor.

In addition to developing an understanding of the kinds of art that children do naturally, experienced teachers avoid assigning a new, untried technique to their classes. The teacher's confidence and effectiveness are heightened immeasurably if he or she has explored ahead of time the materials and tools that are available to the students and has created successfully with those tools.

It is a goal of every effective art teacher to guide his or her students toward a fuller aesthetic awareness of their environment—for example, to see beauty in the commonplace, such as droplets of morning dew glistening in a moisture-laden spider's web. Students are highly impressionable and susceptible to visual influences over which teachers and parents have little control. Television and MTV, movies, computer and video games, musical recordings, makeup, magazine illustrations, recording covers, posters, cars, clothes, and package design clamor for their attention, shape their developing taste, and help to form their cultural values. While students' discriminative choices often differ from those of adults, an effective art teacher can help guide students to consider aesthetic choices. In teaching art criticism, art history, and aesthetics, top-notch teachers of art use as many audiovisual aids as possible. These include original works of art, reproductions, films, photographs, slides, video recordings, magazine articles, colorfully illustrated art books, and examples of student work. Although little or no money may be budgeted for purchasing visual materials such as slides and reproductions, the dedicated teacher purchases them out of pocket and taps the resources of libraries and museums, spending about 45 minutes a day in planning time. (Chapter 10 discusses still-life arrangements, and Appendix D lists some audiovisual sources.)

The Teacher's Positive Personality, Rapport, and Respect

A positive, cheerful, and outgoing personality is a major asset for teachers of art. Teachers must learn in sometimes difficult and trying situations to be patient, calm, and resolute. Children want to believe in their teachers. They need the security of a teacher's abiding confidence in the worth of the subject being taught. Students come to rely on their teachers for help with important choices in resolving perplexing problems, and they become skeptical of those who confuse them with vague generalizations or those who place all the responsibility for decision making in their hands.

Teachers of art should learn to listen to children's descriptions of their experiences, both real and imaginary, with sympathetic interest. They should avoid a detached, keep-your-distance approach. Instead, their commitment, concern, and excitement for the project must be evident in their actions, words, and facial expressions. Veteran teachers learn to cultivate a ready sense of humor, which can help to alleviate many tension-fraught situations. Teachers who really care about children do not talk down to them; neither do they underestimate their potential to excel.

A teacher's success in the art class often is based on the empathic rapport that can develop between instructor and students. Getting to know the students is especially important because of the one-to-one relation-

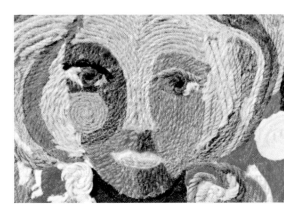

Illustrations from Frank Wachowiak's university classes.

College and university students preparing to teach art should explore varied art materials and techniques. The knowledge they gain will build the confidence they need to guide children's art production endeavors. **Top row:** *Oil pastel, plaster relief, tempera batik.* **Bottom row:** *Oil pastel, yarn collage, crayon engraving.*

ship demanded in a creative atmosphere. Name tags and a seating chart (with movable tabs to expedite changes) will hasten memorizing the students' names. Once teachers establish a climate of cooperation and mutual understanding, their ability to challenge their charges becomes their teaching strength. Teachers who have a greater sense of their effectiveness produce higher achievement gains in their students. These teachers believe If I try hard, I can get through to the most difficult, unmotivated students.

One can immediately sense the electric involvement, purposefulness of endeavor, and genuine rapport that exists between students and a teacher when visiting a classroom in which qualitative art learning is taking place. The special quality that distinguishes dedicated teachers of art from average instructors is their ability to respond intelligently, sympathetically, and purposefully to the children's creative efforts. They can communicate with the students both knowledgeably and honestly regarding their progress in art. The best teachers evaluate their students' work seriously and objectively; their critical attention gives the work importance and significance in the students' eyes. These teachers show sincere respect for what the individuals are trying to do as they strive to give form to their ideas. Most important, they take the students seriously as artists.

Chapter 4

TEACHING STRATEGIES

The Art Room: Appearance and Atmosphere

An art teacher begins establishing a qualitative art program even before a school year begins. A student's first impression of the classroom or art room is particularly critical, reflecting as it does the teacher's art convictions and his or her awareness of design as a vital environmental influence and conditioner. Indeed, the room's impact on students during their first visit is, in effect, the first art lesson a teacher gives. Prior to the start of the school session, the art teacher must work to make the classroom orderly, yet inviting. Above all, it must be visually stimulating. Attractively mounted artwork by children should brighten the walls. Hanging mobiles of fish, shells, birds, or butterflies created by preceding classes adds a surprising element of color in motion. The creative teacher relies on a variety of eye-catching resources, including bulletin-board exhibits, found-object displays, living plants, animals or birds, art-book displays, hobby collections, antiques, and selected original works of art and craft. Resources such as these help to make the art room a perpetually changing world of wonders.

A word about maintaining a productive atmosphere in the art classroom: Experienced teachers know there is no single solution to the varied behavioral problems with which they must cope. Veteran instructors of art generally find it expedient to begin classes with a serious, organized approach, which can be modified later if the situation warrants. This is better than allowing so much uninhibited freedom that it is impossible to bring the class under control when necessary. If students suspect that their art teacher is unconcerned when they waste time with idle chatter or horseplay, they will develop a self-defeating, laissez-faire attitude in class.

Courtesy of Baiba Kuntz, Glencoe, IL.

The room teaches. Attractive bulletin board displays help stimulate students' achievement. The color chart over the board is used to suggest why certain colors go together. It shows the beauty of related colors combined with accents of others. Some of the most sophisticated color usage reproduced in this book was done in view of such a display.

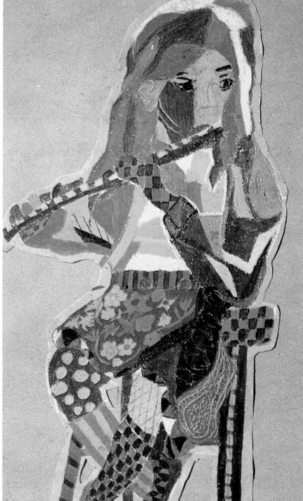

Courtesy of David Hodge, Oshkosh, WI.

The art room was decorated with these colorful figures to stimulate other classes (see page 246). They were drawn from class models on large 24- × 36-inch colored construction paper and colored with oil pastels. Then they were cut out and mounted on construction paper of a complementary color. Two eighth-grade students cooperated on the coloring of each figure.

Using Nonverbal Instructions

The best teachers do not rely on verbal instructions alone. The teacher's spoken, personal interaction with each student should be reinforced by the written and displayed materials. For example, teachers of art can enhance their instructional effectiveness by using the chalkboard or white marker board to emphasize their motivational presentation and to outline the specific objectives of a project. Students entering class can read the instructions on the board and proceed to their work without wasting time. The board can be used to identify and clarify the various possibilities and steps of the project. Evaluative criteria in the form of questions posted on the board allow students to make their own evaluations of their in-progress work (see Chapter 13). Using the board minimizes students' dependence on their instructor and discourages the refrain of "Am I finished?"

Chapter 4: Teaching Strategies **31**

Planning the Distribution, Collection, and Organization of Materials

Crucial to an art project's ultimate success is housekeeping. The teacher must organize the classroom or art room facilities so there will be adequate working space, a sufficient supply of materials and tools, varied storage facilities for both projects in progress and those retained for exhibition, a diversity of display spaces, and effective cleanup facilities (see Appendix A).

The distribution of student work in progress, art supplies, and tools should be planned carefully before the class begins so that valuable time is not wasted. To expedite the return of artwork, have students put their names on their work at an early stage. Materials can best be distributed either by a student-monitor system or by having students come up by tables or rows to a central supply area. Because disciplinary problems can arise when supplies run short and students have time on their hands, the teacher must ensure that the supply of materials and tools is adequate for the project at hand.

Beginning the Lesson

Getting the class session off to a good start is a major step in creating a productive studio atmosphere. When students come to an art room at the beginning of the period, the teacher should meet them at the door. A positive, cheerful greeting by the teacher can start off the class in the right mood. If some of the incoming students are boisterous, the problem can be resolved before it gets out of hand.

Before they provide motivational material or give demonstrations, experienced teachers usually wait until they have every student's attention. Once the students are focused, start the class with something novel, different, or unusual. Avoid starting a class in the same way day after day. Instead, vary the opening activity by bringing different resources to class to show and discuss. Bring a painting—perhaps one of your own artworks. Borrow a sculpture or piece of folk art show. Play a song on a CD or cassette player. Tell the class a special guest is coming, step out of view, slip on an artist costume, become that famous artist. Create situations in which structures can be discovered. Teaching does not require you to limit yourself to transmitting structures that may be assimilated at nothing other than the verbal level.

In striving to make sure the students understand the project's objectives, sometimes the teacher prolongs the motivational session too long.

Three to five minutes may be ample time to arouse interest and show one or two exemplars of historical art. Be alert for those unmistakable signs of student disinterest: the shuffle of chairs, the tap of pencils, the whispered conspiracies, and the faraway looks. Teachers must learn to stop before students reach their fatigue point. Students need information, but they also want to get into their work. Perceptive teachers can detect when students are only half listening, or are more intent on some distracting gadget they possess than on their teacher's remarks or instructions. When expert teachers spot wandering prodigals, they may bring them back with a pointed question, a reprimand, or simply a pause and a meaningful look in the offender's direction. Also, when a discussion is held before studio activity, it is recommended that teachers wait to distribute materials and tools until the discussion is over, because students naturally are tempted to explore the materials at hand instead of giving their full attention to their teacher's presentation.

Getting the Design Off to a Good Start

The first few minutes of creative work are critical. Here, the teacher lays down the parameters of a successful work and puts into place the main compositional features. Just as a push is needed to set objects into physical motion, a push may be needed at the initiation of the working period. The first three minutes immediately following the motivation, when students pick up their art media for the first time, are crucial. While most students will be eager to do art, some may be overcome by uncertainty or fear. Students who are insecure about their own creativity may not be able to self-start. Some may sit perplexed, overcome by waves of confusion, self-doubt, and inadequacy. One way to spur such students into creative action is to give them one specific task to do. For example, the teacher may say to a student who requires direction, "To begin, place a line for the head at the top edge of the paper and a line for the feet at the bottom edge." Guided-drawing techniques at the start can get students working—drawing goggles for a subsequent undersea picture or drawing roller-coaster curves and then turning these into an amusement park.

Left to themselves, some students—perhaps those who daydreamed while instructions were given—will get off to a poor beginning and make mistakes that threaten their ultimate success. For example, some will draw tiny figures too small to paint or cut out. Or, instead of getting the overall picture put into place, some will use too much time and worry about drawing one small detail. They will insist on erasing one object repeatedly to "get it right," having set an unrealistically high goal for themselves. Try to forestall such problems by giving instructions or mate-

Get the design off to a good start. "Make the clown's hat touch the top of the page and his feet touch the bottom edge." This statement helped the children to create a composition that effectively filled the page and offered sufficient room to show important details. In addition, making the figures large helps to eliminate the problem of filling up empty background space. Crayon encaustic then was used for the paintings.

rials that will prevent their occurrence. For example, to prevent fussing with and erasing timid pencil lines, have the students draw bold outlines with yellow chalk. Instead of criticizing the negative, focus on the positive. Upon seeing a problem, hold up as a model a student's artwork that avoids the mistake.

Nurturing Creativity During the Working Period

During class, the teacher should not only keep students focused by calling attention to the instructional objectives, but should also look for creative uniqueness. Model, instruct, reinforce, question, and explain strategies for thinking in new ways. Look for student work that shows imagination, elaboration, and new variations. Use these exemplars to stimulate others to arrive at their own individual solutions. Hold up a student's work and

refer to it to call the class's attention to the particular creative inventiveness in evidence: "Look at how this composition fills up the paper. Four dancing figures are repeated, and the arms and skirts of several touch the sides of the paper, here, here, and here, to give the design a feeling of unity. I wonder in what ways other artists are giving their designs unity?" Two notes of caution are in order, however. First, the teacher should be careful not to embarrass the student whose work is singled out. Second, while the class is working seriously, the teacher should not constantly interrupt with calls to "look at this." Even so, there are many times that it is appropriate, when attention flags, for the teacher to use students' exemplars, as well the teacher's exemplars and reproductions, to rekindle the fires of motivation. (See Chapter 14 for additional ways to stimulate the creativity of students.)

Strategies for Fostering Perseverance

Perseverance, which probably contributes as much as anything to a successful artwork, is central to the qualitative method. In their desire for instant gratification, too many students race through assignments; the

Perseverance contributes much to the quality of an artwork. Students too often stop short, when extra effort could make the difference. Here, in contemporary artist William Sapp's 8- × 10-foot piece entitled Dogpack (1992) are not just a few clay figures but a thousand.

One way to ameliorate lagging student interest is to intersperse long and short projects. Many art projects by students of Beverly Mallon of Chase Street Elementary School in Athens, Georgia, take three, four, or more periods. But shown here is a quickie filler project for second graders—a pastel of a fantasy rooster on black paper, cut out and mounted on white paper decorated with a border. The artworks of animals were auctioned off at an Athens Humane Society fund-raiser event. All were sold, and the students received recognition over the PA system and in the school newsletter. Students learned both the importance of public service and the value others place on their artwork.

resulting lack of sustained effort regrettably brings with it little or no gratification. It is a mistake to equate speed of execution with freedom of expression, because a genuinely spontaneous and sparkling quality in a work of art is not achieved easily. Even in the primary grades, many successful projects can stretch over a month in duration. Teachers can hold students' interest and maintain an effective and productive atmosphere in their classes by continuing to emphasize the project's objectives that unfold session after session and by reminding students of the ultimate satisfaction to be achieved in an artwork that is done well.

One major problem that an art teacher is likely to encounter is students' lagging enthusiasm once the initial excitement of a new project or technique has waned. Almost every class contains students who are satisfied with only a superficial effort, who do not develop a real concern for the subject matter involved, or who find it difficult to persevere. They insist that they have exhausted the possibilities of the project, even though their

classmates still are busily involved. Here, the challenge for a teacher is to find the right balance between what these children may be willing to settle for and what they are capable of if given sensitive teacher guidance.

At the outset of a project, if the teacher collaborates with the students to stimulate their interest in setting and reaching objectives in both expression and design, children will be less likely to rush through their work. Perseverance is reinforced when students are internally motivated. For example, when students want to express something that is personally meaningful, they will work for a long time. This is why developing instructional objectives that encourage the expression of feelings is so important. For upper elementary and middle school students, posting the process and evaluative criteria on the board allows the teacher to function effectively as both a classroom manager and a facilitator for individual students. When questions arise, the teacher can clarify and resolve them for the entire class by referring to the posted criteria rather than by taking time to repeat those criteria to each student.

Encourage the students to go farther— to "weave" the figures into their pictures, to tuck some objects behind others, to create rhythm.

Courtesy of Joyce Vroon, Trinity School, Atlanta, GA.

Both perseverance and a sense of personal involvement can be increased by relating art projects to the students' personal interests and values. Fifth-grade student Sarah Nix.

Saturday Children's Classes, courtesy of Frank Wachowiak, Athens, GA.

The teacher encouraged these students to go further and add more figures. Then, students were encouraged to break up the empty background space in inventive, beautiful ways. Illustrations on this page are by upper-elementary-grade children. They took turns modeling with sports equipment and musical instruments in the center of the room.

Encourage them to make their pictures swing, to have rhythm through repeating forms. One way to encourage a child to do more is to combine praise with suggestion. For example, a teacher may say, "Now Mandy is starting to draw in the children; I wonder how many will be in the line by noon?" Mandy likely will respond to the teacher's expressed faith by putting in many figures.

Likewise, a suggestion offered to one student often will trigger fresh ideas for others who have reached a creative impasse. Using students' work in progress, call attention to compositional requirements as well as variations in expression. To the child who says "I spoiled mine," reply "the only way a picture is spoiled is not to do it in your own, personal way." Another method to stimulate extra effort is to have students anticipate a special show of their work. For example, ask the kindergarten teacher if she would let your class come in for a few minutes to show their artworks.

At the upper elementary and middle school levels, the practice of writing brief, constructive remarks on the back of a student's work or on slips of paper attached to that work will promote perseverance. Although time-consuming, this strategy for evaluation can help the conscientious teacher give individualized instruction. It also allows the teacher a chance to evaluate studio performance during a time that is relatively free of distractions and other responsibilities. It strengthens the possibility that every student in class will receive specific, individual help at some point during the project, and it provides students with a definite working direction for the ensuing studio period.

While many lessons may proceed with the majority of students roughly at the same stage, in today's inclusive classroom it may be that everyone will not be doing exactly the same project and assuredly not at the same rate. The range of student abilities will require multi-level teaching and perhaps adaptive technology. If paraprofessionals are in the room to attend to the needs of students with disabilities, caution them to not "do" the project for the student (see Chapters 12 and 13).

Cleanup and Evaluation

Cleanup procedures should be planned in advance to ensure that enough time has been allotted and that the process will occur in an orderly fashion. Because cleanup comes at the end of the lesson, when students are ready to do something else, and it often requires several students to be out of their seats at once, planning is necessary to avoid problems. For example, confusion and possible disruptive behavior at the sink can be prevented by sending students from one row or table at a time to that facility.

Courtesy of Barbara Thomas, Whit Davis School, Athens, GA.

Well-planned procedures for distributing and collecting supplies will facilitate both the production of artwork and cleanup, as shown by the basket and tray for materials.

utes of class or at cleanup time. Let the students know that they will be advised one student at a time, and remind them to take turns when conferences are necessary.

Unless children are given permission by the teacher to move about, they should remain in their assigned seats during class. In large classes, students should take turns obtaining and returning materials and tools, either by tables or by rows. The quality of artwork produced generally diminishes as the amount of students' unguided socializing increases; therefore, excessive talking, laughing, whistling, running, throwing things, chewing gum, propping of feet on desks, table hopping, and crowding at sinks should not be tolerated.

Students eager to test their power will act out in mock fighting, challenges to authority, and subversive tactics. They learn quickly to take advantage of an instructor who makes idle threats and fails to carry them out. Problems of student apathy, disinterest, and errant behavior are heightened by insufficient lesson planning, meager motivational material, too little visual stimulation, insufficient knowledge of the technique, weak rapport between teacher and student, and a lack of conviction by both regarding the worth of the art experience. To minimize disruptive behaviors, explore all possible avenues of motivation and persuasion, of reason-

If time remains after cleanup, the teacher should use it to good purpose and not let the period end with idle chatter. The after-cleanup period can be a summing-up or an evaluation session. This is a time to come full circle and demonstrate how the instructional objectives have taken form in the students' work and produced positive results.

Classroom Management

It is vitally important that the teacher always be aware of what is going on in the room and be at strategic stations at critical times. In other words, the teacher needs to have eyes in the back of his or her head. This means that during materials distribution, for example, the teacher should be near the supply area. When lecturing, the teacher should avoid facing the chalkboard or standing in front of the glaring light of a window. An effective instructor moves among the students during a studio activity rather than staying at his or her own desk. Likewise, an experienced teacher does not allow a bevy of demanding and questioning students to distract him or her from monitoring the class as a whole, especially during the opening min-

Courtesy of David Harvell, Fourth St. School, Athens, GA.

In this elementary classroom are posted five rules: (1) Listen. (2) Respect others. (3) Be polite and helpful. (4) Follow directions. (5) Take care of the room and materials. The first offense results in a warning; the second and third offenses result in varying lengths of time out.

ing and strategic reconciliation. If disciplining students is necessary, do not act hastily. Never mete out punishment during the heat of a crisis. Admonish the errant students and tell them you will discuss the infraction with them after class. Once you have stipulated a punishment, whether it involves changing seat assignments or sending students to the principal's office, put it into effect. (See also strategies for Students with Behavior Disorders in Chapter 12 on students with disabilities.)

Sometimes those who cause problems in class may be having problems at home. To reach such students the empathic teacher may use a "door-opener": "Why don't we talk awhile" or "What you are saying sounds serious. Tell me more." Often, the student will share the problem with a teacher who simply listens passively, nods, and acknowledges with "I see."

Teachers realize that students have a need to communicate. Talking in class is to be expected, especially during studio activities; however, when the conversation becomes so loud and disruptive that it prevents concentration on the project, teachers must take action. If they shout "Quiet!" or "Settle down!" or rap a desk with a ruler, ring a bell, or clap their hands, they may be successful in calming the class, but probably only for a few minutes. Experienced teachers prefer to use constructive approaches such as redirection and positive reinforcement. Calling the class to attention, they emphasize some aspect of the project that needs amplification. They also might hold up a student's work in process and point out specifically creative solutions that were achieved. (Prepare and photocopy in advance some remarks and rewards to clip to students' artworks ahead of class time.) By using positive strategy such as this, teachers maintain motivation and order while they avoid being seen as martinets in the eyes of their students.

In summary, during art sessions in which the teacher builds respect for serious endeavor and excessive, boisterous socializing is minimized, students' performances are of a consistently higher caliber than those of students in highly permissive situations. A class is less likely to be bored or cause disturbance when it has been guided to see the many possibilities of the project and has been richly motivated. Motivation is the subject of the next chapter.

Courtesy of Melody Milbrandt, Valdosta, GA.

Students work intently, facilitated by the cigar box containers full of crayons that afford students a wide choice in colors as they enrich their watercolor paintings.

Chapter 5

ART MOTIVATION

Most children need some form of stimulating motivation, either visual or verbal, to achieve high-quality results in their studio art endeavors. Students must have something to say if they are to give it visual form. The introductory phase of an art lesson should kindle the spark that ignites curiosity and piques interest. It is unfair to expect students to be challenged or excited by a teacher saying "Draw what you want today," or "Paint the way you feel." Some of the many successful ways to begin an art project include the following:

• Showing visual materials on the theme selected
• Viewing examples of previous work
• Guiding a class discussion in recalling a past experience
• Conducting a field trip to enrich the students' knowledge of the subject selected
• Playing recordings or tapes to create the mood of the particular visual theme
• Demonstrating the technical process with student participation
• Calling attention to a bulletin board or chalkboard presentation prepared for the project
• Having a guest speak, perform, or model for the students
• Using poems, stories, lyrics, and music as motivational enrichment

Inspiration for children's art expression comes from many sources. It may spring from their experiences at school and at home, from their playground activities, or from their visits to special places. It may come from nature and science or from topics in social studies; these are the subjects of the following two chapters. It may come from internal wellsprings, in which case the teacher's role is to nurture it. No matter what the source of inspiration, however, the responsibility for reactivating motivational experiences and giving them the immediacy to stimulate students into art expression is primarily the teacher's. With motivational procedures planned in advance, students can experience art class as a time of purposeful significance and excitement, a unique and rewarding period of the school day.

Personal Experience

The most vital and successful art project motivations usually result from vivid and meaningful personal experiences. The teacher's role is to help the students graphically clarify the significant aspects of the experience. Two main types of personal experiences can be used for art lesson motivations: recalled experience and direct perception.

Recalled Experience

In recalled experience, children do not actually see the objects before their eyes; rather, they recall them in their minds. Teachers must activate the children's store of knowledge and help them tap into their recall powers. Perhaps students have visited some special place, such as an aquarium or a farm, or have seen a circus, carnival, parade, dog or cat show, or sporting event. Perhaps it is an experience they regularly have, such as playing a musical instrument, sport, or computer game.

Because some children are not able to recall enough specific attributes of an event or an object, they may complain that they do not know how to draw it. The teacher must then help them to recall their experiences by asking questions such as *Who? What? How? Where? When?* and *Why?*

Campus School, University of Wisconsin, Oshkosh. Courtesy of David Hodge, Oshkosh, WI.

Recalled imagery of riding one's bicycle makes for a vivid picture. The everyday interests of young adolescents give them motivation to create art. These include sports, bicycling, rock celebrities, TV and movie idols, electronic games, and dancing. In the mixed-media collage by a middle school youngster, notice how the rider fills the space and the wheel motif is repeated in the background to create unity. Areas of analogous color comprise the background, and a feeling of motion is created by the bent back of the cyclist and the flowing scarf.

The known and the remembered are delightfully combined in this Greek child's depiction of the terraced countryside. It shows the boat pulled up onto the beach, the houses lining the meandering road, distant islands, and the sun peeking around the mountain.

The "what" is the overall experience that the child is being asked to recall—for example, a scary dream. To revive the "what" and "how" in students' minds, ask the children to physically act out the experience, using their bodies to recreate what was frightening in the dream, such as spiders or ghosts.

The purpose of *"where"* and *"when"* is to make passive knowledge active. To continue the dream example, ask the child to describe the room and the setting, its location in the house, who uses the adjoining rooms, the time of day or night, what else can be seen in the room, and the feeling the experience gave. The purpose of asking *"who"* is to give the child an opportunity to express self-identity and relationships with others. For example, a child may say, "I am in bed with my teddy bear in my arms, and Papa has tucked me in."

The *"why"* question is for the teacher. Teachers should ask themselves why this particular theme is considered to be important enough to warrant being the subject of the child's artwork. In the scary dream example, the hope is that by representing and sharing the frightening event with the group, the individual will gain a feeling of personal control over its scariness. A theme of playing on the playground may be chosen to promote an individual's feelings of group belongingness. Or a lesson topic might be chosen to stimulate a certain type of artistic representation. For example, depicting "my street" and "ring-around-the-rosy" would stimu-

"Where" can motivate an entire artwork. "My Bedroom" is an excellent topic for recalling significant things in a student's life. Here, student Catie Trezise very thoughtfully shows herself, her three cats, her wall decorations and furniture. Rather than just solid colors, teacher Barbara Bluhm of Maine taught the students to make graduated, blended colors with oil pastel.

A Philippine child recalls a favorite game, "jumping over the stick." She used her schema for profile and frontal views to depict the figures in this joyful watercolor of an important activity. The figures up front are drawn larger and those in the background smaller. In the small figures in the lower corners, realistic requirements yield to decorative requirements.

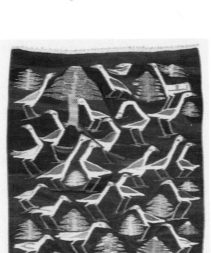

Children near Cairo, Egypt, create weavings directly from memory. They use no prior drawings and often weave with the image sideways. Weissa Wassef's world-famous experiment in creativity has brought wealth to the villagers. **Left:** *An 8- × 10-inch weaving of village animals, trees, and bird by Amal, age 11.* **Middle:** *At age 16, Amal created this sophisticated 12- × 14-inch design of ibis and trees.* **Right:** *Rowhia Ali, who had been considered the most talented of the child weavers, is now 55 years of age. She recently created the 42- × 66-inch Bedouins Entering the Village at Night.*

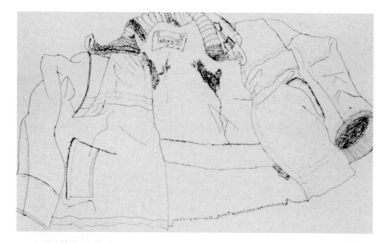

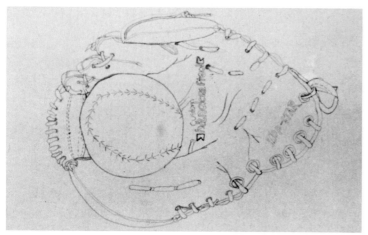

Courtesy of Baiba Kuntz, Glencoe, IL.

late the use of foldover drawings, and depicting "what's inside my body" (or "inside my house") would stimulate the representation of transparency or X-ray images.

The power and charm of designs that young children create based on their personal experiences are nowhere better illustrated than in Weissa Wasse's project, Weaving by Hands (see page 41). Young children in a small Egyptian town (Hourranie, near Cairo) created beautiful designs and transformed them into utilitarian and aesthetically satisfying weavings of significant economic value.

Direct Perception

While recalled experience is one kind of motivation, another is direct perception. Long before we are cognitive beings, we are aesthetic beings, responding to the world through touch, taste, smell, sound, and sight. One of the teacher's greatest challenges is to turn students into *noticers*—avid observers of color, structure, and design in their environment. The teacher can enrich students' lives forever by helping them to become aware of the pattern, beauty, and variety in nature. Children who note the unique cornice on a door, the intricate shapes on a violin, the subtle patina on an aged sculpture, the moving reflections in water, the varied cracks in dry mud banks, the shadow of a tree on the snow, and the veins in a leaf or dragonfly's wing can bring deeper insights to their art expression. Help students to delight in nature's colors, textures, and patterns by asking, "What else does it remind you of? What else can you show me about its structure?" To elicit a detailed, richly expressive response, there is no better motivator than direct contact and immediate observation of a given object. Thus teachers should emphasize drawing experiences based on things that can be perceived directly. Lead your students to look intently at everyday things, to see the unusual in the usual. By doing so, they will become inquisitive explorers for the rest of their lives. (See Chapter 20, Drawing.)

Direct perception is the other way to draw. The most common everyday object is a likely subject for direct perception drawing. Objects with special significance, like the warm fur-lined jacket, the sturdy hiking boot, and the professional baseball mitt and ball, stimulate even greater interest. Items that specifically relate to or fit the human body possess unique, lifelike qualities and natural contours that lend themselves most beautifully to dynamic, effective drawing.

Combining Recalled Experience and Direct Perception

A general tendency is to use recalled experience more often in the primary grades and direct perception from still lifes, nature, and models more often in the later grades; however, both methods effectively supplement each other. Students can be encouraged to add things from their memories or their imaginations to the background of a picture derived from direct perception. Indeed, mature artists often blend the two methods. Artists doing a scene from memory frequently use real objects or photos to acquire supplemental information. The French painter Marc Chagall did still-life paintings from bouquets of flowers and then, from his memory, added simply drawn human figures to the backgrounds.

Still Lifes as Artistic Arrangements

The elementary classroom or the art room can be the child's first, and often most enduring art lesson. Stimulating, eye-catching still-life arrangements should be on view for sketching purposes. Students should be encouraged to contribute to the store of found objects and nature's treasures in the classroom. The teacher's organizational ability, however, usually is needed to create a source of beauty and stimulation; what may be a source of exciting motivation to one person may be just a source of clutter to another. Whereas the next two chapters point out ways that still lifes can be integrated with other school subjects, still lifes also can be arranged solely as sources for artistic, eye-catching motivation to promote students' perceptual skills.

Different kinds of fabric—both plain and patterned—and large, colorful quilts and bedspreads can be draped against and tacked to a cork bulletin board. Pin the material to create bunches of fabric balanced by draped swags. Pin up an array of colorful hats against the drapery. Invite students who are willing to remove their shoes to stack them up for a still-life arrangement. Lunchboxes, bookbags, raincoats, and umbrellas usually are readily available. For late spring, a still life pertaining to pleasant summer activities (beachballs, floats, a thermos, and picnic supplies) will pique interest. Boots, shoes, shoulder pads, hats, caps, helmets, and gloves provide interesting organic shapes for drawing. A Western theme of boots, saddle, and harness brings to mind exciting associations. Objects associated with fun and pleasure, such as plastic toys and teddy bears, also are good choices to hold interest. Likewise, still lifes can be made of colorful desserts, á la the artist Wayne Thibaud. Sports equipment pertaining to skiing or skating can be combined with modeling by students, taking turns being draped in colorful cloths or costumes within the still life. A visually interesting understructure can be made by stacking several chairs or stools, with some sticking out at different angles, and weaving some drapery or beach towels in and out of the openings. In middle school, following a contour drawing of the setup, you might suggest that the students paint the negative shapes instead of the positive ones.

Have students participate in building a color environment as a motivation for painting in tempera and watercolor. Make it a class "happening." Incorporate colored tissue paper, crepe paper, fabrics, beach towels, ribbons, colored streamers, fans, banners, balloons, posters, party hats, beach balls, and Day-Glo materials. If the arrangement is near a window, use colored cellophane to create a stained-glass effect. Teachers will find many occasions during the year to use the following resources in still-life arrangements to enrich their art programs:

Fluorescent paint and papers
Fish netting and glass buoys
Window-display mannequins
Wallpaper sample books
Theater costumes and makeup
Tissue paper in assorted colors
Full-length mirror, face mirrors
Sports equipment
Contemporary posters
Duck decoys
Model cars and airplanes
Plastic-foam wig holders
Old fashioned hats, shoes, and purses
Texture table, felt board
Spotlights for illuminating still lifes
Bicycles, motorcycles, and helmets
Stained glass
Acetate or acrylic plastic in varied colors

Bulletin Boards and Art History

Plan exhibits and bulletin-board displays that relate to the art objectives. Bulletin boards and displays should be changed often, allowing students to appreciate completed projects and whetting their interest in further art endeavors.

What student in May would not be stimulated by anticipation of pleasant summer days, foreshadowed and recalled by this still life of beach balls, sand buckets and shovels,

Frisbees, kites, scuba diving goggles, figures, and scenes? Second-grade student Gregory Paulus.

Bulletin boards, videotapes, and reproductions of paintings, sculptures, prints, and crafts illuminate and intensify the objectives of the lesson. Color slides of art, crafts, and architecture; of design elements in nature and in constructed objects; of creative work by children worldwide; of examples illustrating the technical stages in a project; of people in active work, in sports, and in costume; and of animals, birds, fish, insects, and flowers can

Fourth-grade student Jenny Guillaume. Courtesy of Joyce Vroon, Trinity School, Atlanta, GA.

Cowboy boots, hats, jackets, and riding equipment capture the imagination and bring to mind the mystique of the Wild West.

Teacher Susan Whipple, Grace Christian School, Medford, Oregon.
USSEA art collection of Dr. Anne Gregory, Los Angeles School District.

Watercolor felt tip markers are richly and beautifully used by student Sarah Dody in this scene of a home by the snowcapped mountains.

be strong motivations. Books, biographies, and periodicals can lead to a project's richer interpretation. (See Part 3 for an in-depth discussion on incorporating art history, art criticism, and aesthetics.)

The Art Medium

The materials, tools, and techniques of the various art projects can themselves be the special catalysts that fire students' efforts. The teacher's demonstration can challenge the students. In the primary grades, introduction of new, vibrant colors in oil pastel, tempera paint, watercolor felt-nib markers, crayon, and construction paper elicits enthusiastic response. Likewise, colorful tissue paper delights upper elementary children working in collage when they discover new colors through overlapping. In the upper grades, the teacher can stimulate students' interest by introducing them to melted crayon for encaustic painting, discarded tiles for mosaics, waxes and dyes for batiks, plaster for carving sculpture and bas reliefs, glazes for ceramics, and wire, plastic, wood, and boxes for construction projects (see Part 4).

Critics of art education practices have recently called attention to the proliferation of media and techniques in school art programs, citing their deleterious effects. Although some of this criticism is justified, it

Courtesy of Joyce Vroon, Trinity School, Atlanta, GA.

New materials such as plaster-of-paris strips over a wire armature will motivate upper-grade students, eager to depict their interests. Here is fifth-grade student Natalie Bennett's piece, California Beach or Bust, Surf or Die.

An unusual medium that adds interest is drawing with pastels on black paper. Here an autumn still life with pumpkins is drawn by fourth-grader Rachel Nimmons.

The many colors of colored pencils were put to good use in a still-life drawing of jelly beans and their glass containers. An unusual marblelike paper added further interest. Fourth-grade.

usually is not the new materials and techniques per se that are to blame. Instead, the fault lies in how the materials are used: *as the sole motivation and purpose of the lesson.* The solution is to teach for qualitative art excellence and incorporate a range of valid lesson objectives. Any teacher can testify that a poorly motivated student, equipped with the newest and most expensive art gimmick, may produce a careless, nonartistic monstrosity, whereas another individual, using only discarded remnants from a scrap pile, may create an object of singular beauty.

Amount and Timing of Motivation

Because most children can absorb and retain only a few ideas at a time, avoid overwhelming them with an avalanche of suggestions. Motivations should be provided in small doses. Rather than swamp the students at one session with a plethora of ideas, introduce, if possible, a new and exciting attention-getter each time the art class meets or when interest flags. Rather than read an entire story for motivation, read a brief passage, or show the pictures while talking through the plot. Timing is of utmost importance in successful motivations. The teacher must sense when students have reached a fatigue point and need richer incentives to ensure progress in their work. Because students are most receptive at the beginning of a period, this is the best time to introduce new motivations, materials, and tech-

niques; teachers should not interrupt a busily engaged class to point out something that could have been handled at the outset. Time allotted for motivational sessions should be budgeted so that children will not feel cheated out of their studio or activity period. Plan the entire time sequence of motivation, discussion, demonstration, studio time, and evaluation both imaginatively and economically.

Exhibitions

Having one's work put on exhibition is motivating! As teachers, we can introduce students to this important aspect of the art world. One principle is that the further away from the classroom, the more selective the exhibit needs to be. In the self-contained classroom, every student's work might be exhibited. Each student might assume ownership of a designated place, identified by the child's large name label. Even high places and very low places can be assigned. In the school hallway, only the most significant works of a child need be exhibited.

At some time during the term, every child should have his or her artwork on exhibit. Some teachers save each student's work in a folder, from which they select pieces for exhibition. Then, they send all of the works home at special times of the year, such as Mother's Day or the winter holiday.

Top left: Courtesy of David Hodge, Oshkosh, WI. *Top right:* Courtesy of Frank Wachowiak, Athens, GA. *Bottom:* Courtesy of Baiba Kuntz, Glencoe, IL.

Sharing students' artwork with the community and the larger public provides valuable social interaction. Teachers of art can help children to develop such interests, which can provide life-long leisure satisfaction. **Top left and right:** *Middle school art exhibit at annual Art Education Conference, University of Iowa, Iowa City.* **Left:** *Notice the colored mats and aligned arrangements in this art display.* **Bottom:** *Observe the high degree of artistic organization in this elementary school art bulletin board. It contains sunflowers by Grades 3 and 4 and sunflower paintings by grades 5 and 6.*

To display group projects, one good way is to bring a fairly large, dead tree branch into the classroom. Mount it against a light-colored area of wall or a bulletin board. Not only does it provide unmatched subject inspiration for contour- and line-drawing projects, it is ideal for displaying paper sculpture or papier-maché birds, butterflies, and painted eggs and fish.

To avoid displays that look disorganized, align the pieces horizontally or vertically. Traditionally, artworks are mounted with a border that is three to four inches wide on three sides and about a half inch larger on the bottom. Check with school administrators for school policies on how work is to be hung on the school walls. Can tape be used, which might

Courtesy of Joyce Vroon and Marlee Puskar, Trinity School, Atlanta, GA.

This display of "Stars" paintings by third-graders was made interactive by it being necessary to lift the papers to uncover the celebrity's name.

Courtesy of Barbara Thomas, Whit Davis School, Athens, GA.

Avoid disorganized displays. Alternating columns and rows of underwater pictures, origami, and stained glass pictures make a stunning, varied, and colorful hallway display.

pull off the paint during removal, or are tacks or staples preferable, which will leave tiny holes? Another consideration is the audience. Should the work be hung at the eye level of the teachers and adult visitors, or at the students eye level?

Although a permanently installed hanging strip limits the level at which the work is hung, any type of fastener can be used in it. Another option is permanent display panels of composition board. Tacks and staples can be freely used in these, although excess use of any flammable boards may violate fire codes. As an alternative, a few 4- to 8-foot, foam-core display boards can be attached along their edges with duct tape to make a lightweight, temporary folding display area that is suitable for school open houses.

Move exhibitions into the community for even greater motivational power. Tell the students that some of their work from a project will be exhibited at a store, a branch bank, or a restaurant. At holiday time, display children's art in the local post office. Exhibitions hung in unusual places will get attention. Works can be displayed in the windows of a vacant store, for example, or murals can be painted on fences or walls.

Although commercial exhibitors usually pay a fee, school art often can be exhibited free at community events such as fall festivals, county fairs, and arts and crafts exhibits. Middle school students can take part in the local museum's exhibitions by serving as junior docents for children's tours. Hospitals have underwritten the production costs for a full-color calendar of children's artwork advertising the hospital's departments. A

Courtesy of Marlee Puskar and Joyce Vroon, Trinity School, Atlanta, GA.

Displays can be made more exciting and communicative by adding related three-dimensional objects to the display's background. Here, egg containers and straw enrich this display of third-grade students' rooster paintings.

newspaper has an annual design-an-ad contest at Halloween. Exhibiting students' artwork in the community is a way to bring recognition to your school and to your students.

PART 3

CURRICULUM FOR
AND NATURE OF THE LEARNER

Courtesy of Claire Clements, Athens, GA.

Chapter 6

Educational Psychology Considerations on Children's Learning and Creative Development

The first chapter in this part provides a background for considering child development in art. The subsequent five chapters give specific curriculum recommendations by grade levels: first and second, third and fourth, fifth and sixth, and seventh and eighth. The final two chapters of Part 3 give curriculum recommendations for children with disabilities and for gifted children.

Mind, Eye, Heart, Hand, or Context?

Mind, eye, heart, hand, or context (used as metaphors)—which of these controls the art learning process? Do children draw what they know, or do they draw what they see? Is it knowledge or vision that guides the drawing process? In general, young children draw what they know. Older children in our culture tend to draw more of what they see. Young children tend to pay little or no attention to the object and instead use a scheme, a product of individual cognition. During elementary school, children increasingly do attempt to draw objects more as they appear. Cognitive and developmental psychologists have made the case for a connection between children's art and their intellectual growth. Yet even older children may rely upon visual constancies—the remnants of their earlier cognitive schemes—for representing an object. These stereotyped "ideas" must be overcome for the child to "see" and draw an object with a degree of accuracy in representation. Young children can be exposed to drawing the figure or still life; however, teachers must accept the efforts of those still employing their own fixed schema of how to represent something, rather than attempting to capture its visual appearance.

Educators concerned with perception, called perceptualists, have emphasized children's ability to see, and especially to see differences. They stress vision, figure-ground relationships, and seeing, describing, and depicting differences within art's formal elements and principles.

In contrast, cognitive psychologists emphasize the mental processes in the child's constructing knowledge, while contextualist educators place importance on the making of choices within a given societal context. The five orientations are *not* mutually exclusive; experts, as well as new teachers such as yourselves, have differing degrees of acceptance of any of these orientations. Indeed, powerful thinkers such as Jean Piaget have provided theories that account for several of these orientations.

Moving beyond the scribbling stage, the young child begins to use geometric shapes to make representations. Butterflies in the Garden shows a wonderful, intuitive use of color in the multihued flower petals and cheerful use of background washes. White crayon lines are especially effective in crayon resist.

Constructivism

Piaget's psychological theory of intellectual change, *constructivism,* refers to the self-constructed nature of knowledge. Children are to be seen less as problem solvers and more as problem seekers or raisers—developers of strategies for manipulating information. That is, when students are tied to facts, we prevent their inventing and discovering for themselves. Education's value is measurable largely in terms of how well it permits the learner to go *beyond* the information given. Learners need to discover the means by which to make meaning out of experience and the knowledge they have gained. (For some art examples, see Chapters 15 and 16 on Science and Social Studies Integration). Through art representation, the child can find new ways to represent meaning.

These ideas gave rise to *Discovery Learning,* which focuses on creating the possibilities for the child to invent and discover knowledge. One variation of such ideas was in A. S. Neil's school, Summerhill, where the learning decisions were made by the students, who were considered to be innately wise and realistic. Effective discovery learning requires emphasizing objectives constantly and asking reflective, "springboard" questions—those that contain an element of controversy or contradiction. Identifying contradiction, identifying novel problems, taking risks in problem solving, and building a representation of the world are central in art making and art criticism. When a child seriously draws an object or writes about a concept, discoveries are made, writing and drawing are aids to learning. Discovery learning is not about haphazard, aimless goings on.

Piaget's theory focused on how the changes in children's thinking come about. The large changes in children's development are the sensorimotor period, the period of concrete operations, and the period of formal operations. These bear a rough resemblance to stages in art education: scribbling and manipulation of materials: learning how to represent things and ideas through art media: and, in middle school, increased intellectual examination, such as in art criticism, art history, and aesthetics.

Piaget emphasized the rational mind's central role in forming the knowledge structures necessary to bring stability and order in understanding the world. He believed there was at work in the individual's knowledge-gathering capabilities an equilibration process," rational and conscious that was used by the individual to construct systems of order. The individual's mental change occurs not just from mental reflection, but also from the action, exploration, and interpretation; hence, the individual *constructs* knowledge. It is for this process that the constructivism theory is named.

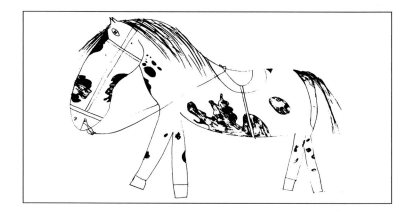

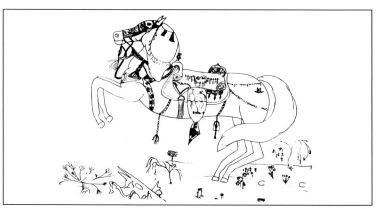

From the book, *Heidi's Horse,* by Sylvia Fein, Exelrod Press, Pleasant Hill, CA. Courtesy of the author and publisher.

These drawings, made by the same girl at ages 7, 9, and 10, illustrate increasing refinement in drawing horses.

Saturday Children's classes of Frank Wachowiak and Mary Sayer Hammond, Athens, GA.

Learners can find ways to create meaning from art experiences. Here, the bright and varied colors of insects and gardens are fused into a personal representation. Art criteria of varied shapes, informal balance, and border-touching are applied. **Top left:** *This tissue collage by a first grader is given movement and unity by colors moving from a red area in the upper left to a white area on the right edge.* **Top right and bottom:** *A fifth-grader applies colored tissue to a marker drawing on 18- × 24-inch white construction paper.*

In earlier times, a child had been considered to be a blank slate or empty tablet (tabula rasa) onto which the information was written. But constructivists view knowledge not as objective truth, but as transformative and changing. Rather than there being "one correct interpretation" to an artwork, an artwork's interpretation is more or less relative. Constructivists believe that, for true learning to occur, students must construct their own meaningful, personal knowledge bases under the guidance of a teacher who encourages active learning. Certainly, making an art representation of a thing is a clear way to construct and show to oneself and to the world what one understands about that thing.

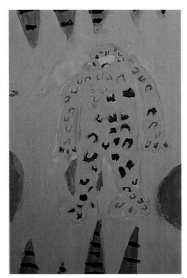

A meaningful, personal learning base can be exemplified by students' drawings of personal myths. This integrated art lesson was done after students studied Greek mythology and wrote their personal myths in language arts class. Here, sixth-grader Burton Dodd's powerful Hulk-like blue monster is seen through the eyes of its adversary's dragon-like teeth.

Effort in achievement of personally meaningful goals is shown in this fifth grader's oil pastel, "I become a hero on that special day." Teacher Debra Belvin, Bearden Middle School, Knoxville, TN.

Meaningful learning, the personal expression of a learned skill, is shown in this depiction of "Something I Am Proud Of." Here, the joy of achieving in soccer.

Before the constructivists, the behaviorist psychologists had emphasized how the environment could shape the individual through positive and negative reinforcement. For the stimulus response psychologists, knowledge was a passive kind of behavior, as in operant conditioning, and was elicited by stimulus and strengthened by response. The developmentalists, on the other hand, had a theory of innate biological unfolding, like a bud unfolding to become a flower. But the constructivists believed these theories were insufficient to explain how the sources of changes in interpreting the world came about. They believed it was through the individual's revising theories, based on the individual's experience in the world.

Educational psychologist Jerome Bruner led the cognitive revolution that rejected behaviorism's constraints. His bold dictum, "Any subject can be taught effectively, in some intellectually honest way, to any child at any stage of development," pointed out how early learning experiences form the basis for later learning. The task in the early years of school, then, is to put the material into the child's natural way of thinking, that is, using the senses along with concrete objects. An outstanding example of this in architecture occurred when, a second-grade boy, Frank Lloyd Wright, and his mother worked together with Froebel blocks. He and his mother worked together at the task for years. So strong was this influence that his final words were, "Put blocks in the young child's hands." Attendant to this developmental idea, Bruner believed knowledge was acquired in a spiral manner. Sequential art curricula that revisit art concepts year after year show an application of this idea.

Role of the Social Context

Piaget and another constructivist educational psychologist, L. S. Vygotsky, believed that teachers should encourage students' verbal interaction with peers to develop their thinking about issues. In so doing, the children are forced both to confront the views of others and to learn to express and defend their own ideas. They learn by interacting with a more experienced play partner, a peer, a teacher, or a parent. For example, Montessori education combines classes of three grade levels. There is little evidence that

Courtesy of Baiba Kuntz, Glencoe, IL.

The educational power of working in pairs (or dyads) is shown here in this pair of wrestlers. Seventh-graders Michael Schmidt and Matt Siegfried worked side-by-side on their wrestlers of Sculpey for weeks, finally putting them into the same wrestling ring.

Iowa City Laboratory School, IA. Courtesy of Frank Wachowiak and Ted Ramsay, Emphasis Art, first edition.

Students working in a group have artistic and language interaction as they jointly develop their "jungle." Intermediate elementary grade children made the 18- × 36-inch group collograph. A paper punch created patterns in the leopard and on the bushes. Pinking shears were used to cut the palm trees. Additional cutout holes, as well as little squares and triangles of paper, also were pasted onto the cardboard plate; see especially the gorilla's frenetic background at left. The plate was then printed.

The social context can be a powerful catalyst for learning. Here busy upper elementary youngsters work on a group project, a reduction linoleum print. Step One: In this variation of the regular lino print process, the students first cut away selected areas of the linoleum and pulled several prints using a red printing ink. Step Two: While the prints were drying, the youngsters gouged out additional sections of the block. Step Three: The cleaned

plate was inked again in green and printed over the first red edition, with care taken to "register" or match the second printing over the first. Step Four: While the two-color prints dried, students cut away the final selected areas. Then they used black ink for the third and last impression. The completed print is shown.

creative learning arises spontaneously and in isolation; the imagination develops especially well through pretend play with peers.

Although teachers traditionally have been accustomed to valuing the silent classroom of children working individually on tasks, the constructivists' ideas of social learning instead urge teachers to appreciate the developmental role played by guided communicative language interactions. This book's chapter on art criticism and aesthetics shows specific ways that this is done through questioning, generalizing, and hypothesizing what will happen next in the picture. In one method, *reciprocal learning,* the teacher and students take turns summarizing the main ideas in the picture.

Educational psychology has swung away from thinking of the student as an isolated problem solver toward thinking of the student as learning in a social environment. Buzz groups, dyads, educational games, working in teams, and group mural projects are a few manifestations of this. Cooperative learning—an idea supported by constructivists—requires children to be dependent on each other to achieve a learning

goal, for example, to prepare a report or mural or to construct a tower of a certain height.

Likewise, in the fine arts, attention is increasingly being paid to how learning and creativity operate less as the purview of the individual and more as within the verbal interaction of a social context. Some examples: While inventing cubism, Picasso and Braque felt "rather like two mountaineers roped together" (Berger, 1965). Paul Cezanne and Emile Zola, when young, were buddies. Mary Cassatt's creative genius was catalyzed by close friend and mentor Edgar Degas. Many of the abstract expressionist painters spent hours talking together in the evenings. Jacob Lawrence received his art inspiration in art classes at Harlem's first art center. Judy Chicago worked collaboratively with numerous women artists on The Dinner Table project. Such examples challenge the myth of a person-centered view of creativity and emphasize instead the social, family, and school context. As the student integrates give-and-take reciprocity of discourse, the student's consciousness is restructured by the social context.

Courtesy of Frank Wachowiak child art collection.

Imagination is not just for frivolous fantasy. It also can set the stage for generating ideas useful in real contexts. The world of the future is illustrated in pen and ink by upper elementary youngsters from Saga, Japan.

Courtesy of Beverly Mallon,
Chase Street Elementary School, Athens, GA.

How we will live and communicate in the future is shown in fifth-grader Brett Bessinger's Millennium *scene of a red spaceman interacting with jets, spaceships, and communication satellites.*

Much current educational psychology emphasizes context. For example, some cultures and contexts have not been concerned with showing realism while others have. Murals would not exist without willing owners of walls; school symphonies wouldn't exist without a supply of instruments and taxpayers willing to hire the teacher. Advertising art would not exist without advertisers and advertising media. Creativity is not only culture dependent, but also domain specific and field specific. Domains and fields are sociological concept systems that either allow or thwart the development of the individual's conscious and unconscious functions. In other words, development moves from the outside in as well as from the inside out.

But operating in real-world contexts should not mean disregarding the imagination's positive educational role. Imagination is not merely as frivolous fantasy of minor importance. Imagination assumes an important educational role when we think of it as students generating meaningful patterns of ideas that are useful in a real context.

Role of the Emotions: The Intuitive and the Nonrational

In addition to seeing and knowing (the eye perceiving and the mind constructing reality and operating within a context), there is a third element that guides children's drawings and learning—the feelings, which we metaphorically call "the heart." Psychologists interested in the link between self-esteem and learning have found that youngsters with high self-esteem performed better. In viewing a class's drawings, one sees the children's distinct personalities infusing both the objects shown and the very drawing styles. Educators who believe the expression of feelings is art's main purpose emphasize the emotional and psychological basis for art expression (see also Chapter 14 on the affective domain).

Emotions do guide actions and are shaped by them. The elementary school age child must develop an emotion-filled eagerness to learn new skills and win recognition through successful performance, or the child risks developing a sense of failure and inferiority. This elementary school-age crisis of a sense of industry inferiority was explained by psychologist Eric Erickson. His theory of psychosocial development stages explained how social factors influence feelings and behavior. (Erickson had been a high school dropout who wandered around Europe studying art until age 25, when he studied with Freud.)

Non-rational impulses, which may well be ill-defined, play an important role in the individual's change and growth. Piaget's equilibration mechanism accounted well for the human tendency to learn logical, rational, and stable structures, but it did not account well for the nonrational, or

We understand experience with both our conscious and unconscious mind. Fifth-grade students were asked to depict a dream. Here, the act of swimming is used to depict feelings of danger and helplessness.

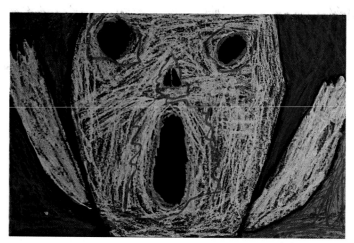

A dissonant, chaotic situation appears in third-grader Josh Schaefer's scary white face of a Halloween mask. Students love the macabre. Oil pastel on black paper.

This personal myth, set against a dark stormy sky, shows two enormous, dangerous lightning bolts crashing at the bare feet of a calm young girl, dressed in a primitive style dress. Language arts, writing, art, and study of Greek myths were integrated.

for innovations in the humanly crafted world. We "know" about things with *both* ideas and feelings. We understand with both the logical, linear, and rational as well as the emotional, intuitive, and nonrational.

Art can provide vicarious experiences in dealing with dissonant, chaotic situations, and these experiences, in turn, can help individuals deal with the dissonance they encounter in their everyday lives. Children's drawing violent monsters and Dungeons and Dragons superheroes and fighter planes while vocalizing "akakakakakak" give psychological voice to their creators' coping strategies.

Art and creativity are often considered functions of the right brain, while the left brain controls activities more amenable to tests, according to some researchers on brain functioning. Although many neurophysiologists are skeptical about the hemispheric separateness of right and left brain functions, the notion may serve a useful purpose in highlighting the importance of educational activities such as art. Like other dichotomous systems from years past, such as Viktor Lowenfeld's visual/haptic dichotomy, this dichotomy widens the scope of what is legitimately thought of as education's proper role. Likewise, Howard Gardner's theory of multiple intelligences also opens the door for a respect for multiple ways of knowing about the world (see Chapter 13, Giftedness).

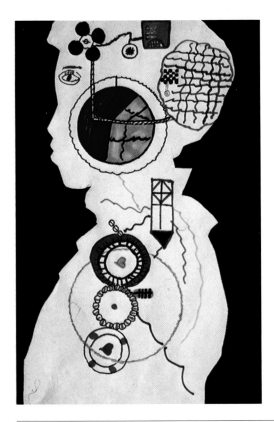
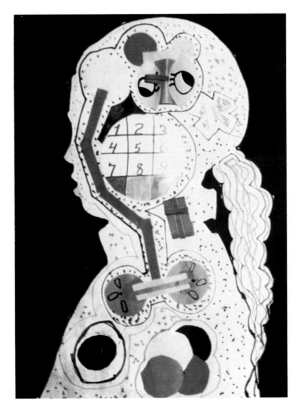
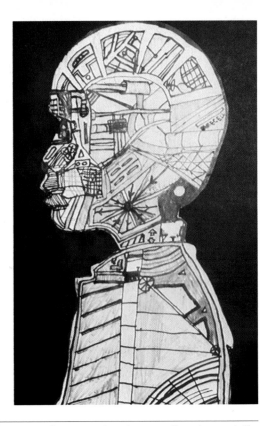

Fifth-grade students, whose knowledge about perception, evaluation, and aesthetics is increasing, created these X-ray silhouettes. They show how the opportunities and challenges of technology—for example, radio transistors, motors, battery watchworks, cameras, computers, and television—have affected them. Materials employed were 18- × 24-inch white construction paper, watercolor markers and crayons, wallpaper samples, scissors, pencils, and paste. A film projector lamp was used to create the student's shadow, and the silhouette was drawn by outlining the student's profile in pencil on the white paper. The completed drawings were cut out and mounted on dark-colored construction paper.

Transformation

As art is made, the brain's different mental functions—the rational, the intuitive, and even the irrational—are brought together. The rational processes are complimented by the fluid, nonrational, noncategorical thinking that occurs outside of conscious awareness. Art's bringing together these different mental functions into harmonious interplay can serve to transform the individual as well as society.

Transformation and novelty are important goals of education. David Feldman calls this tendency of mind to provide novel constructions the "transformation imperative." Humans have a tendency to intentionally transform their physical and social world. They want to bring into the world new conditions that will make it a more satisfactory place. Crafted objects that have already been made serve as models for innovation. Art classes provide children with exposure to such objects and especially to the process of transforming things and ideas through art to make a more meaningful world.

Like young kittens, young children are curious, toying with the boundaries around them and engaging in novel activities. Children gain pleasure from the manipulation of symbolic forms. Our educational task is to keep this playful analogical thinking growing, rather than dwindling, throughout the school years. Analogical thinking reaches back into the individual's rational and nonrational thoughts and emotions. It combines previous experiences in unusual ways to generate new patterns of meaning. Teachers should try to develop in their students an equilibrium between analogical and logical thinking. In this endeavor, art classes can help. Art classes catalyze the imagination as students generate ideas and designs to solve a problem in the context of art creation or art criticism. Art activities can stimulate students' imaginative, creative, and transformative potential—essential to our nation's greatness.

*Second-grade students transformed ideas of normal architecture into "funhouses"—fantasy creations designed and colored to convey pleasure and delight. **Left:** a house shaped like a Coke® bottle, with a taco-shaped patio for outdoor cooking. **Center:** a riot of hearts and stars add excitement to this huge funhouse; **Right:** a tall ladder leads up to this boatlike creation.*

Children's Similarities and Variability

Children everywhere have much in common. They react in similar ways to their environment. They laugh, cry, play, act, sing, and dance. They delight in seeing and manipulating bright, colorful objects, in playing games, and in manipulating machines and vehicles. They respond to sympathetic, supportive voices and to loving, nurturing hands.

Likewise, children everywhere draw in much the same manner during their early developmental stages. Long before we learn how to respond to the world cognitively, we respond to it aesthetically through touch, taste, smell, and sound. Preschoolers begin with random, haphazard marks and then move on to explore different types of scribbles. Acquiring more control and the desire for representation, children become able to shape their scribbles into simple, geometric shapes, which then develop into semirealistic interpretations. Contrasted with later stages, in which development is much more variable across cultures, the early stages of artistic development (up to 5 to 7 years of age for children without developmental disabilities) are universally determined; they are strongly similar across different cultures and times.

While universal patterns of development govern the early stages of expression, forces of the specific culture and its educational and enrichment programs play greater roles as children mature. As anyone who has looked at children's art would attest, the complexity of children's graphic imagery varies with the stages of their mental, physical, psychological, and social development.

Furthermore, no two children are alike. Because no two children are alike, it is difficult to generalize about them by grade or by age. Students in the same class may come from different backgrounds and economic levels, and they may have had totally different day-to-day experiences. Their problems and needs are unique. Even identical twins, who may confuse their teachers with surface similarities, have different personalities, different feelings and reactions, and different mental and creative abilities. Likewise, some fortunate students may have had abundant experiences in working with art materials, whereas others may have had only limited creative opportunities.

Courtesy of Baiba Kuntz, Glencoe, IL.

By the eighth grade, children are quite differentiated and variable in their representations in Sculpey® modeling clay. **Top left:** *a strong, self-reliant cowboy with chaps, lasso, mustache, and rocks, by Jonathan Honor;* **Top center:** *a strong, green haired, red bearded figure wearing contemporary baggy jeans with yellow stitching, by Lucas Simpson;* **Top right:** *a one-eyed general with the Union Jack and sword, claiming new land for the kingdom, by Dan Millner;* **Bottom left:** *a very artistic girl painter with thick black braids, dotted overalls and shirt, poised to commence work on her Miro-esque painting on its easel, by Amanda Ip;* **Bottom center:** *an old wizard in a beautiful star-studded cape parts the crashing waves, by Alison Eckenhoff;* **Bottom right:** *a young child, well protected with yellow slicker, rainhat, boots, and umbrella, is accompanied by a duckie, by Dena Gilman. Magazine photos on the walls provided a vague sort of motivation. Students worked for weeks on their characters.*

To understand and help children to grow through art, however, the teacher must be aware of those characteristics that have been identified with certain age groups. Art strategies for children with special needs—those with significant mental or physical handicaps and those who are gifted—are discussed in Chapters 12 and 13, following the chapters on the various grade levels.

Stage theory should be used only as a descriptive, however, and *not* as a prescriptive device. Stages are "external" not "internal"; a person does not "have" a stage. Rather, a stage is a commonly available structure of thought, like "gender" and "race." Like them, stages can be stereotyping and limiting. A teacher should keep in mind that stages may be skipped and even reversed. Even within one drawing, indications of several stages may be found. Lowenfeld's stages—the scribbling stages; the preschematic stage (first representational attempts, 4–7 years); the schematic stage (achievement of a form concept, 7–9 years); and the gang stage (dawning realism, 9–12 years)—have been criticized for these reasons.

Grade 1 girl

Grade 1 boy

Grade 2 girl

Grade 2 boy

Grade 6 boy

Grade 7 boy

Children's development in art is sequential. It generally moves toward showing more realistic proportion, more muscles, gender characteristics, and detail; however, there are numerous exceptions to the "typical" sequence. After leaving the scribbling stage, children at first draw tadpolelike figures in which single, straight-line limbs protrude from the head. By first grade, most children conceive of the head as a separate circle, from which hangs a body drawn with a triangle or square. Attached to this are straight limbs with two sides, rather than just being a stick (grade 1 girl). Then, the phenomenon of bending limbs becomes graphically realized, and curved, sausage-type limbs are drawn (grade 2 boy). Joints develop,

Grade 3 boy

Grade 4 boy

Grade 5 girl

Grade 6 girl

Grade 7 girl

Grade 8 girl

Courtesy of Frank Wachowiak, Iowa City Elementary Laboratory School, except grade 1 girl, courtesy of David Harvell, Athens, GA, and grade 7 girl, courtesy of Baiba Kuntz, Glencoe, IL.

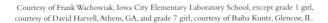

and knees and elbows then are drawn as the locations of the bending (grade 3 and 4 boys). The limbs become progressively more fused to the body (grade 3 boy and grade 5 girl). Overlapping of limbs over the body can be seen (grade 2 and 4 boy, grade 6 girl and boy). Proportions change from the three-heads-high figure (grade 2 boy) to the five-heads-high figure (grade 6 boy). The form of the neck, arising from the torso, becomes more clearly realized. Hips and muscles become more clearly represented (grade 6 girl and boy). Foreshortening appears (grade 8 girl's writing arm), and three-quarter views may appear (grade 8 girl's face).

Further, stage theory fails to account for how cultural influences can shape development. In school, the child is taught to accept culturally approved systems of drawing and to ignore those that the culture does not approve of or value. Artistic expression is not a driving force that seeks improvement, nor is it an unfolding of predetermined abilities. Instead, it is bound to the time and place of its creation, and it reflects the creative options available at that time and place.

Educational psychologists have documented "U-shaped declines" in creativity (although there is little unanimity as to when such decline occurs—in primary school, intermediate school, or middle school). Some researchers say the young child's early prowess in graphic symbolizations submerges by ages 8–11; this is called the U-shaped development in graphic symbolization. Perhaps this slump is due to inhibitions caused by the child's inner demands for photographic realism. Regrettably, after these slumps, only a few resume their creative efforts. Except among those who go on to become adult artists or who have outstanding art teachers, often there is little development in drawing skills beyond this stage. Alas, education too often brings with it increased criticality. Some say that this critical preference for what is safe and conventional is not a loss, but instead shows an increase in evaluative skills. However, while mastery of rules obviously benefits an individual, in too many instances it simultaneously inhibits the individual's existing abilities and capacities. (For example, untrained folk artists' creations may have a raw freshness judged superior to educated artists' artworks.)

While art teachers may fret over a diminution in artworks' imagina- ... kids don't see it that way. Five-year-olds prefer the realistic drawings ...-year-olds to their own. Eight- to ten-year-olds, in the conventional ... of middle childhood, have as their main art goal to be as realistic as ...ble. Only on reaching roughly age twelve can children entertain the ... that there are other things in art besides realistic drawing skill.

Later is not better. Artwork from earlier stages in a child's life is not inferior to later work. A younger child's work, filled with exciting, unpredictable naiveté, may show more giftedness than that of an older child. The spontaneity, beauty, and naiveté of a child's artistic expression at age 10 may never again be seen in that unique form in that child's work. Just as with fine art produced over centuries, fine art from the distant past is not inferior to more contemporary artwork. Instead, the work from each time shows the distinctive characteristics of that time.

The spontaneous and intuitive visual expressions of young children are so wonderful and so filled with wonder that they have influenced many noted artists such as Jean Dubuffet, Juan Miro, Paul Klee, and Karel Appel. Pablo Picasso said, "Once I drew like Raphael but it has taken me a whole life to learn to draw like a child" (de Meredieu, 1974).

Courtesy of Beverly Mallon, Chase Street Elementary School, Athens, GA.

Later is not better. Many adult artists would give a lot to be able to design like this kindergartner. It seems almost unbelievable that a kindergartner could create this rhythmic collage design of Matisse-like doves with such sensitivity to positive and negative shapes. In three 35-minute periods, kindergartners learned how to put triangles together to create diamond shapes and how to draw doves. First, they drew triangles and doves. Next, they traced over and over these shapes (to develop facility in writing). Then they cut them out, arranged them, and glued them down.

Chapter 7

A SEQUENTIAL CURRICULUM FOR KINDERGARTEN

This chapter and several that follow address students' development at the following two-year periods: primary grades 1 and 2, intermediate grades 3 and 4, upper elementary grades 5 and 6, and middle school grades 7 and 8.

Courtesy of Beverly Mallon, Chase Street Elementary School, Athens, GA.

The newness of drawing the school's butterfly garden with chalk outdoors motivated this kindergartner's painting of three powerful bluebirds soaring through a garden of beautiful tall flowers reaching up to the sun. Another day the children worked indoors painting the 14-inch × 18-inch artworks.

Each time period is discussed three parts: (1) in a table listing developmental characteristics of the age group and their implications for the teaching of art; (2) in a description of children's artistic development in terms of their use of shape, size, color, space, shading, ways of drawing objects, the human figure, and favorite subject matter; and (3) in teaching procedures for the areas of art criticism, art history, aesthetics, and art production.

Kindergartners' Developmental Characteristics	Implications for Instructions
Are interested in new things and eager to learn, but have a limited span of attention and are easily fatigued.	Preserve and stimulate their natural curiosity. Expose the children to many manipulative materials and encourage their interest in using art materials.
	Provide for changes of pace and location in different parts of the room. For example, begin by doing art, then sit and discuss each others' art.
Are easily excited.	Need little or no motivation.
Are prolific workers for a short period of time. Want to see immediate results.	Take into account the child's intense but short attention span in planning lessons.
Can answer speculative questions, such as "What would happen if …?"	Talking about an art reproduction, kindergarten students can speculate on what happens before and after.
Can sing complete songs from memory; can chant and move rhythmically to a beat.	Can paint to music; can sing while making art.

Courtesy of Beverly Mallon, Chase Street Elementary School, Athens, GA.

Using mirrors and guided instruction, kindergartners are capable of drawing self-portraits. They drew in pencil first and painted on a second day: a girl with thick black braids; a figure with circular blue earrings, eyes, and mouth; a boy with stick-up hair; a girl with a huge smile, neat hair, and a white floral patterned dress; a girl with a perfect triangular dress with head perched atop; and a girl with surprised eyes and lush eyelashes.

Kindergartners' Developmental Characteristics	Implications for Instructions
Some play alone, while others play cooperatively. A developmental sequence follows: *solitary* play (no awareness or interaction with another) *onlooker* play (near others and aware of their play, but not entering into the other's play) *parallel* play (independently working on a common activity, such as putting puzzles together and building with blocks) *associative* play (using each other's toys and asking questions) *cooperative* play (for example, playing hospital requires defined roles and a division of responsibilities of doctor, nurse, and patient)	To promote cooperative play, have more than one of an object, for example, two baby strollers. Do group projects only when each child can do his or her individual part independently. Let the children help around the room.
Learn social and interpersonal skills while playing. Can understand needs for rules and fair play.	Teach children how to comfort each other and give encouragement to others about their art. Large boxes such as refrigerator boxes can become houses, stores, boats, planes, and trains, providing venues for cooperative play. Puppets and simple puppet stages also promote cooperative play.
Like to do pretend play.	Seek opportunities to do pretend play activities, since they develop both cognition and imagination.
Desire the approval of classmates and teachers.	At sharing time, have the children tell about their pictures. Encourage them to comment on things they like in peers' pictures.

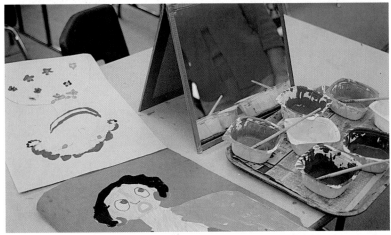

Children painted and cut out the first letter of their first names and combined them with their self-portraits. **Top:** *this boy's anger and anguish over his home situation might be reflected in his self-portrait.* **Middle:** *12-inch-square mirror tiles, which can be purchased at any home decorating store, had their edges taped with duct tape for safety and were then taped together to form a tent shape so that children on each side of the table could draw their self-portraits. Note how the premixed colors of tempera paints were distributed.* **Bottom:** *Note the circular nose and eyes; how well observed are the braided hairdo, eyes, and teeth!*

Courtesy of Barbara Thomas, Whit Davis School, Athens, GA.

Various techniques were used in kindergartner Derek Looney's illustration for The Rainbow Fish. *An initial pencil drawing was then outlined in marker, after which watercolor and a touch of sparkle were applied.*

Kindergartners' Developmental Characteristics	Implications for Instructions
Have strong need to get and give love.	Ask "Who is there with you in your drawing?" Show that you respect their art.
Have a playful attitude toward the environment, its objects, and experience. Like to use an object in several ways; have an easy and rapidly changing interchange between what is real and what is fantasy.	Encourage the interplay of reality and fantasy, and their dreams of grandeur shown in their art. Don't put down their dreams of grandeur (for example, "I am the strongest").
Like to pretend and engage in make-believe stories about the characters in their pictures.	Use puppet plays and made-up stories. Ask, "What would this character in your picture say?"
Can imitate movements of animals, evoking associations and imagination.	Use movement to motivate an art experience; for example, moving like a rabbit can stimulate drawing a rabbit.

Kindergartners' Developmental Characteristics	Implications for Instructions
Delight in fantasy, imaginative games, dances, stories, and plays.	Use psychomotor games and role-playing exercises and fantasy to stimulate their art. For example, ask, "If snow were like jelly beans, how would my yard and house look?"
Are developing awareness of their bodies.	Use games ("Simon says touch your head, tummy, ears") to help children to want to represent body parts in their artwork.
Are interested in moving and using their bodies. Like to climb into large boxes and under tables, run and hide from someone, play ring-around-the-rosy, and put together and take apart objects.	Involve the child's sense of one's body. Ask, "When swinging on a swing (or riding a bicycle or climbing a tree), which parts of your body feel it?"

Courtesy of Beverly Mallon, Chase Street Elementary School, Athens, GA.

A 2-inch border was drawn on the paper first to be used later for a decorated border. This four-period lesson involved pencil drawing on the first day, going over the figures with markers on the second day and also writing; watercoloring the figures and making watercolor experimental patterns to be used for the border on the third day; and pasting on the border on the fourth day. Kindergartner Eduardo Rojas drew "Hermano and me going for a walk with Papa and Mama," accompanied by a watermelon, a baby, and a picnic. Note the unique sawtoothed grass.

Kindergartners' Developmental Characteristics	Implications for Instructions
Can manipulate objects appropriately; for example, knows to rock a baby and push a car—not vice versa.	Develop desirable work habits: Teach the proper way to use a paint brush, markers, and clay, as well as how to clean a table.
Can spend hours in sand and water play, dredging rivers and sailing boats, constructing mountains, and making small boats to sail. Can sustain ideas from day to day.	Provide a sand table, a water table, and props to use. Encourage children to play together and to talk and listen to each other.
Desire to discover and to test their conceptual and physical powers. Are self-reliant in expressing their ideas.	Avoid projects that are to be made "one right way," such as a Pilgrim or a turkey, for example. Praise students when they have arrived at their "own way" of drawing something.
Have feelings that are easily hurt.	Respect their artwork; don't "correct" their drawings for being visually inaccurate. Accepting their art expressions and treating them with respect can build feelings of self-worth. Likewise, treating with respect their verbal expressions of the meaning of their art can build their self-respect and confidence.
Need outlets for wishes to dominate, destroy, or make a mess.	Provide opportunities for manipulating blocks and wood scraps and the like and playing in water, mud, and clay. (Yet, don't let objects be dirty or broken; teach good housekeeping.)
May experience a lack of confidence by determining that another child is the "class artist."	Praise children for arriving at their own unique solutions. Praise individual expression.

Artistic Development and Drawing

Drawing development is highly variable, especially during kindergarten. Some kindergartners will be scribbling or will just be coming out of the scribbling stage. Many will be drawing using diagrammatic forms between scribbles and symbols. And children who are advanced in their ability at making graphic representations will be making symbolic representations more like those of first- and second-graders, as described in the subsequent chapter.

Some common configurations seen in kindergartners' art range from disordered scribbles to ordered scribbles to geometric configurations to combining these into tadpolelike figures to a clearer understanding of trunk and limbs.

Preschoolers begin with random, haphazard marks and then move on to explore some of several kinds of scribbles (Kellogg, 1970). These include the following:

- Patterns of marking in strokes
- Patterns of dots
- Vertical, horizontal, diagonal, circular, curved, and waving lines
- Placement of patterns on the page, such as overall, quarter page, centered, in halves, along a diagonal axis, and following the shape of a two-corner arch, a one-corner fan, or a two-corner pyramidal form

Rather than thinking of these as *scribbles*—a term that has negative connotations to some people—one can think of them as presentations, in contrast to children's later *re*-presentations. Following random manipulation comes controlled manipulation, as the child discovers more consciously the ability to repeatedly go back and forth, up and down, diagonally, and around a circle.

Developing out of the scribbling stage, children move beyond scribbling's back-and-forth scrubbing motions and learn to draw simple geometric, schematic diagrams. Upon acquiring more fine motor control and the desire for representation, children introduce the geometric symbols of the circle, square, triangle, and rectangle into their artwork.

An understanding of triangular and curved shapes can develop into zigzag and wavy lines in bands, along with decorations, to create an attractive artwork.

A circle will be used for a person's head, the sun, or a flower blossom. (In fact, the telephone doodles of some adults often are of such diagram-like presentations of nonobjective, geometric markings.) Radiating lines from the circular forms represent limbs and sun rays. Common at this stage is the tadpole figure—a circular or oval form with sticks protruding to represent limbs. Some writers call such post-scribbling diagrams pre-symbolic or preschematic; that is, the child has not yet settled upon one defined symbol for or method of drawing a person (or house or animal). At this stage children confidently and proudly give their drawings titles; one minute afterward, however, they are likely to rename their artwork.

Kindergarten students exaggerate the sizes of things and people important to them. They usually draw themselves bigger than their parents. Hands, and even arms and legs, may be omitted. Drawn objects usually are not in correct size relationship. For example, in a drawing of "Me and the people in my house," the child is drawn the largest. Don't focus on size or omission of arms, hands, and legs—these will be learned later; instead, enjoy such disparities. Most children pass quickly through these early stages of visual representation. Hence, enjoy their representations while they still conceive in this spontaneous flowing development from scribbles into conceptual symbols, and later into dawning ideas of representing natural appearance. All too soon, the harsh standards of realism destroy the child's satisfaction with the symbols. Rather than forcing children in the manipulative stage into the higher stages, help them to feel good about their artistic efforts, pointing out their features.

Courtesy of Jackie Ellett, Fort Daniel Elementary School, Gwinnett County Schools, GA.

Four kindergartners prepare to discuss their paintings. The two students in the background probably can tell stories about the shapes they have created; the two students in the foreground appear to have achieved a concept of a girl figure and an animal.

Courtesy of Melody Milbrandt, State University of West Georgia, Carrollton, GA.

Notice the precocious artist's larger size, the body schema of a tapering rectangle for the torso with bent elbow arms, the lollipop tree with apples, and the use of sophisticated analogous colors.

Also enjoy the nonnaturalistic use of color. Kindergartners choose colors imaginatively, not realistically; do not insist that objects be their natural color. Children this age use color without regard to its local use or identity—it is so related to feeling and expression. Urging the child to use realistic color representation is to deny the child his or her own feelings. Whatever color strikes the child's fancy suffices; for example, a face may be painted blue or green. In fact, many mature artists have striven to emulate the kindergartner's freedom in selecting colors nonnaturalistically. Thus, praise and relish the wild color imagination shown, for it will not last long.

As figure drawing ability progresses in children in this age group, the idea of a body that is differentiated from the head develops and the limbs move downward to grow from the shoulder area rather than from the head. Fingers are added to the ends of the stick arms. Gradually, each limb grows to comprise two lines suggesting the arm's or leg's inner form. In coming up with a way to depict a figure, a student's combinations of symbols often differ greatly from those used by his or her classmates.

Some kindergartners arrive at the concept of using a baseline at or near the bottom of their pictures. From floating figures eventually develops an awareness of a groundline or line upon which figures and objects can stand. This may be either the bottom of the page or a separate baseline.

Drawing

Drawing clarifies, focuses, and increases children's comprehension. It communicates to the world some idea of the child's understanding. Discourage erasing and help the children to develop confidence in their ability to put their ideas down on paper. Thick kindergarten pencils, markers, and ballpoint pens are good for drawing. As regular-sized crayons can cramp kindergartners' hands, use the extra stout crayons, if available. Teach children to store a marker's cap on the marker's end and, when through, to replace the cap over the felt tip securely. (Because of harmful fumes, do not use permanent markers, especially with young children in the elementary school.)

Students draw things intuitively as they know them: the sky as a ¾-inch-wide blue band across the top of the picture; the yellow sun that appears in part or whole in the upper corner of almost every drawing. In such symbolic representations, the symbol prevails over what is visible to the eyes. Even kindergarten students who are advanced in their representational skills usually show little awareness of overlapping (or representation of things behind or blocked from view); that is, they draw both the outside and the inside, as in a transparent house or in legs visible through pants or a skirt. Kindergartners who are advanced in visual representation will devise a variety of interpretations for the human figure, a house, a tree, and animals. They discover the relationship between objects and color and seek colors close to those they know flesh and tree trunks to be. Like

Courtesy of Melody Milbrandt, State University of West Georgia, Carrollton, GA.

This kindergartner boldly used black paint to draw the figure and snowman. The legs, arms, large boots, gloves, snowman's twig arms, and tassel hat show excellent awareness, perception, and representational skill.

many children in first and second grades, advanced kindergartners develop their way to portray a front view figure, a side view figure, a sitting figure, a girl, and a boy. Don't dictate adult forms, but encourage the children to perceive and discover.

Children at this age require little or no motivation by the teacher, though an occasional "What else did you see? Was someone else there with you?" may spur a child to remember another object or figure that might be included in the picture. Help him or her to be inwardly motivated and to use personal symbols. Avoid asking questions that may divert children's attention from their work. Indeed, suggesting what to draw may confuse those unsure of what to draw until pencil hits paper. If a child runs out of ideas, suggest that the child review his or her past drawings. As they are being reviewed, the question "What is that?" is fine to ask, especially for four- and five-year-olds. In the unusual circumstance in which a child does not know how to begin, however, the teacher can motivate the child by saying, "What is it you want to make? Which color would you like to begin with? Do you want to make it big or small?"

Avoid giving one's own ideas as corrections, such as "The sky should reach the ground" or "That is only a bunch of scribbles." Do not comment on size disparities. While it is important not to dictate or overdirect the creative efforts of the kindergartner, it is essential that a teacher demonstrates how to get and handle supplies and finished work. Likewise, he or she must reinforce proper behaviors: "I like how you always put your brush back in the right jar of paint. I like the way you share materials." However, though it may take self-control to withhold feeling about paint being wasted, colors mixed to "mud," and paintings messed over, be careful not to ascribe negative attitudes, such as about messiness.

Avoid cute, follow-the-directions, gimmicky assembly projects geared to impress parents. Although such projects often are shown in kindergarten teaching magazines, especially at holiday time, too frequently they teach next to nothing about artistic expression. They merely reinforce in the child's mind the idea that adults know the correct way to do things and that children cannot arrive at their own solutions; instead they must copy exactly. Such one-right-way projects frustrate children because they condition them to accept adult concepts that children cannot produce on their own and teach them to regard their own ideas as unacceptable. This deprives children of opportunities for decision making and individual expression.

An art project that is not at the child's stage of visual representation is a subtle lie and a plagiarism. In many "tricky" projects, for example, the teacher does inordinate amounts of cutting beforehand (which the children would benefit from by doing themselves), and then requires the children merely to assemble the pieces in the right order. While "following directions" is doubtless reinforced through assembling a head with features, or a body with limbs, such projects involve little creativity. Follow-the-directions projects promote doing without thinking; they are the antithesis to creative expression.

Although it can be desirable to show a method for assembling, for example, a figure, other approaches should also be shown or encouraged. Children might come up with alternative ways to put together the figure, or they might place three eyes on the face of the figure. We believe there is educational value in encouraging different solutions, not in teaching just-one-right-way projects. Representation should come from the child, with the teacher's guidance, and should reflect the child's ability in conceiving of the human form.

Regarding display, a principle that generally applies is the younger the child, the more attention on the process and the less attention upon displaying the product. Also, if you display some work, you must display the work of all children in the group or class. With kindergartners, do not emphasize taking the work home; instead, let the child make that decision.

Help the child to think in positive self-statements: "I am able to think of new ideas. I am a capable person. I enjoy drawing in my own special way." In fact, some educators believe that art examples should never be shown to a child since the educational goal is to develop the child's self-confidence—not to imitate an example. However, the kindergartner's stage of visual conceiving examples may be used if introduced casually and briefly as just one of many possible ways to do the artwork. Then the

Kindergartner Annabelle Barbe first drew this watermelon-eating family scene in yellow chalk. Next, watercolor, and then black marker and other marker colors were added. In the fourth period, squares made during the watercolor experimentation were shared with classmates and used for the decorative border, interspersed around the text, "Me and my dad with my neighbor Casey eating watermelon with a bluebird."

teacher should encourage and praise as the children discover their own approaches. Children *do* learn by imitating, yet the danger of copying is that it leaves the kindergartner feeling insecure about his or her own powers.

Note, however, that it is not necessary to praise every product. Lavish praise can be harmful in that it can communicate falseness and misunderstanding. Superlatives of indiscriminate praise do not recognize individual accomplishment and do not build a sense of self-worth. Excessive praise can lead children to want to please adults rather than to please themselves. Respect the product, but don't overemphasize it.

Make descriptive comments about the artwork and relate them to the child's learning and accomplishment by recognizing what the child has done: "You were really concentrating on that" or " What an interesting way to use the brush—like a bird hopping around" or "Green!" or "You mixed all those colors together and made the color of tree trunks" or "What a big strong shape!" or "You invented a new color. Can you give it a name?" or "What a lot of circles!"

Likewise, encourage parents to show interest in their child's work. Suggest making comments such as, "So many different kinds of lines in it!

I enjoy having a chance to see your work." "How did you do it?" since it focuses attention on the process rather than on the product. To share these ideas with parents, write them a letter in which you remind them that their reaction may affect their child for years to come. Caution them against both ridiculing questions and indiscriminate praise. Instead, urge them to commend their child for what he or she has done—not for what he or she is. Separate the child from the act and praise the act, not the child (the child already is okay). Urge parents to provide a safe climate in which their child can feel relaxed and accepted in his or her artistic expressions.

Painting and Other Media

(Also see detailed chapters on the specific media in the latter half of the book.)

Painting

Painting with ½-inch brushes is often recommended in order to help kindergartners to convey boldly the strong, clear configurations they have created. Children can readily paint or draw when seated on the floor. If space permits, 18- × 24-inch paper is best for painting, for the large paper lets the child get his or her whole body into the act of painting. If space permits, easels help the artist to appraise the creation from a distance. They may take up too much room, however, especially in the crowded "temporary" trailer-classrooms in which art is sometimes taught.

To minimize drips and facilitate expression, the consistency of the paint is important: it should be like heavy cream—not water. Teach the children to tap their brushes against the inside of the jar to lessen drips. To facilitate the child's discussing the work with his or her parents later, write on the back of the painting what the child says it depicts.

A good way to provide paint for the children's use is to have four jars of different colors in a cardboard box, with a different brush for each color. Likewise, small shallow dishes or trays, such as furniture casters, can be filled with a tablespoon of each color and held in a larger tray. (Alternately, each container may have several brushes in it; to avoid muddy colors, instruct students that brushes are not to be switched to other jars of different colors.) Fill the jars only to the depth of the brush bristles to help prevent paint on hands. Smocks made of adults' shirts can help to keep clothing protected; using plenty of newspapers to keep paint off floor surfaces will keep custodians happy. Have ready several buckets of warm soapy water in which the children can wash the brushes and in which trays can be soaked. The brushes should be rubbed on the hand or on soap to remove paint from the brush's metal ferrule and then placed upright to dry.

Courtesy of Melody Milbrandt, State University of West Georgia, Carrollton, GA.

Sponges were used to paint the black cat's body and the light blue background of this kindergartner's cat. Triangles and lines were collaged on for the face.

Courtesy of Beverly Mallon, Chase Street Elementary School, Athens, GA.

"We're not gonna' make a real cat!" was the motivation for this "Crazy Cats" project, which emphasized the differences between realistic cat colors and fantasy colors. In the first period, the teacher directed the kindergartners' drawing of the trunk, legs, etc. In the second period, playful patterns were painted to decorate the body. In the third period, the animal was cut out and glued onto an 18- × 24-inch contrasting colored paper.

A project such as painting a box or a board a solid color can be a challenge that is appropriate for kindergartners; when dry, the board or box can subsequently be decorated with patterns, using oil pastels or paint. With holes drilled into it, it can be used as a pencil holder.

After studying Matisse's paper cutouts, kindergartners cut out the shapes of fish, seaweed, and water, and arranged the parts in their designs.

Cutting, Pasting, and Collage

By 4 to 4-½ years of age, most children can cut along lines without much failure or frustration. A six-year-old who has trouble may have a perceptual motor problem. Tiny hands have too often been asked to use scissors with which even adults would have difficulty, with blades that do not contact each other well. (To assure a pair of good scissors per child, some schools encourage the parents to send a good pair to school.) Also, have a few pairs of left-handed scissors available. If the number of pairs of scissors is inadequate, teach a lesson that uses paper tearing. Instruct the children to determine whether the paper has a grain that makes it easy to tear in one direction but difficult to tear in the other direction. Concerning the mechanics of cutting, urge the children, as they bring the blades together into the paper, to press the finger-hole handles together sideways so that the blades are pushed together and make a clean cut. It seems that children have a natural tendency when cutting to snip a tiny shape right from the center of a new piece of colored paper, thus relegating the remainder to being a scrap. To prevent such waste, emphasize the frugal use of resources, the beauty in using recycled materials, and the wisdom of finding an appropriate size scrap from which to cut a desired shape. In addition, teach scissors safety. Remind students to place scissors down on the desk before waving their hands to get the teacher's attention.

When the skill to be learned is gluing or pasting, kindergartners often need to be taught the mechanics: how much glue or paste to use, and on which surfaces to apply it. Some youngsters—uninitiated into gluing with squeeze bottles of white glue—delight in squeezing out great streams of it on the paper, using about ten times more than is required for strength or is desirable in terms of the teacher's later stacking of the work papers.

White library paste can be purchased in lieu of glue, or nontoxic wheat paste can be prepared. A recipe for homemade flour paste is ½ cup flour and ⅔ cup water mixed with ½ teaspoon powdered resin. A cornstarch paste can be made by bringing ¾ cup water, 1 tablespoon light corn syrup, and 1 teaspoon white vinegar to a full boil, then mixing ½ cup cornstarch with ¾ cup cold water and adding it to the boiling mixture. Let the mixture stand overnight. It makes one pint of paste. A few drops of oil of wintergreen or oil of peppermint as a preservative will make the paste last for about two months.

To facilitate collage activities, organize trays or shoeboxes of many found treasures. Wallpaper and cloth scraps, metal foils and textured papers, feathers, and yarn with which to adorn pictures help children to become aware of contrasts in solid versus patterned papers, dark and light coloration, and rough and smooth surfaces.

Fingerpainting

Fingerpainting is an excellent means by which children discover types of lines. As mentioned earlier in this chapter in the discussion of kinds of scribbles, for example, children may draw fan shapes and parallel lines. Teach them about using the edge of their hands as they paint. Fingerpainting can be done directly on washable Formica-type table surfaces as well as on paper; surfaces may be dampened to facilitate the paint's movement.

Prepared fingerpaint is available, but a homemade fingerpaint is easy to make; the simplest way is just to add paint to liquid starch. Another formula combines equal amounts of liquid starch and soap flakes, such as Ivory®, with color. If using powdered starch, dissolve ½ cup of it in cold water, then add 4 cups of boiling water, along with ¼ cup of soap flakes, the color, and ½ teaspoon glycerin. Likewise, wheat paste can be used: add 1-¼ cups nontoxic wheat paste and ½ cup soap powder to 4 cups of water, beat, and separate into jars to which you add powdered or liquid tempera paint colors. Three or fewer colors are sufficient.

If a record of the fingerpainting experience is desired, make monoprints by pressing sheets of newsprint or wallpaper samplebook pages, which may first be dampened, onto the painting before it dries. Protect the floor with newspapers. Follow up the fingerpainting activity by discussing types of lines and movements made by the children's fingers and the edge of their hands. Finally, children may find that cleaning up is as pleasurable as making the painting: use a bucket of soapy water, a big sponge, and a rubber squeegee for the task.

Chalk

Chalk is easy to use, and messiness is not an issue if it is being used outdoors on the sidewalk or playground. Some school districts specifically prohibit the use of chalk inside a classroom by an entire class due to the amount of suspended particulates generated. To be used inside in a less dusty way, one can "paint" with chalk by first painting or sponging the paper with water or starch diluted to half strength. The children then draw on the paper with thick chalks. Another way to "fix" the chalk and prevent its getting onto clothing is to dip the chalk into buttermilk while drawing. (When finished, to prevent this dipped chalk from getting hard and unusable, rub its ends on a piece of screen or concrete to clean it.) Using dark colors of paper gives chalk drawings a dramatic effect.

Clay

Because of its three-dimensional "realness," clay is a particularly good medium for drawing out a shy child and encouraging the child to talk about what he or she has made. For the young child, clay activities should be mainly a touching and feeling experience. Hence, for initial experiences, be particularly careful about the clay's consistency. If it is too sticky, it will be difficult to model and may also be unpleasant for the squeamish child. Rolling out the wet clay on a piece of burlap or heavy cloth quickly removes the excess moisture. Note, however, that if the clay is too dry it will be difficult to model. Clay may remind some children of too recent toileting conflicts; colored and scented claylike doughs and manufactured claylike products (see below) can avoid the problem.

Clay can be pulled apart and smoothed together repeatedly, knocked down and rebuilt, punched with holes or pinched and built up. Clay can be made into a snake, a cup, or a dinosaur. Products should not be contrived by the teacher, however. Don't hurry the children through the exploration; rather, give them the freedom to represent their own experiences. It is not necessary that they create a monster or a bowl. Children love to make tubes (snakes) and balls (eggs) and concave shapes (bird nests) and to tell stories featuring their clay creations. Children who have come to possess the ability to make figures can be taught how to attach appendages, such as legs, onto their forms by scoring and smoothing the pieces together. Volcanoes of clay can ooze red streams of lava. Children can shape animals, pumpkins, chickens, and ornaments to hang from a tree branch in the classroom. Do not feel that all pieces must be saved or fired; if clay is limited, better to reuse it.

Clay cleanup can be facilitated by using a piece of moist clay to pick up pieces that have fallen to the floor or are scattered about on the table. Only after all loose bits of clay are gathered up in a dustpan should water be used on the table. Damp sponges and dry paper towels can help to dry up the inevitable thin film of clay. For additional suggestions about clay maintenance and clay finishes, see the chapter at the end of the book.

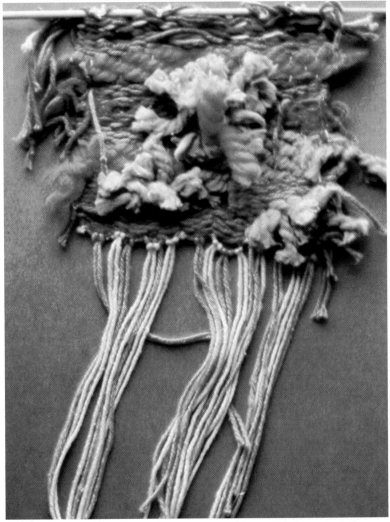

Courtesy of David Hodge, Oshkosh, WI.

A weaving by a kindergarten child, using a variety of yarns of different sizes and with some cut loops extending forward.

Modeling Mixtures

A Playdough®-like mixture can be made of 1 cup of salt, 2 or 3 cups of flour, and 1 teaspoon of salad oil to alleviate stickiness. Cook the mixture in a saucepan on the stove, adding just enough water so that it releases from the sides of the pan and, when cooled and kneaded, such that it won't stick to hands. (For a salt and cornstarch dough, heat 1 part water and 3 parts salt; slowly add 1 part cornstarch; stir well and knead.) Coloring the doughs is optional, as is adding oil of peppermint and cream of tartar, which help the mixture to keep for several months. After being modeled, the mixture can be left to dry and set. Baking it for one hour at low heat will lend additional hardness. This mixture, called baker's clay, often is used for ornaments. If making ornaments, give each child a golf-ball-sized piece of baker's clay to model. Remember to insert a hole at the top of the child's ornament, through which a string or ribbon can be threaded to hang it. New wet-setting clays and other modeling formulations are available at arts and crafts stores; although more costly, they are clean and easy to use and clean up.

Other Three-Dimensional Activities

Puppetry is an excellent way for children to overcome shyness and develop public speaking ability. Puppets can be made in many ways, the simplest of which are: (1) a paper plate painted to be a face and stapled to

Courtesy of Jenni Horne, Tyrone, GA.

A three-dimensional project done by the kindergartners creates a sculptural form of circular strips.

Courtesy of Jenni Horne, Fayette County Schools, GA.

An appreciation of how a quilt is made up of smaller squares was conveyed by pre-K children designing their own quilt.

a tongue depressor stick; (2) a paper lunch bag painted with a face and put over one's hand, or, alternately, stuffed with newspaper to make it three-dimensional and then tied to an inserted stick that is held; (3) a face drawn onto a finger with marking pens, with a scrap of cloth loosely tied around it for a scarf. More complex puppets can be made from a stuffed sock, a Styrofoam ball, or a little tube fitted to the finger. Other three-dimensional activities that also are recommended for developing perceptual discrimination and eye-hand coordination include construction with boxes and tape, parquetry designs, stringing of beads, and building with blocks and Legos®.

Art Criticism

At the kindergarten level, helping children learn how to talk about art can be considered a part of learning to perceive and conceive. Visual awareness is a hallmark of general intellectual development. Not only can children sort, they can describe categories for sorting. They look through the art to vicariously experience the art's content. They pay little heed to style, composition, or multiple meanings—awarenesses that come in later grades. As kindergartners, however, they can attend to and question the nature of visual phenomena, such as color and shape.

Art criticism is a term used to describe a way of talking about not only fine art but also about one's own art and that of classmates. At the kindergarten level, art talk can deal with what we see, what it is called, how it appears, what colors and shapes and textures it has in it, and what ideas it brings to mind. As the children talk about art, accept their approximations and their weaknesses in logic. Time permitting, some of them can report on their painting or clay work at the daily reporting period. They can name the colors, the shapes, the objects and forms, and, if time permits, they can use fantasy in telling stories about their works. Likewise, they can learn to appreciate the work of others through the teacher's encouraging them to "Tell what you like in others' work."

Needless to say, art criticism is not a license to make *critical* remarks about an individual's artwork. Making comments to a kindergartner such as "Don't you know that the sky meets the ground?" or "Can't you see that the arms come from the body, not from the head?" would discourage that child.

Art History

Art history can be introduced effortlessly by showing art and talking to the class about reproductions. Children like to look at pictures, to hear the teacher tell about them, and to tell about them themselves. However, if this art is discussed before students begin drawing, the teacher should take care not to overly influence students' work. It is sufficient merely to say, "Here is how an artist, J. B. Murry, did his artwork about water. He used long lines and decorations of other colors. I'd like to see how you make art in your own way." Not all art educators agree that art should be shown to young children as a drawing motivation, lest the children come to feel that their effort is insufficient. If fine art is introduced as a drawing stimulus for the children, use art that appears to be near the children's stage of visual conceiving, such as folk art or art from prehistoric civilizations, which may bear a surface similarity to young children's ways of representing forms. The teacher who obviously values each child's unique way of drawing and can reinforce individuality in expression can benefit children through the brief, matter-of-fact use of clear, appropriate exemplars.

Aesthetics

Discussions about aesthetics are not beyond kindergartners. For example, the teacher may ask, "Is it okay for art to show scary things and ugly things, or is it better for it to show mostly nice things and pretty things?"

Courtesy of Beverly Mallon, Chase Street Elementary School, Athens, GA.

The teacher briefly showed the kindergarten students a painting by folk artist J. B. Murry, which she determined was at the children's general stage of visual comprehension. A child then made this beautiful painting, full of pattern and smiling faces.

Or, in relation to a discussion of pattern in clothing, a teacher might ask an aesthetics question such as "Can decoration be called art, or does art have to show some real thing, like people and animals?"

Suggested Subjects or Themes

With kindergartners, usually no suggestions are necessary; the child is eager to make art. Allow freedom in choice of subject matter. It is desirable that the child not become dependent on teacher motivation, but, rather be able to focus independently on personal ideas to express. Because some children will be in the scribbling and presymbolic stages, avoid unnecessary domination, such as dictating that they draw a horse one day, a tree the next, a snowman the next. If there is a need for a topic to get the children started, common experiences such as playing on the playground, or with a pet, or with "the person who takes care of you" are good starter topics, as are suns, birds, houses and trees, and exciting occasions, such as a heavy snowstorm, fall leaves, and a field trip to the fire station. "A Favorite Way to Use Water" is a wide-open motivation that gets many differing artistic responses (spray it at a friend, jump in ocean waves, splash in the tub), and it might come after an actual experience with water on "Splash Day" at school.

Courtesy of Melody Milbrandt, State University of West Georgia, Carrollton, GA.

In this painting of a tree in a snowstorm, the kindergartner carefully observed how tree limbs diminish in size.

Chapter 8

A SEQUENTIAL CURRICULUM FOR GRADES 1 AND 2

This chapter and several that follow address students' development at the following two-year periods: primary grades 1 and 2, intermediate grades 3 and 4, upper elementary grades 5 and 6, and middle school grades 7 and 8. Each time period is discussed in three parts: (1) in a table listing developmental characteristics of the age group and their implications for the teaching of art; (2) in a description of children's artistic development in terms of their use of shape, size, color, space, shading, ways of drawing objects, the human figure, and favorite subject matter; and (3) in teaching procedures for the areas of art criticism, art history, aesthetics, and art production.

Developmental Characteristics

The left-hand column of the following table lists some of the developmental characteristics of first- and second-grade children. The right-hand column lists some implications of these characteristics for art teaching.

Developmental Characteristics of First- and Second-Graders	Implications for Instruction
Are active and easily excited.	Use almost any topic as motivation.
Enjoy working with their hands.	Use hands-on art activities as vehicles for correlated learning.
Take great pride in their work.	Display work in the hall.
Exhibit strong feelings of possessiveness.	Be aware that some children may cry if their work is kept for an exhibit.
Are eager to learn.	Teach them many ways to see and draw. Do not underteach.

Developmental Characteristics of First- and Second-Graders	Implications for Instruction
Want to be first.	Assign special responsibilities: "You may be the scissor monitor today."
Have a limited span of interest and are easily fatigued.	Give a series of objectives *throughout* the lesson rather than all at the beginning.
Have feelings that are easily hurt.	Point out several alternative ways to draw something, with each conveying different qualities, rather than just one right way. Praise when students arrive at their "own way" of drawing something.
Are alternately cooperative and uncooperative.	Give "road signs" to foreshadow how long each phase will be, when the phase will stop, and what the next phase will be.
Usually can grasp only one idea at a time.	Give instructional objectives throughout the lesson instead of all at the beginning.
Delight in imaginative games, dances, stories, and plays.	Use psychomotor games and role-playing exercises.
Like to pretend and engage in make-believe.	Use puppet plays and made-up stories about the characters in their pictures. ("What would this character in your picture say?")
Desire the approval of classmates and teachers.	Encourage the children to tell about their pictures at sharing time.
Often live in their own secret world.	Use fantasy as a motivation. ("If I were a … , what would I be like?")

79

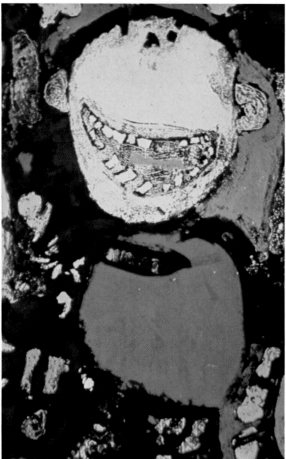

Courtesy of Frank Wachowiak and Ted Ramsay, University Elementary School, Iowa City, IA.

In these attractive, first-grade tempera and India-ink portraits can be seen the characteristic features often found in very young children's art. These include circle heads; the figures *from 2-1/2 to 3 heads high; the bodies comprising circles, squares, and triangles; and the sausage limbs.*

Developmental Characteristics of First- and Second-Graders	Implications for Instruction
Are interested in new things to touch and taste.	Use tactile motivations, such as rabbits, toys, turtles.
Are fascinated by moving and mechanical devices.	Arrange wind-up toys as still lifes. Use visual-perception devices such as kaleidoscopes.
Enjoy TV, illustrated books, movies, picnics, school field trips, new clothes, pets	Ask children to do art criticism of book illustrations. Have them draw after field trips and draw pictures of pets.

Art Development

The adjacent table shows how children ages 5 through 7 employ various art elements. The left-hand column shows early development and the right-hand column later development. At these stages, enormous variability and change occur in children's art development. Although the table is written in the form of instructional objectives, it is not meant to be prescriptive. Beauty and expression can be achieved in many ways—not through only one teacher-prescribed "right way." Representations consisting of scribbles can be as expressive as those depicting clearly defined objects, such as houses. As stated earlier in this book, skills developed later are not necessarily better than those possessed by a kindergartner.

Changing colors on the teacher's signal in a game of "Pass the Paint Please" is a clever way to maintain young children's attention. A good topic for this rotating color painting is "A Flower Garden from Above."

	Early Art Development: Ages 5 and 6	*Subsequent Development: Ages 6 and 7*
SHAPES	Student will draw the geometric symbols of the circle, square, triangle, oval, and rectangle. Student will employ a basic symbol, such as a circle, to depict varied visual images—the sun, the head of a person or animal, a table, a flower blossom, a tree, a body, and even a room. Students will use combinations of symbols that very often differ from those their classmates use. Student will depict simplified representations and is not too concerned with details.	(Because child art develops so rapidly during this period, this column deals with the development of some 6-year-olds, but especially of 7-year-olds.) Student will change slowly from geometric, symbolic interpretations to more specific characterization and delineation. Student will use more details in depictions—hair ribbons, buttons, buckles, eyeglasses, necklaces, rings, shoelaces, purses, fingernails, patterns, and wrinkles in clothes.
SIZE	Student will use emotional exaggeration of size, enlarging things that are important to him or her and omitting features that are not. For example, children may draw themselves bigger than their parents or omit arms and hands if they are not needed in their depiction. Size also may be determined by the need to fill an empty space or the desire to show a clear relationship.	Student will approximate more representative proportions, although figures still may be three heads high (the proportions of the Peanuts cartoon character, Charlie Brown) rather than the subsequent five heads high.
COLOR	Student will use color in a personal or emotional context without regard to its local use or identity. For example, a face may be painted blue or green.	Student will use color in a local, stereotypical way. For example, tree trunks are brown, and the sky is blue.
SPACE	Student will employ a baseline as a foundation on which to place objects such as a house, a tree, or a figure. The bottom of the page sometimes substitutes for the baseline. Student will draw both the outside and inside of a place, a person, or an animal, as if in an X-ray or transparency. Later, student may use a second or third baseline higher on the page.	Although distant objects often are drawn the same size as closer objects, student will begin to place distant objects higher on the page. Students will use a foldover technique, turning their papers completely around as they draw, to show people on both sides of the street, diners around a table or a picnic lunch, people at a swimming pool, or players on a baseball field.

Three strong figures overlap a big red house and fence in this first-grade student's painting in analogous colors.

A still life of flowers motivated this second-grade student's crayon and watercolor painting.

The tiny figures in the background give the scene a feeling of great distance. For her "What I am Proud of" painting, second-grader Samantha Bubes depicted her pride in her roller blading. Notice the charming way that the sun's cheerful face echoes her own face. Also note the careful, thorough use of markers.

Courtesy of Frank Wachowiak and Ted Ramsay, University Elementary School, Iowa City, IA.

Courtesy of Melody Milbrandt, Valdosta, GA.

A second-grade student uses a schematized way of drawing the human figure to show the joy of giving friends valentines. Notice the sausage-like arms, swinging leg, and the bold outlining in black after the colors are applied.

This busy child is not a slave to realism. Four eyes are called for—two to keep track of the hair brushing and two to keep track of the simultaneous teeth brushing. What could be more expressive! Figure schemes are energetically explored. This Picasso-like black crayon self-portrait, 12 × 18 inches, is by a first-grade girl.

	Early Art Development: Ages 5 and 6	*Subsequent Development: Ages 6 and 7*
SCHEMAS FOR DRAWING OBJECTS	Students will draw things intuitively as they know them: the sky as a band of color at the top of the page, the sun that appears in part or whole in an upper corner of almost every picture, the railroad tracks that seldom converge, the leaves that are wider where they attach to the branch or stem, the tree with a very wide trunk to make it strong, the eyes high up in the head, and the mouth as a single, curved, happy line.	Students will draw objects as they know them to be rather than how they see them at the moment, such as a table with four legs when only two are visible from their vantage point, or a house with three sides when only one is visible from their sketching station.
THE HUMAN FIGURE	Students will devise a variety of interpretations or schemata of the human figure, house, tree, animal, and so on, depending on their experience.	Student will begin to use characteristic apparel and detail to distinguish sexes, such as skirts and trousers, and differences in hair styles.

Art Criticism, Art History, and Aesthetics

By ages six and seven, children are beginning to try to figure out what an artwork is, and to make their first interpretive efforts. Of course, their ideas of what is logical may not conform to the standards of adults' logic. They look through the visual rendition. They do not see the style, or the composition, or the multiple meanings that things can carry. They begin to develop a language for art criticism, with the names of the formal elements. For example, they can match photos of textures to real textures. They can describe how things are the same and different.

In this initial stage, a goal is to expose the students to large amounts of material in order to establish a knowledge base. The goal is twofold: (1) to teach students how to experience the delight and values shown in the arts; and (2) to contribute to the students' general perceptual and conceptual knowledge that operates tacitly in a broad range of situations in and out of school. One caution is to avoid the reductive bias of presenting only clear instances, rather than showing the complexity of knowledge. Require students to examine their own knowledge to come up with answers. This approach is in line with education's shift from being curriculum-centered to being learner-centered.

"Do you like this painting? Why?" This kind of art criticism is appropriate to the level of students in Grades 1 and 2. For children at this age, subject matter is most important. If they like the object portrayed, they will like the picture. For example, in responding to Albrecht Dürer's drawing of a hare, the children like it because it's cute or because they like rabbits. When speaking, children do not differentiate between the world of

Courtesy of Barbara Thomas, Whit Davis School, Athens, GA.

Studying the artist William Johnson's use of enlarged body parts, third-grade student Kelisha Scott did this colored drawing of the cook skillfully using his hands to flip pizza at the school's partner Pizza Hut.

Courtesy of Barbara Thomas, Whit Davis School, Athens, GA. Student: Courtney Daniel.

Three-dimensional Vincent van Gogh's Starry Night *was the motivation for this first-grade student's cut-paper and crayon-resist version of the radiating starlight.*

pictures and what the pictures represent. They like pictures of things they like and reject pictures of things they dislike or fear. Indeed, understanding the difference between appearance and reality develops gradually. For example, one first-grader, needing to assure himself that he had not created a frightful lion, told the class with some uncertainty in his voice, "It's not a real lion."

In addition to their preference for pictures of things they like, children at this age like pictures that are clear and vivid. Clarity of perceptual cues and orderly organization of elements are very important. First- and second-graders look through the visual rendition; they do not see the style, the composition, or the multiple meanings. Their perceptions are limited to a single interpretation. Talking about art reproductions helps to develop their skill in drawing inferences. They can scan and take in whole scenes to figure out situations, characters, and narration. They can predict what a scene would be like if they were there and how they would feel about it. Because they cannot imagine the scene in an alternative way, art inquiry is limited to what is shown rather than also incorporating how what is shown could be changed. By the second grade, however, the children's preferences grow beyond like or dislike of a subject to include personal experiences as important factors.

Children between ages 5 and 7 are particularly drawn to the effects of color. From the first class meeting, begin teaching this age group perception of the art elements, especially color awareness. Emphasize the child's everyday surroundings: the classroom, clothes, books, artwork, and posters on display. ("If you have anything turquoise around your desk—maybe a notebook or a bracelet—hold it up.") Help them to identify the primary and secondary colors, Introduce the warm, sunny colors such as yellow, orange, pink, and red, as well as the events associated with them—the circus, county fairs, parades, Mardi Gras, and autumn harvest. Likewise, talk about the deep, cool colors such as green, turquoise, blue, and blue-violet and the images they evoke—the mysterious night, the ocean depths, the rain-wet jungle, and the deep, dark forest.

Take advantage of the many stimulating games, toys, and devices available for developing color awareness: the prism, paint chips, the color wheel, and the kaleidoscope. If a rainbow can be seen from the schoolroom window after a rainfall, use this natural phenomenon as the basis for a discussion of the color spectrum. Encourage color matching and sorting exercises using found materials such as scraps of art paper, wallpaper, magazine illustrations, cloth, and yarn. Store the color collection in shoe boxes, one box for each color. When the children are using paints, encourage them to create new colors by mixing colors on wet or moist paper and naming their new color inventions.

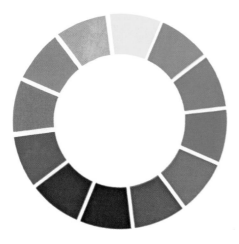

Complementary colors are those opposite each other on the color wheel; analogous colors are those side by side.

Have children explain the meaning and contribution of the following terms: color, shape, line, pattern, repeat, and texture. Encourage them to describe pattern and texture in clothing, in school surroundings, and especially in nature's bark, fur, fish scales, and plumage. Just as talking about art helps to promote their artistic creativity, artistic creation helps them to talk about art.

Teachers should exploit all means at their disposal, including the marker board and bulletin board, to call the child's attention to art project–related vocabulary.

Children between ages 5 and 7 should know the following basic art terms: black, blue, bright, brown, brush, cardboard, chalk, circle, clay, coil, construction paper, crayon, dark, dot, drawing, easel, eraser, fingerpaint, glue, green, grey, hammer, ink, kiln, light, manila paper, mural, nail, newsprint paper, orange, oval, overlap, paste, pastel, pen, pencil, pink, pinch pot, purple or violet, rectangle, red, ruler, scribble, shape, square, stripe, tempera paint, tissue paper, triangle, watercolor, weaving, white, and yellow.

Designing, Drawing, and Painting

Something big, something small.
Something short, something tall,
Something dark, something light,
Help to make your drawing right.

This rhymed stanza helps to remind young children to add variety to their compositions. In most instances, the *more* images, shapes, or ideas the students incorporate in their compositions, the more unified their drawings become. "Who else was there?" and "What else might have been on the ground?" are helpful prompts.

As children join the community of picture makers, they begin to understand the demands of representation. They like to paint simple images, using themes such as a favorite toy or "What I like to do when it rains." For children whose abilities have developed beyond the scribbling stage, discourage their rushing to finish or scribbling in backgrounds haphazardly. Children love to use their pictures to tell stories, and both pictures and stories can change over time. Children often make several representations of the same subject—for example, the family's new baby. Some can write their own titles and stories; in other cases, they need help to put their ideas into words.

One common sequence in making a drawing or painting is, first, a house, then a tree, then a flower, then a person, and then a pet. Drawing the chimney at right angles to the slanted roof shows that, while children can recognize the correct vertical orientations, they prefer the perpendicular orientation in their drawings.

Courtesy of Frank Wachowiak and Ted Ramsay, University Elementary School, Iowa City, IA.

A first-grade child uses the circle-square figure schema in her drawing of pets and friends. Figures are shown with no elbows and no shoulders, which would distract from the figures' crosslike forms, but the cat has well-defined elbows and shoulders. Pattern in clothing is depicted by stripes, plaids, and even a floral design. The multicolor crayon engraving technique requires considerable patience. Because it calls for the application of several layers of crayon, use a small size of heavy oaktag. Begin with a light hue, such as yellow or pink, and build layer on layer through darker colors to a final brown, dark blue, or black. Lakewood Elementary School, Ann Arbor, MI.

Introduce your students to various tools for making linear images. These include pencil, ballpoint and felt-nib pens, crayon, oil and chalk pastel, brushes, school chalk, a nail for crayon-engraving projects, or fingers for finger painting. Praise their discovery of various line patterns: stripes, plaids, circles, stars, spirals, radiating lines, and zigzags.

As mentioned previously, children this age like their pictures to show clear and vivid relationships. One good way to achieve this is to use large brushes: ¼-inch, ½-inch, or larger. Another way to show clarity is to draw objects against an empty background. Passing the paint containers every few minutes also works well. During this period, floating objects gradually will diminish, replaced by figures on a stand line or a baseline. Later, the children may move to the use of multiple stand lines. At this age, however, it is too early to introduce overlapping.

Some children will make the delightfully charming foldover drawings. They will show figures arranged in a circle or on both sides of the street and upside down on one of the sides. Games such as ring-around-

Courtesy of Joyce Vroon, Trinity School, Atlanta, GA.

Here, the walking figures and cabin cruiser are seen as if from the side, while the rowboats and sidewalk are seen as if from the top. Showing both the top and side views in one scene is called mixed-plan-and-elevation drawing. *This, and foldover drawings, which show the events upside down on the other side of the street, are charming ways by which artists represent what is known rather than what is seen. Conception and perception work together in this Taiwanese primary-grade child's telling about events at the water's edge.*

Courtesy of Joyce Vroon, Trinity School, Atlanta, GA.

The outside shape and inside rooms of the child's house, from basement to attic, are shown in Millie Rhodes's X-ray or cross-section view.

the-rosy can be used to stimulate these charming representations. For the children, foldover is a quite satisfactory method of design representation, because it tells very clearly what is occurring.

Another pleasing representational device that appears in some drawings is X-ray drawing or transparency—seeing the figure through the clothes or seeing through the walls to what is inside the house. As children grow older, this way of representation diminishes; children say they do not do it that way anymore. Transparency does not mean that children think clothes are transparent; instead, it comes about because they draw the figure first and then dress it, like using paper dolls. This representational device is used in some other cultures, such as Australian aboriginal art, and can be employed as a motivational material.

Introduce first- and second-grade children to line drawing, the variety of shades, light and dark value, color, and pattern. Encourage drawing based on their personal experiences and observations, but welcome and praise imaginative expression as well. In addition, provide many opportunities for them to draw from real objects. These might include plants in and around the school, pets brought to class, flower arrangements, toys and dolls, classmates as figure-drawing models, self-portraits, depictions of the

Courtesy of Sharon Burns-Knutson, Iowa City, IA.

This remarkable self-portrait is a contour drawing. A second-grade child from Iowa City patiently delineated what she observed. Guide children to look carefully and see freckles, collar stitchery, and patterns in the hair. This portrait reveals once again what drawing skills youngsters are capable of when they are encouraged to become aware, observe details, and draw slowly and deliberately.

Courtesy of Joyce Vroon, Trinity School, Atlanta, GA.

Using mirrors, these primary-grade students draw and paint themselves in fancy hats. Art by third-grade student Natalie Long.

Courtesy of Frank Wachowiak and Ted Ramsay, University Elementary School, Iowa City, IA.

"On our street" was the subject of this colorful colored construction paper collage by a first-grade child. The class first discussed shapes of houses, garages, churches, synagogues, and stores, then of trees, bushes, hedges, fences, sidewalks, telephone poles, traffic signs, billboards, mailboxes, pets, cars, and trucks.

family in various settings, community helpers, and subject matter observed on field trips. Provide large-size paper or newsprint so that details the children consider to be important can be shown. In figure drawing, the size of the drawn head often determines the size of the body. Encourage the children to fill the page.

Collage (Cut and Paste)

Students in this age group also need to develop their scissors skills. Invite them to cut simple, basically geometric shapes out of construction paper. Make sure to have scissors available that are designed especially for left-handed children. Encourage the beauty of torn paper edges. The privilege of using pinking shears and scissors with scalloped and patterned edges can be a special reinforcement. In addition, provide opportunities that involve pasting little shapes onto big shapes, such as those cut with a hole punch. Point out how contrast is achieved by pasting a light-colored shape over a dark-colored shape and vice versa. Demonstrate how to use paste and glue economically and effectively. A felt board can be employed to introduce children to the countless possibilities of cut-out shapes and how they can be juxtaposed. Cooperative murals employing the cut-and-paste technique, in which each child contributes one or more parts to the whole, are very satisfying projects (see Chapter 20). Almost any theme lends itself beautifully to collage making at this stage: flowers in a garden, animals in the jungle, fish in the sea, birds in a tree, and butterflies in flight.

Printmaking

Simple repeat prints result in colorful, all-over patterns. These can be made with vegetables, found objects, clay pieces, erasers, cellulose scraps, and hands and fingers. In most instances, colored construction paper is recommended for the background printing surface. Other possibilities include colored tissue paper, newsprint, wallpaper samples, brown wrapping paper, and fabric remnants. Printmaking activities with children at this age are somewhat limited because first- and second-graders do not possess the necessary skills for complicated techniques. Emphasize space filling when trying plastic foam meat-tray prints with incised relief created by pencil pressure. Monoprints, too, are wonderful projects for this age group.

Ceramics

For success, sufficient clay must be available; a ball of clay about the size of a grapefruit is recommended for every child. The clay must be of the proper malleable plasticity as well. If it is too sticky, it should be left to dry a while. Allow the children to discover clay's potential. Encourage them to

Saturday Children's Classes. Courtesy of Frank Wachowiak, Athens, GA.

For primary-grade children, delightful prints can be created using plastic foam meat trays as the printing plates. Trim off the curved part of the tray. A preliminary drawing with a felt-nib pen or soft-lead pencil is recommended. Make the impression by pressing a blunt-pointed pencil into the tray. Water-base black printing ink, rolled out on the engraved tray with a brayer may be used.

squeeze, pinch, poke, and stretch the clay. Show them how to make coils and how to form the clay into small balls or pellets. Guide the children in the creation of simple, familiar forms. Suggest they hold the ball or lump of clay in their hands as they manipulate it into the desired shape. This procedure discourages the tendency of some children to pound the clay flat on their desks. Primary-grade children can control the relatively simple sculptural forms of an elephant, hippo, cow, horse, rabbit, turtle, pig, dog, cat, whale, or resting bird. They enjoy manipulating the clay in either an additive or a subtractive way. Teachers prefer the subtractive way (pulling features out), because it results in a form less likely to fall apart.

This first-grade student painted her fantasy wish to be able to fly like a bird.

An animal with a figure or with its young is a popular ceramic theme. Additively constructed pieces can come apart in drying and jostling. Therefore, emphasize heavy legs, firmly attached with roughening and smearing of the clay at the points of attachment. Japan.

Construct simple pinch pots from a lump of clay the size of an orange, and bisque-fire the pots if a kiln is available. Ask the children to hold the clay ball in the palm of one hand and to insert the thumb of the other hand into the middle of the clay ball about halfway down. As the children rotate the clay ball, they should push and pinch their thumb and fingers along the inside and outside of the ball in overlapping pinches. Caution them not to make the wall or bottom of the pot too thin. Also, because the marks of their fingers and thumb often add an attractive texture in itself, discourage the use of water to smooth their clay.

Suggested Subjects or Themes

The following topics are suitable for children of ages 5, 6, and 7 (Grades 1 and 2):

Playground games
Fun in the snow
Fun in the fall leaves
A flower garden with insects
My pet and me
Stuffed animals
Animals in the zoo or jungle
Farm animals
Noah's ark
Kings and queens
What I like to do when it rains
What my parent and I like to do together
My make-believe wish
Skipping rope
Our community helpers
Butterflies in a garden
Fish in the sea
Land of make-believe
My favorite toy
Clowns (for pattern)

Courtesy of Melody Milbrandt, Valdosta, GA.

In this first-grade student's painting of a clown, an initial crayon drawing was then gone over with watercolor.

Chapter 9

A SEQUENTIAL CURRICULUM FOR GRADES 3 AND 4

Although children's art at all developmental stages has a unique beauty, some people refer to the third-grade and fourth-grade years as the "golden age of child art." Just as roses are most beautiful at the moment halfway between bud and full flowering, children at this time create art that reflects the charm of newly discovered representational concepts along with signs of a move toward realism. Abstraction and realism are in a state of happy coalescence, and children's belief in their expressive powers is not disturbed by the anxiety about "not looking right" that comes later. By this time, most children have developed methods of drawing that satisfactorily communicate their meaning to adults. Their schemes may be based partly on concepts and partly on perception. Early forms such as a lollipop tree, which once seemed okay, yield under increasing perceptual input to become more novel, fresh forms. Beneath the surface, however, the conceptual model still has an influence, and the child who uses a conceptual scheme should not be made to feel inadequate. This child's vision may be driven more by intuitive design decisions. Rather than settling for stereotypes, the teacher should instead encourage students to put visual discoveries into representational forms. For example, the teacher might say, "Does anyone see anything around the mouth that we could draw? Juan says he sees half-circle lines at the edge of the mouth. How can we draw these?"

Developmental Characteristics

The left-hand column of the following table lists some of the developmental characteristics of third- and fourth-grade children. The right-hand column lists one or more related art instructional objectives for each characteristic.

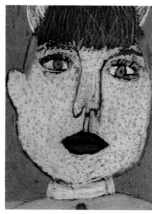

Courtesy of Sharon Burns-Knutson, Cedar Rapids, IA. Students: Elizabeth Browning, Caleb Rucker, and Jenna Lindberg.

These fourth-grade students were encouraged to observe details in their oil pastel self-portraits.

Developmental Characteristics of Third- and Fourth-Graders	Implications for Instruction
Have improved eye–hand coordination.	Students will draw from peers posing as models.
Have better command of small muscles.	Students will draw details of clothing and features.
Are becoming aware of differences in people.	Students will show differences among figures and objects in their artwork.
Are gradually learning to become responsible, orderly, and cooperative.	Students will share, distribute, and collect art material.
Begin to form separate-sex groups.	Give art motivations for both boys' and girls' interests.

Developmental Characteristics of Third- and Fourth-Graders	Implications for Instruction
May start to join gangs and cliques.	Students will depict their friends in their art. Use peer approval to modify behavior.
Enjoy comic books.	Students will create their own comic book characters and superheroes.
Are growing in critical skills, self-evaluation, and evaluation of others.	Students will use instructional objectives to evaluate their work.
Are now able to concentrate for a longer period.	Projects may span more than one period if new objectives are brought forth.
Are developing an interest in travel.	Students will describe how historical artworks relate to a culture.
Are interested in the life processes of plants and animals.	Students will draw from life, taxidermy models, and pictures of flora and fauna, and they will describe how their drawings show the specific features of plants or animals.
Are developing a sense of humor.	Students will discuss aesthetic issues raised by art cartoons.
Are becoming avid hobby fans and collectors.	Students will discuss their collections in terms of art criticism: "The picture shows his batting strength."

An intermediate-elementary-grade boy, who incidentally was in need of braces, did this fantasy oil pastel resist of an imaginary creature; part animal, part bird, part fish, and part insect. The white shapes of the head and ears are repeated in the spirals of the tail and hind legs. Star, flower, and leaf forms fill the background.

A developmental issue, especially important at this time, is whether the child develops feelings of competence or inferiority. Elementary students need generous amounts of encouragement to complete assignments and generous praise for their good performance. While regular classroom activities develop children's skills in reading and math, children may develop feelings of inferiority about their drawing ability if they are not given encouragement and instruction. Hence, do not be afraid to teach art skills and to help students win recognition and praise through their artwork.

Art Development

As observed previously, note that skills developed as a child matures are not better than those that a younger child possesses. In other words, later is not better. The stages described in this section are descriptive and not prescriptive.

SHAPES	Students will draw and compose with more conscious, deliberate planning, and they will show more naturalistic and realistic proportions.
	Students will select and arrange objects to satisfy their compositional design needs.
COLOR	Students will mix and experiment with an expanded range of colors, including tints and shades.
	Students will discuss the mood and effects of warm and cool colors, both within a painting and in the environment.
	Students will use analogous colors (those adjacent to one another on the color wheel).
	Students will neutralize (dull a color) by mixing it with the complementary hue (opposites on the color wheel).
	Students will describe the effect of subdued colors next to bright, intense colors.
SPACE	Students will create space and depth by employing vertical placement, diminishing size, and overlapping shapes.
	Students will describe how the horizon line can be used to show distant space.
OBJECTS	Students will select and arrange objects to satisfy their compositional design needs.
THE HUMAN FIGURE	Students will show action in their drawings of people and animals.
	Students will draw with more naturalistic and realistic proportions; more will use the five-heads-high figure.

Third-grade children show their individuality in these large (12- × 24-inch) tempera self-portraits. Notice especially the spirit and the wonderful complementary and analogous colors in the self-portrait with orange and purple eyes, purple and green fingernails, and green lips and eyelashes! Beautiful! Here again, qualitative, in-depth teaching strategies are the key to such successful artworks. These strategies include mixing a varied range of tempera hues, making sure the children devote time to doing preliminary sketches, and encouraging the imaginative use of color.

Art Criticism, Art History, and Aesthetics

The second and third grades are the stage of beauty and realism—the golden age of child art. The child believes the purpose of art is to represent something. He or she wants objects to look real, with clarity and good definition. Indeed, the more realistic and clear the artworks, the better the artworks are liked. Children in these grades feel that artwork should be recognizable pictures of handsome, valuable, interesting items. They do not

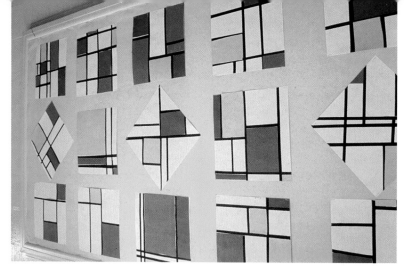

Third-grade students studied Mondrian's paintings as a motivation for making their designs.

care for pictures showing anything weird or ugly. In responding to realistic art, children comment, "I wish I could draw like this." In fact, this hankering after realism is so strong that, when confronted by abstract artwork, the children try to find a specific image in it.

Second- and third-grade children take a longer time to look at art. They now have the linguistic skills to express the concept that artworks are

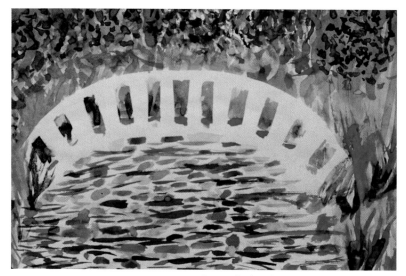

Studying Monet's paintings of his water lily garden at Giverney, fourth-grade students first cut a stencil for their bridges before doing their Impressionistic painting.

different from the thing itself. ("It is a picture of a rabbit" rather than "It is a rabbit.") Students can identify events depicted in artworks, and they can describe both likenesses and differences between pictures. They can accept their peers' differing representations as being valid art expressions and recognize style in each other's works. They can tell about the colors, shapes, lines, and textures in an artwork. In addition, children this age can recognize different media and techniques in various works of art. Likewise, they can identify the forms of artwork: sculptures, ceramics, landscapes, portraits, and architecture. In discussing artworks, they can identify objects and make associations about them. For example, they can rank in order a series of objects, such as figures by age, or animals by power. They can describe how two classes can be combined into a larger group. They can describe some criteria for art, and they can plan an art exhibition. Of course, many of the above abilities depend upon exposure and education, such as found in a quality art program.

The following words can be added to the children's growing art vocabulary: background, balsawood, batik, brayer, cellophane, ceramics, collage, collograph, color wheel, complementary colors, composition, cone, contrast, contour line, crafts, cube, cylinder, engraving, foreground, form, found material, hue, inking slab, intensity, landscape, masking tape, monoprint, mosaic, negative shape, papier mâché, plaster, plywood, positive shape, poster, pyramid, radiation, rasp, scoring of clay and paper, shade, sketch, slab, slip, spiral, staple, still life, stitchery, tie-dyeing, tint, unity, value.

Drawing, Designing, and Painting

Children like to depict clothing—their favorite outfit or occupational clothing, such as a police uniform. Group projects comprising students' individual works can demonstrate the power of working together to create projects of large size and scope. Continue to call attention to the immediate and visually stimulating subject or image for drawing. On sketching excursions, scout for the unusual site—the pictorially exciting vista with multifaceted structures, interesting towers and spires, and varied foreground and background breakup. In representing distance and overlapping, children often change color and size to show space and its vastness. Suggest new directions in design such as the following:

• Overlapping shapes
• Achieving distance through diminishing sizes and placement of objects higher on the page
• Creating pattern and textural effects contrasted with quiet or plain areas
• Drawing the lines with varied weights and in varied ways

At this stage, and certainly by the fourth grade, children can be introduced to observational drawing and basic contour-drawing techniques. For an immediate visual stimulus, begin with simple, easily recognizable,

Courtesy of Joyce Vroon, Trinity School, Atlanta, GA. Jessie Maxwell, Grade 4.

The fascination that uniforms hold can be seen in fourth-grader Jessie Maxwell's study of mass and movement in a marker drawing made from a newspaper photo.

Courtesy of Jackie Ellett, Fort Daniel Elementary School, GA.

Fourth-grade students learned about overlapping, perspective, and pattern in architecture as they drew from slide-projected city scenes.

objects: fruit, vegetable, shoe, glove, helmet, cap, cowboy hat, baseball mitt, football, or water pitcher. As the students' skill and confidence in contour drawing increase, introduce a combined arrangement of several objects in which the items overlap. Guide the children to look carefully and intently at the objects and to draw very slowly and deliberately.

Explain about inner contour lines. For example, with a flower, suggest that the children begin in the middle with the core, adding one petal at a time, rather than with a hasty and general outline of the entire flower. In other instances, such as with a banana or okra, begin with the outer contour line and then add inner contour lines to clarify the form. A few children can even draw oblique planes and use overlapping.

A soft lead pencil is best for contour drawing. Kindergarten pencils are recommended. Erasures should be discouraged; instead, a second, cor-

This fourth-grade student shows a keen observation of nature. Note the changes in size and direction of the leopard's spots on this decorative plate employing a marker drawing.

rective line more carefully observed is suggested. The students may stop at critical junctures, reposition the drawing tool, and then continue drawing.

Direct the children's attention to nature and its variety of lines, shapes, textures, colors, patterns, rhythms, and contrasts. Help them see examples of radiation, emphasis, and unity in natural forms. Urge students to bring interesting natural objects (taxidermy specimens, roots, weeds, fossils, honeycombs, bird's nests, pods, pinecones, seashells, and coral) into class to be used in discussions about artistic perception and for inspirational still lifes.

Color Awareness

Introduce art projects that demand multiple color choices:

- Make collages using colored construction paper, colored tissue paper, wallpaper samples, paint chips, and assorted color fabrics and felts.
- Weave with colored papers.
- Color with crayon or oil pastel on colored construction paper.
- Make mosaics with colored tesserae on a colored or black background.
- Create a color environment or happening in the classroom, combining, for example, crepe paper, balloons, beach towels, hula hoops, paper fans, colored cellophane, ribbons, scarves, umbrellas, posters, and fabrics.

Pattern was the focus of this third-grade student's cat drawing. Interest is created by the bold black-and-white diamonds in the floor, the patterns in the cat's fur and the wall moldings, and, for a finishing touch, the background three-dimensional dot pattern using T-shirt paint.

For her stuffed animal still life, Christy Kelly plans to use many premixed containers of paint in a variety of tints and shades.

Encourage students to mix and experiment with an expanded range of colors, including tints and shades. Discuss the mood and effect that warm and cool colors give within a painting and in the environment. Call attention to the analogous colors (those adjacent to one another on the color wheel). Now students often are ready to tackle the intricacies of color neutralization (dulling a color) by mixing a color with its complementary hue (opposites on the color wheel). They also can appreciate the subtle contrast of subdued colors next to bright, intense colors.

Collage

Introduce cut, tear, and paste projects that require the creation of texture and low-relief effects. These can be accomplished by folding, crimping, pleating, fringing, weaving, braiding, and curling the paper. Direct the children's attention to positive and negative shapes. Suggest how the positive shape—obtained by cutting a motif (star, leaf, heart, cross, diamond) from a piece of paper—and the negative shape—the paper that remains after the shape is cut out—can be juxtaposed in a collage design. Introduce colored tissue paper, either cut or torn, as a collage medium. Urge the use of light-colored tissues first, building up later to the sparing use of darker colors as accents. Encourage color discovery by suggesting that students build several tissue layers. Collage projects in tissue lend themselves beautifully to nonobjective designs and depictions of dreams and moods. Children also can make collages interpreting sounds: whisper, shout, swish, rattle, squeak, roar, and thunderclap.

Printmaking

The vegetable, clay stamp, and found-object print media introduced in the primary grades now can be augmented with oil pastel as a final, rich embellishment. Likewise, a variety of printmaking processes, which are

Studying Henri Matisse's paper cutout pictures, fourth-grade student Amy Wallace made this joyous collage.

Courtesy of Joyce Vroon and Marlee Puskar, Trinity School, Atlanta, GA.

A collage display is made from third-grade students' brass fastener action puppets.

explained fully in Chapter 24, now are manageable. These include the glue-line print, the collograph or cardboard relief print, and the string or cord print, in which string is glued to a cardboard plate, inked, and printed. An excellent medium for greeting-card designs is the plastic foam meat-tray print (with sides cut off to make a flat surface). On the foam tray (or similar ¼" thick polyurethane foam insulation material from a building supply store), lines are engraved with a pencil and the tray is inked and printed. The engraved lines will appear white in the completed print. In the monoprint technique, a sheet of plastic laminate or of glass (with edges taped) is inked with a brayer. The composition then is created by scratching through the paint with a stick, Q-tip, edge of a cardboard piece, eraser end of a pencil, or wood chopstick. Then a sheet of paper is placed over the inked surface, pressed down, and pulled off carefully.

Ceramics

Review with third- and fourth-grade children the knowledge that they have gained in earlier school years about clay: where it comes from; its properties, such as plasticity; its possibilities; and its limitations. Describe the importance of ceramics in the everyday life of both ancient and con-

temporary cultures. An exploratory session in clay manipulation is again recommended to help students appreciate the following:

- Hardening clay is difficult to model.
- Clay that is too moist sags if the supports of clay or rolled paper, or the "fifth leg" under the stomach of an animal, are not sturdy enough.
- Appendages break off when the clay piece dries unless they are securely joined to the main structure with clay-scoring or slip-cementing.
- Textures, patterns, and details can be made in clay with fingers, pencils, and assorted found objects.
- Solid clay pieces over ½-inch thick may explode in the firing kiln unless openings are made through which the air inside can escape.

In pottery making, children can make the basic pinch pot into a larger container or an animal's body by joining with clay-slip two pinch pots of the same size. Cut out openings, and add feet and spouts for more complex pots.

Suggested Subjects or Themes

These topics are suitable for children of ages 7, 8, and 9 (Grades 3 and 4):

Inside me (imaginative X-ray)	Totem poles
Fun on the jungle gym	Action poses
Sports poses and still lifes	Design in nature: radiation
The circus parade	A tree house
The merry-go-round	Tree of life
The house where I live	Imaginary animals
Rare birds	Prehistoric animals
Animals and their young	Teddy bears
Flowers from above	The insect world
Autumn leaves and trees	Playing a musical instrument
The pet show or pet store	Still life of interesting objects
A magic forest	Flower market or fruit market
The wedding	The toy store or Santa's workshop
Western objects	The circus in action
Here come the clowns!	Space voyage
Washing the family car	Self-portraits
Food we like to eat	Sunken treasure
Boarding the school bus	A special place to go
A quiet activity at home	

If I were a balloon seller, a juggler, a tightrope walker, a ballerina, a scarecrow, a skydiver, an astronaut, a clown....

Courtesy of Baiba Kuntz, Glencoe, IL.

Fifth- and sixth-grade children created these sophisticated self-portraits with an animal or bird. The drawing was first done in gold or silver crayon on black construction paper. Then, oil pastel was used to create the complementary and analogous color areas. Notice the perceptive and sensitive handling of the eyes, eyelids, hair, and face planes. Iowa City Schools.

Chapter 10

A SEQUENTIAL CURRICULUM FOR GRADES 5 AND 6

After the strong beginning most children experience in the primary and middle elementary grades, when almost all children feel they can do art, a period of plateau or decline may occur during the upper elementary grades. It is not known whether self-doubt is the cause of this decline, or whether the decline is the result of self-doubt. To be sure, the best art, whether realistic or abstract or primitive, is characterized by assuredness and verve, and this confidence seems to be shaken in the upper elementary grades. Children's criteria of what is good in art outrace their abilities. They come to feel that their drawings are "not good enough," and they decide they are "no good in art." These attitudes underscore the importance of discussions about aesthetics, what makes quality in art, and whether realism is or should be the only goal.

We believe that the guidance and encouragement of a sympathetic, knowledgeable teacher can prevent students from languishing on the same creative plateau for years. Without a teacher's guidance and encouragement, children's cognitive and affective growth in art, employment of visual resources, command of the vocabulary and language of art, and use of formal elements may remain static or even retrogress. This eventually may lead to discouragement, frustration, and apathy. Children who are not taught art skills may develop into adults who feel limited in their ability to make and discuss art.

However, under the guidance of a teacher who helps them to create and appreciate the beauty they create and who gives them good reasons to try, children will grow in their ability to be careful delineators, to represent overlapping and receding spatial planes, and to use these concepts in their contour drawings, drawings of buildings in nature, and imaginative drawings of the fantastic. Another approach that is especially suited for those who doubt their art ability is to use art topics in which students express themselves and their values through symbols, dreams, and metaphors—in other words, art that expresses their uniqueness as individuals.

99

Developmental Characteristics

The left-hand column of the following table lists some of the developmental characteristics of fifth- and sixth-grade children. The right-hand column lists one or more related art instructional objectives for each characteristic.

Developmental Characteristics of Fifth- and Sixth-Graders	Implications for Instruction
Begin to concentrate more on individual interests.	Students will depict their individual collections, their clothes for special occasions—for example, baseball uniforms, ballet costumes, scout uniforms.
Are now interested in activities that relate to their gender.	Students will use methods of art criticism to describe and interpret art works showing preadolescents.
Vary in maturity, with girls more developed physically and emotionally than boys.	
Are becoming more dependable, responsible, self-critical, and reasonable.	Students will use their own evaluation of their artwork—describing both strengths and weaknesses—as a guide toward making changes in it.
Are interested in doing and making things "right"; try to conform to ideals of "good" behavior.	Students will explore using the methods of realistically showing deep space. Students will be able to conform to their group's behavior policies.

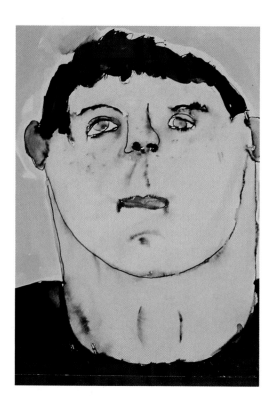  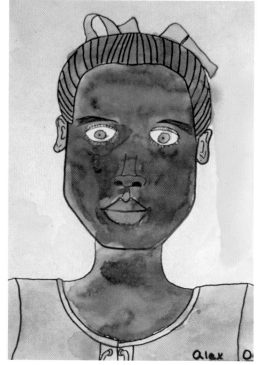

Courtesy of Melody Milbrandt, Valdosta, GA; Baiba Kuntz, Glencoe, IL; and Joyce Vroon, Trinity School, Atlanta, GA.

Left: Self-portrait of a fifth-grade boy was done in ink and watercolor. *Middle:* Fifth-grade student J. Ryan Lapatka did his self-portrait in conté crayon on grey paper. *Right:* Fifth-grade student Alex Owen used permanent marker and watercolor for his portrait of a classmate.

Developmental Characteristics of Fifth- and Sixth-Graders	Implications for Instruction
Develop interests outside home and school—in their community and in the world at large.	Students will describe how the arts are incorporated into their community.
Begin to criticize adults and anyone in authority.	Students will debate the art judgments of experts.
Are undergoing critical emotional and physical changes.	Students will depict their physical appearance and emotions in their art and writing.
Become more involved in hobbies and collections.	Students will create an art display or representation of a hobby
Begin a phase of hero and heroine worship.	Using examples from art history, students will describe a favorite artist's life.
Often enjoy being by themselves, away from adult interference.	Students will create personal art notebooks/diaries showing their inner lives.
Enjoy working on group projects.	Students will cooperate with a group of peers in planning and executing a group project.
Are developing a sense of values, a sense of right and wrong.	Students will debate issues in art ethics. ("Who should own and display Native American art—big city museums or tribal museums?")
Are increasing their interest and work span.	Students will work on an art project for three or more hours.
Tend to form separate gangs or cliques according to their interests, sex, ethnicity, neighborhoods, and family status.	Students will identify and interpret historical art exemplars representing groups with which they identify.

The principal developmental focus coming into play for children around this age is one of identity versus role confusion. Can the child find a meaningful place in the world and in the world of work? Promote their development of a sense of identity through group art projects that focus on community occupational roles, including the many occupations artists have.

Art Development

The level of mastery that individuals achieve when developing expertise is closely intertwined with the effectiveness of the instruction they receive. Without a teacher's guidance, children's growth and interest in art

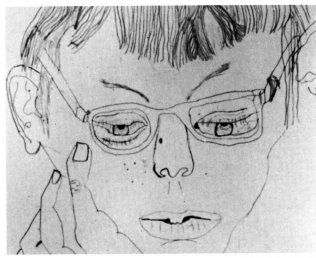

The self-portrait of this upper-elementary-grade boy is a contour drawing, patiently delineated.

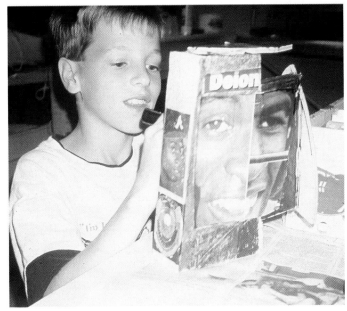

Fifth-grade student Brian Davis uses a piece of wood as a foundation for a Marisol-like collage sculpture of his sports hero, Deion.

and their use of formal elements, in the way they perceive artistically and in how they discuss art may remain static. Fifth- and sixth-graders do develop some unique abilities, to which the illustrations throughout this chapter attest.

The following table gives some general, stage-related descriptions of children's art development at this age.

Art Development	Enabling Activities
Become increasingly critical of their drawing ability and often are so discouraged with their efforts they lose interest in art class unless they are wisely and sympathetically motivated and guided.	Students will describe well-drawn and expressively drawn parts in each others' artwork. Students will describe and use design principles in creative crafts. Students will show more interest in art history.
Develop a growing curiosity to experiment with new and varied materials, tools, and techniques.	Students will use specialized tools and techniques, such as linoleum-cutting tools, plaster carving, weaving, and stitchery.
Experiment more with value contrast, neutralized colors, patterns, and textual effects.	Students will neutralize colors and create both pattern and texture effects.
Begin to use rudimentary perspective principles in drawing landscapes, buildings, streets, train tracks, fences, roads, and interiors.	Students will use vanishing area perspective as well as appreciate other ways to create depth.
Become more interested in their environment as a source for their drawings and paintings.	Students will draw scenes of historical interest and natural beauty in their community.

Art Criticism

At this age, students can identify the major compositional features of an artwork. They can suggest alternative ways to make something and can express critical judgments about artworks. For example, one student said, "It needs to have a black dog in the painting." Encourage them to hypothesize about the motives that underlie behavior: "Why did the artist do it that way?" Fifth- and sixth-graders will be able to compare and contrast works in terms of both form and expressive meaning. They can describe how the elements work together to convey the ideas, and they can learn to

The perspective lines (lines receding into depth) of tables, trucks, and buildings in this 11-year-old student's drawing of the Bilecik, Turkey, market do not go to one vanishing point. Instead, the lines head to a general area in the upper right corner, in a method called isometric perspective. This technique, in which the perspective lines diverge as they go back in space, is called inverse perspective *and is used in much Near Eastern art.*

see beyond the subject matter and use terminology to identify the style and mood. They can describe what things are like in art, although they do not use metaphors (e.g., "icy person") until later. They can identify symbols used in artworks.

Likewise, children at this age can describe artists in their community. Plan opportunities that promote independent action by students, such as interviewing community artists or other students. Promote their growing multicultural awareness by analyzing works from a wide variety of cultures.

Children also like to know about illustrators' tricks of the trade, such as zoom lines and ways of depicting muscles, and they are interested in studying how artists and illustrators use such conventions. For example, students might brainstorm about what is necessary to make a good depiction of a villain or a princess. A bulletin board, onto which students pin up examples they bring in, can show symbols for power, violence, speed, and motion.

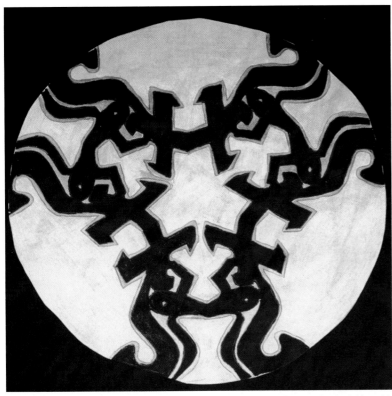

From a linear design of the student's initials, an attractive design using trilateral symmetry developed.

Fifth- and sixth-grade students should be able to use art terms such as the following in discussing artworks:

Design: harmony, motif, gradation, symmetry, asymmetry, emphasis, balance, composition, repetition, rhythm, simplicity, unity, variety
Shape: concave, convex, conical, pyramidal, exaggerated, geometric, biomorphic
Representation: foreshortening, proportion, symbol
Color: analogous, monochromatic, shading, harmony, spectrum, neutralization, transparent, opaque, translucent
Eye movement in a picture: circular, straight, spiral
Size: microscopic, telescopic

Space: narrow, wide, horizon line, perspective, vanishing point, vanishing area
Texture: granular, pebbled, regular, irregular

Art History and Aesthetics

In art history, students will be able to identify major figures and masterworks. They can explain how two styles of art differ and can arrange examples of historic styles into chronological sequence. Encourage them

Frank Stella's artwork motivated four students who worked together on this cut paper collage with craypas.

to think more deeply about experiences and about the motives that underlie behavior: "Why did the artist do it that way?" They will be able to explain different art criteria—those based on aesthetics, and those based on nonaesthetic criteria such as money or subject matter. Because students of this age tend to value things according to size, expense, complexity, and power, the teacher can present reproductions of artworks that are especially large, costly, or complex, or that depict powerful individuals.

The art preference of these children is for realism and "super" realism—a preference that peaks at age 11. In response to realistic artworks, students will say, "I wish I could draw like that." They are puzzled by pictures showing objects as they are not, or as they "should not" be. They call

From a study of Nigerian art, fifth-grade students used the counter repoussee metal-working process.

Studying Egyptian tomb figurines, fifth-grade student Kristin French first rolled a slab of clay around a tube. Clay was added for the arms and legs, and the tube's top was covered. A ball of clay was used as the head, and a draped covering and hieroglyphics were added. The piece was painted with green acrylic paint, a black wash was applied, and the figure was glued to a scrap of wood.

these depictions "weird" or "ugly." They feel that the things in pictures should be recognizable and valuable, neat, and interesting. At the same time, they are beginning to comprehend on an intellectual level (although often not on an emotional level) why an artist might show something other than a realistic rendering. They can and do use visual and verbal metaphors.

Students in the fifth and sixth grades are sensitive to the idea of "system," of a "right" way to do things. They try to adopt the rules and the codes necessary to survive in society. They want to know the right ways to count, read, and do math; the proper ways to play and to work; the codes of right and wrong. Because of the firmness of their convictions and their awareness of rules concerning the way things are supposed to

Courtesy of Sharon Burns-Knutson, Cedar Rapids, IA.

Nigerian art also motivated this project in aluminum tooling by fifth- and sixth-grade students. Bold geometric designs have been used and stain has been applied to bring out the relief.

Drawing, Designing, and Painting

Students now can be careful, expressive, and observational delineators. They begin to include shadows and receding planes in paintings. Scout out challenging sites to draw, such as nearby building construction and demolition sites, Victorian-style homes, and gardens. Because it may be inconvenient or difficult to leave the school grounds, find interesting locations around the school to observe and draw: the lockers, halls, gym, entrance, kitchen, or playground. Students can be guided to create variety, space, and movement in their compositions by the imaginative placement of images, objects, or motifs within the picture plane. Encourage them to put figures or buildings on different foreground levels and to

Courtesy of Joyce Vroon, Trinity School, Atlanta, GA.

Fifth-grade student Ben Faulkner's pen drawing of a roller blade shows the careful delineation of rounded forms turning away out of view.

be, their language contains many "shoulds." ("That's not what a good drawing of a car should look like.") The teacher of aesthetics can use these "shoulds" to raise contested issues about the nature of art. ("Should good art take a lot of time to make?") Encourage students to think of questions about meanings and values. Ask them to clarify their statements, to give reasons to support their positions, and then to examine the reasons they gave.

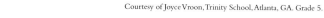
Courtesy of Joyce Vroon, Trinity School, Atlanta, GA. Grade 5.

Metaphors present a way to share one's feelings. Art class can provide a venue for expression: wearing a false face (by Michael Selik); an intricate maze (by Grant Arnold); and a nest of snakes in a jungle of vines (by Matthew Parker).

doubt before it takes root. Continue practice in contour drawing, but introduce new approaches such as fantasy, nonobjective, and optical-art themes. Interest in the surreal shows up in the use of macabre and bloody images. Children can use metaphoric images—for example, an isolated tree for loneliness and despair. They can use metaphors in their designs for record album covers and billboards. Lead students to discover the many different ways they can use line as pattern to enrich surfaces and vitalize backgrounds. Students become absorbed in the tricks of the trade; they like learning the conventions of comic book illustration, such as thought bubbles, overly defined muscles, and stars and steam to depict violence. Reward their out-of-school independent efforts in drawing, for these provide learning opportunities that otherwise wouldn't exist.

When your students paint with color, reinforce learning about complementary, monochromatic, and analogous color harmonies. Discuss tints and shades, the directions for neutralizing colors, the color spectrum, and the color wheel. Continue to build color awareness by calling the students' attention to color usage in their everyday world: billboards, magazine and recording covers, athletic uniforms, storefronts, and automobiles. Use mood music as a background for free, expressive painting.

Collage

Recapitulate previous learnings, such as the use of positive and negative shapes. Recommend using partially three-dimensional effects through paper folding, fringing, pleating, spiraling, and curling. Introduce paper scoring to students who are ready for more skillful challenges. Demonstrate the scoring technique: place paper to be scored on a thick pad of newspapers, use the blunt point of scissors, the pointed end of a wooden popsicle stick, or a similar tool to indent the curved line into the paper, then carefully fold along the indented line. To enrich students' collages, encourage them to scout for found objects such as wallpaper and rug samples, fabric and ribbon remnants, yarn, old greeting cards, and discarded building materials.

Collage-like techniques are possible with computer art that permits the instant scanning of photos or with clip art on the computer and the recombination of images in collage-like ways. Likewise, film images taken by the students themselves and photos from magazines can be combined in imaginative ways. Indeed, photography is a popular new medium to introduce at this age. Students love to take photographs of the environment, city scenes, and signs.

Courtesy of Carole Henry, Athens, GA.

Many students are highly impressed by the ability of cartoon superhero artists to depict an exaggerated play of light and dark, revealing exaggerated muscles. Hilsman Middle School.

terminate them at varying heights in the background. Shapes can be juxtaposed or overlapped to create unity and space-in-depth.

Sadly, inability to achieve satisfactory realistic results leads some children mistakenly to conclude, "I am no good at art." Challenge this self-

Courtesy of Baiba Kuntz, Glencoe, IL. Grades 5 and 6.

From a preliminary drawing, an attractive disposition of the basic shapes of an imaginary house is glued down, then architectural details and landscaping are added.

Sixth-grade students captured the texture of a billboard's multilayered torn surface, the expressive surface of a graffiti-covered wall, and the diagonal pattern of sunlight and shadows falling across a colonnaded and trellised entry. Students: Ashley Wagner, Catherine Overend, and Devon McClure.

Printmaking

Although the various printmaking processes introduced in previous grades—vegetable and found-object print, glue-line-relief print, polystyrene print, monoprint—can be repeated successfully at this age, the maturing students now will respond to more complex and challenging techniques. Linoleum printing is a favorite because of the opportunity to use a variety of gouges. Because more tools, materials, equipment, and time are required for advanced printmaking, see Chapter 24 for guidelines on inking, printing, and cleanup.

This woodblock print of a child model playing a recorder is by an upper-elementary-grade student in Japan. It shows carefully delineated fingers, as well as lines around the mouth to indicate the blowing. Removing the background created an attractive texture. Japan.

Ceramics and Crafts

Ceramic homes in clay relief are very successful at this age. Popular themes include animals and their young, animals in combat, portraits and self-portraits, clowns, acrobats, and mother and child. Students now place strong emphasis on realistic portrayals and the achievement of correct proportions and characteristic detail. Toward these ends, the teacher must be prepared to offer sympathetic and supportive guidance when called on. In most instances, recalled images alone will not supply the child with sufficient visual data. Build a library of photographs and slides showing exemplars of ceramics and crafts through the centuries. Neither overpraise the purely realistic approach they admire nor harshly criticize it; instead, introduce students to a variety of styles and interpretations. Many crafts are popular at this age. Creating simple jewelry also is a favorite activity.

Courtesy of the International Collection of Child Art, Illinois State University, Normal, IL.

Maori chief by a New Zealand student, age 10.

Mirrors help students achieve success with projects like these life-sized clay-relief self-portraits. Upper-elementary-grade students are concerned with realistic portrayals showing correct proportions and details.

Suggested Subjects or Themes

These project suggestions are suitable for children of ages 9, 10, and 11 (Grades 5 and 6):

At the gas station
A view from a plane
Bicycle race
Horse show
Warriors in armor
Undersea marine life
At the swimming pool
Dreams
Values
Cartoons
Winter carnival
Cities in outer space
Self-portraits

Portraits of classmates
Traffic jam
Landscape, cityscape, or seascape
Nature study on a theme of adaptation and survival
The marching band
Ball game, track meet, or scout jamboree
Amusement park showing time, space, and motion
The shopping mall
Disneyland, Six Flags
Motorcycles
Renowned sports figures
Still life of musical instruments or sports equipment
Crowds at the county fair and 4-H competitions
Still lifes of watches, hair bows, typewriters, telephones, old tools, and old objects
Still life of beach paraphernalia, scuba-diving equipment, or roller blades
Bags and packaging from fast-food restaurants

Chapter 11

A Sequential Curriculum for Grades 7 and 8

Vygotsky writes that adolescence is filled with the tension between intellect and affect, that is to say, between adolescents' increasingly self-critical attitudes and the emotional vicissitudes of puberty which they are experiencing. Their overly critical attitudes lead many to abandon their creative efforts.

Middle school students move into a changed academic world. For the first time, they may have a different teacher for each subject they take. If they come from the typical elementary school situation in which the classroom teacher taught art, it will be their first contact with a specialist art teacher. In American schools, just a little over half of the students this age participate in visual arts classes. Regrettably, in some schools students involved in band or orchestra programs cannot take art. Also regrettable is that, in general, students draw less as they grow older. For a fair number of adolescents, however, a new synthesis occurs. Their newly developed technical facility is joined to their vision of what they need or want to express.

Middle school students are experiencing a renaissance of intellectual inquisitiveness that in some ways may never be matched again. Although they are less inhibited than upper-elementary-grade children, they are highly critical of their own performance. Yet they are more willing to tackle new processes and new materials. They are technically more proficient. Their ability to capitalize on suggestions is heightened, and they can enter into critical discussions on art design and structure with a keener sensitivity and sharper argumentative skills. They are highly impressionable. Their cultural horizons are expanding, and they may carry with them for the rest of their lives the preferences and prejudices regarding art that they develop in these middle school years.

Courtesy of David Hodge, Oshkosh, WI.

This middle school student is intent on his ceramic creation. For many youngsters, there is no greater satisfaction than hand building structures out of clay. The simple, basic pinch-pot form has been enriched by the addition of a foot, neck, handles, and an embellishing relief pattern.

112

Developmental Characteristics

Developmental Characteristics of Seventh- and Eighth-Graders	Implications for Instruction
Feelings of alienation cause need to be accepted by their peers. This acceptance often is more important to them than the teacher's approval.	Students will work in small groups to determine a project, to carry out the project, and, subsequently, to discuss the project and related fine art examples.
Experience a change of identity, feelings of loss, and inner conflicts. Unpredictable behaviors may intensify.	Artwork and talking about art are ways to explore and even work through alienated and conflicted feelings.
Consider bad taste what society considers good taste and vice versa.	In class discussion, students can critique fashion styles from different times and cultures.
Often are more inclined to daydream, to watch rather than to perform.	From a study of art history books, students will describe an imaginary day in the life of an artist.
To establish a sense of their identity, students need to begin considering vocational areas.	Point out vocations related to the arts, and have art history units on artists' personalities and careers.

Painting a design for a music cover may reveal that middle school students' opinions about the quality of rap music are different from the teacher's. Nevertheless, the teacher can lead them to consider how the artistic solutions of artists such as Wassily Kandinsky and Peter Max may be applicable to their own designs.

Developmental Characteristics of Seventh- and Eighth-Graders	Implications for Instruction
Although it is unacceptable behavior, some may disparage or bully peers or, conversely, be bullied or disparaged.	Show art exemplars of persecution and discuss the feelings of the people who are depicted.
Begin to emphasize their appearance and grooming. Popularity is now an issue. Intensely curious about the pubertal changes in their bodies.	Students will create a clay head in three dimensions of themselves or of a classmate. Study art's role in puberty rites, e.g., mask-making.
Possess varying degrees of physiological and sexual maturity.	Students will interpret artwork showing persons of this age.
Are becoming more self-conscious regarding their changing physical characteristics. Feel that people are concerned about their appearance.	Students will be able to draw caricatures of their prominent features. Discuss famous stars' features when the stars were teens.
Are fascinated with their names.	Do name or initial designs as prints or collage.
Are in constant communication with their friends about dates, parties, TV shows, movies, music, classmates, and teachers' and parents' foibles.	From a personal record of phone doodles, students will describe the design variations and use these ideas as the basis for a T-shirt design.
Because of an egocentric viewpoint, may have difficulty in distinguishing between their own points of view and those of others.	Art criticism in which different views are expressed can help to lessen egocentrism.
Are unable to commit to decisions. May experience a loss of sense of identity and a snobbishness or scorn or rebellion against authority.	Use integrated learning experiences, challenging and exciting projects, and active and cooperative learning.
Frequently model their behavior and appearance after sports stars, television personalities, rappers, recording artists, and movie stars.	Students will be able to draw from photos of persons whom they admire.
Are developing their interest in sports, music, or other arts.	Students will draw their own collections of souvenirs and mementos.
Often are unusually sensitive to other people's problems, but do not know how to help.	Students will create a work of art to share with another person and give emphatic feedback to another student about art.
Have a personal fable that normal laws of nature don't apply to them, and a belief in their immortal and unique existence.	Discuss art history examples of superheroes (e.g., Greek gods) interacting with normal people and discuss real life consequences.

Courtesy of D. Hodge and F. Wachowiak, University of Wisconsin,
Oshkosh Campus Laboratory School University High, Iowa City, IA.

Developmental Characteristics of Seventh- and Eighth-Graders	Implications for Instruction
Are trying to develop a code or sense of values.	Students will interpret a work of art in terms of the moral dilemmas for the persons represented.
Form status groups and cliques, using "accepted," "tolerated," and "rejected" categories.	Students will interpret artworks by diverse groups, and, looking at pictures of alienation, explain what the artists were trying to communicate.
Seclude themselves from family and children.	As an out-of-school activity, draw one's room,
Have a growing desire for new and exciting experiences.	Students will be able to depict exciting, imaginary adventures through art.
Fluctuate between childhood and adulthood in their interests, insights, abilities, and judgments.	Students will describe art careers in the community.

Emotional Vulnerability

Young adolescents have tender feelings, and direct criticism of students' artwork in front of their classmates can be humiliating. Avoid sarcasm and belittling remarks at all costs. Writing as an adult, Georgia O'Keeffe recalled the painful humiliation she felt when, at age 13, she was criticized by her art teacher in front of her classmates for drawing a plaster figure's hand too small. "At the time I thought she scolded me terribly. I was so embarrassed that it was difficult not to cry" (O'Keeffe, 1988). Teachers may also embarrass students by praising their work too lavishly in front of their peers. To avoid public embarrassment whether correcting or praising students, give individual, in-process critiques.

Circle self-portraits in oil pastel on colored construction paper by middle school students. By using a circle format and emphasizing imaginative use of color and form, the teacher created a new artistic design challenge. Flags, flowers, camouflage, and birds serve as auxiliary ways the artists have conveyed their interests.

apathetic or cool in their response to art. Once they become caught up in the excitement of a creative, productive, and qualitative art program, however, they become enthusiastic converts to art's adventures, challenges, and personally satisfying rewards.

During middle school, teachers really begin to see the personalities and idiosyncrasies of the students reflected in their behavior and their art. While students can be conformists, they also can be fiercely independent. They may try out a role for a week: the extrovert, the loner, the risk taker, the methodical planner, the procrastinator, the idol seeker, the plodder, the perfectionist, the maverick, the dreamer, the braggart, the idealist, and the quiz whiz. The next week, a different role might hold appeal. Personalities depicted throughout art history (such as Albrecht Dürer's knight on a horse and Renaissance depictions of David and Hercules) can be related to some students' fantasies. Students' rites of passage are acted out in real fights, mock fights, and challenges to authority. This is a time of increased awareness and self-consciousness, sensitivity to the differences in

Courtesy of Davis Publications and Teddy Oliver, Marietta, GA.

A 12-year-old has expressed pain and humiliation in this oil pastel, My Mother Just Spanked Me. From "Middle School Expressions," by Teddy Oliver and Robert Clements, School Arts Magazine, *September, 1983.*

Emotional swings and moodiness in children are not unusual; some students may reject their own excellent artwork. Drawings of jeans, T-shirts, sneakers, and hairstyles considered as contrary to the adult culture's norms can express adolescents' need to be separate from the dominant adult culture. Especially if their art experiences in elementary school were limited, unsatisfying, or unrewarding, middle school students may be

Red Barn, Lake George, New York, 1921 (oil on canvas, 14-1/4 × 16-1/4 inches) Georgia Museum of Art, Eva Underhill Holbrook Memorial, Gift of Alfred Holbrook.

Georgia O'Keeffe remembered for decades her middle school teacher publicly rebuking the realism of her figure drawing in front of her classmates. Her paintings are acclaimed for their bold shape patterns.

Courtesy of Fay Brassie, Athens, GA.

In a design for a jacket, this middle school student has expressed yearnings for love, joy, and the banning of rules.

their behavior, you may notice a shortness of temper or a lack of affect. For such students, art expression may serve as a beacon warning that a person is in trouble emotionally. Students' verbalizations during art criticism and art interpretation often provide a forum for other students to speak out about what is on their minds. Very general and wide-open art topics, such as "crying" or "oppression," may provide a way to express, through art, what formerly seemed to be unmentionable. The teacher of art may be able to help the young person cope with problems—not as a psychologist but as a caring friend with whom significant events may be shared. Through the school counselor, the art teacher also may be able to help individuals or their parents contact agencies skilled in dealing with serious emotional or family life problems.

Not only can art announce to the sensitive perceiver an individual's distress, it can play a major role in restoring a person's balance after a traumatic situation. Art creation as well as discussions about art can help students feel better about themselves. Problem solving through art provides an opportunity for the "person within" to emerge. Interestingly, applying the principles of good design—balance, proportion, variation—seems to foster those same qualities in the artists. For example, during art creation, the individual may find help through being able to share visually, at what-

others, identification with a peer group, and heightened emotional responses. Possibly as a means of self-searching, a preadolescent likes to draw portraits and self-portraits and capture their own and their peers' changing self-image.

Going steady, having crushes, engaging in sexual activity, and being subjected to physical and sexual harassment and abuse are emotionally charged situations in which some older students may find themselves. Other events fraught with the potential for creating feelings of guilt are the divorce of parents, an abortion, or the death of a loved one. Feelings of worthlessness, incompetence, ugliness, anger, guilt, and complicity interfere with the development of students' positive self-concepts. Teachers used to say that the schools' biggest problems were students' talking in class, chewing gum, making noise, running in the halls, and getting out of turn in lines. Today, however, far more serious problems are endemic. By being a friend to the student and expressing personal concern, you may play a pivotal role in the student's life at a critical time. Through your teaching and encouraging, the art program may provide a vehicle for the student to express his or her conflicts or develop positive attitudes of achievement.

When students are going through emotionally trying situations, you may see a decline in their ability to concentrate on art expression. In

Courtesy of Joyce Vroon, Trinity School, Atlanta, GA.

Painting "A Dream" may be a way to gain insight into the messages from one's unconscious mind. Fifth-grade student Pierce Lowrey.

The emotional side of middle school art is shown in this soft firebrick sculpture and this drift-wood sculpture. Here are seen the creators' sensitivity to others, their forming of significant relationships with others, their heightened emotional responses, and their self-searching.

ever level is comfortable, the event that needs expression. Likewise, through talking about the art of others, the individual may be able to give voice to personal feelings and break out of his or her aloneness and grief. A student's art accomplishment can help others to see that person as an individual of worth. In turn, the achievement helps that individual acquire a sense of pride and self-worth.

Art Criticism

A new and genuinely different way of thinking about art comes into being in the seventh- and eighth-grade years. The criterion of realism is replaced by those of intention and message. Given artwork containing expressive themes, students will talk about the expressive qualities of the artwork. They can recognize style and can contrast the treatment of theme

in two or more artworks. They understand metaphor and mystery, and they can identify multiple meanings in represented objects. Students also can formulate and try many alternative hypotheses in explaining an artwork. For example, they can deductively reason: "Pretend to be (a famous artist) and solve a contemporary problem."

Accompanying the rapid changes in their bodies and their own search for identity is a shift in their understanding. Seventh- and eight-grade students can recognize that expression of the experiences of others and of one's self is subjective. Reassure students that they need not share their own personal artworks publicly unless they so desire. Perhaps because expression characterizes this stage, there is less concern about realism and the beauty of a subject. Pictures now can be seen as metaphors for ideas, and emotions can be valued for their ability to inspire feelings. Social commentary art, such as that by George Tookers, helps them to express feelings of justice. Students can speculate on the artist's mood. They can imagine alternatives to what a picture shows and speculate on different scenarios. These exercises in expression allow students to feel an identification with accepted, mature artists. In another exercise, students can role play contrary-to-fact propositions; for example, they can pretend to be an art museum director and make judgments about a variety of artists' works.

In addition, students will be able to discuss the aesthetic quality of an artwork or a utilitarian object. For example, students can judge the effectiveness of the designs of athletic shoes, T-shirts, and motorcycles, as well as analyze how such objects suggest ideas and feelings.

Art History and Aesthetics

Adolescents' ability to think abstractly and to reason about ideas increases dramatically at this time. Children in the seventh and eighth grades can consider the logical possibilities in a problem. They make guesses about what might be going on behind the depicted scene, and they can discuss symbolism, deeper meanings, and double meanings.

Students of this age also have the ability to conduct inquiry from several vantage points. That is, they can role-play different parts, such as art critic, artist, disgruntled client, or government official. Working individually or in small groups, students can report on artists' careers. In staged mock debates between artists they can address issues in art, such as whether paintings should show realism or depict emotion. Some terms to discuss are expressivism, realism, aesthetics, anatomy, judgment, value, art critic, censorship, metaphor, spontaneity, and craftsmanship.

During this new stage of aesthetic response, students can investigate questions of content and social significance. Because art is an expression of

Exciting color projects to stimulate color awareness can be motivated by showing the work of Judy Pfaff, such as her 1986 Apples and Oranges. *Mixed media, 113 × 72 inches.*

its creator, ask them to discuss how the artist uses color and design to show emotion. Students also are able to consider more abstract aspects, such as style and composition, and they understand that other students' perspectives can be different from their own.

To tap their interest in expressive works of art, expose them to Van Gogh's life and letters. Show them works about the suffering of women and children during wartime by Kaethe Kollwitz, Francisco Goya, and Max Beckman. Expand their knowledge and appreciation of master drawings and paintings by artists such as Leonardo da Vinci, Albrecht Dürer, Rembrandt Van Rijn, Rosa Bonheur, Paul Klee, Henri Matisse, Pablo Picasso, Louise Nevelson, Andy Warhol, Katsushika Hokusai, Georgia O'Keeffe, William Hogarth, Romare Bearden, Peter Brueghel, and Mary Cassatt. Students love the artworks of Red Grooms and Grant Wood.

Call students' attention to the cave drawings at Altamira and Font du Gaume as well, to Benin bronzes, and to the tribal-huntsmen renditions of African and Australian native cultures. Show them the sumi-e ink drawings of China and Japan and the expressive graphics of the Inuit and Native Americans. Students should be able to match artworks to styles. One appropriate task is to identify the artwork that does not belong in a group.

Middle school students, coming as they often do from different elementary schools, will bring varied backgrounds in art vocabulary. Vocabulary words that have been suggested in previous grades should be reviewed and new words added as they are introduced:

Through drawing classmates modeling, students can express indirectly something of their own nature. Here, a middle school youth captures in a contour-line drawing a quality of openness and searching. The drawing also conveys an understanding of the human form, the chair, and folds of clothing.

Art history and criticism: expressionism, neo-expressionism, op art, pop art, African sculptures from Yoruba, Benin bronzes, Zaire nail art, Chi Wara antelope sculptures, surrealism, cubism, Renaissance art, impressionism, symbolism, double meaning

Drawing and painting: conte crayon, sienna, spectrum, stipple, umber, montage, ochre, watercolor wash, distortion, encaustic, fixative, foreshortening, gesture drawing, hatching, converging lines, crosshatch, caricature

Printmaking: baren, bench hook, burnish, etching, intaglio, printing press, proof, relief print

Photography, film, and video: negative, fixer, plate, tone, daguerreotype, cibachrome, playback, wipe, fade, establishing shot, zoom shot, soft focus, montage, slow disclosure, low-angle shot, freeze frame, long shot, pan, superimposition

Sculpture: armature, assemblage, bas relief, solder, sandcore, sepia, stabile, incised relief, repoussé, patina

Art Development

Art Development	*Implications for Instruction*
Choose subject matter for art expression that relates to human-interest activities, community and worldwide events, and current projects in ecology, medical research, space, and undersea exploration.	Students will use current events as the setting for their art expression. Students will explain the art principles they used in depicting the sociological, artistic, or scientific event.
Attempt shading and cross-hatch techniques to make drawn forms appear solid, cylindrical, and believably realistic. Experiment with perspective drawing.	Students will use shading and cross-hatching to create the appearance of three-dimensional form. Students will be able to apply some perspective concepts.
Are self-conscious and self-critical about their drawing ability. Supportive instruction contour and gesture as well as drawing helps them to become increasingly skillful in figure and animal drawing.	Students will use gesture and contour drawing to capture the feeling and dynamics of the posed human figure.
Are ready to interpret complex compositions, such as richly orchestrated still lifes and multifigured events and celebrations.	Students will apply design principles of repetition and variation to draw an organized composition from a complex still life or from many figures in action.

Art Development	*Implications for Instruction*
Are mature and skillful enough to handle a variety of challenging crafts: photography, glazed ceramics, repoussé, plaster reliefs, sculpture in hard materials, and woodblock printmaking.	Students will use craft processes for personal art expression.

Drawing, Designing, and Painting

Students like their work to have expressive content—to convey a mood and have a message. They are interested in finding a powerful means to convey an experience or an idea. Whereas younger students showed scenes, adolescents now use scenic natural forms to communicate their attitudes toward life. They can study symbols and work into their designs motifs for peace, freedom, evil, or envy.

Most students at this age have a love–hate relationship with drawing; while on the one hand they seek realism, yet, on the other hand, they are often frustrated by their inability to attain it. Elaborate still-life setups with models in expressive apparel stimulate their interest and, hence, their desire to accurately represent the model's positions and clothing. Line drawings of cartoon characters, mythical animals, and sports events are popular, as are cartoon portraits. Using shading, stippling, hatching, crosshatching, and washes, they can begin to comprehend and depict the effect of spotlights on models. They will need guidance and reassurance, however, in handling color values and using cast shadows and reflections.

Students interested in creating depth in their pictures will begin to realize the importance of creating avenues into the composition. This is done by using lines and shapes that terminate at the boundaries or borders of the paper and lead the viewer into the picture. A bonus is that the more avenues created, the more opportunities the student has to employ a variety of colors, values, and pattern in the resulting shapes. Perspective may be introduced as just one of many ways that artists create the illusion of depth; however, only a tiny fraction of students can work out realistic perspective showing space and depth. Thus, unless a student specifically requests help, it is wise not to introduce regimented perspective rules or foreshortening techniques at this stage.

Inverted perspective sometimes now appears, and the beauty of this method should be pointed out—for example, in Persian art. Some students will want their drawings to "look right" and will request specific assistance in making their toppling, meandering fences stand straight.

Perspective is shown in this 10-year-old girl's street scene from Tehran, Iran. Diminishing sizes are seen in the street vanishing around the bend, its dotted centerline, the curved fence, and the street-side buildings.

They want their sidewalks to lie flat and their roads to disappear believably over a distant rise or hill. To help them achieve these effects, show them that fence posts are drawn parallel to the sides of the page, division lines in sidewalks are drawn at angles directed to a distant vanishing point, and roads or highways diminish in width as they move away toward the horizon.

Older middle school students often are enchanted by the mechanical, mathematical aspects of perspective drawing. The illusion of space gives some students, especially those who do not like to draw, a feeling that they have done something of note. Their enthusiasm should not be dampened, but the teacher can point out the compositional limitations of a rigid reliance on perspective. Similarly, it is all right for students to strive for "right" proportions in their figures, but the instructor must help them to realize that drawing something "realistically right" does not necessarily make it "artistically right." Especially now, when the expression of feelings is so important, students can be shown that many artists throughout time who either did not know of or ignored the rules of perspective and proportion still produced art of great impact and beauty.

Middle school students are mature enough to respond to the many subtleties and complexities of color harmonization. Review the processes for making tints and shades and the techniques for neutralizing colors. Challenge the students to use color principles in designing CD covers, monograms, posters, logos, book jackets, store-window displays, room decor, and stage designs. Call attention to how color is used in artworks for conveying emotion. Discuss the psychological effect of color on people, the colors emphasized in packaging and advertising, and the colors of ceremonies, celebrations, rituals, and rites of passage. Analyze how various countries and cultures use differing symbolic color meanings.

Taking ideas from contemporary color and light shows, students can be encouraged to construct their own color "happenings." They can use found materials such as ribbons, yarn, wrapping paper, kites, cellophane, balloons, hula hoops, confetti, crepe and tissue paper in assorted colors, giant paper flowers, fabric samples, and beach towels. Other exciting projects to stimulate color awareness can be motivated by examining such artists as Victor Vasarely, Richard Anuskiewicz, Marc Chagall, and Judy Pfaff. For example, students can construct toothpick-and-box sculptures painted in bold tempera or fluorescent colors and make miniature stained-glass windows using scrap colored glass, colored tissue paper, or stage gels.

Printmaking

The simple prints that children enjoyed in earlier grades—vegetable and found-object prints, glue-line-relief prints, collographs, monoprints, linoleum prints—can be done with satisfaction and success during middle school. More complex subject matter and themes also now can be employed in a variety of printmaking processes. As always, the organization and monitoring of inking, printing, and cleanup are of special importance. At this grade level, sophisticated printmaking techniques such as woodblocks can be undertaken if teachers are experienced in supervising advanced printmaking techniques. Use nontoxic, water-based inks rather than oil-based inks.

Ceramics and Sculpture

Because students may come to middle school with varying backgrounds in clay experimentation and creation, provide for several sessions to review clay exploration. Discuss the importance of clay to the lives of people in other cultures.

Discuss art visuals of ceramic pottery and sculpture from ancient as well as contemporary cultures. Include Greek vases of the Hellenic period, Chinese Tang figurines, the outstanding life-size ceramic warriors and horses unearthed at Xian, Japanese Haniwa creations, and clay vessels in the form of human figures from Mexico and Peru. Library copies of *Ceramic Monthly* can bring the students up to date on the newest developments in the field of ceramic pottery and sculpture. Put up a "potter of the week" display on the art-room bulletin board so that students will become familiar with pioneers and innovators such as Shoji Hamada, Dan Lucero, and Peter Voulkos.

Seventh- and eighth-grade students can engage in more complex and challenging clay construction and modeling than was possible in the early elementary years. If glazes and adequate kiln facilities are provided, students can experiment with safe ceramic glazes to give their works

Larger-than-life clay portraits from Japan capture the human figure's expressive potential. Observe the heavy supporting neck and the freely applied dabs of clay to create the form.

glowing color. A popular sculpture activity begins with wire armatures that are attached to a block of wood for a base and covered with plaster-of-Paris strips to form expressive figures in motion: rock musicians, surfers, and sports figures, for example.

Crafts

Crafts such as weaving, stitchery, hooked rugs, papier-mâché, puppetry, and simple jewelry are especially popular at this level (see Chapter 28). All of these hands-on activities should be included in a qualitative, progressive elementary and middle school art program. For example, weaving can progress from simple paper weaving in the primary grades to sophisticated, hanging woven panels in the middle school. The story quilts of Faith Ringgold and of Harriet Powers can motivate exciting sewn applique banners and quilts. Mask construction, simple puppets, and stitchery can be offered at all levels. Papier-mâché, paper sculpture, leather and metal tooling, marionettes, and jewelry are best reserved for upper elementary grades and middle school. Then, many students also are ready for challenging subtractive sculpture projects in soap, balsa wood, sandcore, leather-hard clay molds, plaster-of-Paris blocks, and soft fire-

Hooking a rug can bring pride and satisfaction to middle school students.

brick. They will enjoy additive sculpture employing toothpicks, wood scraps, wire, metal, driftwood, and found objects. Specialized craft vocabulary terms such as the following should be taught: glaze, gouge, greenware, grog, leather-hard clay, mat, mat knife, mixed media, mold, raffia, reed, tesserae.

Collage, Photography, and Computer Art

The collage process—which can be expanded to include montage and assemblage, and combined with new media—provides middle school students a host of opportunities to use the principles of art. These include variety in shapes, contrast in values and color, and overlapping to create unity. Collage allows students to express through art their personal concerns about attractiveness and intimacy as well as their social concerns about world problems such as ecology, hunger, drugs, and war.

Review with students the fundamentals of the collage process: how to identify and exploit positive and negative shapes, and how to create subtle space through overlapping. Show them how to achieve three-dimensional effects through paper folding, scoring, pleating, fringing, and curling. Preliminary drawings or sketches are recommended for collages when the subject matter deals with landscapes, figure studies, or still lifes. In themes from the imagination or in purely nonobjective interpretations, the direct cutting, tearing, and application of the shapes to the background may be encouraged. In both approaches, however, the pasting or permanent adhering of materials should be delayed until the students, with the teacher's guidance, can make those compositional changes—additions, subtractions, and revisions—that are necessary to enhance their creations.

Both new and found materials have expanded the range of collage creation immensely. Photographs taken by the students and images scanned into the computer, altered, and printed, as well as computer clip art, can be combined in imaginative ways. Explore the possibilities of colored tissue on white or colored cardboard, colored sections from magazine ads, wallpaper samples, and fabric remnants. Incorporate nature's store of colored and textured wonders: bark, leaves, seaweed, sand, feathers, butterfly wings, dried flowers, seeds, and snake skins. The collage is an excellent first project of the year for middle school art classes. It does not put as much pressure on the students as an assignment in drawing or painting, and it is not stressful to cut out elements and put them together to make a whole design. Every student in class can succeed in making a collage. See Chapter 27 for recommendations concerning photography, video, and computer art.

Courtesy of David Hodge, Oshkosh, WI.

Vehicles are a popular topic with middle school youths. Students created collages from detailed drawings of an open-doored van parked on the school's premises. Gas pumps and logos were added to enhance the compositions.

Suggested Subjects or Themes

These project suggestions are suitable for children of ages 12, 13, and 14. Visual resources are absolutely necessary. For additional ideas, refer to the themes recommended earlier for grades 5 and 6, which can be adapted to the middle school. Middle schools may comprise sixth through eighth grades, or even include the fifth grade as well, and this variation will affect the suitability of topics. Nonetheless, some themes, such as a bouquet of flowers, self-portraits, and animal pets, can be recommended without reservation through the eighth grades.

Environmental problems and
  solutions

The Olympics

I wish

Great moments in music or ballet

Great moments in theater, literature,
  or science

Great moments in sports

I would like/I would not like

Customs and costumes of the world

The weather's mood

Sadness in the world

Legendary heroes and heroines

Helicopters, planes, or air balloon
  races

A vivid dream

Skateboards and snowboards

Oppression and conformity

Landscapes

Illustrations of selected stories and
  poems

Dream cars, motorcycles, and boats

Historical costumes

Flying trapeze act

The electronic-game arcade

A cry for help

String quartet

Fashion show

Wrestling match

Chapter 12

ART FOR STUDENTS EXPERIENCING COGNITIVE OR PHYSICAL DEVELOPMENTAL DISABILITIES

Eight Concepts in Special Education

Approximately 12 percent of students in American public education are in special education programs, and they are entitled by law to instruction in art as well as other content areas. Children with mental and physical disabilities (in learning, hearing, vision, and mobility), as well as those who use mental health services, now are integrated into classrooms of children without disabilities. Given this, every public school classroom teacher and art teacher is increasingly called upon to serve in his or her classroom youths who have disabilities; currently, 85 percent of teachers teach children with disabilities. Hence, all art teachers must be prepared to respond to the needs of students with a broad range of abilities.

In this chapter we will discuss eight important concepts in the area of special education: inclusion, people-first language, developmental disability, normalization, age-appropriateness, partial participation, empowerment, and human worth.

Courtesy of Beverly Mallon, Chase Street Elementary School, Athens, GA.

This dynamic painting of a cat was created by a student who was diagnosed with behavior disability and learning disorders and who was mainstreamed into a third-grade class.

Inclusion

After the passage in 1975 of Public Law 94-142, the Education for All Handicapped Children Act (renamed in 1990 the Disabilities Education Act) was passed. It mandated the regular education initiative for students with milder disabilities, and it promoted the integration of children with severe disabilities. The law mandates testing, individualized educational plans, parental consent, confidentiality, least restrictive environment, and educational programming for youths with developmental disabilities. Students must be served within the regular classroom unless specific social or physical barriers interfere with the child's learning. Inclusion is being implemented to the fullest extent possible. For example, in New York City, 40 percent of students with significant mental and physical disabilities are taught in regular classes with nondisabled students. Over a third of students with disabilities spend from 60 percent to 90 percent of their time in regular classrooms.

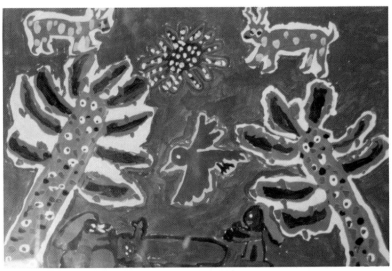

Courtesy of Beverly Mallon, Chase Street Elementary School, Athens, GA.

A fifth-grade girl in special education painted this marvelous design titled "The Healing." Perhaps some of the child's African American artistic heritage and Pentecostal religious beliefs are evident in the artwork's rich patterning and religious power. At the center bottom can be seen a moving scene of two small figures ministering to a prostrate figure in bed. Stags and sun fill the painting's upper portion. Even the trees bow to the heavenly bluebird's power.

People-First Language

In your speech, use people-first language. Do not refer to "the blind" or "the retarded," thus implying that these individuals belong in a class that is set apart; instead, speak of "persons with disabilities in seeing or learning." It is a matter of human decency and respect. As another example, "persons who use a wheelchair for mobility" is more respectful than "crippled people." Further, do not focus on what someone cannot do, such as a child who "can't draw." Instead, focus on capability, such as a child who can "vocalize about the patterns he or she draws." Negative language continues old attitudes of exclusion and a "them vs. us" perspective. Likewise, positive language fosters positive attitudes and helps to promote independence, self-help, and community integration. Terminology changes rapidly, but at this time the term "with disabilities" usually is preferred to "exceptional, challenged, or handicapped." Even more important than terminology, however, is having an attitude of acceptance and faith in the individual.

Developmental Disability

A developmental disability is a severe, chronic disability of a person that:

• Is attributable to a mental or physical impairment or combination thereof
• Is manifested before age 22
• Is likely to continue indefinitely
• Results in limitations in three or more areas of life activity: self-care, language, learning, mobility, self-direction, capacity for independent living, and economic self-sufficiency
• Reflects the need for individually planned treatments of long duration.

Normalization

Normalization is the use of means as culturally normative as possible to establish personal behaviors that are as normative as possible. It does not mean that all people should be the same. Normalization is the idea that all people in a society should have, as far as possible, equal opportunity to live, work, and play. It means that students with disabilities in your art class should be treated as much like all other students as possible.

Age-Appropriateness

A concept related to normalization is age-appropriateness. Teachers of art frequently have been criticized for having older special education students do activities that are deemed to be "babyish." Strive to keep your choice of topics and media age-appropriate. For example, do not have older students do pudding painting; instead, use an adult material such as paper pulp. Test whether an activity is too childlike by asking yourself whether nondisabled persons of the same age would want to do it. When using art materials such as crayons, which some people may associate with primary school, emphasize how they have been used by famous artists, such as Picasso. (This is a good strategy even for persons without disabilities.)

Partial Participation

For students with especially severe disabilities, keep in mind the principle of partial participation. Is there some way in which the student with a disability could participate in the lesson? Perhaps a student without language

Illustrations from *Art and Mainstreaming*, a textbook dealing with art instruction for exceptional children in regular classrooms, by Claire B. Clements and Robert D. Clements, University of Georgia, Athens, GA.
Courtesy of Charles C. Thomas Publishers, Springfield, IL.

Printing designs and shapes with potatoes, sponges, and erasers provides an unusual experience in aesthetic discrimination and fine-motor coordination. In addition, the decorative patterns that result can then be used for gift wrap, for greeting cards, and for covering boxes.

Human Worth

Every individual is a human being of worth. Each child presents potential, and it is the teacher's job to unearth that potential. As teachers filled with openness, patience, and belief, it is our job to unlock the potential within each person. Art teachers especially, charged with nurturing creativity in the individual, must model and teach respect for human diversity. Humanistic education's goals are to value people and to believe in every human's potential.

General Teaching Strategies

For most children in elementary and middle school, the teaching guidelines proposed in this book should prove to be adaptable and effective. For children with special needs, however, other teaching strategies may be needed. This chapter provides some practical approaches to help teachers meet the challenge. First, the good news: the art class or studio atmosphere is the best of all possible environments in which to work with children having developmental disabilities. Each child is accepted, and his or her

could hold up the art reproduction that the class discusses. A student without sight could work with another child in cleaning the paintbrushes with soap. Even if a student cannot do all of the steps in a process, you or another student can arrange for the individual to do those that he or she can. However, because the child may need longer to do a certain step, the sequence may need to be changed.

Empowerment

Another important concept in special education is empowerment. It is very easy for helpers to "overdo" for individuals with disabilities. In fact, many children both with and without disabilities are masters at getting extra services from adults, using the familiar refrain "You draw it for me." To foster independent achievement, the less assistance the teacher or aide offers, the better.

Knox Wilkinson, an artist with mild mental challenge, has successfully shown his work in museums throughout the nation and world. He is involved in efforts to help others achieve through art, and his design of two birds here is an announcement for a Very Special Art Exhibition.

Facing page: Drawings depict children in a variety of art activities that build self-worth. **Left to right, top:** *Construction with wood scraps from lumber yard; costumes and hats designed for a parade; paper masks.* **Left to right, bottom:** *Simple cardboard-and-string mobile; train engines and trucks constructed from discarded grocery cartons.*

potential is respected. Each child can excel in some way, and every child can be an achiever.

The importance of the teacher and his or her role cannot be emphasized enough in the context of teaching children with special needs. All attributes of the dedicated teacher that we have spelled out so far—empathy, knowledge, tact, confidence, resourcefulness, understanding, equanimity, and patience—are important in the successful management of a classroom that includes students with disabilities. Precedence, if any, must be given to the qualities of understanding and patience. Some general strategies for teachers who are experiencing inclusion for the first time include the following:

1. Accept the children as they are.
2. Familiarize yourself with the disabilities of special children assigned to your class. Use the student's out-of-school interests as guides for suitable activities.
3. Ascertain whether a progress chart has been recorded on the students by a previous teacher. Note the art experiences and projects with which they have been successful.
4. Help the parents to promote their child's life-enriching recreation and leisure skills by advising them regarding art materials their child enjoys using. Suggest art and hobby materials they might acquire for use in their home and inform them of community arts class offerings.
5. If teacher aides are assigned to help you with the students with disabilities, involve the aides appropriately. Do not let the aide sit idle, but, more importantly, do not let an oversolicitous aide do the project for the individuals.
6. Keep your own progress report on every child with disabilities. In a few school systems, the art teacher must write and implement individualized educational plans (IEPs) for each student with developmental disabilities. This involvement in the IEP process is a valuable educational practice in making art fundamental for all students.
7. Consider carefully your teaching procedures for students with disabilities. Will you use free-choice projects, in which children choose their own subject matter, materials, and time limits? Will you employ the unit or project method, in which the same art activity is planned for students both with and without disabilities? The latter approach usually calls for individual adjustments to meet the needs and abilities of the student with disabilities.
8. Ask the child if there is something that could be done to facilitate his or her participation in the activity. ("How can we make it easier for you to do the project?")
9. Enlist the aid of students without disabilities—especially those with proven abilities and stable, pleasant personalities—to help their classmates with disabilities.

Projects that may be undertaken successfully with children with some kinds of special needs. **Top:** *Three-dimensional animals constructed with folded and cut tagboard.* **Bottom:** *Stable constructed of found materials.*

10. Above all, do not permit those children with disabilities to participate in copying or tracing artwork. Help them to create their own imagery, even though this imagery may differ from that of the other students in the class. Even when children's graphic expression consists of scribbles, they have feeling for the patterns their marks make. They have made something that did not exist earlier in the world.

The following sections describe specific teaching strategies and tactics to follow in working with students who have developmental disabilities. Keep in mind that even if the students with disabilities have normal or above-average IQs, they probably will require some nontraditional teaching strategies and adaptation of materials.

Teaching Students with Learning Disabilities or Hyperactivity

In teaching the child with learning disorders or hyperactivity, at all times proceed deliberately, methodically, and calmly. Give directions or instructions slowly and clearly, using simple language at a rate that the children can assimilate. Make sure, if possible, that you have the child's attention when explaining something. Students with learning disabilities often look as if they understand, when in fact they are confused. In spite of very clear instructions, assume that misunderstandings may exist.

Prepare lessons to meet specific needs—hand-eye coordination, fine or gross motor skills improvement—and to meet identifiable objectives such as color or shape naming. Demonstrate more, and talk less. Employ visual symbols and models. To hold the child's attention, speak in a well modulated tone of voice. (Certainly, all students could benefit from such a tone.) For youths with attention deficits, use colorful teaching materials.

Although the teaching materials should be colorful, the room surroundings should show a calm, ordered environment. A teacher can help in this by doing the following:

• Keep changes to a minimum.
• Consider limiting opportunities for choice.
• Consider minimizing the number of materials used.
• De-emphasize group activities.
• Give immediate reinforcement.

Students having problems in math, such as dyscalcula, may find measuring a challenge, for example, when measuring a mat.

Be prepared for emotional outbursts. Heed when a child may be close to losing control, and change the situation before that point is reached. Give "road markers,"—notices that an activity will terminate or change in a few minutes. These signal a student that he or she must get ready to move on to another activity.

Consider reordering seating arrangements so that a child is not distracted by viewing others. Working in a carrel may help a child to concentrate. The student could sit up front in a corner or behind a partial screen. Likewise, a temporary folding screen could be placed on a child's desk to form a baffle or cubicle. Try to create seating arrangements and projects that encourage staying in the seat—for example, looking at an art history book while seated in a beanbag chair out of view of most distractions.

Teaching Students with Vision Deficiencies

Most students with vision deficiencies in school classes will not be totally blind, but rather will have some residual vision. As a teacher of art, a subject involving considerable visual/motor coordination, you may be among the first to notice that a student in your class might have a vision deficiency. If you suspect something may be amiss, notify the school nurse or parent. The following behaviors or conditions might be indicative of a vision deficiency:

putting head close to artwork to see it
tilting head or thrusting head forward to see artwork
squinting or frowning
rubbing eyes
focusing with difficulty
becoming irritable when doing precision art assignments
red rimmed or encrusted or swollen eyelids
watery eyes
crossed eyes
recurring sties

Also listen for the following complaints:

complaints of not being able to see well
complaints of headache following close work
complaints of eyes itching, burning, or feeling scratchy
complaints of blurred or double vision

To encourage a child's participation to the maximum extent possible, the following approach can help them to achieve success. Increase the amount of contrast between the drawn lines and background. Broad-line markers of vivid colors and brightly colored crayons are preferable to markers and crayons of more subdued values. Some media, such as puff paint and glue-line prints, will leave a raised line that can be felt. Black paint can be added to white glue for drawing on white paper, and a bold raised line will be left when dry.

For those who supplement vision with touch, use large contrasting (black-and-white) sheets of paper. However, some students will prefer tinted paper, which minimizes glare. Other techniques, such as printing on plastic-foam meat trays and drawing on heavy aluminum foil with a dull pencil, will leave a recessed line. Art media that make noise, such as squeaky brayers and markers, or that smell, such as scented markers and paste, can add interest.

An emphasis on three-dimensional work is often beneficial, employing projects such as jewelry making, weaving, and pottery.

Figure sculptures of pipe cleaners or wire and polymer clay can be used to emphasize good posture. Topics such as "a call for help" can foster the expression of feelings. Making texture maps and box sculptures can communicate the individual's concept of himself or herself as a person capable of moving around the home and community.

Teachers can help by asking a child whose vision is deficient what light level is most comfortable for him or her: near a window, in bright light, or in subdued light. Provide optical aids such as magnifying glasses. Allow the child extra time for eye rest. Your school may permit printed material for the child to be photocopied at a greater magnification. Make eye contact as you address the students. Sit on a chair or stool so that your face will be nearer to the child's eye level. Do not address the class while facing the chalkboard or standing in the glare from a window.

Consistently storing supplies in the same place helps students with vision deficiencies to find what they need. In order to foster independence, require students with vision deficiencies to help care for the art materials. For students with partial vision, light shows can use colored gels and projectors.

Encourage interpersonal interactions between blind and sighted peers; for example, assign a sighted student to serve as a helper. In looking at art reproductions, have the partially sighted child sit close to the front of room and be given the opportunity to examine the print at the distance and in the light level that is best for him or her.

Teaching Students with Neurological and Orthopedic Disabilities

Students with neurological and orthopedic disabilities are likely to have frequent absences. If the child is hospitalized, send work home but don't make demands that the child cannot meet. Provide the parents with suggestions about possible art projects. And, on the child's return to school, make the student feel welcome. Spend time helping the class to develop realistic attitudes about infirmities and teach them how to interact with peers with disabilities.

School absences can affect not only academic performance, but also social and emotional development—especially self-esteem. Students may be excluded from class activities or rejected by peers. Hence, treat these students as worthwhile, competent students who have interests and needs similar to their classmates.

Because students with neurological and orthopedic disabilities may have received pity or overprotection, never expect them to do less than that of which they are capable. Develop reasonable objectives and expect their attainment. However, recognize that, because of fatigue, they may not be able to do all activities or to finish activities on time.

Borders, boundaries, and holding devices may help students with disabilities perform various tasks. Plastic meat trays can hold clay and small objects, and cafeteria trays can be clamped with a C-clamp to a wheelchair work surface. Masking or duct tape can be used to tape down water containers and to tape a brush to a child's hand. Individuals with severe limitations in movement can pull a string to move a mobile and can make patterns in salt, sugar, or millet on a colorful tray. Further, using a rasp to carve blocks of balsa wood can provide both exercise and an art experience. Also, students can press papier mâché into a greased mold to create sculptural forms.

An occupational therapist on the IEP team can be a resource in knowing how to secure and in getting adaptive equipment.

Teaching Students with Hearing and Speech Disabilities

For students with hearing and speech disabilities, emphasize art projects such as self-portraits to help them overcome their self-consciousness. Likewise, working with a buddy on a joint project will help to reduce feelings of insecurity. To encourage their use of residual hearing, have students sit on a wooden floor and bang on a drum, or paint to music. Develop language skills by staging plays with puppets and masks, using a model grocery store to serve as a setting.

To promote normalization, remind nonhandicapped students that 30 percent of school age youngsters are likely to have deaf relatives.

However, some students with hearing disabilities may be indistinguishable from their nonhandicapped peers in behavior. A child with a hearing impairment may appear to be inattentive and to daydream, seeming reluctant to participate in class activities. Another child with a hearing disability might have developed mannerisms such as looking as though she understands when, in fact, she does not. Students with impaired hearing may have frequent absences from school because of earaches or sinus congestion, which can be a source of temporary or permanent hearing loss. Likewise, allergies and head congestion also can temporarily reduce hearing.

Allow students with hearing disabilities the opportunity to move their chairs as needed in order to hear better or to see the teacher's face for speechreading. Speak naturally for students who are speechreading. Don't slow down or exaggerate mouth movements. Recognize, though, that they may need to hear a term repeated many times and in many ways. Help students with hearing disabilities to find seats away from humming fans or boisterous students, and try to keep background noise to a mini-

A twelve-year-old boy diagnosed with mild intellectual disability did this cheerful artwork to the Beatles song, "Here comes the Sun, I say it's alright." In the first period, the sun was drawn with hot colors. Then oil pastels were used to color the artwork. Circular shapes, triangular shapes, and serpentine shapes were emphasized by the teacher.

This unique composition of a kicking judo athlete with his head going off the page was the original idea of an intermediate level student diagnosed with mild intellectual disability. Notice the proudly earned black belt in the center of the picture.

mum. Give students with hearing disabilities an outline of the art assignment, or have a classmate take notes using carbon paper.

Encourage students with speech and hearing impairments to talk about their artworks, perceptions, and out-of-school activities. When they are speaking, listen attentively and show your active interest through facial expressions. Don't inadvertently look away while they are speaking. Also, don't finish their sentences for them. To promote their talking, ask open-ended questions including *How, why, where,* and *when,* rather than questions that can be answered *yes* or *no.* And, to overcome their shyness about speaking and to help them understand their assignments, encourage them to ask questions. Positive self-esteem comes from full participation in the student art community. The key is to minimize discrimination, stigma, and difference.

Teaching Students with Cognitive Disabilities

Levels of cognitive retardation vary, from mild to severe to profound impairment. Each stage has its own requirements. At the stage of profound retardation, an appropriate goal is that the student be aware of movement and sensation and be able to handle art materials with enjoyment.

Wonderful jumping action is shown by the outstretched legs and the bouncing braids in this primary level special education student's basketball scene. She wears two gloves, so much the better to catch the ball. During the first period, motivation consisted of jumping and using hands to catch; also, the figure was drawn in pencil. In the second period, a fantasy background was painted in with neon watercolors. In the third period, markers were used to add detail.

Strive for projects that are both age-appropriate and ability-appropriate. Repeat instructions and procedures frequently. Use multi-level approaches, sequencing, adaptation, and much reinforcement. Plan projects that may be broken down into sequential, manageable, and explainable steps. Then do the project one step at a time, finishing one step before explaining the next step. Allow sufficient time for the completion of each stage; it may be necessary for early finishers to do filler activities while others complete a step. Do not begin a new step, however, until the previous one has been completed.

In an inclusive classroom, you must help all the students. If a lot of repetitive one-on-one instruction is necessary, then a teaching assistant is indicated. You cannot devote all your time to one or several children.

Teaching Students with Behavioral Disorders

Let the students, especially those with behavioral disabilities, know you expect reasonable standards of conduct in art class. Communicate your expectations clearly and firmly. Then, provide consistent consequences for inappropriate behavior. When students feel connected to what is going on in the art classroom, they are more likely to engage in responsible behavior. Hence, devote classroom meeting time to establishing and discussing standards of behavior. This is what inclusive schooling strives for.

Behavioral psychologists urge teachers to try to "catch children being good" and to reinforce their good actions. Some teachers object on ethical grounds to the use of behavioral techniques, such as token economy, contingency contracting, and group-based contingencies, while others believe such procedures are a humane way to help students to achieve in the classroom. How do you feel about this issue? Use unexpected rewards, such as displaying artwork outside the principal's office. Provide reinforcements such as letting the child arrange a bulletin board, pronounce the art vocabulary words, or sketch a tray of toy figures.

Empathize with the students and show that you understand the lesson's difficulties: that the classroom space is cramped when students are doing large pictures, that the temperature in the room is uncomfortable, that hard work is required to color in the whole background.

It can be helpful to students who have problems for the teacher simply to be empathic and to listen passively, acknowledging their concerns. Saying "I see," nodding, and smiling are ways to communicate your attention and understanding. If you suspect the problem may come from a home situation, however, encourage the student to tell you about it, asking him or her, "Would you feel comfortable sharing what it is?" When a teacher discovers a problem that is beyond his or her area of expertise, it should be referred to the school counselor or psychologist. Knowing when to refer is very important.

Courtesy of Beverly Mallon, Chase Street Elementary School, Athens, GA.

A student with behavior disorders and mild intellectual disability made this thrilling geometrically dynamic painting. Note the visual push and pull of the rooftops as shapes alternately advance and recede. Objects which are on top of, behind, and beside other objects usually shift from moment to moment. The teacher showed the class a crazy quilt, which students then sketched in chalk. In the second period, the students painted in the squares. In the third period, the students painted in the patterns and details. This child was particularly involved, "Because my Gramma makes quilts."

Rather than issuing blaming "You" messages, express your feelings using "I" messages. For example, "Because your noisy, out-of-seat behavior showed disrespect for and ignored the art class rules, I am angry." Three steps in giving effective "I" messages are: 1) a non-blaming, non-judgmental description of the behavior; 2) a description of the tangible effect the behavior is having on you, the teacher, and on other students; and 3) a description of how this behavior is making the teacher feel.

To prolong attentiveness, consider using projects that might imply monetary value (glazed ceramics, leather work, crafts), and tools should be manual arts tools (hammers, gouges). Art media should offer active resistance (linocuts, carving). In addition, the project should have three dimensions. Emphasize experiences that deal with kinesthetic manipulation and multisensory stimulation.

Be aware of the difficulties that students with disabilities have in tolerating changes in routines. Further, recognize that some are easily distracted and have short attention spans, and that many require constant praise and encouragement. Brief, one-session projects demanding minimum memory recall may be necessary. Longer projects may be appropriate as well, but only if broken down clearly into separate steps, presented one at a time. Also, remember that, like all students, those with disabilities respond more enthusiastically when their art experiences are successful.

Using Art for Community and School Integration

Persons with disabilities are not a separate group from the community at large. They are citizens with the rights of all citizens. Congress has passed the Americans with Disabilities Act, guaranteeing these individuals rights to equity in employment, housing, and community services. Some ways the art program can promote positive community attitudes follow:

Encourage these students to participate in community activities so that they may see themselves as, and be seen by others as, active members of their community. Involve them in activities about their own cultural heritage in particular.

Be alert to opportunities such as art exhibitions in which your students with disabilities can participate. A Pilot Club or similar civic organization in your community or state may sponsor activities in which your students could receive recognition. Make arrangements for students with disabilities to attend community art openings and art festivals.

Display the students' work attractively and elicit supporting response from their peers. Remember that their projects, which may differ in appearance from the art of students without disabilities, can bring pride to the school, delight to parents and visitors, and an enhanced sense of self-worth to the participating students.

Ascertain whether the student, parents, or caregivers are being served by community organizations whose purpose is to provide support for them. For example, perhaps there is a support group in your community for young people requiring mental health services. Many communities have a quasi-governmental, centralized resource with a name such as "Help Line" or "Community Connection" that puts people in touch with social service agencies and support groups appropriate to their needs. Certain community service organizations may provide special equipment as well. (For example, the Lions Club offers services to people with vision difficulties.)

Be an active advocate for accessibility. When setting up art exhibitions, have certain pieces designated for touching. Position large-print labels at the proper height. Integrate alternative forms of communication, such as Braille and Blissboards (boards with pictures to which a person points to communicate). Art teachers can help children without speech to draw their own "talking books."

Photo: William Bengston

From "The Problem with Martin Ramirez," *Clarion*, Winter 1986. Collection of Gladys Nillson and Jim Nutt.

Famous Hispanic-American artist Martin Ramirez hid his artwork behind the radiators in the mental institution where he spent his adult life, until the artistic power and rhythm of his works were discovered by an art teacher.

Experiences and Objects That May Appeal to Students with Physical or Cognitive Disabilities

Painting

Cutting

Pasting

Rolling beach balls

Opening packages

Toys

Construction (wood, boxes, found objects)

Meat-tray boats

Weaving

Balloons

Fingerpainting

Figure drawing

Pets and animals

Flowers and trees

Dressing up, costumes, and uniforms

Kinesthetic activities

Decorating the classroom

Puppets

Piñatas

Fanciful hats

Marching and parading

Printmaking (with vegetables and found objects)

Big cardboard cartons to hide and play in and to transform into vehicles

Fish in aquariums

Clowns

Making music with assorted concocted instruments

Bright colors in paper, cloth, yarn, cellophane, and ribbons

Noisemakers and horns

Modeling mixtures

Singing

Masks

Face make-up

Drums

Pantomime

Painting to music

Use of mirrors

Mobiles

Kaleidoscopes

Kites

Specialized Materials

Familiarize yourself with the many specialized devices, tools, and materials now used in art classes by children with significant physical disabilities. The school's special education coordinator may be able to help you in requisitioning the following materials for your students:

Four-holed scissors that both student and teacher can manipulate simultaneously

Fat-handled brushes (1- or 2-inches wide) or brushes that have handles wrapped with masking or surgical tape to provide a better grip.

Giant color crayons, felt-nib markers (water-based), kindergarten-size pencils with soft lead

Glue sticks (which may be easier to use than squeeze bottles of white glue)

Painting stretchers assembled together and placed on desks around the perimeter of the in-process projects so that students can judge their work's boundaries; other possibilities are plastic meat trays and cafeteria trays

C-clamps and duct or masking tape to hold artwork onto wheelchair trays; specially designed art boards for wheelchairs

Duct tape for taping a brush to a child's hand

Forehead pointers

Mouth wands or rubber spatulas with brushes or markers taped to them

Posters and instructional signs with giant-size letters and numerals

Cameras and computers adapted for special use by those with disabilities in vision, movement, and coordination

Touch table, touch box

Flannel boards and pegboards

Building blocks in assorted shapes and sizes

Magnifying glasses and colored gelatins

Wood or plastic colored beads and sticks in assorted sizes

For additional found or recycled materials useful in art classes, see Appendix

Chapter 13

GIFTEDNESS AND ART THINKING

This chapter discusses giftedness in general, relates general-intelligence approaches to artistic giftedness and creativity, gives strategies for the teacher, and offers suggestions for outreach into the school, home, and community. Gifted and talented students are part of the greater school community and should have appropriate adaptations and challenges made for them in the regular art class setting. Admission into a school's gifted programs often requires a score on the Stanford Binet Intelligence Test of 120 to 130 points, as well as teacher recommendations, high grades, and acceptance by a review committee. Some experts feel the intelligence test is overly weighted toward skills in math and reading comprehension, with areas such as art ability going unmeasured. One alternative to the IQ test is the Torrance Test of Creative Thinking, which considers four aspects of creativity: fluency, flexibility, elaboration, and originality. As a teacher, you can nurture these four desirable characteristics for all children by talking with and questioning your students as they create their artwork and by urging them to produce lots of different and unlikely ideas.:

Fluency: "How many can you show?"
Flexibility: "Can you think of another way to look at it?"
Elaboration: "Can you tell about this in more detail?"
Originality: "Make it your *own* way, and show the special idea that you have."

Since creativity is so domain specific, and it is not a trait or a capacity that pervades all of an individual's activities, it is doubtful that creativity can be assessed. To characterize creativity as simply a set of abilities that incorporate fluency, flexibility, and originality leaves many other aspects of creativity unaccounted for.

Another way to look at intelligence comes from Harvard psychologist Howard Gardner, who does not believe that there is one monolithic kind of intelligence. Instead, he describes eight distinct forms of intelligence, or ways of "information processing" (1990):

• Linguistic
• Logical and mathematical
• Interpersonal (knowledge about other people)
• Musical
• Spatial
• Bodily kinesthetic
• Intrapersonal (information about oneself)
• Naturalistic

Gardner does not consider artistic thinking to be a separate form of intelligence. Instead, seven of the forms can be directed to artistic or nonartistic ends. (Bodily kinesthetic is not included.) For example, language ability can be used by a poet or a lawyer. Kinesthetic ability can be used by a dancer or a surgeon. Spatial ability can be used by a sculptor or a sailor. You can bring these concepts into your classroom for all students in the following ways:

• Linguistic intelligence can be related to art through discussions of art criticism, art history, and aesthetics. Encourage students to give their artwork a title and to write about it. See Chapter 17, Reading and Writing.
• Mathematical intelligence can be related to art through the study of geometric forms such as icosahedra in three-dimensional constructions, fractal geometry in computer art, linear perspective, and topological

Fifth-grade student Kristen Richardson paints her imaginary bird. A branch in bud and one bird are silhouetted against the full moon while another watches after a nest of eggs and a hatchling. School has ended for the year; everyone has gone home for the summer, and two gifted students paint on, intent on finishing their tempera birds. Pride can be taken in the finished artwork.

surfaces in mapmaking and Escher prints. See Chapter 15, particularly the section on math.

- Knowledge of other people (interpersonal knowledge) can be shown by empathically discussing the art of others. Students can give encouragement to peers for their art and can depict interpersonal relationships in their own. See Chapter 16.
- Musical intelligence can be related to art through painting while listening to music, creating music to accompany a certain painting (such as Moussorgsky's "Paintings at an Exhibition"), and studying how various

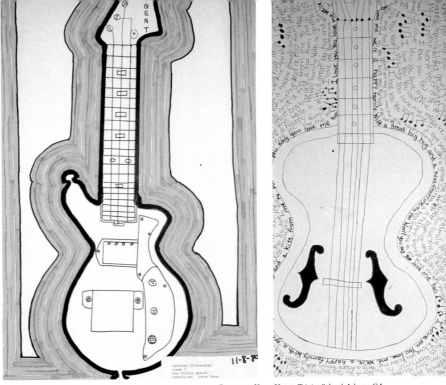

Courtesy of Joyce Vroon, Trinity School, Atlanta, GA.

Left: One way that musical ability and interests can be integrated with art is by drawing musical instruments. Fifth-grade student Courtney Clinkscales carefully draws an electric guitar and then outlines it in bands of alternating, vibrating colors. *Right:* After drawing a guitar, Tyler Grubb adds song lyrics, written around the guitar's outline in successive rows.

Sky and Water, 1938, woodcut, M. C. Escher, (1898–1972). National Gallery of Art, Washington, D.C., Cornelius Van S. Roosevelt Collection.

In this M. C. Escher print, the dark bird shape is transformed into water. The white fish changes into sky. Although Escher was a poor math student, his prints showing transformations from two- to three-dimensions have been hailed as having much significance, especially for mathematicians. Today, students in math classes often create their own similar transformation designs.

cultures have expressed themselves through music and art. See Chapter 18, Related Arts.

- Spatial intelligence is the area that is related most closely to visual art. It can be cultivated by exploring ways of creating and analyzing space in art, especially in architecture and sculpture, but also in all art ideas dealing with space—for example, perspective. See Chapters 28 and 29 on Architecture and Sculpture.
- Intrapersonal intelligence is awareness of the subtle interplay between cognitive and emotional processes that guide one's behavior. This form of intelligence can be given expression in art classes by discussing the meaning of one's own art or of masterpieces and by considering questions of aesthetics. See Chapter 16, particularly the section of Psychology.

• Naturalistic intelligence can be related to art by the artists' experiencing and depicting observed natural phenomena. Examples are the notebooks of Leonardo da Vinci about natural phenomena, John James Audubon about American birds, and J. M. W. Turner about cloud formations. The photos by Romain Vishniak of microscopic life are another manifestation. See Chapter 15, Science and Art Integration, for examples of student projects.

Creativity

New studies in creativity focus on problem solving, problem finding, and on the creation of products. The four stages in the creative act are preparation, incubation, inspiration, and verification. Creativity is no longer seen so much as an individual activity conducted more or less in isolation. Instead it is increasingly being viewed more as an interactive dialectical process among talented individuals, domains of knowledge and products, and the judges. No person, act, or product is creative or noncreative in itself; judgments of creativity are made by knowledgeable judges.

When people are involved in creative activity or play, self-consciousness disappears, the sense of time becomes distorted, and the activity becomes enjoyable in itself. A balance of challenge and skill is achieved, action and awareness are merged, and distractions and worry are put aside. Psychologist Mihalyi Csikzentmihalyi found that adults' play (such as mountain climbing, gardening, chess, or art making) had the following characteristics: 1) able to concentrate on a limited stimulus field, 2) in which individual skills can be used to meet clear demands, 3) thereby forgetting personal problems, 4) and one's own separate identity, 5) at the same time obtaining a feeling of control of one's environment, 6) which may result in a transcendence of ego-boundaries and consequent psychic integration with metapersonal systems. This sixth point can also be stated as creativity being based on the belief that the individual can transform the world.

Gifted students frequently go beyond the assigned project, doing extra work on their own. This depiction of Olympic athletes was done by a fifth-grade student independently following her completion of the class project shown below. To create a feeling of ancient marble, she created marbelized paper using chalk floating on water. She then traced her figure drawings from the artwork she did in art class and combined them with Grecian columns. The 1996 Olympics were a big event in Athens, Georgia, as three events were held there and are shown in the pictures: rhythmic gymnastics, soccer, and volleyball. The bottom picture shows her first paintings of the figures, cut out and applied onto a background of interlocking pastel shapes. On doing a second version of her picture, perhaps she felt that a more classical style of depiction could more adequately capture the Olympics' classical ideals.

Courtesy of Beverly Mallon, Chase Street Elementary School, Athens, GA.

Courtesy of Baiba Kuntz, Glencoe, IL.

Seventh-grade student Beth Savitsky rendered this abstract face and figure in acrylic paints after studying Miro's use of fantasy. Note the secondary colors and the graduated purple background.

Saga Prefecture, Kyushu Island, Japan.

These fish drawings are by primary-grade children. What imaginations these youngsters possess to invent and elaborate so skillfully.

Characteristics of Students Gifted in Art

In the qualitative approach to art, all students are encouraged to develop many of the characteristics possessed by persons talented in art. Talented students have greater persistence and are able to work both longer and with greater concentration. They find pleasure by encountering complex, challenging problems. They can become absorbed for hours in a medium. Worries and cares drop away and they derive deep, personal satisfaction from their art involvement. Some or all of the following characteristics are true of people gifted in art:

- First reveal giftedness through their very early drawings and may develop a personal style of representation early in their school years.
- Use a greater amount of detail, pattern, and texture in their artwork than do most children. Some of this elaboration is observed and some is imagined.

A superb pen-and-ink drawing of lush foliage by a gifted sixth-grade Japanese girl.

- Possess a richer store of images and ideas from which to draw, heightened by their acute observation.
- Often possess a photographic mind, with vivid recall of events engaged in or observed that distinguishes their efforts, which are characterized by a richness of details.

- Master certain technical aspects of drawing—perspective, foreshortening, volume, shading, overlapping, spatial handling, movement—much sooner than do their peers.
- May choose subjects of fantasy for their art compositions, with complex themes involving intricate structures and a host of participants.

- Are open to new experiences with new media, techniques, and tools.
- Show great interest in the art world and the lives of contemporary artists and craftspeople. They may visit art museums and even may carry a sketchbook to record their impressions.
- Rather than merely reacting to occurrences in the world, their creativity leads them to take a proactive stance toward them.
- Learn quickly to employ the vocabulary of art both effectively and confidently and to criticize and evaluate their art production for design.
- Usually prefer drawing, painting, printmaking, and collage to step-by-step craftwork.
- Use color imaginatively, making up their own palette by combining the hues provided to the class.
- Are oblivious to distractions when engaged in their art, and often resent interference.
- Generally are highly self-motivated and driven by a need to fashion art products on their own—after school, at home, and even during other classes.

Teaching Strategies

The teacher can encourage gifted students by providing a supportive environment. Students feel this is more important than any instruction they receive. Overpraise is to be avoided, however, because it can lead to peer resentment. Be aware that learning occurs from "Novice to Expert"; by analyzing experts' performance, novices can see differences among them. This is a familiar idea in arts' education where, centuries ago, the apprentice system was used. Perhaps you are the expert role model who can guide a child, or perhaps you can put the child in contact with an expert.

A good approach is the minimal one of leaving the student to follow his or her special direction—in effect, underteaching. The teacher can provide challenges through multimedia techniques and subject-matter assignments that demand imaginative solutions and interpretations. For example, an assignment might be to depict a famous person when young, experiencing the first intimations of her or his future role in life. Although a teacher should provide challenges, on no account should you rush the gifted child into advanced forms of expression.

Letting the child pursue his or her own endeavors may pose problems for the teacher who uses the project method, in which all students in class engage in the same subject-matter assignment using the same technique. To allow gifted children the special privilege of working on their own subject choice, at their own pace, while their classmates are required to stay with the assigned project, is not recommended. A wiser procedure is to challenge gifted children to stretch the possibilities of the assigned project or theme to their fullest. Remind gifted students that there are many moments outside of class when they can soar creatively and imaginatively in subjects of their own choosing, and encourage them to share with you some of those outside efforts.

Model creativity yourself in your teaching. To keep the creative spark alive, each day surprise the students in your class. Write down how you surprised others and personally seek out surprises each day. Ask, "What would happen if …?"

Extending into the School, Home, and Community

The teacher can foster students' creative growth not only in the art class but also in the school at large, the home, and the community. Find ways to extend art activities into the community and the individual's ongoing daily life. Community integration may be especially helpful to creative students because of their tendency to be more socially reserved, aloof, and distanced. They also are more questioning, skeptical, and opinionated. People may express negative attitudes toward them, and both peers and adults may perceive them as smart alecks.

To foster the creative and social growth of talented students, consider forming a club or an organization for your gifted students, who might find kindred spirits in such a group. Together, they can discuss and share their artwork and go to special events, such as museum openings. They can contribute artistically to the school's special functions, perhaps by painting a set for an assembly program. Middle school youths can be organized into a chapter of the National Art Education Association's National Junior Art Honor Society. Because males and females need role models with whom to identify, provide gifted students with role models from both genders and from diverse cultural backgrounds. Do not enter gifted elementary and middle school children's art into competitions, however, because such external competitions can undermine creative interest and performance. For the one child who is reinforced by a prize, 10 or 100 children will have confidence in their nascent ability undermined. Especially shun coloring contests of pictures drawn by adults.

The home environment is extremely important in encouraging creativity. Studies of creative individuals found that often at least two generations had participated in the creative field. Creative adults report that when they were young they were exposed to environments in which they were encouraged to ask questions and to test their ideas by active experimentation (Note that these also are the tenets of the constructivist educators.)

Gifted students can stretch the possibilities of the assigned project to the fullest. A middle school student did this colorful simulated mosaic employing cut and torn colored paper for the tesserae. Note the gradations of blue in the harbor's water. The subject is Sakurajima Park, with a view of an erupting volcano on a nearby island. Kagoshima, Japan.

At a parent conference, share with the child's parents your notice of his or her special giftedness. Direct parents' awareness toward community art enrichment programs for children. An art specialist with hundreds of students each year might use a letter to parents to give notice of artistic giftedness and offer suggestions for how to nurture it. An example of such a letter follows:

To the Parents or Guardians of _____ :

Teaching at Anniston and Mayberry Elementary Schools for the past two years, I have had the opportunity to observe the art achievement of over a thousand students. You probably are already aware of your child's giftedness in art; however, I felt it to be my professional responsibility to bring to your attention my notice of and appreciation for the quality work your child does in art. Giftedness is rarely loudly announced; many geniuses as adults showed no spark of giftedness when young (for example, Einstein, Churchill, Tolstoy, Kafka, and Proust). Picasso was poor academically. As a general trait, artistic giftedness in children is shown by their being able to concentrate longer, having a lot of ideas to express, and including a lot of detail to make their drawings more elaborate. They are more self-directed, draw more realistically earlier than other children, and use art materials more creatively.

Some talented children have profited from several art-enrichment programs in our community. Although as a school employee I cannot endorse any one program, I wanted to bring their existence to your attention if you wish to look into their suitability in meeting your child's needs:

Mayberry Recreation Department, Lyndon House Art Center, classes for children ages 4–12, Tuesdays and Thursdays, 3:30 to 5:30 PM, 10 sessions, cost of $20 a term. The YMCA has art classes for members, Saturday, 10–12 AM. Alachua County Junior College has a gifted program on Saturday mornings that sometimes has classes focusing on the arts (546-9990). Private art teachers of whom I am aware in the community are Martha Menendez, 546-7783, and James Jackson, 543-3454. In addition, there are probably more programs of which I am unaware.

Please contact me at school at 543-9087 (between 2:30 and 3:30 PM is best) or at home at 548-4543 (between 7 and 8 PM) or by e-mail : fjones@home.com, if I can be of help to you concerning how we might work together to further your child's artistic creativity.

Art Teacher, Anniston and Mayberry Elementary Schools

Teachers who discover talented children are fortunate. They witness what children can do in art when they extend themselves to their fullest potential. Teachers can derive clues from the creative solutions that gifted children employ to help them motivate other classmates. What teachers see and learn from the characteristics and working habits of talented children is what they emphasize in a qualitative art program. They see keen, sensitive observation; rich imagination; persistence, patience, and concentration; and above all, art that is engaged in by the child both seriously and purposefully.

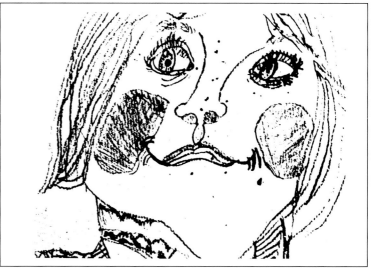

Courtesy of Sharon Burns-Knutson, Cedar Rapids, IA.

The teacher of art should call parents' attention to gifted students' abilities so that the children may receive enrichment instruction and the gift be nurtured. Gifted first-grade children have produced these detailed contour-line drawings. They reveal once again what youngsters are capable of achieving in drawing skills when they are encouraged to become aware. First-grade children can notice jewelry details, barrettes, freckles, eyeglass hinges, creases of skin around the eyes and at the mouth's sides—even the oval on the upper lip below the nose and the wrinkles in the lips.

PART 4

ART'S CONTENT: INTEGRATION WITH OTHER SUBJECTS

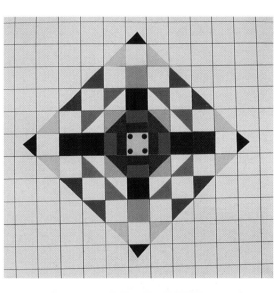

Courtesy of Baiba Kuntz, Glencoe, IL. Seventh grade.

Previous page: *Mathematical objectives integrated with art objectives can be explored through making patterns. Here patterns are made from clay-coated Chroma® paper, pasted to 13- × 13-inch stiff paper ruled into a 1-inch grid. Begin in the middle and work outward.*

Chapter 14

INTRODUCTION TO INTEGRATION AND THE COGNITIVE, AFFECTIVE, AND PSYCHOMOTOR DOMAINS

Introduction to Integration

Most art has content, that is, it is about something. Perhaps it is about a flower garden filled with buzzing insects, or an early culture's celebrations, or us in our community. It can be about geometric designs or visual fields, or about a visual response to music. Art often has rapprochement with fields such as science, social studies, reading, math, and the other arts. It often is enriched by the interrelationship. Can anyone think of art that has no content?

Teachers frequently have students write about and discuss what they have learned. We urge teachers to have students draw and make art about what they have learned. Let the students put their knowledge into their own visual images as a way of showing how they have integrated the learning into themselves!

But the relationship between art and other disciplines is not always a happy marriage. Because some school systems have a lack of enlightenment about art learning and considered it to be far less important than social studies, reading, math, or science, correlating art to the cognitive learning found in other subject areas can be anathema to art teachers. Friction also can occur when scarce art supplies, and scarcer student art-learning time, are used primarily for another purpose, which may

An example of an integrated lesson involving art and science is this colorful felt flower mural. The 3- × 6-foot mural hangs in the school's main display area in the front hallway. Fifth graders sketched in the school's outdoor butterfly garden and then came up with the design; an assembly line of students was developed to produce the mural. The white picket fence gives visual organization to the design. The 3-D effect was achieved by the use of starch to make the fence. Flowers protrude from the wall. Each table of four students worked together as a company to produce the most and best quality of flowers, just like a real business.

Courtesy of Beverly Mallon, Chase Street Elementary School, Athens, GA.

147

barely qualify as an art learning experience. With the current integrated-curriculum approach, however, there is a strong movement to make art "part and parcel" of every school subject.

When the art considerations are serious and fused to the theme and stated clearly, significant art can result. One example of a valid objective that correlates science with art is: "Students will create a design, employing repetition of pattern, based on three different kinds of insects." By doing correlated art projects, teachers of art have succeeded in actually gaining art-learning time and in offering qualitative art experiences to students. Some teachers welcome correlation, so long as that activity is not a substitute for formal art instruction.

Making the case that art is an area that should be part of a common, general education designed for the future nonspecialist citizen, the National Art Education Association (NAEA) recommends that there be "one hundred minutes of art class time a week in the elementary school, with art taught as a subject in itself." In addition, the NAEA says that "time, space, and materials should be provided for supplementary independent and individual art experiences in the regular classroom."

It is crucial that arts-based and arts-related goals be preeminent in arts education. Yet there are more instrumental ends for the arts, as well. These will be addressed in the next four chapters, which deal with the integration of art with specific academic subjects. For example, the next two chapters discuss science/art integration and social studies/art integration, respectively. Both science and social studies offer opportunities to motivate learning in art; likewise, the study of art can motivate learning in science and social studies. Indeed, integration of art with other academic disciplines can provide a synergistic effect, wherein the whole is greater than the sum of its parts.

Integration through the Cognitive, Affective, and Psychomotor Domains

Before turning our attention to art education's relationship to various academic subjects, let us first consider a simpler way to consider education: in the affective, the cognitive, and the psychomotor domains. These domains comprise the three major categories of a system titled Bloom's Taxonomy of Educational Objectives (1954)—an approach to learning that is widely used in many schools that require written lesson plans. Briefly, the cognitive domain deals with the factual information that students learn in school, as well as with higher-level skills such as analysis and synthesis. The affective domain deals with the role that the emotions play in learning. The psychomotor domain deals with how the movement of the body is involved in learning.

Courtesy of Lawrence Stueck, The Design of Learning Environments, Ph.D dissertation, 1991, University of Georgia, Athens, GA.

Fourth-grade children converted their classroom into a model city. They designed and constructed their own buildings: a bank, court, post office, newspaper building, etc. Subjects were taught through an integrated curriculum.

One of the main virtues of the Bloom system is that it calls attention to the affective and psychomotor domains, which tend to be neglected in schools. The system also emphasizes higher-order thinking, which is less amenable to simple measurement and is more like the thinking done in art. The three domains cut across the disciplines. Because the fusion, like many experiences we encounter in "real" life, combines knowledge, body movement, and emotions, fusing all three into any one subject or lesson makes the learning in that subject very powerful. To ignore two of the three areas may make what remains "just boring facts," "just jumpin' around," or "just a bunch of talk about our feelings."

Each domain is considered to have several levels, or stages, within it, ranging from basic to advanced. For example, in the affective domain the levels are, from lowest to highest, as follows: receiving or willingness to attend, awareness, responding or willingness to participate actively, valuing,

and organizing values. When education critics say that too many "low-level objectives" and not enough "high-level objectives" are used, they are referring to Bloom's Taxonomy.

We begin by examining the cognitive domain.

The Cognitive Domain

Much of schooling centers upon cognitive objectives. Indeed, some teachers of art would say too much, particularly of the lower-level skill of knowing, as evidenced through rote memorizing, identifying, and matching. However, most educators also feel that too little emphasis is spent on the higher cognitive levels, such as applying knowledge to new situations,

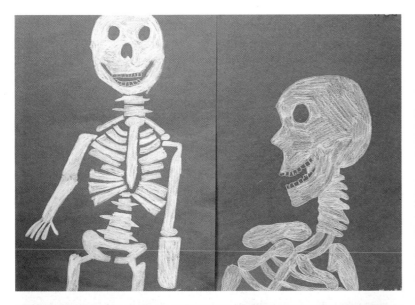

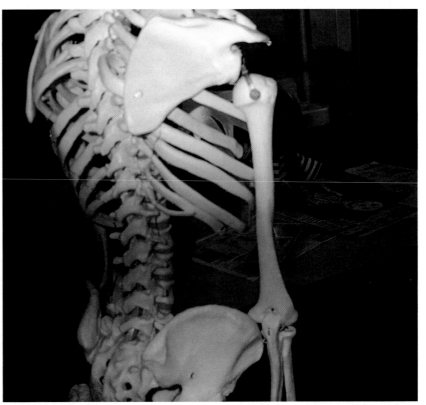

Courtesy of Joyce Vroon, Trinity School, Atlanta, GA. *Top left:* Fourth-graders Eric Dudiak and Laura Flynn Heller.

Cognitive learning is evident as fourth-grade students analyzed the skeleton's three-dimensional structure and synthesized this knowledge into their two-dimensional renderings. Language arts integration occurred when the art teacher featured the celebration of Dias de las Muertos in the hallway display.

Courtesy of Yung Fu Elementary School, Tainan, Taiwan. Courtesy of Frank Wachowiak and Ted Ramsay, University Elementary School, Iowa City, IA.

Kids can leap like frogs. Note the kids in different poses, side view, back view, seated. Psychomotor reenactment of catching frogs may have preceded the making of this delightful watercolor painting. One color, blue, predominates. Four tints and shades of green, from blue to yellow, are used for the carefully observed leaves and frogs. The child is fortunate to have an excellent art teacher who appreciates what children can accomplish by striving for design excellence.

analyzing, synthesizing, and evaluating. Teachers are often at a loss as to how to evaluate such higher-level thinking. Art activities offer wonderful opportunities for demonstrating application of the higher-level skills.

Numerous examples of such opportunities will be given in the following four chapters dealing with art's relation to cognitive objectives in science and math, social studies, reading, and the related arts. Cognitive objectives

Courtesy of Beverly Mallon, Chase Street Elementary School, Athens, GA.   Courtesy of Beverly Mallon, Chase Street Elementary School, Athens, GA.   Courtesy of Robert Clements, Athens, GA.

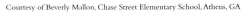

Psychomotor acting out of the motions before beginning the drawing enhances the children's kinesthetic knowledge. Arms are flung high, and legs leap into the air. **Left and Middle:** *These collages of a New Year's Eve celebration used decorative foil papers and confetti from the school's holiday giftwrap sale samplers.* **Right:** *Energetic boys dance to the music with marimbas as they decorate the large paper with paint on their feet.*

within the field of art—especially in art history, art criticism, perception, and aesthetics—will be discussed in Part 5.

The Psychomotor Domain and Multisensory Area

Some educators and many students believe that children spend too much elementary school time sitting at desks or tables. By doing so, they miss out on opportunities to learn through their bodies. Moving our bodies and using our other senses can stimulate learning in all subjects, including art production and art criticism activities. For example, a lesson plan objective might be as follows: "Students will be able to take the exact pose and facial expression of Van Gogh's Dr. Gachet, and they will tell the class something that he might be thinking about Vincent."

Psychomotor approaches also can be used for aesthetic experiences in and of themselves. Acting out a picture is one way in which kinesthetic awareness can trigger artistic awareness. For example, one objective is that, by using their bodies, students will be able to stimulate awareness of what they have perceived. For example, they might be given the following instruction: "Show with your body how cats clean their bodies. How can we show this tongue licking the paw in our drawing?"

The Bloom Taxonomy lists these psychomotor stages:

1) perception,
2) readiness to act,
3) ability to copy an instructor,
4 and 5) ability to carry out simple, and then complex, movement patterns with confidence,
6) ability to modify and adapt established patterns to meet special situations, and
7) ability to create new movement patterns.

Can you conceive how these stages relate to art teaching?

Psychomotor exercises are used in many progressive children's programs at museums to arouse interest in artworks. They have children respond nonverbally to the artworks, using their bodies and creative movement. Using an art reproduction, you can use many of these same ideas in your classroom:

Courtesy of Beverly Mallon, Chase Street Elementary School, Athens, GA.

Courtesy of Robert Clements, Athens, GA.

Courtesy of Joyce Vroon, Trinity School, Atlanta, GA.

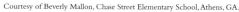

*Left: Children twirl scarves overhead to awaken their awareness prior to depicting the Olympics' rhythmic gymnastics event. The twirls in the chalk background are echoed in the twirling scarf. First period, pencil drawing; second period, chalk background; third and fourth periods, paint. Note the girl's strong body, arms, and legs. **Middle:** Whitney Leet's "Proud of"*

*picture shows the child's pride in doing handstands on the bars. Note the unique U-shaped arms and legs and the hair hanging down, also the thorough all-over marker coloring. **Right:** Imagining being in the Olympics, gifted first-grader Lewis Jones imagined himself making basketball hoops. Notice the unusual side view that he invented with no teacher instruction.*

- Using your imagination, place yourself in the picture. Move the way the people shown are moving.
- With a friend, act out a dramatic skit showing what the subjects are saying and doing.
- Show what you see through sounds, impromptu drama, human sculpture, and free movement.
- Take the exact pose and facial expression of the subject, and tell what are you thinking.
- Recreate the sounds you think you might hear, using your voice and hands for drumming.
- Imagine the smells that are in the air.
- With your friend, go on a "treasure hunt" around a room in the museum to find the pictures that depict certain items on a list the teacher has prepared.
- Become human sculptures, and use free movement to recreate the essence of the picture.

Multisensory stimulation, such as olfactory awareness of aromas, also can be a strong motivator of art and learning. ("Sniffing a jar of ground cinnamon, students will show in their artwork the events of which the smell of cinnamon reminds them. Show how the figures looked as they mixed ingredients, did the baking, and ate the baked goods.") A popular auditory stimulation is painting to music. ("Painting to the rhythm of *The Nutcracker Suite,* students will represent the music's measured regularity and variation in their paintings of dancers and soldiers in motion.") In fact, some art teachers make calm, classical music a staple feature during working periods.

Objectives and Evaluation of Affective Goals

Why bother with feelings in a book about teaching art? Just phrasing the question in this way suggests that emotions are something bad, something

Courtesy of Jackie Ellett, Fort Daniel Elementary School, Gwinnett County Schools, GA.

Using a brayer to ink the surface of the fish and make a print is an unparalleled multisensory experience, also providing psychomotor and perceptual stimulation.

Likewise, cultivate the ability to take affective pleasure in the challenge of solving art problems or making art products. Feelings often motivate art and sustain its production over the long periods necessary for creation. If something is important in an emotional sense, then the creation of art becomes a way of taking action to share the importance of the experience. Many artists root their art in concerns of life and death, nature and living beings, and the expression of feelings. Art can give voice to our inner needs and desires. It can give shape to our hopes, fears, ideals, and our very sense of self (see section on psychology in Chapter 16).

Few would disagree with affect's importance in art, yet many novice teachers have a particularly difficult time conceiving of affective objectives. Perhaps this difficulty comes from their having been taught to keep feelings to themselves. In order to help a teacher overcome this difficulty and wed affect to art learning, six kinds of affective objectives are described.

Courtesy of the Art Education Archives, School of Art, University of Georgia, Athens, GA.

"How did you feel at the event?" The wedding of an older sibling made an emotional impression on this upper-elementary grade artist, who then captured the ceremony's sacred feeling in her tempera painting.

regrettable to be pushed aside, something that gets in the way of productive working and living.

Yet just the opposite is true. Feelings are the engine that drives us as we decide what actions to take. Emotion is a state of aroused feelings or agitation. The creative imagination needs to have access through art, fantasy, play, and daydreams to affect-laden thoughts—even though they may contain frightening and puzzling sexual and aggressive content. Fred Rogers of *Mr. Roger's Neighborhood,* teaches his young audiences that "it is okay to have scary, bad dreams." Indeed, the role of dreams in our psychological functioning is just beginning to be understood.

Affect is a broader concept than emotions; affect includes emotions, drives, and feeling states—those that are temporary and those that are pervasive. Concerning the identification of pervasive feeling states in children's development, L. S. Vygotsky urged educators to attend less to the child's ideas and more to the child's internalized, private speech; that is, ask Is the child giving himself or herself a positive message of "I think I can" or a negative message of "I always mess up"? Or, is the child conveying an emotional deadness, an inability to say "Whoopee!"? In educating for affective growth, cultivate students' ability to experience affect itself by asking them questions such as the following: How did the person feel when the event happened?

Affective Objectives in Art Lessons	Representative Statements by Teacher or Students
Students will express personal feelings in their art production.	The feeling I'd like to put in my mask is one of super power.
Students will express feelings common to their age.	Fear of scary things in the closet was something I felt strongly when I was your age.

Courtesy of Joyce Vroon, Trinity School, Atlanta, GA.

Personal feelings can be expressed in a picture of one's dream. In sixth-grade student Paul Freschi's dream picture, the figure confronts devils, flames, a dead end, and a maze of high yellow walls.

Courtesy of Beverly Mallon, Chase Street Elementary School, Athens, GA.

Affective goals can be involved through children giving artworks they have made as gifts.

Affective Objectives in Art Lessons	Representative Statements by Teacher or Students
Students will show feelings about external events in their art.	Mary's being in the hospital makes me want to do something to try to make her feel a little better.
Students will express their personal feelings indirectly via art criticism.	The people in the picture appear to be afraid of the storm that's approaching, as though bad things are going to happen to them.
Students will indirectly share personal feelings by peers' interpreting their artwork and through art history examples.	Does anyone get a different feeling from the way the trees and clouds are painted in Bernardo's picture?
Students will express feelings about sharing art as gifts.	What will you say when you give your art to someone special to you? What do you think that person might say to you?

Clay Dinosaurs: A Sample Lesson Plan Combining Cognitive, Affective, and Psychomotor Objectives with Art Objectives

Education should focus on the integration that occurs within the child—the integration of the child's emotional, psychomotor, intellectual, perceptual, and aesthetic experiences. Here is a sample lesson plan containing eight types of objectives. Such a rich, integrated plan enables students with a wide variety of learning styles, emotional needs, and life needs to become involved in producing quality artwork. It also enables them to understand how their art is to be evaluated:

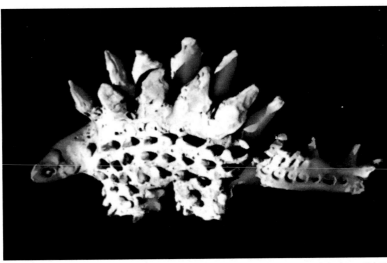

Courtesy of *Emphais Art* second edition, University Elementary School, Iowa City, IA.

Many kinds of instructional objectives can relate to this third-grade clay dinosaur lesson.

Clay Dinosaurs, Primary Grades	Enabling Activities
1. Art production (specific art skills to be learned)	Students will pull head and leg forms from a ball of clay to construct a dinosaur. Students will form eyes, ears, mouths, and tails.
2. Artistic perception (where we see specific art elements in daily life)	Students will describe similar structural forms in nature, such as other animals, tree branches, tables, and post-and-lintel construction.
3. Art history (interpretation of similar artworks by artists of other times)	Students will describe animal forms shown in reproductions of Aztec pottery, tell how the legs were made, and describe the animal's expression.
4. Art criticism (discussion and interpretations of students' works)	Students will describe differences in each other's creations, identifying those that look delicate, ferocious, or strong.
5. Aesthetics (discussing ideas about art)	Students will discuss whether scary and ugly things can be art, even though some people think art should be only about what is beautiful.
6. Affective (dealing with emotional needs)	Students will describe how their dinosaur makes them feel, their dinosaur's personality, how it interacts with friends or enemies that try to hurt it, whether it has any children, and what the children are like.
7. Cognitive and functional (correlated to important knowledge about our world and our functioning in it)	Students will be able to match their dinosaurs to photos of actual dinosaurs. Students will be able to describe how their dinosaur's diet and defense mechanisms relate to those the students use themselves.
8. Psychomotor and multisensory (dance, music, vocalization, role-playing, taste, smell, hearing)	Students will mimic the sounds and movements of their dinosaurs, then use these motifs to organize a dinosaur dance.

Chapter 15

SCIENCE, MATH, AND ART

A half millennium later, the world is still in awe of the achievements of Leonardo da Vinci. In his notebooks, he combined science, writing and drawing. Each element is enhanced by the others; each element helps one to understand more about the others.

Both science and art are ways of knowing, both provide new similarities and contrasts, and both go beyond common knowledge to yield new visions about our world. Science and art can show the principles that underlie nature's phenomena. Indeed, science and art share many goals:

Art and science are two complementary approaches to understanding nature. Here, a Japanese upper-elementary-grade child envisions the famous French entomologist Jean-Henri Fabre as a boy pursuing his hobby.

- Developing curiosity
- Building a knowledge base
- Setting and solving problems
- Investigating, fantasizing, and combining objects and ideas in new ways
- Observing natural phenomena
- Visualizing mental images

John Dewey wrote, "Art—the mode of activity that is charged with meanings capable of immediately enjoyed possession—is the complete culmination of nature, and 'science' is properly a handmaiden that conducts natural events to this happy issue" (1934). Dewey not only reverses the traditional hierarchy that places science over art, he also denies any rigid dichotomy between them.

Use drawing in as many aspects of the science lesson as possible—drawing specimens, mapping, charting, and illustrating experiments. Help children to sense what the fields have in common by calling attention both to the design structure and the scientific explanations of nature's phenomena. For example, symmetry is an important principle of growth in nature, and it can be studied by using a small hand mirror to draw one wing of a butterfly or one side of a petalled flower. Folding over the half-drawing and tracing or monoprinting then brings out the bilateral symmetry. The following are some other patterns common in nature:

- Symmetry in five directions (as a starfish or snowflake)
- Radial patterns (as in daisy petals)
- Spiral patterns (as in spiral whelk shells and the series of leaves going up a stalk)
- Fractal patterns (wherein the part recapitulates the structure of the whole, as in branching trees and meandering rivers)
- Fibonacci series (as in the seed arranged in a sunflower head)

On a large sheet of paper and over a very light pencil drawing of every petal of a flower, fifth-grade students Anneke Heile and Renée Davis used watercolor to capture the overlapping forms, in the style of Georgia O'Keeffe.

Help students to see analogies between things. Ask, "What does it remind you of?" Our perceived experience of what we see is extended by meanings drawn from what is remembered. Our immediate visual experience is supplemented by what our imagination brings to mind. Urge careful observation in creating the artwork. Tactfully discourage students'

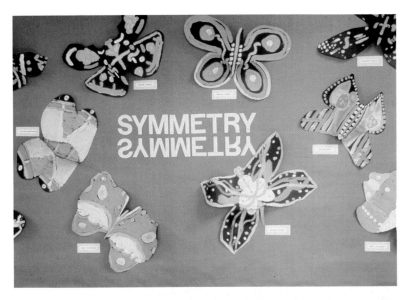

Few natural objects surpass butterflies as an instrument for the study of bilateral symmetry. **Top:** *Second-grade students' art is shown in an attractive display on symmetry using butterflies painted on black paper, with the lettering mirrored.* **Bottom:** *Second-grade student Nikki Foster folded a paper diagonally and transferred the shapes from one side to the other, then diligently applied oil pastel.*

Courtesy of Joyce Vroon, Trinity School, Atlanta, GA.

A brown-and-white hamster brought to class in a cage afforded second-grade student George Sheerer a live nature drawing experience.

Courtesy of Claire Clements, Athens, GA.

In drawing from nature, try a change of art medium; this perky bluebird was rendered in stitchery.

use of visual stereotypes, such as lollipop trees and V-shaped flying birds. Let the students' vivid imaginations help them to see, feel, and represent their own reality, sparked by the phenomena before their eyes.

To show art/science integration in action, this chapter covers many of the concepts taught in the elementary school science curriculum and gives suggestions for art/science integration. For recommendations on how to teach specific art media, see the chapters in the last half of the book, especially the sections in Chapter 20 on still lifes and animals. Note: The section on Mathematics Integration is included under M in the alphabetical list of Science topics.

Courtesy of Joyce Vroon, Trinity School, Atlanta, GA.

A chalklike artists' material, conté crayon, was used by third-grade student Quincy Smith for his animal drawing done on gray paper, a favorite drawing technique of Renaissance artists. Second-grade student Bingham Jamison drew in pastel this delightful trio of sand birds.

Animal Life

Enthusiastic artistic responses can be evoked by bringing to class live animals as well as terrariums and aquariums with coral and seashells. Bleached animal skulls and skeletal bones make excellent studies for line drawings, as well as vehicles to promote an understanding of anatomy. During the study of vertebrates and invertebrates, classify and draw a wide variety both with and without backbones, such as crickets, butterflies, snails, and earthworms. Draw birds' nests, birds in cages, and mounted birds, fish, and animals; a caution is to first inquire if any student has an allergy to dander or animal fur. Bring from the students' homes, or keep as pets in the room, turtles, rabbits, and guinea pigs; draw these in a variety of art media. Include drawings of the animals and birds along with nature studies of bird's nests and feathers. Make casts of animal tracks. Ecology, camouflage, and types of claws and beaks can be studied by using magazine photos for drawing animals and plants in their native environments. In connection with a study of weaving, try to weave a bird's nest or other container.

Use puppets to engage in artistic and fantasy extensions of science and to illustrate concepts such as predators, commensalism, and mutualism among animals. Sketch the life stages of the brine shrimp, frog, or salamander, and include sketches of the plants and animals that are found around a pond. Before or after a lesson of drawing animals or living things, an art/science card game can be played wherein small groups of students, using art reproductions, (depicting, for example, spiders, fish, mammals, microorganisms) categorize the art reproductions into the taxonomic categories of the animal and vegetable kingdoms—as well as into the various art styles.

Astronomy: Our Solar System

Using a pattern of the star points in the Big Dipper, Big Bear, or Orion (on black paper and using chalk), students will draw their own superheroes or objects in the sky as might be imagined from the star-point locations. Have students draw views of the Earth and Moon in space, imagining they are inside or outside space-travel vehicles and confronting interplanetary life. Our own Milky Way is a spiral galaxy, one of 100,000 million galaxies; spirals also are found in hurricanes, whirlpools, seashells, double helix DNA molecules, and Celtic design—a good springboard to a study of art.

Courtesy of Baiba Kuntz, Glencoe, IL.

In this multisession art lesson, fifth-grade students drew and watercolored themselves in their winter coats. **Left:** *Sarah Wampler added her cat and dog, a squirrel in a nest in a white* snow-covered tree, and white marshmallows floating in hot chocolate. **Right:** *Betsy Ure captured the sheen of her jacket, her multitasseled cap, and her love of basketball.*

Climate

Have students draw their families as if they were people from different climates, in native dress and in their homes. In artworks, show the climate through such features as the northern lights and wavy convection currents above a fire; ask "Where was it? What else can be seen? How does it feel?" Study the art of people from hot and cold climates—for example, African and Eskimo art.

Foods and Nutrition

Have students draw themselves gardening or harvesting favorite foods and berries. Make charts of the different kinds of food that we eat in a week. On a large cardboard pyramid assembled from a cast-off refrigerator carton, students can add their illustrations of favorite foods in each group of the food pyramid. For these, they might draw from a still life of fruits, vegetables, nuts, and grains.

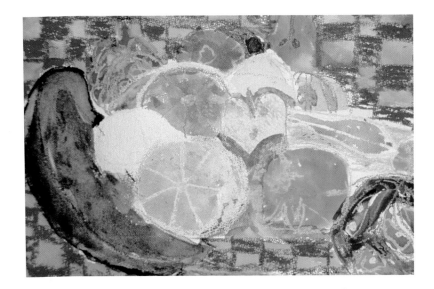

Second-grade student Juliana Ramus studied and drew cross sections of fruits and vegetables along with the patterned table cloth; the background was given a unifying resist coat of light green. After studying Dutch still lifes of fruits and vegetables, students developed their ability with chiaroscuro (light and shade).

Geology

Take a sketching trip, perhaps to a nearby eroded gully, to draw unusual earth and rock formations. Point out the color and surface textures of sedimentary and igneous rocks as well as the effects of water and wind erosion or past glacial activity. From photos, draw cave interiors with stalactites and stalagmites, and imagine an exciting "Tom Sawyer–like" story of students in a cave, finding prehistoric cave art such as that found

Through using a straw to blow paint, student David Williams vividly depicts his geological knowledge of earth's molten interior magma layer.

Courtesy of Jackie Ellett, Fort Daniel Elementary School, Lawrenceville, GA.

Pictographic systems of representing figures used by prehistoric people in their cave art are studied by third-grade students in their recreated, crumpled paper cave.

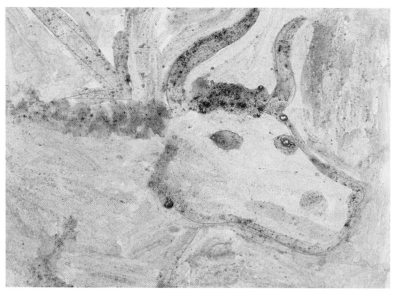

Courtesy of Jackie Ellett, Fort Daniel Elementary School, Lawrenceville, GA.

Earth pigments of iron oxide, charcoal, and kaolin clay, with white glue added, are used in this fifth-grader's study of cave art animal representations.

under cliffs and on rocks throughout the world. From small still-life arrangements, draw the textures, patterns, and colors of rocks and minerals. Discuss the chemical elements that make up pigments—iron red, chrome green and yellow, cobalt blue, lead white, cadmium orange. In connection with a study of fossils, make plaster bas-relief casts of everyday objects.

Human Body, Anatomy, and Growth

After seeing anatomical drawings by da Vinci and Vesalius and making a figure drawing, have students, using tracing paper enabling them to see through to the original drawing below, first imagine, and then draw and label the muscles' locations. On another sheet of tracing paper, have them locate and draw the (real and imaginary) organs inside one's body. Insights into human growth can be gained by drawing oneself from baby pictures or from imagination, doing the good and bad things that the students did at that age. Also have students draw an imaginary view of themselves as adults doing some favorite activity.

Courtesy of Frank Wachowiak, Athens, GA, and Mary Sayer Hammond, Fairfax, VA.

The millions of varieties of insects have unlimited possibilities, as illustrated in this crayon engraving by an intermediate-elementary-grade youngster. It was enhanced in the final stage by an application of oil pastels on the background areas. Bordering lines of black should be preserved to unify the composition. Saturday Children's Classes.

A second-grade student used white clay to construct a spider on its web.

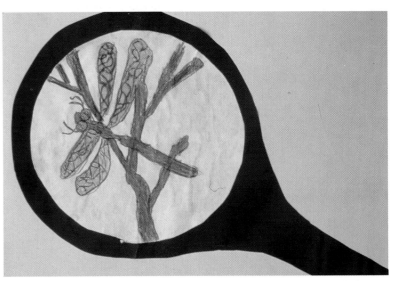

Magnifying lenses are useful for drawing insects. Here, the second-grader also shows the lens.

Insects

Create an imaginary, three-dimensional insect using a variety of materials, then write a description of the creature, describing the physical features that it uses to find food and to defend itself. Draw ant farms and insect and butterfly collections. Using tempera resist, or on dark paper, draw pictures of children catching fireflies at dusk, collecting nature specimens, or delighting in a butterfly garden.

Light and Perception

Just as telescopes and magnifying lenses opened many of nature's secrets for analysis, such perception-enhancing devices likewise can foster science/art integration. Assorted equipment to help expand the students' awareness and visual horizons includes microscopes, prisms, kaleidoscopes, holographs, magnifiers, liquid-light lamps, fiber optics, telescopes, microscopic projectors, computers, mirrors, and black lights. A study of reflections and shadows can be tied in with a study of Monet's water-lily pond paintings and Impressionism, as well as Seurat's Pointillism.

To promote interest in the properties of light, arrange bottles of different colored glass on windowsills or against a light source. Fill some with dried flowers or branches, some clear ones with colored water, and some with strips of aluminum foil. Study spectra in nature by painting rainbows. The concept of mirror images can be tied in with a unit on printmaking, in which the images are reversed. On a sunny day, a student can draw his or her classmate's shadow outside on the asphalt playground or concrete sidewalk, and this distorted image can be decorated. Perceptual distortion and the convex lens can be studied by using narrow olive jars, clear glass marbles, or magnifying glasses. Students can draw the distortion seen in chrome hubcaps, shiny bowls, and other polished, convex surfaces. Study distant perception by making drawings of objects that recede into the distance. Pinhole cameras and shadow-puppet plays also are useful for studying light.

Magnetism

To illustrate magnetism in connection with a study of photograms and light, make photograms of iron filings. Along with an explanation of the photochemical phenomena of photograms, the edges of objects such as fern leaves and lacy objects also can be discussed.

Courtesy of Joyce Vroon, Trinity School, Atlanta, GA.

Courtesy of David Harvell, Fourth Street School, Athens, GA.

The symmetry in octagonal designs is conveyed by making yarn designs popular in Mexico, called Ojos Dios (God's eyes). Rather than sticks, long cardboard strips were used for supports, making it possible to staple the class's work together to make a magnificent hallway display. Another conveyed lesson is that, through combining our individual efforts, we can achieve greater goals than anyone can achieve individually.

Using cameras, sixth-grade students Hadley Hughes and Alex Davis were able to study the effects of sunlight and shadow on textured and patterned surfaces.

Courtesy of Beverly Mallon, Chase Street Elementary School, Athens, GA.

Knowledge about mathematical symmetry is applied in these swirling hex designs of 8-, 6-, and 16-pointed star forms. Shapes can be combined to form other shapes; arcs are combined to create circles, rectangles reside inside triangles. Third grade.

Mathematics

Measuring with Rulers

Math tools and forms can be used in art; for example, mechanical drawing instruments, including compasses, triangles, and T-squares, can be used to make geometric designs. Rulers are used to measure for paper weaving. However, like so many craft projects, they become much more like art when the lesson has been enriched by bringing in the imagination and emotions (for example, designing cloth patterns that Martians would like, constructing cardboard box looms or weaving placemats to celebrate special occasions.) Rulers can also be used to measure squares to be cut out and decorated for borders. Students can decorate a dozen or so squares, trade them for classmates' squares, and paste them around a painting to make a beautiful border.

Scale and ratio, the relationship of numbers of one size to those of another size, can be employed in enlarging pictures. For example, an artwork of the student or a magazine picture of a masterwork can have a grid of 1-inch lines ruled on it or traced over it through a semi-transparent piece of paper (and each square numbered), then a huge paper can have 1-foot squares ruled on it and numbered, and then the student draws the outlines one square at a time.

Estimating can be taught by looking at art reproductions and estimating how many figures, animals, or buildings are shown, and the objects' sizes, ages, and, art historically, the century in which the picture was made.

Parquetry Blocks

Colorful parquetry blocks teach how shapes can be combined into larger shapes. Forms of beauty and power can be created by nesting forms within or adjacent to each other: Triangles can become squares and six-pointed stars, squares can build rectangles, and triangles and squares together can form isometric, three-dimensional illusions. Frank Lloyd Wright attributed his lifelong design ability to his using parquetry shapes and blocks when he was an 8-year-old.

Geometry, Math, and Art

The Platonic solids are the cube, the tetrahedron (a 3-sided pyramid, with 4 triangles), the octahedron (with eight triangles), the dodecahedron (with 12 pentagons), and the icosahedron (with 20 triangles); students can find and describe examples of these in architectural reproductions and in box design. The perceptual qualities of cylinders, prisms, and cubes are explored

The mathematician Benoit Mandelbrot figured out the mathematical formulas for nature's branching and dividing forms. Now, using these formulas, computer programs can draw branching trees, meandering streams, and forming clouds. Artists and people sensitive to nature have long intuitively sensed these relationships. Sixth-grade student Michael Selik's photo shows the fractal branching of tree limbs creating dramatic silhouettes against the heavy winter sky.

by Montessori preschoolers. Plane geometry is artfully and imaginatively shown in early American quilts. Just as the quilters did, teach students how to geometrically construct a five- and six-pointed star, and correlate this lesson to the design of snowflakes. The theme of stars can be further integrated by a discussion of Van Gogh's "Starry Night." Fibonnacci series, seen in the arrangement of seeds in the heads of sunflowers, can be discussed from a mathematical point of view. Also, discuss the geometrical background of such forms as tetrahedra and icosahedra.

Math, Sculpture, and Architecture

Plans for architectural and industrial design illustrate how buildings and objects drawn in two dimensions can be transformed into three-dimensional objects. For example, a dome can be considered either an arch rotated 360 degrees or a bisected sphere. Math books illustrate polyhedral structures, from cubes to the soccer-ball-like icosahedra, and these forms also appear in books on three-dimensional design, most notably in Buckminster Fuller's geodesic dome. Students can write or discuss geometrical analyses of Michelangelo's buildings. Likewise, they can design

and write a geometrical analysis of three-dimensional paper sculptures they make, describing the arches, rectangular solids, and other three-dimensional forms. Groups of students can describe the geometric shapes shown in art reproductions, such as in the St. Louis Arch and other examples from modern and ancient architecture. Hexagons and octagons appear in snowflakes, beehive cells, Chinese lattices, and Moorish mosque tile designs from the Alhambra. Perspective appears in art as early as in ancient Roman wall murals. It flowers in Renaissance art, for example, in works such as Leonardo da Vinci's "Last Supper," paintings by Andrea Mantegna, and prints by Albrecht Dürer.

Tessellation and Topological Surfaces

In order for shapes to tessellate, their corners must equal 360 degrees. Triangles, quadrilaterals, and hexagons, such as in honeycombs, tessellate. One way students can make their own tessellated designs is to cut sponges into these shapes and pack them together into geometric patterns. More than one shape can be used to make up a tessellation: for example, a

One can sense aesthetically the mathematical and architectural relationships in nature's intricate forms, such as how beautifully the calyx shelters the flower.

Courtesy of Joyce Vroon, Trinity School, Atlanta, GA.

Our sensibility to artistic shape has been forever changed by Alexander Calder's work. After studying Calder's work, second-grader Wesley Long combined Calder-like shapes in paper and collage. He then drew straight and curved parallel marker lines to create an illusion of surfaces folding into themselves. The rhythm of the nearly parallel lines makes the paper seem to vibrate.

soccer ball is a combination of regular pentagons and regular hexagons. In science, the study of tessellation is important in the analysis of crystal structures. Tessellation and packing patterns appear in Islamic temple decorations from a half millennium ago. They resurface in the twentieth century in the prints of M. C. Escher (who, incidentally, was a poor student in mathematics). Some math resources for the construction of tessellation grid patterns are "The Mathematics of Islamic Art," a 20-slide set from New York City's Metropolitan Museum of Art. "MECC Tessel Mania," is a CD-ROM for children to make their own tessellations (phone 1-800-68-MECC, ext. 529). A variation on tessellations is to have students make a tangram—a Chinese puzzle wherein a square is cut into triangles and quadrilaterals which are then combined to represent people, animals, and objects.

Mathematicians have proven that four colors are sufficient to color the countries on any map such that no adjacent countries are the same color; students can replicate this famous experiment. The continuous curving transitions and ribbon edges of Mobius strips can imaginatively become the basis for depictions of fantastic amusement park rides. Alternately, a sequence of steps in an action scene can be drawn on both sides of a strip of paper and folded into a Mobius strip, to make a continuous, never-ending story.

Computers

Using computer three-dimensional modeling programs, two-dimensional polygons can be transformed into three-dimensional polyhedra. Computers use mathematical formulas in doing iteration, interpolation, and resolution rations; a shape or line can be copied, swept, replicated, or arrayed. Fractal geometry, the mathematical foundations of which were discovered by Benoit Mandelbrot, is given beautiful form in computer art programs, as well as in nature's forms of meandering streams, branching trees, and cloud formations.

Paper Folding

Origami from the Orient and paper airplane construction teach one about bisecting surface planes diagonally and about the interplay of top and bottom surfaces. However, to be an art expression, it is necessary to extend the lesson to bring in the imaginative, the fantastic, and the personal. For

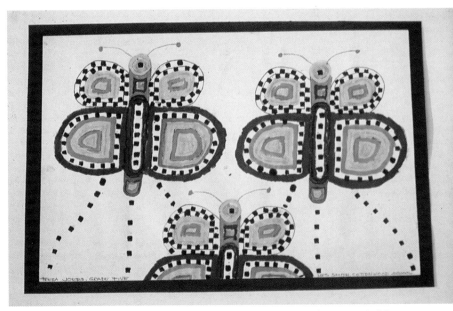

Mrs. Smith, Cottonwood School. Teresa Joers, Grade 5.

Symmetry takes on a sense of playful charm as these three butterflies harmoniously grace the world with their delightful checkerboard patterned bodies and wings.

example, the folded construction can be attached onto a drawn picture, depicting how one personally relates to the subject: a jet for my friend and me to fly, space stations from which engineering feats and intergalactic exploits occur, swans on the lake in the park where my family picnics on Sunday afternoons. Symmetry, explored through paper dolls (folding, drawing, and cutting a row of figures holding hands and touching feet), can become an artistic expression by then using markers to draw different emotions on the figures' faces and the corresponding clothing that could elicit such emotions. A wall/ceiling border can be made by connecting the students' chains of figures. In other words, for math and art integration, the mathematical means should be fused to expressive ends, which can kindle the imagination.

Molecules

Using Styrofoam, colored modeling clay, or colored table tennis balls and toothpicks, make models of the elements; then make fantasy sculptural (undiscovered) elements. Also make models of human figures, and relate this to the study of modern sculptures.

Plants and Botany

Still lifes of plant specimens can be used to call attention to the ecological devastation faced by plants and animals—for example, the fact that 250,000 of today's plant species will vanish in the next few years. Especially in rooms with few windows, large potted plants of assorted foliage brighten up a classroom. Draw the process by which insects help a flowers' pistil, stamen, and anther to create fruit. Have students draw their favorite tree (maybe their backyard treehouse), and then draw and label its visible and underground parts. Make a close-up sketch of its leaf. Using a

Courtesy of Frank Wachowiak and Mary Sayer Hammond, Athens, GA.

A science perception objective might be: "Students will observe and be able to draw a variety of leaves." Leaf terms might be "opposite and alternate, simple and compound, with margins, entire, serrate, or dentate." Children gathered a variety of leaves and drew them in crayon using a bold contour-line technique, emphasizing the veins but not coloring in the spaces solidly. They filled up the white paper in an allover design, the leaves turning in all directions, some touching and some overlapping. Then, using their watercolors and brushes, they applied the transparent colors over and between the leaves.

*Top: Over a freely painted background of delicate tints and shades, the camellia's leaf veins and petals, stamen, and anthers are drawn in pastel. **Bottom:** Third-grade student Kristin Dudley drew this riotously energetic picture of leaves accompanied by butterflies.*

Eighth-grade student Laura Gutterman drew her own hand and amaryllis bulbs.

fast-growing plant such as a sweet potato, draw its stages of growth each week. The unusual shapes of sweet-potato vines and other tuberous roots are an artistic challenge. Properties of leaves, leaf edges, and shapes can be studied by sorting and identifying those with different edges and shapes

and then making a composite drawing to show this variety. Along with a discussion of the concept of photosynthesis, both live and dried flowers and plants, such as Indian corn, decorative gourds, locust pods, and fall weeds make a wonderful autumnal still life for drawing.

Simple Machines

Arrange still-life setups of antique Americana hand tools and farm implements, such as corn shuckers, cotton gins, and cherry pitters, along with objects such as bottles, lanterns, lamps, clocks, and musical instruments. While studying machines and how they work, have students use hand tools for craft and sculpture projects. For a study of balance, ful-crums, and levers, draw children seated on a teeter-totter. While studying axles, draw or make toy vehicles. While studying energy-creating machines, make pinwheels, and study or draw windmills and water-wheels.

Sound

Draw a still life or students modeling with musical instruments. Make and decorate homemade musical instruments, such as drums and bottle xylophones. Play recordings of music, dramatizations, poetry, sounds of geographic regions (city and country, nature's forces, forest and jungle), and sounds of machines, planes, ships, trains, circuses, and amusement centers to enhance art/science lesson motivations. Cassettes combining sounds of the jungle or the seacoast with gentle music can be good motivations for drawing.

Courtesy of Joyce Vroon, Trinity School, Atlanta, GA.

After studying Ben Shahn's contour line drawings, fourth-grade student Drew Powers emphasized thick and thin lines in this drawing of old-fashioned telephones shown where else but on telephone book pages. **Right:** *After discussing Claes Oldenberg's sculptures, Sahra Robinson made a soft sculpture of a boom box radio cassette player.*

Courtesy of Joyce Vroon, Trinity School, Atlanta, GA.

Toxic waste is the subject of fourth-grade student Eliot Brusman's modern-day adaptation of Grant Wood's American Gothic.

Technology and Energy

When viewing and discussing the artistic merit of outstanding computer art, have students use computers to create art (see Chapters 19 and 25).

Use videotaping to record scientific phenomena, such as pollution in the neighborhood. Make drawings of facilities and equipment associated with energy, such as power plants and solar collectors.

Water

View Paul Klee's paintings of underwater life and make artistic charts of the ocean food chain using a combination of real objects (such as preserved dried fish) and photos of microscopic life, large fish, and mammals. Draw from a still life of sea creatures and objects that float on or in the water or are found on the beach (coral, seaweed, and seashells), then add figures and other sea life and paint the sea in the background. Using crayon resist, draw a *20,000 Leagues Under the Sea* picture of what can be viewed from an underwater-exploration vehicle. When studying water evaporation, make watercolor paintings while outdoors on a sunny day. In relation to topics of water pollution, oil spills, and Brownian motion, students can make marbelized papers that later can be used in other art projects.

Courtesy of Joyce Vroon, Trinity School, Atlanta, GA.

Wave action on the surface of water, as well as the effects of sunset reflections, are depicted in sixth-grade student Elizabeth Leaque's impressionistic painting in complementary tints and shades of orange and blue.

Imaginative underwater themes, á la Jules Verne, intrigued the Japanese children who painted these rich interpretations of oceanic exploration and adventure. When youngsters are capable of producing such rich visual statements, why allow them to settle for stereotyped, minimal results?

The interactions of water and wind, light and shadow, swan and reflection are poetically shown in sixth-grade student Mary Margaret Murphy's photograph. After a look at Currier and Ives winter scenes, this snowy scene of the student and friend ice skating on a frozen pond was painted.

Weather, Wind, and Air

After showing Leonardo da Vinci's drawings and Turner watercolors of clouds and storms, draw a storm and/or cumulus, stratus, and nimbus cloud formations and weather forecasting equipment. Draw the snow-plows, road-clearing equipment, and sandbagging used to ameliorate the weather's effects. Include in these drawings activities that children do under adverse and pleasant weather conditions. Along with discussing art-

Cloud formations, shown in Virginia Simm's photo of a figure silhouetted against the heavy clouds, are one of the most visible manifestations of wind and air. The wrath of Hurricane Hugo and its effects on beach surfaces and structures are captured in sixth-grade student Kempton Mooney's series of photos.

works showing umbrellas in use, make a still life by hanging a variety of colorful and overlapping umbrellas and raincoats from the ceiling and walls. Umbrellas from the Far East are especially attractive. (*Caution:* Don't hang anything from light fixtures.)

Display Japanese, Chinese, Indian, and Indonesian kites, balloons, and banners. After a study of the principles of fight, have students make, decorate, and fly paper airplanes, parachutes, and kites. After a study of early American weathervane designs, design windvanes (perhaps of animals, such as a favorite cat or dog). Pieces can be cut from oak tag and attached to both sides of a soda straw, which is then pinned, through a bead that can revolve, to an upright dowel rod (or the eraser of a pencil, sunk in a spool glued to cardboard).

Archimedean spirals, which resemble the neat spiral peel of an orange, can be cut from paper and hung above a lamp. They will rotate as effortlessly as birds and gliders float upward on thermal currents; this can lead to a study of Alexander Calder's mobiles. Tornadoes, which spin counterclockwise in the Northern Hemisphere, have a corkscrew structure called a helix, also found in the metal waste from a drill cutting soft metal, in grain harvesters, in the DNA double-helix molecule, and in spiral staircases—a link to the study of architecture.

Many artists throughout time have been interested in nature and scientific phenomena; likewise, they have been interested in human beings' interactions with each other in their diverse cultures. Thus, the next chapter examines the integration of art and social studies.

By using imagination, wind can be shown indoors where there is little; on a table, three girls pose as if holding kites. (Notice also the beautifully organized, stimulating classroom environment.)

Chapter 16

SOCIAL STUDIES, MULTICULTURAL INQUIRY, AND ART INTEGRATION

This chapter begins by examining the social studies curricula across the grades. It then discusses art's integration with seven specific social studies disciplines, from anthropology to sociology. Finally, the chapter concludes by exploring multicultural inquiry—an important perspective in today's schools, and a topic that cuts across all of the social studies disciplines.

Culture is the common possession of a body of people who share the same traditions. It is the complex whole that includes knowledge, beliefs, art, morals, law, and customs. One important means of transmitting, maintaining, and analyzing any culture is through the visual arts; hence, art plays an important role in social studies education. The arts are integral to the study of culture, and they are a common denominator in world civilizations.

One current social studies text contains 600 reproductions of artworks, showing how the new methods in teaching social studies emphasize the interconnectedness of political, social, economic, and artistic issues. Art can be integrated with the teaching of social studies concepts such as self-determination, location, and human/environment interactions. Likewise, topics from social studies can be used as vehicles for learning about light and dark, texture and color, dominance and subordinance, carrying through a motif and varying a theme, diligent workmanship, and ingenious imagination.

Courtesy of Melody Milbrandt, Valdosta, GA.

Third- and fourth-grade students painted this mural showing their understanding of Native-American styles of dress, artifacts, housing, and decoration.

Social Studies Curriculum Across the Grades

It is helpful to begin by reviewing the social studies subjects currently taught in the elementary school years. This chapter is written mainly for the elementary classroom teacher who wishes to integrate art's motivational power with social studies learning. It is structured to give the art specialist an overview of the concepts covered in social studies. Some important concepts that are taught include the following:

Power and status
Personality and motivation
Conflict and cooperation
Dependency on others
Dependency on the environment

Fourth St. Elementary School. Courtesy of David Harvell, Athens, GA.

Charlotte Country Day School. Courtesy of Alice Ballard Munn, Anchorage, AL, and Diane Rives, Athens, GA.

When art considerations are serious, integrated art and culture lessons are of value for learning in both areas. The study of ancient Egyptian culture comes alive through art expression. **Left:** *Life-sized paintings of mummy sarcophagi create a display of grandeur and majesty in* the elementary school's entrance hall. **Middle:** *Glazed ceramic sculpture of the Egyptian ibis-headed scribe deity, Thoth.* **Right:** *A first-grade student's painting of Nut, the star-studded deity of the night.*

Freedom, diversity, and equality
Property
Change
Social behavior and roles
Human needs
Justice
Scarcity
Truth

The general movement in the social studies curriculum across grades is one from the smallest unit to the largest unit: that is, from the family and neighborhood to the community to the state and nation and, finally, to the world. Because the danger in this approach is ethnocentrism, curricula usually intermix the study of other cultures. The Task Force on Social Studies for the Young Learner of the National Council for the Social Studies recommends the following sequence:

Kindergarten: a main goal of socialization, along with the names of one's community, state, region, nation, the basic time elements, the meaning of basic symbols, and classroom rules.

First grade: school and family life, rural/urban, working cooperatively in groups, contributions of different family members to the family as a whole, working together to solve problems, and seasonal changes in the local environment.

Second grade: the neighborhood, communications, major kinds of transportation, consumption of goods and services, and how groups work to solve problems.

Third grade: the community, its history and its problems, a person's responsibility to the community, and contributions of various ethnic and cultural groups to it.

Fourth grade: regional/world geographies, with the home state as an example; comparison of land forms and characteristics of the home state are compared with other regions.

Fifth grade: close neighboring regions, the Western hemisphere, basic rights of citizens, major American historical events.

Sixth grade: world cultures, Native Americans.

Seventh grade: a global view of the changing world, especially outside the Western hemisphere.

Eighth grade: American economic/social history, and its effects.

A Cape Town, South Africa, scene of a farmer plowing his fields has clear areas of glowing color.

Before examining art's integration to seven specific disciplines in social studies, let us first examine seven general strategies and methods that cut across disciplines:

- personalized responses
- hands-on art activity
- danger of social studies/art integration
- drawing a still life arrangement
- use of models and speakers
- sketching trips
- using art reproductions for art criticism and social studies

Personalized Responses

Because social studies/art integration projects often center around some other person or some remote event, always seek to motivate the student's *personal* response: "If you had been there, how would you look, how would you solve the problem, who would be with you, what objects would you take with you, what clothes would you wear?" Seek to involve the students immediately, both in thought and feeling. As art often deals with the expression of personal feelings, urge students to put themselves and their

daily activities into their representation of the earlier culture's figures. Their personal experiences and multicultural perspectives are primary.

To draw on what is familiar to the students, begin with their own beliefs, values, and community. Note, however, that appreciation should not be disseminated in a top-down manner. Rather, strive to make the classroom a more democratic place by incorporating the neglected group's

Multicultural understandings are acquired as these students from many lands work together, side by side, on a mural.

subculture. Organize students from differing cultural backgrounds into small groups, and have them explain why they like the art that they do. The art program you provide for your students can help them to feel pride in themselves and connectedness to their own cultural backgrounds, to other people, and to other cultures.

Hands-On Art Activity

Creative, hands-on art activity can promote social studies in many ways. For example, students can make paintings of cultural celebrations and discuss diverse customs. Puppet plays and dioramas can illustrate clearly what students know about other cultures. Teachers should also provide opportunities for students to express ideas through art construction—to draw their conceptions of things, to cut out labels and paste them onto drawings, to construct models and dioramas. These can be models of artifacts, buildings, and communities, land forms, coal mines, off-shore oil-drilling rigs, and open-pit mines. Students can exhibit sewing, soap carving, paper-bag dolls, a television set with a paper-roll program, baskets, jewelry, holiday decorations, pottery, playhouses, tie-dyed fabrics, block printing, bulletin boards, posters, knitting, stitchery, and quilting. Other media can be photography, computer art, sculpting, construction of two- and three-dimensions. Representations employing coloring, modeling clay, and collage also can be valuable. The art activity must be done in depth, however. For example, a poster should be done in conjunction with a serious study of poster design; that is to say, the overall design and lettering must be bold and the background interesting, as in the World War II posters of Ben Shahn.

Doing an artwork in the style of another culture can teach one about that culture's way of looking at phenomena. Of course, simply making a kachina doll will not necessarily result in multicultural understanding; without discussing the culture, such an activity may be considered a mere pastiche of surface appearances. Thus, when doing a contemporary version of an earlier culture's style, be sure to discuss the sociopolitical issues of that culture. Both the teacher and the students should contribute what they already know or have researched or surmised about the culture.

Danger of Social Studies/Art Integration

An important caveat for teachers is that poor instruction in both art and social studies can be the result if the art/social studies integration is haphazard. Regrettably, poorly planned, stereotypical procedures in both art and social studies are too often used. The results may be execrable, look-alike exercises, such as sketchily colored-in outlines of one's palm and fin-

Courtesy of Melody Milbrandt, Valdosta, GA.

Medieval life is shown in these artworks. A maiden awaits her knight outside her well-protected fortress. Note the limited palette used in this third-grade student's painting of fighting knights.

gers for a Thanksgiving turkey. Teachers must eschew such overused, impersonal activities as dittoed patterns of pilgrims and presidents' profiles, wherein the art method (uncreatively coloring dittoed patterns) violates the social studies goal (assimilating into oneself something about

Courtesy of Baiba Kuntz, Glencoe, IL.

Fifth-grade student Laura Richart captured with eight colors of Sharpie® markers every fold pattern and ruffle of this 19th-century dress.

Courtesy of Baiba Kuntz, Glencoe, IL.

A study of figure drawing is combined with a study of 19th-century dress as fifth-grade girls took turns modeling, a half period at a turn.

In fact, art/social studies assignments in which the teacher sets higher standards than those students will meet naturally, and that require more effort than routine work, can result in students' most memorable learning experiences. In such projects, students sense the unity of thought, personal feeling, and expressive action that results from an aesthetic experience. Hence, the social studies/art integration suggestions offered are intended to be used in tandem with the qualitative art instruction principles and methods given throughout this book.

The following suggested social studies/art integrated activities do not supplant the regular art instruction period but, rather, they supplement it. The National Art Education Association recommends that, in addition to 100 minutes a week for art, other time should be devoted to art as it relates to other subjects.

Drawing a Still-Life Arrangement

The study of a culture can be the focus of a still-life arrangement that you and your students put together. To teach students about the design motifs and indigenous art materials used in other cultures, artifacts from particular countries and regions can be collected for display or borrowed from a

the personal, creative initiative of the subjects studied). In short, if no art instruction is provided, little or no art learning will occur; art materials will simply be used up. Do not use art exercises as a way to fill an unplanned 15 minutes.

Help your students to develop a feeling for their cultural heritage through drawing a still-life arrangement incorporating Americana. When children sensitively capture in their drawings an old coffee grinder, railroad lantern, kerosene lamp, mantle clock, antique sewing machine, steam iron, architectural gingerbread, and assorted old musical instruments, these objects take on new meaning. Widen your students' cultural horizons by introducing them to a host of exciting artifacts from many cultures as subject matter for their art expression.

Courtesy of Deborah Lackey, Atlanta, GA.

Through drawing a still life of artifacts from the Southwest Native-American culture, fifth-grade students' learning about styles of decoration can be integrated with their knowledge of the culture's customs.

museum or curriculum materials center. Perhaps students' parents can lend masks, wood carvings, costumes, textiles, ceramics, toys, dolls, fans, puppets, and kites for the still life. In addition, travel agencies may be able to provide large, colorful posters. Merely drawing an object from another culture will not integrate the learning, however. Teachers can help to define the nature of a culture by having students discuss how the culture has treated groups such as children, women, captives, and the elderly, and from whence its wealth has come.

Early Americana can be studied through travel posters of cities' historic buildings, as well as through large, colorful bedspreads or quilts hung against a wall or draped on a counter for still-life backgrounds. Use costumes such as leather jackets and fancy dresses for student models who sit or recline in the still-life arrangements, and add picturesque farm implements for historic interest. Still lifes can be constructed around other themes such as the following:

Central American pottery
Colorful paper umbrellas from Japan
Kites, fans, and bells from the Orient
Masks: African, Indian, Malaysian, Indonesian, Mexican, Chinese opera, Mardi Gras, clown, Japanese Noh or Bugaku, Greek drama

Eskimo sculpture in soapstone or whalebone
Indian kachina and Japanese kokeshi dolls
Navaho rugs and San Blas Indian molas
Musical instruments from around the world
Puppets, toys, dolls, and wood carvings from around the world

Use of Models and Speakers

When studying another region of the world, invite guests to talk and pose while wearing the region's ethnic costumes. Ask the guests to share the cultural artifacts from their collections. While drawing the visitor in costume, students can ask about the native customs and the attitudes held there with regard to immigration. Also invite guests and parents with interesting occupations and hobbies and work costumes to model while they chat with the students. If your school is in or near a major city, the country's embassy might be able to put you in touch with people who have objects they would be willing to lend for school use, and such individuals might be willing to come and talk while modeling in costume either for, or with, the students. The students themselves can take turns wearing special hats or clothing, such as Indian and African tie-dyed shirts or fire personnel uniforms, and can take turns serving as models posed in

Courtesy of Joyce Vroon, Trinity School, Atlanta, GA.

A student model coyly poses wearing a richly patterned silk kimono, with fan and umbrella and pussy willow flowers.

Watercolor landscape painting is studied along with the use of the fan in East Asian culture.

Take the students on sketching trips to where different cultures may be studied. Here, Amish wagons are captured by art professor David Hodge.

a still-life arrangement dealing with the social studies material being studied. (See drawing from a model in Chapter 20.)

Sketching Trips

Sketching trips can help students gain insight, through art, into issues of historic preservation, trade balances, technological innovation, and community growth. (See the section on outdoor sketching in Chapter 20 for art principles and methods.) Before or during the trip, discuss sociopolitical issues as well as the site's aesthetic qualities and how to create an attractive drawing—for example, use of foreground, middle ground, and background. Of course, it is prudent to visit the sketching site before the class trip to check procedures and to secure field-trip approval from authorities. Possible sketching trip destinations include the following:

Natural history museums
Construction sites
Manufacturing facilities
Fair or arts festivals
Bus and train stations
Shopping malls
Local art studios

Fire stations
Historic buildings
Historic monuments or statues
Art museums
Bridge sites
Boat marinas or wharves

Using Art Reproductions for Art Criticism and Social Studies

Art criticism *per se* is discussed in Chapter 21; its use in connection with social studies is examined here. Artwork themes can be discussed with regard to values, such as loyalty, conflict, equality, tolerance, and control (and/or the conflict of these values). One might ask, "How does the artist convey who is in control? What conflicts might be on the characters' minds?" In artworks discussed in class, show a willingness to address issues of racism, sexism, and inequity. When showing the class materials from diverse cultures, tell students what you know about the artist's life, class, and ethnic origin, and have them hypothesize how issues such as life circumstances, gender, and ethnicity might have affected the artist's work.

Courtesy of Joyce Vroon, Trinity School, Atlanta, GA.

A discussion of the last century's attitudes toward death, its sentimentality, and its love of classical culture might be sparked by sixth-grade student Billy Welsh's photograph.

Hypothesizing, evaluating, and synthesizing—skills at the top of Bloom's Taxonomy of Educational Objectives—can be readily practiced using art reproductions. "What happened before? What will happen afterward? What culture practice changed before or after this scene we are looking at? Can you explain the meaning of this scene in terms of whether it is or was good for the society? Is this a good picture? Why or why not?"

Art reproductions and postcards are easy to handle and store, and they are used more often than real art objects. Real objects, of course, have more presence; however, students can sort postcards of artworks, photographs, or other reproductions by region or society and describe the overall stylistic concepts that a group of cards from one culture have in common. In noting these shared characteristics, students might describe something that they know about that culture. Learning about the art style of a particular region or time can be facilitated by sets of art-reproduction cards made for playing an artistic version of Old Maid. "From a pack of cards find all the artworks made, for example, in the Orient, or during the Industrial Revolution, or in this century."

Interpreting artworks allows each person to reflect on his or her understanding of life. With no one feeling personally threatened, social interaction can easily occur while students and teachers talk about art. With teams of students from diverse backgrounds, discuss how the values

Courtesy of Marlee Puskar and Joyce Vroon, Trinity School, Atlanta, GA.

Egyptian artifacts and wallpaper design accompany the students' Egyptian paste jewelry in this display.

of other cultures are shown in the artworks, and compare these values to those of the students' own culture.

A game of picture detective can be played with pairs of students; one explains something about the picture in a sentence or two, the second interjects related points, and then they switch. A Go-Fish format also can be used; students must remember the physical location of works that go together and try to acquire sets. Such games can be played by pairs of students, in classroom learning activity centers, or by those who have finished an assigned activity early.

Thus far in this chapter we have overviewed social studies curricula across the elementary grades and discussed strategies for integrating art and social studies (personalized responses, hands-on activities, still lifes, sketching trips, and art criticism). We shall now examine ways to integrate art with the goals of seven specific social studies disciplines. Art study and expression can give insights into the methods and issues of anthropologists, economists, geographers, historians, law officers, psychologists, and sociologists.

Anthropology

Anthropology is the study of a people's symbols. Cultural anthropology analyzes cultural traits and artifacts. From examining and making drawings of artifacts, students can imagine what life was like in another country. When studying objects, ask, "Of what were the artifacts made? What purpose did they serve? How well do you think they met that need?"

African culture is examined through a papier-mâché constructed mask decorated with beans and broomsedge.

Third-grade students, studying Anasazi pottery of the Ancient Puebloans, created these ceramic pieces decorated with black-marker Native-American designs.

In teaching about another culture, note that it is disrespectful to emphasize only one aspect of that culture, such as weaponry (tomahawks) or inhumane practices, while neglecting a culture's nurturing and civic contributions. In general, it is not helpful to exoticize a culture or people or to label them primitive. This only makes a culture seem strange or foreign. Emphasizing the "grossness" of foods or "weirdness" of clothing communicates that "they're strange" and not at all like us. Just as the concept of race and racial characteristics lead to false stereotypes and harm, there are dangers in homogenizing many national groups into one, for example, combining Puerto Ricans, Mexican-Americans, and Cubans into one category—Hispanic or Latino.

Some suggestions for integrating art and anthropology in the classroom follow:

- Fold a piece of paper in half lengthwise. In one column, list schooling or coming-of-age rituals in some place or time; in the other column, list the practices in our own community. Compare and discuss what was listed.
- The activities that people perform and the objects used at various times of the day and in different seasons can be illustrated. Likewise, concepts of time can be reinforced in early primary grades through a display showing the students' illustrations of their activities at different times of the day.
- In kindergarten, students can sort sets of artwork reproductions into time categories: now/then, first/second/third, night/day, summer/fall/winter/spring, before/after, or morning/noon/evening.
- Students can draw today's artifacts, such as expensive designer sports shoes, and generalize about our society from the artifacts that students choose to draw. The crafted objects of a society reflect its values.

Courtesy of Joyce Vroon, Trinity School, Atlanta, GA.

One kind of service industry work can be suggested by this janitor's cart, tools, and supplies. After studying Duane Hanson's realistic polyester figures of actual people at their jobs, third-grader Taylor Dryman made this carefully observed marker drawing using bold primary colors.

Courtesy of Joyce Vroon, Trinity School, Atlanta, GA.

Even animals are commodities in third-grade student Edgar Crossett's representation of a pet store with checkout counter.

Economics/Vocations

Economics deals with the distribution of material wealth and with the structures that exist to provide jobs and services. Some suggestions for art integration are to illustrate an individual plan of economic action—draw or make a collage of what you would invest in "if you won $20,000." An understanding of concepts of monetary value can be gained by discussion following children's drawing make-believe choices of "being given an amount of money to buy presents."

Many artworks can be used to illustrate economic concepts. Art criticism of artworks, such as George Caleb Bingham's "Fur Traders Descending the Missouri" (which the artist had first titled "French Trader and Half-Breed Son"), Honoré Daumier's "Third Class Carriage," François Millet's "The Sower," or Duane Hanson's life-size polyester resin and Fiberglas figures, such as "Tourists" or "Cleaning Lady," can bring out the interrelationships of resources, suppliers, consumers, and economic needs.

Objects of scarcity, exchange, and consumption could make up a still life for drawing. Advertising can be analyzed for how art is used to motivate buyers. A sketching trip to a local business or construction site can show types of resources: natural resources, capital resources, and human resources. Drawings and diagrams can be made to show how rail lines, highways, airports, industrial complexes, and geographic factors interact. Fold the classified ads section of the newspaper into fourths, then, in each section, draw a career choice of which you are aware. Categorize these drawings of careers into those of persons who make things, fix things, create, and work with ideas.

Weaving discussion of career choices into art lessons at relevant points is a natural way to help children begin to think about careers involving art. A teacher might say, for example, "These ceramic animals you made this

week are as interesting as those at the downtown art fair last weekend." Comments such as these get youngsters thinking about art's role in many careers. Occupational value and economic value become of increasing concern to older students as they approach the time when they will begin to consider career options. A teacher might say, "Can you describe some occupations that use the skills found in this lesson?" (for example, measuring, designing, making color choices). "Many people make their livings by being designers of things like the racing automobiles that you have drawn."

Geography and Map Reading

Making maps helps students to learn content as well as map interpretation skills. Students' motivation for reading maps can be enhanced when they design their own map symbols. A group of students living near each other can make neighborhood maps using their own symbols for houses, streets, trees, government buildings, fun places to go, fast-food restaurants, and parks and playgrounds. To reinforce symbolization, students can match their symbols with photographs of the buildings or objects. Students also can draw maps from their homes to their favorite places and decorate them personally with significant details of what they see along the way. In the intermediate grades, make maps of regions and transportation arteries

Advertising art graces the highways and night sky in this sixth-grade student's artwork with its postmodern emphasis on an economy of consumption rather than production.

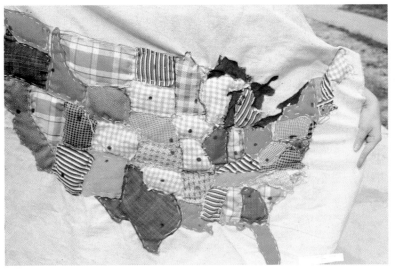

Working in a group, students sewed and quilted their individual states together to make e pluribus unum.

Courtesy of Joyce Vroon, Trinity School, Atlanta, GA.

Students related medieval life to their own concerns and to the art of metalworking in these metal repoussées showing a closed-up castle with a fallen knight. Claire Turner shows a

knight in shining armor astride his decorated horse. Subject matter and media come together in this medial project when both armory and metalworking were at their heights.

around one's city; use out-of-the-ordinary art materials, such as cut yarn pieces or cardboard relief, to foster a different type of artistic thinking. With these regional maps, encourage students to consider how major rivers, landforms, and highways affect the development of the area.

The study of transportation can be integrated by having students sketch vintage automobiles parked in the school parking lot and bicycles brought into the classroom, with a student modeling as the driver and backgrounds drawn from photographic views of bridges, modern cloverleaf intersections, and historic photos of downtown roads. For a very large map, students working in small groups in an out-of-the-way corner of the

room can use a mixture of sawdust, glue, vermiculite, plaster of Paris, and water on a large piece of cardboard or plywood to make a raised relief map of a part of the world. To make comparisons between geographic areas, students can draw differences in climate, transportation, foods, customs, and home architecture in two areas of a paper. After studying the street names in the area, students can draw imaginary portraits of the individuals (see "Drawing Faces" on page 253). Creatively illustrate the name of a famous place to show something about it. Students can sort art scenes into those showing such concepts as settlement, village, town, city, suburb, metropolis, and megalopolis. Art reproductions can be examined regarding the landforms, people's clothing, tools, homes, weather, roads, and transportation that are shown.

History

There are many ways for art projects to make history vivid in students' minds. To foster creative thinking about peoples' motivations at a certain time in history, have students hypothesize about the artists' intent; for example, for prehistoric peoples' cave art, have students communicate the prehistoric artists' message by reenacting the painting in dim light inside an empty refrigerator carton or other large box. Students can draw scenes showing themselves in historical events and add their own captions. Have students sort pictures or art reproductions, into chronological order and interpret what is happening in them. Draw and describe public buildings in the community, sort them into chronological order by age, and discuss

Joyous holiday parades and celebrations, such as this Taiwanese boy's depiction of the lion parade, not only bring the community together, but also help to create the community's very cultural essence and spirit. Note how the 10-year-old boy has captured the joy and excitement and how the figures' eight legs give away the secret of how the creatures move.

the values conveyed by the architecture. In two clay figures or on two halves of a sheet of paper, have each student contrast his or her life with that of a person from a historical period. Illustrate a problematic situation, such as a slave's dilemma about whether to run away, or an immigrant's dilemma, or an army general's dilemma. Encourage students to create personal solutions. Illustrate famous people's names in creative ways. Use pictograms to recount historical events. Put on a puppet play showing varying scenarios of how an event might have unfolded, and enact contrasting feelings toward the event. Make applehead dolls, add yarn hair, and dress them to represent historical figures. Then add an accompanying illustration of an event in that famous individual's life.

Illustrate what you may have been doing, in reality or in fantasy, when a noteworthy historical event occurred. Make a mural depicting historic events, and tell another class about it. Illustrate time lines to show the development of tools, inventions, and the arts. Illustrate grids with names of cultures listed down one side and concepts of house, headdress, and food listed across the top. Of course, making models of ancient monuments, castles, cathedrals, and kon-tiki rafts, building dioramas and displays, and creating masks, embroidery, engravings, and costumes for role-playing stimulates students' imaginations, especially when personalizing occurs and art principles are emphasized.

Law-Related Education

Law-related education deals with concepts such as equality, fairness, honesty, justice, power, property, responsibility, and tolerance. It addresses issues such as family law, consumer law (e.g., shoplifting), and community-safety law (e.g., bike helmets). Political science is concerned with examining rules, both good and bad, and taking the rights of others into account.

Many art reproductions illustrate such issues. Students can debate the merits of the issues, both from the artist's point of view and from the students' position. For example, Diego Rivera's contrasting murals "Night of the Rich" and "Night of the Poor" and Luis Cruz Azaceta's "Oppression III" illustrate issues of corruption and humans' cruelty to each other.

Likewise, students can illustrate examples from their lives of their own legal awareness, from raw power to group values to a belief in principles. Students can do figure drawings of a police officer who models while talking about community law problems, or of a uniformed member of the military who talks about issues of international law. Children in primary grades can make puppets in law-related education, such as for enacting issues concerning classroom rules (raising one's hand to speak, for example) and in trials conducted on law-related issues, such as the trespassing trial of Goldilocks vs. the Three Bears. Further, students can draw and discuss how people on the playground show that they do not

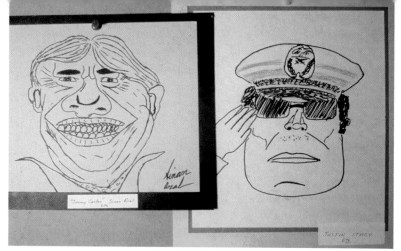

Courtesy of Joyce Vroon, Trinity School, Atlanta, GA.

Sixth-grade students practiced the art of characterization in their drawings of President Jimmy Carter and a general.

Courtesy of Joyce Vroon, Trinity School, Atlanta, GA.

Combining a study of Stuart Davis's art and the showing of a personal goal or favorite activity, a student produced this exuberant soccer design.

approve of certain behaviors. Young students can illustrate rules for safety on the playground swings, and older students can make posters illustrating the pros and cons of community issues, such as gun control and airport or city dump relocation. Incorporate text in speech balloons, as are used in cartoons, into the drawings. After examining the symbols and stereotypes in political cartoons, older students can draw their own cartoons of politicians and world leaders. From the intermediate school years to young adulthood, the law-and-order orientation is strong; older students can research and debate the rightness or wrongness of actions in art history episodes, such as Michelangelo's breaking his contract to paint the Sistine Chapel ceiling.

Psychology

Psychology is concerned with how an individual perceives the world or behaves based on those perceptions. Social roles (such as leadership, aggression, and submission) and personal social needs (such as acceptance and belonging) can be brought out through students making artworks on topics such as the following:

• What I do to please my parents
• Relationships with my siblings (or peer)
• Relationships with school peers

Topics such as "I am happiest when I—," "How I feel inside," and "The things I value" may be too broad and require narrowing and focus during the motivation period—for example, "What (*about siblings, about food, about*

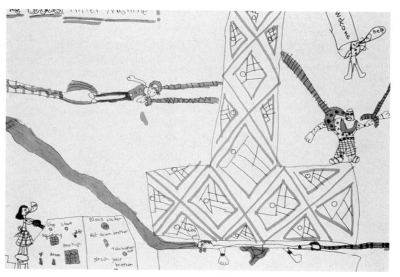

Courtesy of Joyce Vroon, Trinity School, Atlanta, GA.

One's feelings of frustration toward one's siblings have been expressed in this work called "A Brother Killer Machine," which may derive from an examination of torture machines used throughout the ages.

Courtesy of Joyce Vroon, Trinity School, Atlanta, GA.

Illustrating "A metaphor for my life," this student wrote: I am walking through the checkerboard of life's moods and feelings, stepping through the red of happiness and the black of sadness."

Courtesy of Joyce Vroon, Trinity School, Atlanta, GA.

Recalling a vivid dream, Michael Selik drew himself rapidly proceeding through an endless hall of mirrors.

Courtesy of Sharon Burns-Knutson, Cedar Rapids, IA.

Using a hand mirror and oil pastels for her self-portrait, fourth-grade student Johanna Siska expressively delineates her purple turtleneck, her red-orange eyeglass frames, and her long straight hair, which dips dramatically over one eye and is caught back on the other side to show her pearl earring.

the playground) makes me feel happy, sad, or mad?" Self-expression as a goal can be brought out through the teacher's eliciting and praising unique expression. "Because you are a unique individual, yours should not look like anyone else's. Make it your own way." One goal of social studies education is that students respect others. To have such respect, it is first necessary that one respects oneself, and creative expression in the arts is an excellent way to build self-respect and a positive self-concept.

Individuals' differences can be brought out through self-portraits that show personal interests, values, likes, and dislikes (see the section of self-portraits on page 253). Students who hold certain aesthetic values can

Student Lindsey Dole, Teacher Susan Whipple, Grace Christian School, Medford, Oregon.
USSEA art collection of Dr. Anne Gregory, Los Angeles School District.

In this 12- × 18-inch marker drawing, a little blue bird flies skyward under a blue-patterned angel's watch, as a giant Miss Liberty looms large but vine-encrusted behind the fortresslike institutions, church, state and home.

debate those with students holding differing values, for example, realism vs. abstraction. Psychology exercises on peer understanding, such as "find out three things about your partner" or "what would he or she do if given $300," can easily be integrated with the art task of drawing one's classmate (see drawing portraits in Chapter 20). When making masks, depict the face appealing for pity or succumbing to force. Have students illustrate what–will–happen–next endings to case-study situations of value conflict, such as individual freedom vs. the common good. Motivate thinking about value-based problems by having one student draw a problem situation on half of a folded paper and another student draw the solution on the other half.

The relativity of perception can be shown by asking for different interpretations of art reproductions. "Does anyone think it means some-

thing different?" The meaning of a painting such as Edvard Munch's "The Scream" can be debated—what might have provoked the depicted feelings, and what psychological strategies could be used for dealing with such emotions? The psychology exercise of brainstorming alternate solutions to a problem also can be used for art teaching—for example, students might work in pairs and discuss how to make their designs attractive and eye catching." The values that are implicit in each solution can be analyzed later by discussing issues of aesthetics (see Chapter 21).

Sociology

Sociology is the study of how people function in groups. In early grades, draw the family and what it does on special days. In middle grades, illustrate the contributions of the people who live in our city or state. Or, divide the class in half, and, using shoe boxes and cartons for buildings, have one group make an urban community and another make a rural community (see the section on box sculpture in Chapter 28). In upper grades, encourage thinking about concepts such as norms, society, values,

Courtesy of Barbara Thomas, Whit Davis School, Athens, GA.

First-grade students studied life in an American town in the 1800s. Richard Fisher's houses show three-dimensional form and their overlapping creates depth.

competition, status, and change. For example, students might draw "If I could change this school in some way . . . " or "If I were the teacher . . . " To study abstract concepts such as status, first examine artworks showing it, then have students make their own drawings showing the concept. As a variant of drawing from an object or picture, try illustrating a concept or an event, working only from a verbal description, such as of the urbanization of an area, child labor in a clothing factory, or the making of steel. A group of students can each draw one event in a sequence, and the whole can be pasted together. Students can then label the drawings with explanatory sentences and take turns explaining them. Illustrations can be made of the outstanding contributions of immigrants from a particular country or region. To bring out the idea of multiple group memberships (recreational, social, religious), have the students make drawings of themselves doing an activity in their different groups, and combine the resulting artworks into a large display. Wonderful pictures that provoke thinking about careers can be made of police officers; firefighters; nurses; performers such as clowns, dancers, pantomimists, and musicians with their instruments; scuba divers; airline personnel; and athletes in uniform.

Sociology and art come together as students think about questions such as the following: Why do the people in our community do art? How is it different from in other lands and at other times? In our area, how does

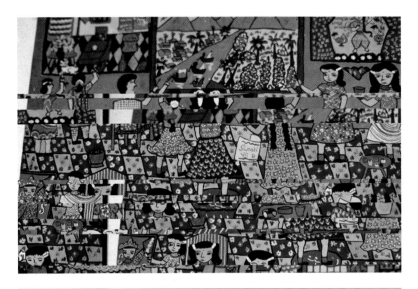

The sociological mileu of the art class is shown as students work jointly on two murals and individual paintings. What beauty is shown in the richly patterned and carefully drawn clothing and floor tiles! Observe the careful depiction of the paint jars and palette on the table. An ordered world, replete with richness and pattern, is depicted by this 13-year-old Indian child.

Courtesy of Melody Milbrandt, Valdosta, GA.

In A Birthday Party at the Skate Palace, *this kindergartner's crayon drawing shows the delightful social interactions and clowning around.*

art bring about a sense of community? How are the varied cultural customs around us shown in the art of our community? How have people in our community and elsewhere, and at other times, used art to mark life transitions and other social events?

Art reproductions can spur discussions of sociological issues. For example, Jacob Lawrence's "Migration Series" documented the changed lives of African Americans in the 1930s as they moved from the South to the North seeking work. Likewise, the polling methods used in sociological studies can be integrated with art inquiry. Students can conduct interviews among friends and family that investigate art-related issues, polling people in their neighborhoods on the merits of a design for a new playscape, public sculpture, or community recreation center. Current events can be studied through an art-news bulletin board to bring out interrelated concepts in the social sciences and art. Students can write or give oral reports on a family member, relative, or neighbor engaged in the arts. These can relate language arts, social studies, and art, and the class as a whole can discuss the importance of the art in the creator's life. Also, photography and videotaping can be used to document individual interviews with artists or community members, or to document the community's eyesores and contrast them with attractive sights.

Multicultural Understanding Through Art

In the Nation and in the Schools

The final section of this chapter concerns multicultural understanding and art. As a topic, it can include all the material previously presented in this chapter, about the curricula across the grades, about the seven teaching methods, and about the seven disciplines. However, since both our nation in general and our nation's schools are increasingly addressing the importance of multicultural understanding, we will discuss it as a separate topic.

Multicultural understanding is not a passing trend. It is a reconceptualization of our nation's "melting pot" concept—of who are Americans, and of how our various cultural heritages will be added to the "melting pot." Will they meld with the overall stock, or will they retain their clear identities?

As the student populations of American schools become increasingly multicultural, teachers of art are building curricula that promote the appreciation of diverse cultures' artistic heritages. Art is a natural area in which to combat ethnocentrism and monoculturalism. The goal is not to add "multicultural" ingredients as new elements to education but to make

Courtesy of Beverly Mallon, Chase Street Elementary School, Athens, GA.

Art projects can help children to understand the shared beliefs and attitudes of people in their society. Here is a detail of a stage background for a multicultural holiday musical. The mural painted on a primed painter's drop cloth by fifth-graders, shows a Native American woman on the left and an African-American man in a Kufi hat on the right.

Courtesy of Jackie Ellett, Fort Daniel Elementary School, Gwinnett County Schools, GA.

Students from many ethnic backgrounds become friends as they create art side by side.

education truly multicultural. The idea is not to abandon an existing curriculum but to expand it to include cultural plurality. For example, migrant workers' children are enrolled in many schools; a discussion of the cultural issues brought to mind by Dorothea Lange's "Migrant Mother" photograph could be enlightening to all in the class.

Help children to understand and acquire the shared knowledge, beliefs, and attitudes common to members of their society. By showing your students' cultural heritages in a positive light, you can help to strengthen their self-confidence. By serving as a source of positive energy concerning students' ethnic heritages, your art program can motivate and develop confidence in at-risk students. Education should help students understand the cultures in which they live; likewise, it should free them from their cultural boundaries. Art can help teach students to respect those who lead their lives in different ways.

Courtesy of Joyce Vroon, Trinity School, Atlanta, GA.

One way students can become familiar with other cultures is to represent persons from that culture in their traditional dress. Here fourth-grader Shelly Jones paints a Native American in traditional costume. Notice the skillfully coordinated use of shades and tints of Indian red and earth colors with accents of bright colors.

Courtesy of Beverly Mallon, Chase Street Elementary School, Athens, GA.

Art can help students to become aware of similarities and differences among people. In her own drawing sketchbook at home, second-grader Annabelle Barbe, whose family is active in the performing arts, did this drawing of a ballet dancer.

The Postmodern Artworld

In recent decades, the artworld has moved away from a primary interest in abstract art elements to exploring social, political, and environmental world problems through combining historical and popular images and new mixed media techniques. The cutting edge importance of art for art's sake, as a contemporary idea, has been eclipsed. Formalism in art—the idea that the formal elements and principles are art's central issues—is under attack, and is considered by some to be irrelevant and even oppressive. The earlier Modern Art movement dealt with issues such as abstraction and abstract expressionism and avoided sociopolitical commentary. The Modern period was characterized by rational, traditional, absolute, and universal values,

Courtesy of Melody Milbrandt, State University of West Georgia, Carrollton, GA.

Is all art political? The plaintive expression on this clay figure dressed in a red yarn skirt might be interpreted as the primary grade child's statement on the historic mistreatment of Native peoples.

unlike the Postmodern period's relativity and conflict. Art's new emphasis is "Aboutness." It is about the society in which it is made. It is about a particular culture's values and political beliefs, to which its creator either acquiesced or resisted.

Postmodernism embraces diversity and plurality and therefore shares some of the tenets of multiculturalism. Postmodern art emphasizes accessibility of the artwork's meaning and de-emphasizes an individual genius's accomplishment. Especially today, there are numerous notions of the nature of art, reflecting less a unified world view and more a minefield of conflicting notions about the nature of art. Art imagery can be a battleground of meaning. It can be a weapon of competing groups in their quest for influence and power. Certainly, it is true that art can be used as an

agent for social change. Some would even go so far as to say that all art is political. Artworks such as Nancy Spero's and Leon Golub's works about brutality, Judy Chicago's and Mary Kelly's pieces about women and motherhood, Kara Walker's cutouts of African-American stereotypes, or Nam June Paik and Joseph Beuys's video about whales show this renewed sociopolitical activism. Of course, it is a mistake to depict this increased activism in too great a contrast; past periods have also done political commentary, for example, from the Modern period, the artworks of George Grosz, Max Beckmann, and Kaethe Kollwitz showed a cultural critique of Nazi Germany.

The Thematic Approach

Two thematic approaches to considering art's subject matter in relation to social studies are using major themes and using contestable issues. The thematic approach focuses on cultural differences and commonalities through exploration of concepts such as adaptation, survival, environment, time, space, and motion. The students explore a variety of resources and consult the Internet, books, and magazines. Groups of students from diverse cultures can work together to arrange art reproductions about such issues into a bulletin-board display. The teacher and students choose an issue to be explored historically through analysis of artworks. For example, today's ecological crises have pointed up the merits of less technologically intrusive ways of living. The Native American sense of stewardship for the earth addresses this need, and thus there has resulted an increased interest in Native American culture. In teaching units about major themes, relate the material to the student's own life experience and the student's own understanding of the current situation in the student's community. Still another way to promote multicultural education is through exchanges of children's art between schools here and in other countries.

Using Contestable Issues

Another way to approach art's subject matter is to use issues about which students can debate. This teaching method fosters the examination of cultural assumptions, a critical attitude toward the status quo, and a nurturance of social change. Present the students with a real-life dilemma related to art and social studies and discuss how to solve it. The controversy might be about a piece of public art, or an artist's actions or financial predicament, or an art theft or forgery, or the return of artwork to the country of its origin. Provide culturally and situationally relevant contexts about an authentic activity.

Courtesy of Sharon Burns-Knutson, Cedar Rapids, IA.

Patterns of crosses, thunderbolts, stripes, dots, and a parade of animals and birds make this full-size replica in acrylic paint of a Plains Indian teepee by fifth- and sixth-grade students an object of wonder and beauty.

Courtesy of Jackie Ellett, Fort Daniel Elementary School, Gwinnnett County Schools, GA.

Contestable issues bring out dissenting opinions and help to make individuals aware of other points of view. Preserving air quality and maintaining a good quality of life in inner-city, high-density housing are issues about which individuals have diverse opinions.

Courtesy of Jackie Ellett, Fort Daniel Elementary School, Gwinnett County Schools, GA.

A study of Southwest Native-American architecture was combined with a study of pastel, complementary colors and use of chiaroscuro to create an illusion of roundedness in this third-grade students' work.

In artworks, students can look for evidence of oppression and social inequality. They can find images that maintain the dominant culture and show another group or gender in subservient and serving roles. Students can try to find artworks showing positive or negative attitudes toward ideas such as the following: that people have the right to live in different ways, that power should be equitably distributed among groups, and that social justice should exist for all. Yet a word of caution: conservative school administrators or parents in conservative areas may not be sympathetic to the contestable issues approach.

No less an expert than child psychologist Jean Piaget believed that students and educators should be searching for conflict, since conflict is a part of all life and is necessary for development. A plant's roots become strong by pushing against the soil. Using art reproductions, art criticism affords a forum to debate the merits of the values shown in artworks. For example, ideas about the power of the state can be debated using Max Beckmann's "Departure" as a starting point toward a discussion of the equitable administration of justice to all people in a community. Important skills to learn are how to respond to conflicts—by acquiescing to the dominant point of view, or by assertively advocating for one's own or minority points of view? Other skills to be learned are in how to express

Surely, part of America's strength is its ability to integrate the cultural contributions of its diverse population. Fourth- and fifth-grade students painted this stage backdrop for a social studies Pageant. Set against a starry, fireworks-filled sky, famous American Freedom Fighters who have changed our society are shown. In this detail, clockwise from the top: Abraham Lincoln, James Madison, Thomas Jefferson, Susan B. Anthony (in red dress), Frederick B. Douglas, Eleanor Roosevelt, and Cesar Chavez.

Your art program can help students feel pride in and connectedness to their cultural backgrounds. Here, elementary school children from Tainan, Taiwan, have depicted their culture's traditional festivals and pageants. **Top and bottom:** *the dragon dance.* **Middle:** *the river festival.*

disagreement agreeably, in a patient, rational manner. Students can do their own artworks about their perceptions of inequities in the community or nation.

The art/social studies program that you provide can help your students to feel pride in themselves and their own cultural backgrounds and connectedness to people in other cultures. Social studies and art share a common interest in perceiving distinctive attributes, in grouping things by shared properties, and in generalizing. Values education can be promoted through art making and art viewing. And there are larger goals—even beyond learning specifically about art and social studies. The study of the arts and humanities enriches daily life, helps one to understand oneself, helps maintain civility, and develops a sense of community.

Courtesy of Joyce Vroon, Trinity School, Atlanta, GA.

Many symbols are evident in this personal myth written and painted by fifth-grader Mary Radford Wyatt. The yellow-and-black striped boat with dark sails seems to portend danger; green-faced spirits blow the wind away from the sailboat; Atlas holds up the boat on the watery globe.

Courtesy of Beverly Mallon, Chase Street Elementary School, Athens, GA.

Young children's drawings can communicate more than their words. Kindergartners wrote and illustrated The Further Adventures of Peter Rabbit. *The child dictated the story, "Peter Rabbit and Flopsy, Mopsy, and Cottontail look at a rainbow while waiting to take a ride on an airplane." Life is one happy adventure! First period learning how to draw a rabbit, second period pencil drawing the scene, third period watercolor, fourth period markers.*

Chapter 17

LITERACY: READING, WRITING, AND SPEECH INTEGRATION WITH ART

Literacy is broadly defined as the ability to read and write. When the visual arts are metaphorically considered to be language, then a concept called *visual literacy* emerges. Visual literacy goes beyond the fine arts to include those in advertising, movies, product design, and popular culture.

The language arts share much common ground with the visual arts. Both subjects focus on means of expression. Both use symbols. Both employ similar methods of critical analysis and interpretation.

We learn through representation. We construct meaning by formulating our own representations. Although usually these are verbal or written,

Courtesy of Joyce Vroon, Trinity School, Atlanta, GA.

Both writing and artwork are used to represent ideas, things, and events. This display is of third-graders' paintings of their favorite storybook characters.

Third-graders illustrate scenes from their favorite stories, "Rotten Ralph" and "Corduroy."

occasionally they are diagrammatic or pictorial. For children who do not yet know how to write and may not possess the vocabulary to use to describe events, drawing can communicate much. Unfortunately, too often some teachers scold children when they are drawing instead of writing. The interplay of the two forms of communication is, in fact, a powerful motivator for both drawing and writing; both the artwork and the written passage offer representations of the same cluster of things—each provides a window into the child's world.

Speech plays an essential role in a child's developing thoughts. The constructivist cognitive psychologists emphasized this relationship of speech and learning and recommended that children work interactively in pairs and groups to solve problems (see Chapter 6). We form our thoughts into speech at the same time as speech forms our thoughts. Thus, language is an important mediator between learning and development. This concept is applied in good art lesson plans, which almost always allow for a time to talk about the art produced, to share the art's meaning with others in the class. Much research has proven how verbalization improves retention of art concepts. Ways to do this "art talk" are explained in Part 4 of this book. Here, however, the focus, inversely, is on ways to use art to promote language arts goals.

Children in the primary grades can illustrate a popular story such as "Rotten Ralph." Alternately, the story can be divided into scenes and each child assigned a particular scene to illustrate. The scenes can be taped together to tell the entire story in a hallway display. Students can exchange paintings and talk about each other's work. Students in the intermediate grades can keep journals filled with their writing and drawings, working synergistically. They can write poems to go with an artwork (of their own or a reproduction) empathizing with the figures depicted. They can write a reflective piece about why they find a certain artwork meaningful. In their writing, they can answer questions about the feeling they had when they saw the artwork and the elements of the work that attracted them. They can even consider and write about their own thinking process as they responded to the artwork (this is a called a meta-cognition approach). Middle school students can write in their journals about their photographs. Encourage them to show in their writings and drawings such major modalities as the passage of time, movement, and different concepts of space, such as cartoonists use, for example, close-ups, distant views, framing through close objects, silhouettes, high views, and low views.

Among our nation's cultural treasures are the quilts by Harriet Powers (shown in the section on collage on page 294). With their bold

Courtesy of Jessica Crosby, Reading for Life Project, Claiborne County, MS, and
the Mississippi Cultural Crossroads, Port Gibson, MS.

Reading and art can augment each other. Famous quilter Hystercine Ranking passes on quilting skills to students as they participate in the Reading for Life Literacy Program, illustrating in quilt form their own stories inspired by books of African-American authors. From a theme in the book, children develop their own story, with the teacher asking questions such as Who, What, When, and Where.

Courtesy of Joyce Vroon, Trinity School, Atlanta, GA.

The word the students selected had to be both a noun and a verb. Here, fifth-grader Corbin Pendleton illustrates the word KISS with Hershey Kisses®. Notice the use of the graphic device of interpenetration of shapes.

Whole Language Approach

The whole language approach to integrated curriculum has recently been gaining acceptance, especially in the elementary grades. It features thematic interconnections between subjects, focuses on inquiry, and encourages a variety of impressive and expressive learning modes. Whole language emphasizes the students' autonomy, and the approach seems to work well for students who are keen on learning.

In children's earliest representational drawings, they employ their natural narrative impulse—the desire to create stories in their drawings and to talk about the drawing event. Drawing precedes writing and is important in the "prehistory" of their writing. The child's drawing first assures that the early writing process is authentically rooted in his or her own personal experiences. Have children draw a picture of a personally meaningful topic of their own choosing and then write about it. Children learn to read and write most easily when they themselves author the text. Indeed, their first texts emerge in the captions and stories that children dictate or write to accompany what they have drawn. Further, children's interest in one another builds as they are able to talk with classmates

geometric design, the quilts integrated her knowledge of historical and biblical subject matter with events from her life. Your students might undertake a quilt project, showing events from their lives, or from a book that they have read. One introduction to the idea of a class quilt project is *The Patchwork Cat.* Have students bring in quilts from home to get design ideas and to plan out the proposed quilt's colors and shapes. Then brainstorm ideas about the class quilt's subject matter and individual artist's squares.

Outside class, older students can do detailed drawings of the stuff in their rooms, drawn from the doorway or while sitting on the bed. A written description to go along with the drawing can give the students perspective on their values.

Integrating writing and art, create word pictures and drawings describing a place that can be seen from the school. Alternately, write word pictures to describe a remembered place, such as "My Bedroom" or "At the Neighborhood Convenience Store." Young children can collaboratively come up with remembrances, which the teacher can record on the chalkboard. Each child can then select a remembrance that is meaningful to him or her to illustrate with written words or a drawing.

Courtesy of Melody Milbrandt, State University of West Georgia, Carolton, GA.

A first-grade student paints an illustration to a story about a dog-boy and chickens.

Tempera paints mixed ahead of time in attractive tones can produce handsome paintings, as in this primary-grade student's painting of a child reading a book about a cat named Gregory.

Drawing scenes from Pandy and the Ball *helps young children to root the story in their personal experience.*

about each other's drawings. The drawing and the accompanying talk about it give the naturally curious young child access into another child's mind and feelings. Employ the child's artistic intelligence; do not limit a whole language approach only to written and verbal communication or by the use of stereotyped clip art visual images.

Having a sketchbook permits kindergarten and primary grades language arts students a forum in which to express their feelings and ideas. Encourage the children to use the sketchbook not just for drawings and writings in combination, but also for diagrams and pictograms. As in early civilizations, such hieroglyphic pictograms can serve in lieu of or can supplement written alphabets. As one example, art, writing, and diagrams can be meaningfully combined in capturing a recalled experience—perhaps a time with a loved one or pet, or in a special place.

Students can "read" a painting, talking about its images and connecting its images to themes and historical context explored during their coursework in history. Use the study of the visual arts to enhance the study of history and culture. (A more extended discussion of how this

Like in Dr. Seuss's stories, the words and pictures seem to arise together in this marker, craypas, and glitter artwork, "Party Trees." In sixth-grader Lindsay's words, "Walking in a magical forest, I saw three trees with weird hairdos, bowties, and necklaces, going to a party, and they invited me. We partied all night long." Notice how the party atmosphere is conveyed by the riot of patterns of squares, circles, and straight and wavy lines. Teacher Debra Belvin, Bearden Middle School, Knoxville, TN.

my neighbor Casey

me and my Dad and

Eating watermelon

Annabell Barbe

with Bluebird watching

Courtesy of Beverly Mallon, Chase Street Elementary School, Athens, GA.

Kindergartner Annabell Barbe drew the picture and wrote the story, "Me and my Dad and my neighbor Casey eating watermelon with a bluebird watching." Faith Ringgold's artwork and the beautiful spring weather were the motivation.

"image reading" can be done is in Chapter 21 on Art Criticism.) Books are available that exemplify integrated learning. Two that integrate reading, social studies, music, and art are *Annabel's Dream of Ancient Egypt* and *The Further Adventures of Annabel the Cat.*

One successful correlational project—Learning to Read Through the Arts—sponsored by the Guggenheim Museum and New York City Board of Education, helped students to recall with all of their senses. It involved art criticism, art production, and field trips, and it helped to improve students' reading scores by one or two months for each month of involvement in the program (Kinder, 1987; O'Brien, 1978).

Acquiring more skill, intermediate-grade children can first outline a story, using only a few words or short phrases. Then they can work these words or phrases into sentences. After the basic writing is done, they can polish the piece. Save an area near the top of the page for an illustration of

The exciting story of Black Beauty *was illustrated by third-grader Devin McGillivary.*

In this picture, called "Word Processing," after making a careful line drawing of an old Corona typewriter, student Eleanor Siegel then wrote a story that she lettered on the background.

After drawing a guitar, Tyler Grubb adds song lyrics, written around the guitar's outline in successive rows.

a scene in the narrative. Alternately, make a colorful, decorated border using relevant symbols. Computer word processing and paint programs are powerful new means for whole language expression.

One way to stimulate students' imaginations for writing and drawing is through scents, for example, the scent of bread baking or of honeysuckle's fragrance that stir memories. Let the scent pervade the classroom, as you share with the students a story and artwork of your own about your scent memory. Then have students draw an image of the item, do calligraphy telling a story about it, and make a recipe or schematic diagram of how the item is made. They can share the finished work with one or two friends and write down what the scent was, and the memory that it evoked.

Chapter 18

RELATED ARTS INTEGRATION

All of the arts foster the growth of cognition. Cognition refers to ways of processing information and becoming aware of self and the environment through sight, sound, taste, and movement. The visual arts deal with form and images and use vision and tactile sensory systems. Dance is primarily a kinesthetic art form. Music is predominantly aural, using sound and hearing, but it also employs bodily or kinesthetic experiences. Drama, the most integrated form, uses action and behaviors that use the aural, kinesthetic, tactile, verbal, and visual ways of knowing. Education should develop the young child's literacy in all of these symbol systems and modes of thought, and by all means of inquiry.

Particularly in the early years of schooling, many cognitive activities occur as physical activities—drawing, moving, or enacting. Perception rather than logic governs children's early views of reality. Children relate to the arts as media for expression and communication at a time when their verbal skills are not fully developed. For young children especially, the arts must be thought of as total and integrated experiences.

The arts develop the child's sensitivity to symbol systems and the ways of thinking employed in each art form. Each of the art forms has its own symbol system, grammar, and syntax with which children can express themselves and their understandings of the world. Although one must take care to not reinforce stereotyped ways of expression, a tree might be represented in art as a lollipop-shaped branching form, in dance by upraised arms waving, in music with gentle blowing sounds, and in drama, as an overshadowing protective being with a deep voice. Interrelating these forms of representation can facilitate learning. Children's early arts experiences will later coalesce into sophisticated reasoning and problem solving.

Interweave the various arts. For example, consider a lesson about stormy weather. Students waving scarves can dance the gusting movements of the wind and rain. Their dance can be accompanied by appropriate

Courtesy of Beverly Mallon, Chase Street Elementary School, Athens, GA.

Before drawing, fourth-grade children danced to imitate festive New Year's revelry and blowing of celebratory horns. One can almost feel the excitement and hear the cacophony of the celebration!

Sixth-grader Kristie Stephens drew a portable cassette player and headset on a musical sheet.

This fifth-grade girl decorated her self-portrait with musical notations—symbols of her interest in music. A study of American primitive portraits preceded the drawing and painting. Notice the sophisticated rendering of the hair, eyes, and nose.

musical sounds. Students can use their voices for the howling wind and shake a sheet of metal to simulate the thunder. They can enact a skit of a family reacting to the storm's approach. They can use chalk and paint to depict the storm's fury. Of course, language arts activities might also be involved and guest speakers, such as weather bureau personnel, could be asked to speak.

Integration in the arts is legendary. For example, a book by Christopher Isherwood was adapted into a play which was later developed into the Broadway musical and then movie, "Cabaret."

Elementary classroom teachers in the primary grades can easily integrate the arts and move from one art form to another as children make music, act, dance, and draw. For example, after reading the story, "Jack in the Beanstalk," ask:

For music: "What kind of musical sounds can we make with our voices that sound like an angry, running giant? This half of the class be the giant, this half show Jack's fright. I will be the conductor."

For drama: "What would the characters say when the maid hid Jack? Can you make up words to show why she risked losing her job to help a thief?"

For dance: "How could we show the chase by moving our bodies around the front of our classroom? Use all the parts of your body and all the

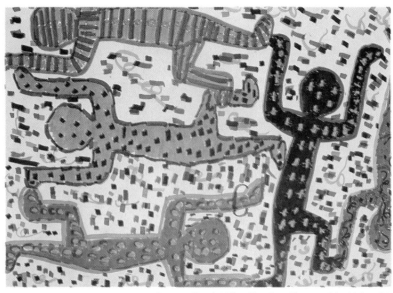

Courtesy of Beverly Mallon, Chase Street Elementary School, Athens, GA.

The teacher said, "I really hammed it up, saying as I danced, 'You've got to groove!'" The students "grooved" about the room and then "froze" when the tape was stopped and thought about the positions of their bodies. They then drew their dancing figure, cut it out, and repeatedly traced it to create the overall design. In another session, the marker drawings on tag board were decorated with squares, dots, stripes, and wavy lines. Keith Haring's figures also were a motivation.

ways you can think to move your body to show the characters' personalities and the chase. Your knees, your elbows, the height of your body. Row 3 be giants, Row 4 be Jacks."

For art: "What scene from the story will you show in your artwork? Make the figures large so we can see the expressions on their faces. How will you show their fingers?"

In many of the world's non-Western cultures, the arts are now and always have been connective and integrative. Colorful sculptural costumes are used in dance and dramatic enactments. Drumming and other instruments create the exciting rhythmic music. Festivals combine music, dance, theater, and visual arts in a symbiotic way.

Likewise, as a school's art teacher, it is likely you will be called upon to have your students make backdrops for school plays and festivals, and perhaps even make special costumes and props. Art teachers often perform service to the school, especially to the related arts areas, and should be credited for such service. When in school, the sculptor Henry Moore recalled with great satisfaction doing such related arts activities with his art teacher and his school buddies. As resident artist at a Renaissance

Courtesy of Sharon Burns-Knutson, Cedar Rapids, IA.

The arts are integrative in many African cultures. Both drama and dance, along with religion and art, employ masks. Here, a student's metal-embossed mask takes its motivation from the magnificent metalwork of the Benin kingdom.

Courtesy of Beverly Mallon, Chase Street Elementary School, Athens, GA.

The art teacher was asked to have her class make a backdrop for the school Holiday Multicultural Musical Festival. The fifth-grade class arrived at a circular design of "People from Around the World," shown in their nation's costumes. The 8- × 8-foot multicultural mural was painted flat on the floor with acrylic paints on a primed painter's drop cloth. Prior to designing their figures, children consulted costume books and the encyclopedia.

court, Leonardo da Vinci staged festivals as a regular part of his work for his patron.

Multi-arts exhibits can combine an art display with students' musical or dramatic performances. At these, students can demonstrate their special art skills through displays in the halls or foyer. School arts festivals can be made more special by having students wear costumes, by serving theme-related food at the opening, or by having a joint exhibition of parent and child art.

Music

Some modes of expression studied in music include listening, singing, playing, improvising, moving to music, and symbolizing through music.

Children love chants and chanting. They can sing chants and songs such as "Ring Around the Rosie," in round form. They can act out the chant. Then they can draw the event with much vigor, and perhaps even connectedness of the figures, having had aural and motor stimulation.

Music elements include beat, rhythm, meter, tempo, repetition, contrast, structure, tone color, and accent. Teach students to identify when an

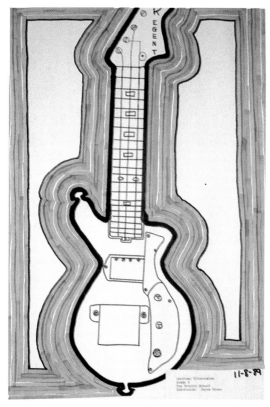

Courtesy of Joyce Vroon, Trinity School, Atlanta, GA.

One way musical ability and art interests can be integrated is by drawing musical instruments. Fifth-grader Courtney Clinkscales carefully draws an electric guitar and then outlines it in bands of alternating, vibrating colors.

Courtesy of Joyce Vroon, Trinity School, Atlanta, GA.

Singing onstage at a big party with lots of guests, standing under three big spotlights, and wearing high-heeled shoes is an exciting experience for second-grader Cameron Weller. The microphone, the boombox, its musical notations, and the singer's expression convey sound in the artwork.

outstanding use of a musical element occurs. For example, students can describe repetition and variation in Ravel's "Bolero." Likewise, teach them to look for repeated elements in artworks.

One of the best known examples of art and music integration is painting to music of differing tempos and tone colors. For example, Respighi's "Fountains of Rome" lends itself to paintings of fountains splashing water. Marches by John Philip Sousa stimulate paintings of Fourth-of-July parades. Have students do the following experiment: Fold a sheet of paper in half and paint one half to fast music and the other to slow music. Show the finished work to a peer. Can he or she tell which halves were painted to each kind of music?

Have students bring in musical toys. Play the toys. Then arrange them into a still life and draw and paint the still life. Draw musical notational

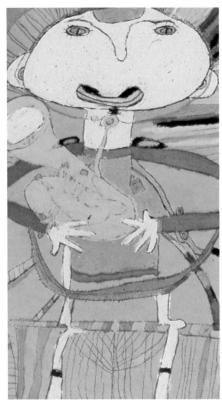

A seated student holding a baritone horn is depicted in a highly original way, especially in how the artist met the challenge of showing foreshortened legs.

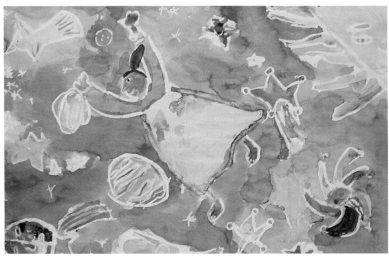

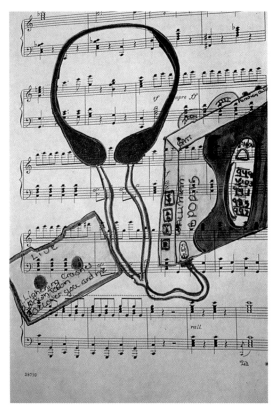

Fifth-grade student Alexandra Robinson drew cassette and CD players onto old music score sheets.

symbols in the background. Have the students draw and paint musical instruments using old sheet music as the background.

Integration also can work in reverse: Rather than painting to music, students can create music inspired by a painting. For instance, Moussorgsky's famous "Pictures at an Exhibition" was composed in response to his seeing specific paintings at an art display. Students might use instruments to create a mood akin to that depicted in a work of art. Using drumsticks or their pencils, students can tap out the rhythms of groups of objects in art-

"I Believe I Can Fly" music was played while students made their designs. Faith Ringgold's book was inspiration for the third-grade child's idea, "One night, in a dream, the sun was smiling at me, and I felt so happy, I felt like dancing on the moon." Children took turns lying on the art tables to see how their bodies looked outstretched. The project, which required five class periods, used a pencil drawing gone over with heavy marker so it could be traced through a sheet of paper, with white oil pastel for the watercolor resist.

Courtesy of Beverly Mallon, Chase Street Elementary School, Athens, GA.

To the sound of nature tapes of ocean waves, third-grade students painted watercolor effects in warm and cool colors. On another day, they tore out warm-colored seashore forms of starfish and sand dollars and collaged them on top. Other themes were outer space and earth.

works, for example, the pattern of clouds, of swaying grasses, of soldiers marching. Then have students apply this knowledge of rhythm in their own artworks.

Symbols used in paintings and in music can be compared. How are darkness and scariness shown in art and in music? How are emotions such as happiness and sadness conveyed in the two art forms?

Dance

Dance can be thought of as occurring in three domains: composing, performing, and appreciating. With young children, focus on the hands-on activities of the first two—especially performing. Students can be made aware of the elements in dance. For example, watching a video of a dance performance, they can identify when dramatic instances of the following elements occur:

• Space (How will the stage's space and the spacing of the characters be used to represent emotions and actions?)
• Time (Will key events be repeated several times?)
• Effort (Where and how will great effort be portrayed?)

• Abstraction (What movements depict the essence of the characters?)
• Representation (costumes, props)
• Alignment (How will the figures be aligned—parallel or diagonally?)
• Axial movement (moving straight to the front, rear, across, or diagonal of the stage)

An exercise in composing can use a simple, familiar story that everyone knows, such as "The Three Little Pigs." Working in small groups, students can discuss how to use the dance elements to plan out a dance about the story.

After studying butterflies and before painting a scene of butterflies in the garden, children can first plan and then enact through the language and symbols of dance the life cycle of the butterfly, snuggled in the cocoon, emerging, flying, finding a mate, escaping birds and storms, etc. In art, students can fold a piece of paper into fourths, sixths, or eighths and draw a series of drawings—one in each square, and taking about five minutes per square—to illustrate these life stages using the language and symbols of visual expression. To incorporate music, the teacher can play music of different tempos while the students draw each stage.

Courtesy of Beverly Mallon, Chase Street Elementary School, Athens, GA.

To be able to leap into the air and touch one's toes is an acrobatic feat! After enacting such movements, children drew and cut out their figures and traced the pieces onto vinyl letter scraps from a sign store. These were then pasted down to comprise the entire figure. Leftover gift wrap samples, from the school's fundraiser, added exciting pattern.

Using mirrors, these primary-grade students draw and paint themselves in fancy hats. Art by third-grade student Natalie Long.

Drama

Drama comprises elements of silence, singing, darkness, light, time, surprise relationships, character, style, variation, pace, rhythm, space, movement, mood, symbol, and meaning. When students make drawings about a play, urge them to incorporate in their representations some of these elements. Performance art uses some of the conventions of drama, but it is clearly concerned with using the body as a discrete visual media.

Make students aware of the art-related professions related to drama. These include design of costume, set, lighting, advertising, and program. Set design is similar to a common art activity—that of building dioramas. Typically, a shoe box is used as the stage. Children decide on the play or story for which they would like to build a set (this way, there can be a variety of plays portrayed), or they first build a set and then write a play to go with the set. To give an introduction to lighting design, they can darken the classroom (or another enclosed area) and use a flashlight—with or without colored cellophane over the lens—to show how the stage is to be lit during certain scenes. Other students could select accompanying music to introduce scenes.

In another activity related to stage lighting, students can use paint or watercolors to paint papers in shades that indicate the atmosphere and lighting of scenes. At another session the students can use black markers to draw the scenes on the papers. Then they can use oil pastels and crayons to color in characters' costumes and other features.

In designing costumes and props, students can sketch the costumes, accessories, and props to be used, employing the symbols denoting the characters, that is, crowns, scepters, tools, and so on. These can then be cut out and placed in the diorama sets. Disregard scale, however.

With kindergarten and primary-grade children, a box filled with top hats, cowboy hats, firefighter hats, wedding veils, fancy ball dresses, cowboy boots, spiked high heels, and props can be used for re-enacting scenes. Older students, dressed in costumes, can model for figure drawing. Students can add special features and captions to their drawings to further clarify the dramatic character whom they have depicted. Another day they can paint in an appropriate background, showing the time of day or night, room interior or outside scene, and animals and props.

Sometimes school classes are bused to see a semiprofessional dramatic production in a local auditorium. Following this field trip experience, they can draw or paint their impressions of the performance. Written captions can clarify the intent of the picture. Older students each can select a favorite scene to depict; then, when the pictures are put on display, the whole play is retold.

In developing related arts activities, as in all your educational planning, try to identify the unique strengths of your students and give them opportunities to do work in those areas. Are there two or three students who have shown particular interest in a given area? If so, have them work as a team, using their special talents to develop a phase of the subject.

Courtesy of Beverly Mallon, Chase Street Elementary School, Athens, GA.

First-graders dramatized the poses that Olympic athletes would take when bringing home their trophies to their countries' rulers. Annabelle Barbe's picture shows the three gold medalists, met at their nation's shoreline, wearing great smiles of pride in accomplishment.

Courtesy of Joyce Vroon, Trinity School, Atlanta, GA.

Drawing caricatures of famous TV and screen personalities is one way to integrate drama and art. Here, the meaning of Mary Flynn Detlefs' caricature is further enriched by a Joker playing card format, alluding to David Letterman's sense of humor.

One way to categorize students' abilities is through Howard Gardner's eight forms of intelligence. The following suggestions apply these various intelligences to a unit on drama:

1. Language: playwriting, writing characters' dialogue.
2. Logical and mathematical: plotting line structures, incorporating math into the dialogue ("Each little pig weighs 20 pounds, so I will have 60 pounds to eat").
3. Interpersonal (knowledge about other people): developing character personality and dialogue.
4. Musical: scoring and performing the background music, choreography.
5. Spatial: designing sets and costumes, planning choreography and blocking (where the characters will be and where they will move from minute to minute), video taping.
6. Bodily-kinesthetic: planning the poses the actors should strike to portray various emotions.
7. Intrapersonal (information about oneself): showing characters' personalities in dialogue.
8. Naturalistic: creating props of animals and birds and trees, painting sets to represent outdoor scenes.

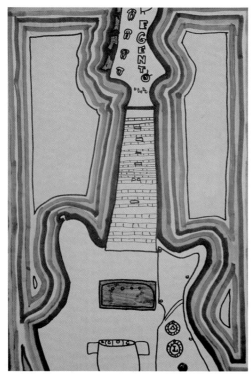

Rhythm in music reflected in rhythm in lines is seen in this rendition of a guitar by fifth-grader Eleanor Siegler. The repeated lines of the instrument's outline seem to echo the guitar's reverberative strumming sound.

Encourage students to make connections among arts disciplines as well as between the arts and other disciplines. For example, while planning an activity in a different discipline, ask, "How would this idea be shown in music? Let's make appropriate sounds to accompany the artwork. If this were a play, what colors of lights would you use on the stage? If we were sculptures frozen as if in a freeze frame, what poses would we be in to suggest this action? Can anyone think of a story that is sort of like this play? How do the plots differ?" By demonstrating this kind of interrelated arts thinking, you model attitudes that foster a rapprochement and interplay of the arts. You lay the groundwork for skills—such as advertising, Web design, TV production, and film making—essential to many America's great industries.

At the heart of learning in the arts is the process of giving form to and making meaning out of personal experience. This may occur through composing or playing music, writing a play, choreographing or performing a dance, or creating an artwork. To be able to use arts elements to express something about one's feelings and experiences is the goal of learning in the related arts.

Oil on canvas, 58- × 86-inches. Reproduced by permission of the Winn Family and the National Trust. This painting hangs in the Nostell Priory, Yorkshire, England.

Previous page: *Looking at art from other times can give us insights into our lives. Almost all young people can identify with the dilemma represented in this painting—that choices must be made about which of our personal interests will receive uppermost attention. How does one choose between competing interests? Whether to play soccer this year or to start hockey, whether to continue keyboard or to start guitar, whether to go camping with Dad or to stay with Mom in town and attend basketball camp.*

Painted in 1794, Angelica Kaufmann's Self-Portrait Hesitating between the Arts of Music and Painting *shows a young woman whose body seems to want to go in one direction and whose head seems to want to go toward the conflicting direction. The Muse of Music and the young accomplished musician tenderly hold hands, while the young woman's other hand seeks the palette as the Muse of Painting points to a higher calling. Which won out, the head or the body? Students could use this picture as a motivation for their depiction of a dilemma in choices of interests to pursue.*

Chapter 19

NEW APPROACHES TO ART APPRECIATION

Today, children have more opportunities to see and appreciate art than ever before. Museums and art centers open their doors to all, and colorful murals now enliven many urban walls. Municipal buildings, subways, and airports display a variety of commissioned public art, and magazines feature articles on art. Bookstores prominently display colorfully illustrated books on art, and art enthusiasts can purchase reproductions at fairly reasonable prices. School textbooks in social studies and literature often are filled with colorful, correlative art visuals, and art councils in the 50 states promote art festivals, exhibits, and "artists-in-the-schools" programs.

Despite a multitude of opportunities to appreciate art in the world about them, many children receive minimal training in learning how to think about, talk about, and do art. They leave school programs feeling like outsiders to the world of art, intimidated at the thought of visiting museums and art galleries. They feel that serious discussions of art ideas are something in which they have no business participating. They think that the study of art criticism, art history, and aesthetics is high-falutin, reserved for those going on for higher education. They have not recognized that art offers everyone a way to investigate the world and its meanings and values.

Toward Civilization, an influential report of the National Endowment for the Arts (1988), described the effect of this attitude on the nation:

> The arts are in triple jeopardy: they are not viewed as serious; knowledge . . . is not viewed as a prime objective; and those who determine school curricula do not agree on what arts education is.

Some educators believe that the activities of thinking and talking about art can give a new intellectual dimension to art appreciation, and they believe that fully implementing these activities would allow art to be accorded a higher place in the school curriculum.

Art Appreciation in the Schools: From Picture Study to Discipline-Based Art Education

The idea that students should study art masterworks and be given instruction in art appreciation is not new. In the mid-nineteenth century, German archaeologist and art historian Johann Winckelmann advised artists to dip their brushes in intellect. At that time in America, a new and distinctly American art was being advocated, one that would be pure, moral, and earnest—an alliance of art, religion, and nature. Educating the child's artistic eye was considered to be an integral part of moral and social education. At the end of that century, the "schoolroom decoration movement" worked to accomplish this by bringing plaster casts of antique sculptures into classrooms. Sepia art reproductions with a patriotic, religious, and moralistic orientation came into the public schools through the "picture study movement." From 1910 to 1920, this movement brought art prints into the schools. These pictures were filled with literary associations on which students could speculate. Works by artists such as Rosa Bonheur, Jean-François Millet, Raphael, and Winslow Homer were deemed to be suitable for young, impressionable minds, and some of these prints, such as E. G. Leutze's *Washington Crossing the Delaware,* still hang in school hallways today.

During the 1920s, formal design elements gained more attention. These were spurred by interest in art movements such as cubism, Roger Fry's writings in aesthetics, and Arthur Wesley Dow's art education writings, which focused on the elements of line, value, and color. During the mid-1950s, four-color printing of large-size art reproductions and 35-mm slides and slide projectors made it possible for masterpieces to be shown in the classroom.

Courtesy of Gwenda Malnati and Eric Hamilton, Athens Montessori School, Athens, GA.

Federal educational legislation also helped. The U.S. Office of Education, through its Arts and Humanities Program, sponsored programs and conferences on how to improve art education. Funds from a booming "Great Society" economy and federal educational enrichment programs (such as the Elementary and Secondary Education Act of 1965) purchased prints and slides for school libraries, social studies classes, art classes, and elementary classrooms. Innovative librarians, teachers, and administrators who sought enrichment sources realized the educational power of such reproductions. Major art museums throughout the nation printed inexpensive reproductions, and the National Gallery of Art in Washington, D.C., made available to the public schools a lending program for art slides, reproductions, filmstrips, and films.

Parallel with the development of printing technology and school enrichment programs was the rapid development in the nation's colleges and universities of the disciplines of art history, art criticism, and aesthetics. Art educators looked at their own discipline and analyzed the elements in its structure. Some argued that art history and criticism were disciplines equally as valid as the actual creation of art. Hence, since the 1950s, national art education conference programs have addressed the question of how to incorporate art history and criticism into school art programs. University-level art texts made the case that art education's primary goal is to help students see art's role in giving meaning to human endeavor and in meeting daily living needs. Aesthetic education's goal was not only to teach students how they can experience the arts for their inherent values and delight but also to contribute to the students' general store of perceptions and concepts. The older term *art appreciation* came to be looked on merely as implying peripheral knowledge. Newer terms, such as *art criticism, aesthetics,* and *aesthetic education,* began to be used more widely (these are explained extensively in the following two chapters).

Foundations took an interest in fostering school programs emphasizing a cognitive approach to art through art criticism, art history, and aesthetics. In 1982, the Getty Center for Education in the Arts was created to investigate the feasibility of having nonspecialist teachers and art teachers, in general classroom settings, teach students skills in the areas of art criticism, art history, and aesthetics side by side with the teaching of art creation. The director of the Getty Center wrote: "If art education is to become a meaningful part of the curriculum, its content must be

Primary-grade students researched and wrote reports on famous artists and delivered their reports in costume. **Top:** *Ersatz Paul Gauguins and Polynesian friend;* **Middle:** *Mary Cassatts, Anna Ancher, and Claude Monet;* **Bottom:** *Leonardos and Michelangelos.*

Talking about pictures can develop thinking about art and life. The painting Road to Eternity is by America's most famous folk artist, Reverend Howard Finster. Why do you think he painted the mountains with sad expressions? Why do you think the artist put pyramids in the background? Is writing all over a picture okay for an artist to do? How can we put the ideas in which we believe into our art?

broadened and its requirements made more rigorous." In 1984, Dwaine Greer gave this movement the label Discipline-Based Art Education (DBAE), by which it has come to be known. Its proponents stressed the need for balance among the four subdisciplines: art history, art criticism, aesthetics, and art production. Although it is not known if these four subdivisions will continue to be the main way that art learning is considered, the curriculum guides of several states have spelled out the content of art in a similar way.

Many art educators from the mid-1960s and after agreed on the importance of these endeavors; however, concern was also voiced regarding if, how, when, and to what degree such activities should supplant or supplement studio activities. Some worried that DBAE could have the effect of suffocating students' artistic creativity, because it emphasizes academic disciplines in which students might have little or no interest without a foundation of experience with art production. Still others objected to the tacit assumption of DBAE that other approaches were fragmented and broken.

Others believed that DBAE did not account for many important functions of art, such as for healing, celebration, social protest, personal transformation, spiritual growth, exploration of the subconscious, and sheer play. In many of the world's non-Western cultures, the arts are connective and integrative and are not readily amenable to DBAE's four-part separation. While DBAE was at first identified with the excellence in education movement, it developed in the midst of another powerful educational reform initiative—multiculturalism. The DBAE movement has been under pressure to incorporate multiculturalism and a global perspective, and it has made efforts to become more interdisciplinary, multiculturally child-centered, and issue-centered. Yet, by its incorporating multiculturalism, some DBAE proponents protest, saying that it has lost its main goal of helping students to understand and appreciate the meaning of works of art. And the debate continues about how to make DBAE more relevant to students' needs.

Art appreciation also is being fostered by the mass media. Television channels specializing in arts, history, and biography show wonderful programs on artists' lives and civilizations' artistic accomplishments. The Web can be used as an enormous resource for students' art research and reports. Yet, for students to benefit from these resources on TV and on the Internet usually requires an adult's enthusiasm and guidance.

Over the past 30 years, this textbook, *Emphasis Art,* has been a strong voice emphasizing the importance of serious, qualitative studio involvement. We believe that studio involvement—thinking and problem-solving in the media themselves—is primary and central. The view of children as innate artists seeking expression, communication, and self-discovery, and having confidence in their own creativity and inventiveness, can be threatened by an overemphasis of academic study.

During the early years of this century, the "father of child art," Franz Cizek, taught that a child understands and enjoys art only to the extent that the child has acquired that understanding through personal efforts. Many art educators today believe that studio art is fundamental to the other disciplines, which are derivative. They believe that studio art production represents the idea of the artist in general education, and that it should precede academic training in disciplines such as art history and criticism.

Thus, there continues to be a healthy professional debate on topics and emphasis in art education. One conception for a sequential approach for aesthetic activities over the years is the following:

• In the early grades, the students should take delight in the aesthetic qualities of objects made by humans and in nature.
• In grades 4 to 6, academic learning moves to the perception of artworks.
• In grades 7 to 9, academic learning should center on the acquisition of knowledge of art history.

Below 10 years of age, production activities should always be central. This should be a time when children have hands-on involvement with the media. Especially during these early years, it is helpful to keep in mind this balance: do not give more to the mind than to the hand. When students are doing perceptual, critical, and historical activities, such activities should be closely related to, and, whenever possible, emerge from, the students' artwork.

General Methods for Art Discussions

The word "conversation" in Latin means change and exchange; "communication" means to share. Unfortunately, too often teachers tend to lecture rather than engage students in a conversational exchange. Your teaching methods will model for students ways to go about talking about art with their friends. These lessons can empower them for their lives, to enable them to feel comfortable going into art galleries and enjoying the artistic experience. The following classroom discussion strategies will be explained in the balance of this chapter:

• Questioning
• Arranging the room for discussions
• Leading discussions
• Focusing discussions
• Keeping discussions concise
• Relating to the students' conceptual stage
• Choosing topics that relate to children's developmental preferences
• Promoting confidence in thinking and talking about art

Questioning

Questioning is a superb way to elicit students' input. Urge students to give reasons for their statements, ask them to disprove alternative explanations, and encourage them to generalize about their ideas. The interpretation of an artwork or thoughts about an aesthetic concept are, and always will be, issues that should be contested. One good way to promote discussion is by asking students "What's wrong with this picture?" This question demands that students put forth their criteria, which then can be debated or contested. Debating and contesting answers are central to the Socratic method of questioning, a method that has been acclaimed for centuries for its ability to give birth to ideas. Of course, avoid questions that get one-word answers, such as "This is an impressionistic painting, isn't it?" Instead, ask open questions, such as "Why do you think this might be an impressionistic painting?" Encourage the students to make inferences, generalize, analyze, and synthesize.

Arranging the Room for Art Discussions

The environment—the climate for viewing the artwork—can help or hinder discussions. If possible, arrange the seating to provide each child with an up-front advantage. To see the reproduction up close, rearrange the chairs into a circle, or seat the children on the floor. Urge the children to come up to the displayed art object and point out the area or detail they wish to discuss. A shy child might be asked to come up front to stand and hold the reproduction. A spotlight on the reproduction can focus students' attention. Avoid reproductions that are too small for class viewing purposes; instead, these can be used for small group discussions.

Leading Discussions

Discussion-leading skill is essential to elicit contributions by many students. Leading discussions can be difficult, especially in large classes and those containing students with behavioral problems. Some will want to monopolize the discussion, interrupting each other and talking over each other. Others will talk so quietly they cannot be heard and, by the softness and slowness of their speech, will invite interruptions. We must keep in check those verbose, verbally domineering students who, by monopolizing a discussion, prevent participation by quiet, shy students. It sometimes is necessary to respond to, or even to interrupt, a monopolizer by saying, "John is saying . . . and we'll discuss this aspect later, but now I'd like to know what some of the people who haven't yet shared their thoughts have been thinking about the idea of . . . (e.g., whether muscles need to be drawn to make a good figure drawing). Through both planned and extemporaneous questioning, you can make art discussions truly exciting and rewarding for every child in your class. Make it a time not just to contemplate, but to interact dynamically with classmates and the art object.

Focusing Discussions

A discussion can go awry if it is not kept clearly focused. Most children enjoy talking avidly about their experiences and reactions. There is no difficulty in getting them to express themselves vocally about the art that you show to them; the main problem is to keep them on the subject, or "on track." If the discussion appears unfocused to the students, too wide-ranging to be helpful to their thinking and acting, they will tune it out. Use your statements to keep the discussion on one central issue. For example, you might say, "Thanks, Juan, for bringing up this idea. It is a related idea, and an important one for us to discuss later, but for now let's see if we can put our minds to thinking about the issue of . . ."

However, be sure to be open to the idea that curricula need not be imposed from above, but can arise spontaneously from the students. Avoid overdetermining the lesson. That students are allowed to take control of some situations builds their autonomy and feelings of empowerment.

Keeping Discussions Concise

Another goal is to keep the discussion concise. Stimulate the raising of issues, but stop the discussion before interest dissipates. Conciseness is important, because so little time is allowed for art in the school schedule. Some students in art classes think of art time as "a time when they get to make things" and resent other activities that seem to be tangential. Keep your art discussions from being long-winded and boring. There are exceptional teachers, however, who can keep large audiences of students vitally engrossed for over an hour analyzing and talking about just one reproduction.

Relating to the Students' Conceptual Stage

In motivating artistic expression, make sure that some of the historical artworks that you present are appropriate for the children's conceptual and developmental stage (see Chapters 7–11). This does not mean that only pictures of scribbles should be shown to scribblers; however, it does mean that artworks in a range that the child is comfortable with should be presented. In this way, you do not frighten the students into feeling inadequate, raising in their minds fears that their artwork will be woefully weak. Students should not feel that the teacher's expectations are unattainable. Using artworks that are visually and conceptually accessible can assist students in seeing alternative and attainable solutions that they can implement.

Artistic activity is a universal human attribute. Nothing in our society more effectively subverts and extinguishes artistic activity than the notion that the artistic product should be a copy of reality or someone else's version of reality. For this reason, often it is best to show historical examples as reinforcement *after* a student has reached a new conceptual and visual stage.

Choosing Topics That Relate to Children's Developmental Preferences

When choosing reproductions and slides for study and appreciation, consider not just their representational ability, but also the natural preferences of the children. Paintings with realistic subject matter to which

Cat and Kittens, ca. 1872 (11¾- × 13¼-inches), anonymous, American. National Gallery of Art, Washington, D.C. Gift of Edgar William and Bernice Chrysler Garbisch.

Consider the children's natural preferences for picture study subjects. "What's wrong with this picture? Why is one kitten mad? In how many places do you see stripes? What does this picture tell us about what life was like over a century ago?"

students can relate usually are more popular with upper elementary children. Subject matter is the primary factor in young children's preferences, and there are strong differences between boys' and girls' preferences. Negative attitudes are expressed toward abstract works and those showing objects they do not like, such as still lifes of dead fish and birds. Young children prefer single subjects; older children can think in terms of more complex groups.

After subject matter, the next most important factor is color. Works that abound in color and contrast are appealing to primary grade children; older children prefer tints and shades and subtle combinations. Middle school students will respond to more complex art themes—to moody, muted colors and abstract, nonobjective compositions. Whereas showing just one or a few pictures is better for elementary students, a variety of examples usually will be more effective for middle school students, because this multiple approach provides an opportunity to analyze contrasting styles and imagery.

Note that purposefully choosing nonpreferred artworks can evoke strong responses, which may lead to heated and stimulating discussions.

Promoting Confidence in Thinking and Talking about Art

Students should not be put on the defensive and made to feel that their verbalizations and artistic representations are incorrect. One goal of discussion is to give those students who have not yet grasped a concept—for example, realism—the "permission" to continue in their own intuitive way of artistic conceiving. ("How would you describe this 'different' quality that Marta's drawing has, and how did her depiction of the sun's personality help give that feeling?")

Art discussions should serve to broaden rather than restrict to a "one right way" system. Discussion should be a bridge between thinking and acting. It should help to promote in the young artist a sense of integration and a feeling of self-worth as an artist. Bounce the discussion back and forth from "what we see" to "how we can make it." In this way, the discussion can reciprocally stimulate both intellectual thought and artistic creativity.

Gamelike Educational Activities

While discussion is the major way to bring about art learning, a second way is through gamelike educational activities. Although research shows games to be no more or less effective than traditional methods, students enjoy educational games as a change from the usual classroom routine.

The game aspect should be easy, and students should first do a practice round. Games may require working together in small groups or pairs—a welcome relief from the usual routine of lecture, discussion, and individual seat-work routines. Students must understand the educational purposes behind the gamelike format, however, lest they feel they are wasting their time or "just playing." Following up with a "debriefing session" discussion is critical in order that students understand the purpose of the game.

Most art games use printed reproductions. A principal source is postcards from art museums and galleries; sorting and matching of these can be done even on a small desktop. Also, the National Art Education Association has published a series of inexpensive art reproductions. Magazine-page–sized reproductions can be found in copies of many popular and art magazines, such as *Artnews* and *Art in America*. Museums and commercial firms specializing in art reproductions have large-size reproductions (approximately 20 × 30 inches) that may be purchased on stiff paper, stiff cardboard, or framed (see Appendix D).

Sets of art postcards can be used to meet art objectives in the following ways:

Art history: Two types of art history objectives are those requiring sorting and those requiring matching. Working in small groups, students sort the cards into chronological order, or match or group those of one art style, such as impressionism.

Art history: Students match art critics' statements from the past to the art images shown on postcards. Some of the critics' statements may seem totally wrong, according to our judgments today.

Aesthetics: Working in small groups, students decide on a single artwork they might theoretically acquire for the school. The underlying instructional objective is that the students will discuss the differences between artistic and societal values in selecting artworks.

Art criticism: Students describe the similarities and differences between artworks depicted and describe overall concepts that cards in a set have in common. Using cards that are sorted into prearranged sets, the learners describe why one of the cards does not belong in the set. This can lead into a discussion of categories, themes, and art elements.

Art criticism: Primary-grade children sort postcards into categories, such as those showing different emotions, those showing realistic or abstract art, those showing past and current times, and so on.

Art criticism: Students hypothesize about the artist's intent. As the students enter the room, the teacher gives each child a card with an artist's name on it. The student then must find the reproduction done by "his" or "her" artist and tell the class "why" the artist painted the picture.

Art criticism: Students identify and describe works by master artists.

Courtesy of Barbara Thomas, Whit Davis School, Athens, GA.

Teacher-prepared educational materials such as "Art Bingo" and discussing solutions in small groups present these upper-elementary-grade students with a change of pace from the usual methods of learning about art.

Commercial sets of art reproductions are available for playing an artistic version of Old Maid; alternatively, sets can be made up by the teacher. The objective in playing is that students learn about an artist's personal

Courtesy of Museum of Primitive Art, New York City, NY.

Courtesy of Frank Wachowiak, Athens, GA; photo by W. Robert Nix, Athens, GA.

Pictures of a mother and child or animal with young can motivate children's creative writing about their family experiences with the birth of a sibling or a pet giving birth.

style. ("Find all the Hokusais, the Romare Beardens, the pre-Columbian pieces, and the Georgia O'Keeffes.") Because such games can be played by students in pairs, they provide an easy change of activity in self-contained classrooms. Likewise, they promote friendships, provide activities for students who have self-directed time, and can be used in classroom learning activity centers.

Further, with the students working in small groups, sets of art postcards can be used for integration with other subjects. In creative writing, for example, groups of students can make up a story using all of the cards in one set. Individual students will tell or write the parts of the story represented in each reproduction. In mathematics, students can describe the geometric shapes shown in the art reproductions—for example, domed architecture, pentagon shapes in Islamic architecture, and sculptures containing icosahedra. (See Chapters 11 and 12 for science and social studies suggestions.)

In both discussions and games, keep in mind the level of the instructional objective. Is mere identification the desired goal? Always try to set some tasks in the upper levels of thinking, such as analysis and evaluation. For example, a higher level of objective—synthesis—can be attained by asking your students "Can you explain in your own words what makes this artist's style special?"

This chapter has overviewed the history and issues of art appreciation, described general strategies for leading art discussions, and listed some gamelike activities that promote talking and learning about art. We proceed in the next two chapters to think about specific ways to teach art history, art criticism, and aesthetics.

Chapter 20

TEACHING ART HISTORY

Conducting Art History Discussions

Art artifacts provide a record of how people of that time acted and what they valued. They define the reality within which the individuals of that period operated. Rather than passing on the "fossilized" processes of cognition, through your teaching emphasize how cognitive knowledge evolves. Ask leading questions to demonstrate how a problem is solved, or initiate the solution and have the student complete it. As discussed here, art history refers not only to the discussion of artworks by masters and ancient civilizations but also to the objects that cultures recognize as having value, such as films, posters, and designed objects. It encompasses art expression by artists of one's own time who live in one's community. The following are some examples of instructional objectives in art history:

- Compare the way you have depicted something—perhaps the design of clothing or a vehicle—with the way that two other artists in history depicted it. Have you used or shown something that did not appear in artworks of past eras?
- Describe works from art history and the humanities with well-known themes. Has the portrayal of the theme changed over time, or has it remained the same? For example, tell about different versions of the Tarzan, Superman, mad scientist, werewolf, vampire, or brute themes. Discuss how women have been shown as Eve or Cinderella, as beautiful and innocent maidens, or as witches. Try to imagine the intensity of feeling and pervasive belief system of a culture that is different from your own.
- Describe how symbolism has been used in art. For example, why was the ruler usually shown seated astride his horse? What ideas does the theme of the dragon express?

- Describe how different artists have given different meanings to the same themes.
- Discuss how ethnic groups, such as Native Americans, for example, have been portrayed in art.
- Describe why you think one artwork style was replaced by a different style. Describe world events that may have contributed to such changes in artistic representation. How does the art of an age say something about its character?
- Describe changing and constant elements in an artist's work, and relate these to changing and constant elements in your own art style.

When children talk about art, they grow not only in vocabulary describing visual phenomena but also in verbal sophistication. Students are weaned from relying solely on their ordinary speech and are helped to form a new art language. Use the vocabulary appropriately. Expand students' vocabulary from their ordinary speech and help them to build a new art vocabulary. New words and phrases such as those in the following list become part of their expanding vocabulary:

Action painting	Dadaism	Mobile
African classical art	Earthworks	Naive art
Art nouveau	Encaustic	Op art
Assemblage	Feminist art movement	Painter's style
Bauhaus	Folk art	Painterly
Caricature	Gallery installation	Patron
Chiarosuro	Genre	Pop art
Critic	Happening	Postmodern art
Critique	Impressionism	
Cubism	Magic realism	

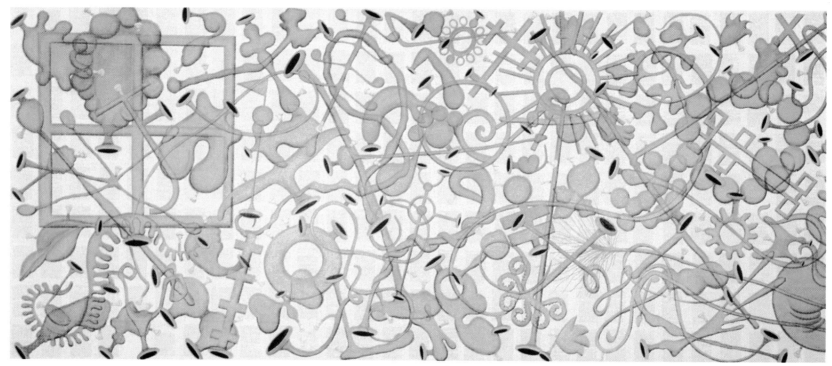

Tim Rollins and K.O.S. (Kids of Survival). Amerika, Land of the Free. A former public school art teacher, Rollins has created a student art workshop in one of New York City's roughest neighborhoods. The collaborative artworks that he and his students create grace major museums throughout the world. A beautiful overall pattern is created by the mysterious abstract forms. They remind one of boxing gloves, trumpets, gears, and windows. What do the forms suggest to you?

Art History Teaching Methods

Perhaps you have just visited a museum or a Web virtual museum; perhaps you just watched a television program about an artist and you want to share with the students your excitement about her work. This is a simple way to make art history material both interesting and relevant—to be interested in the material yourself. Your interest will be infectious. (For Web addresses pertinent to art history, see Chapter 27, on Computer Art.) In addition, teachers have found certain other specific strategies to be useful for adding interest, and we discuss several of these strategies below.

Presentations on an Artist's Life

One teaching method, especially suitable for middle school students who are beginning to look for adult role models, is to have students select an artist to research and role play. The ability to imagine oneself out of the present and into the past or into another culture is an important aspect of understanding art history. Pretending to be the artist, and perhaps dressing up like the artist, the student tells the class the artist's life story. Then, the class questions the actor: What was the artist's personality like? What was the culture like? Where did the artist live? How did people of the time treat the artist? What was the artist's intention in making the art? These presentations can be videotaped and shared with other classes or at a PTO open house. Another teaching approach can be an interview show of a small group of these artist-actors at a supposed exhibition opening or panel discussion. One student acts as the emcee and interviews the participants; other students role-play critics and critique the artists' works.

Quizzes

In a review of art history facts, interest can be spurred through a competitive game. Divide the class into two teams and ask cognitive questions of

Courtesy of Joyce Vroon, Trinity School, Atlanta, GA.

Students took the idea of Grant Wood's American Gothic *of a couple working at their goals, and related it to showing their own interests for their lives. Here Virginia Simms shows a young couple pursuing their goals: sailing, surfing, sunning, beach volleyball, and Frisbee throwing.*

Courtesy of Joyce Vroon, Trinity School, Atlanta, GA.

An attractive display, along with three-dimensional objects suggestive of Native-American culture, is made of students' paintings seeking to emulate the empathy with which George Catlin captured the Native-Americans in their raiment.

each team, for example, the name of the artist, the style of the artwork, or the century in which it was created. The team that gets the answer correct first then has its captain put an X or an O on a large tic-tac-toe game board drawn on the chalkboard.

Correlating Art History and Studio Projects

Art making and criticism, art history, and aesthetics are most successful and most meaningful when they complement each other in an orchestrated, coordinated endeavor. Children's intense, purposeful studio involvement should be related to richly planned art motivations that include art history examples. In this way, their critical faculties in both appreciating and creating art are mutually enhanced.

Teachers have added to children's insights regarding African and Native-American art motifs through studio projects in mask-making. Others have coordinated the study of Egyptian tomb friezes with the making of group murals. Every phase of world art through the centuries can be given immediacy in an art studio environment, from the mosaics of Ravenna in Italy, to the Tang ceramics of China, the illuminated manuscripts of medieval Europe, the Benin bronzes from Africa, the marble sculptures from Greece, the ukiyo-e woodblock prints of Japan, or the wood sculptures of Louise Nevelson. Many teachers have imaginatively combined studio and art history to provide children with a growing treasury of knowledge about art, artists, art styles, and the permeating influence of art in our everyday lives.

It is best if the teacher has access to color reproductions, filmstrips, and color slides. If this is not possible, most public libraries have folio-size "coffee table" art books that contain pictures large enough to show to groups. Sets of large reproductions can be ordered through the school librarian for use by the entire faculty. Some commercial sources of art visual aids are listed in Appendix D; resourceful teachers have collected and organized their own extensive picture and color-slide files. The following table lists some familiar art-education studio projects, along with the names of a few artists whose works might serve as exemplars.

Suggested Art Project	Correlative Art Appreciation
Drawing-painting/ Helping at home or school	Genre paintings of Benny Andrews, Thomas Hart Benton, Jean Chardin, Carmen Lomas Garza, Winslow Homer, Jacob Lawrence, Grandma Moses, Horace Pippin, Norman Rockwell, Lily Martin Spencer, Susanne Valadon, Jan Vermeer, Laura Wheeler Waring, Grant Wood, and Andrew Wyeth.

Matisse display and related fourth-grade marker drawings that incorporated Matisse's lessons.

Suggested Art Project	Correlative Art Appreciation
Portraits and self-portraits	Portraits by Luis Cruz Azaceta, Mary Cassatt, Chuck Close, Domenico Ghirlandaio, Hans Holbein, Leon Golub, Amos Ferguson, Lois Mailou Jones, Margo Machida, Alice Neel, Nick Quijan, Sepik River/New Guinea shaman masks, John Valadez, Elizabeth Vigee-Lebrun, Leonardo da Vinci, Andy Warhol, Hale Woodruff, and Andrew Wyeth. Self-portraits by Max Beckman, Paul Gauguin, Frida Kahlo, Rembrandt van Rijn, Masani Teraoka, and Vincent van Gogh
Objects on a table, chair, or bench	Still lifes by Georges Braque, Bernard Buffet, Paul Cézanne, Jean Chardin, Janet Fish, Audrey Flack, Juan Gris, William Harnett, Margaret Angelica Peale, Pablo Picasso, and Odilon Redon

Suggested Art Project	Correlative Art Appreciation
The landscape or cityscape	Pieter Breughel, Roger Brown, Paul Cézanne, John Constable, Raoul Dufy, Robert Duncanson, Richard Estes, Paul Gauguin, Vincent van Gogh, Edward Hopper, George Inness, Dong Kingman, Kerry James Marshall, Gabrielle Münter, John Marin, Georgia O'Keeffe, Mattie Lou O'Kelley, Maurice Utrillo, and Grant Wood
Fauna	John James Audubon, Bambara Chiwara antelope figures, Rosa Bonheur, Cave paintings at Lascaux and Altamira, Chinese and Japanese animal drawings, Albrecht Dürer, Jean Louis Gericault, Franz Marc, Indian Moghul, Rembrandt van Rijn, Henri Rousseau, and Nellie Mae Rowe
Flora	Rudy Fernandez, Roberto Juarez, Patricia Gonzales, Maria Sibylle Merian, Lowell Nesbit, Georgia O'Keeffe, and Leonardo da Vinci

A study of Georgia O'Keeffe's floral paintings with their dramatic value patterns and abstraction was central to the students' making these cut tissue paper floral close-ups in many tints and shades.

Suggested Art Project	Correlative Art Appreciation
Figure composition	Benny Andrews, Paula Modersohn-Becker, George Bellows, Rolando Briseño, Pieter Brueghel, Mary Cassatt, Robert Colescott, Edgar Degas, Paul Gauguin, Francisco Goya, Gronk, Robert Gwathmey, Keith Haring, Joseph Hirsch, Clementine Hunter, Angelica Kauffman, Käthe Kollwitz, Marie Laurencin, Jacob Lawrence, Henri Matisse, Edvard Munch, Alice Neal, Juane Quick-to See-Smith, Bill Taylor, John Valadez, Diego Velasquez, and Elizabeth Vigee-Lebrun
The abstract, the nonobjective, the surreal, op, pop, and fantasy	Joseph Albers, Hieronymous Bosch, Marc Chagall, Georgio de Chirico, Salvador Dali, Sonia Terk-Delaunay, Arthur G. Dove, M. C. Escher, Minnie Evans, Helen Frankenthaler, Paul Jenkins, Frieda Kahlo, Wassily Kandinsky, George Longfish, Rene Magritte, Joan Miró, Piet Mondrian, Georgia O'Keeffe, Jackson Pollock, Martin Ramirez, Ad Reinhart, Bridget Riley, Tim Rollins and Kids of Survival, Mark Rothko, Frank Stella, Sophie Taueber-Arp, Mark Tobey, and Victor Vasarely
Printmaking: collograph, plastic meat-tray print, linoleum block, glue-line-relief print, monoprint	Albrecht Dürer, Leonard Baskin, William Blake, Mauricio Lasansky, Robert Colescott, William Hayter, Gabor Peterdi, Japanese ukiyo-e artists, Ando Hiroshige, Katsushika Hokusai, Rembrandt van Rijn, and Kitagawa Utamaro
Mask design and construction	African ritual masks; masks of Northern Pacific Indians; masks from Melanesia, Malaysia, Mexico, Indonesia; Japanese Noh play and Bugaku masks; Chinese opera, Greek drama, and Mardi Gras masks
Photographs	Ansel Adams, Tomie Arai, Margaret Bourke-White, Matthew Brady, David Hockney, Dorothea Lange, Sherry Levine, Yong Soon Min, Eadweard Muybridge, Gordon Parks, Adrian Piper, Cindy Sherman, Sandy Skoglund, and Edward Weston
Three-dimensional construction, earthworks, and use of found materials	Alice Aycock, Joseph Beuys, Lee Bontecou, Beverly Buchanan, Alexander Calder, Christo Bessie Harvey, David Hammons, Nancy Holt, Louise Nevelson, Judy Pfaff, Pablo Picasso, David Smith, and Robert Smithson

Cast bronze plaque, 1550–1650 A.D., Kingdom of Benin, Nigeria. The University Museum, University of Pennsylvania. Photo Malcolm Varon, NYC © 1989, Malcolm Varon.

The artistic power of this African chief sculpture is magnified by the surrounding figures and their objects. Seen are his two lieutenants, his secretary, assistant with the spiral cone, his children, and the maces, shields, clothing, and headdresses of authority. Further power and richness are produced by symmetry and repetition. Patterns of dots, zigzags, circles, and interlocked forms add beauty.

Suggested Art Project	Correlative Art Appreciation
Abstract sculpture in plastic block, soapstone, firebrick, balsa wood	Jean Arp, Constantin Brancusi, Easter Island sculpture, Greek Cycladic figures, Judy Chicago, Nancy Graves, Barbara Hepwrth, Henry Moore, Juan Bautista Moroles, Isamu Noguchi, Northern Pacific Indian totem poles, and Martin Puryear
Figurative sculpture	Magdalena Abakanowicz, John Ahearn, Ferdnand Botero, Doug Hyde, Iraqi Abu Temple sculptures, Luis Jimenez, Edward Kienholz,

Suggested Art Project	Correlative Art Appreciation	Suggested Art Project	Correlative Art Appreciation
Figurative sculpture (continued)	"King Mycerinus and Queen Chamernebty," Marisol Escobar, Michael Naranjo, Polykleitos, Alison Saar, George Segal, Rigoberto Torres, Manuel Neri, and "Winged Victory of Samothrace"	Clay pots and containers	Korean Koryo period, ancient Greek vases and jars, Chinese Ming, Pueblo and pre-Columbia pottery, Japanese Jomon ceramics, Thai Sukothai period, Lydia Buzio, Peter Voulkos, and Shoji Hamada
Collage and text	Luis Cruz Azaceta, Jean-Michel Basquiat, Georges Braque, Romare Bearden, Epoxy Art Group, Richard Hamilton, Edgar Heap-of-Birds, Jenny Holzer, Mary Kelly, Barbara Kruger, Henri Matisse, Catalina Parra, Howardena Pindell, Richard Prince, Robert Raushenberg, Kurt Schwitters, and Alexis Smith	Clay figure modeling	Clay figures of Greek Tanagra style; Japanese Haniwa period; Chinese Tang period; Hohokan pottery of Arizona; Mexican, Peruvian, and Guatemalan pre-Columbian ceramic sculpture

Chapter 21

TEACHING ART CRITICISM AND AESTHETICS

Conducting Art Criticism Discussions

In addition to art history and art appreciation, as discussed previously, two other ways of building students' artistic awareness are discussions of art criticism and aesthetics. In art criticism, a major goal is the students' ability to point to evidence in the work to support their interpretations. During the primary grades, encourage the children to ask questions about visual phenomena, to list special eye-catching items in the picture, and to decide what they like. Likewise, have students in the upper grades discuss criteria for judgment (realism and accepted methods for representation) and determine categories of works. Have them hypothesize about how else a picture might have been made or what alternate messages it might have conveyed. Finally, encourage them to bring out questions about social significance.

A highly condensed summary of the sequence of children's development from grades 1 to 8 is:

Personal preference → Realism → Expressive aspects

While visits to art galleries and museums are ideal, it often is more practical to bring art to the students. If possible, use original art; if not, use colorful reproductions, color slides, and book illustrations.

The purpose of art criticism in elementary and middle schools is to develop the students' appreciation and understanding. This purpose should not be confused with art criticism as it might occur in a college studio-art course, however, where the professor's objective is to judge and improve the students' artwork. Students also should learn to distinguish between portrayal criticism and persuasive criticism. Portrayal criticism, such as in the following sequential plan, helps the viewer to slow down and see what the work includes. It suggests that there is no one "right way" to see an artwork. In contrast, persuasive criticism (like some newspaper reviews) is judgmental and argues the worth of the work.

Three different approaches to art criticism and aesthetics used in schools are art elements, themes, and cultures. An example of an art element approach is the way in which various artists use color. An example of a theme approach is artworks showing food gathering in different times and cultures. An example of a cultural approach is the art of the Inuits. The African, Asian, and Native American cultures have values about making and responding to art that do not readily fit into Western academic disciplines and the European tradition. Try to redress the neglect that non-Western cultures have received. The teacher's willingness to help students look at their own and each other's culture is very important; some of the artworks shown should relate to the community and cultural background of the class. Local artists and craftspeople can be invited to visit classes, demonstrate skills, and discuss what it is like to be an artist.

An Approach to Art Criticism

Particularly important in art criticism is that students search for answers in a scholarly way, through inquiry. Students can use this skill for a lifetime, in all kinds of inquiry. Both the teacher and students may not know precise answers. Even if the teacher knows little about a work—who made it, its medium, or when or where it was made—learning can occur as long as an attitude of inquiry prevails. When the students and teacher apply their minds, as if in solving a mystery, successful learning will occur. Any strategy will work as long as the student is motivated to persist long enough to get beneath the surface. Use the format that seems most compatible, following your inner directive. Let the students engage in activities that increase

Cirque, plate II, *Jazz*, 1947 (color stencil in gouache), Henri Matisse, (1864–1954). National Gallery of Art, Washington, D.C. Gift of Mr. and Mrs. Andrew S. Keck.

Wheelchair-bound for the last 13 years of his life, the French artist Henri Matisse was unable to paint and was prepared for his death. Instead, he returned to making paper cutouts, a technique he had used decades earlier for stage decorations, and created some of the world's most life-affirming artwork. What do you see in this picture? How did the artist arrange colors and shapes to make a beautiful design?

receptiveness, using, for example, initial impressions, fantasy role-playing, and copying poses to increase openness (see Psychomotor Activities in Chapter 14).

Art criticism usually occurs in an open, free-form manner. However, four questions can serve as points of reference for an open discussion: What is it, What does it mean, What is its value, and What does it do?

Courtesy of Beverly Mallon, Chase Street Elementary School, Athens, GA.

Emulating the style of a famous artist is one way to teach an appreciation of that artist's achievement. Following a study of Matisse's "Swimmers," fourth-grade students drew their figures on the white, non-sticky backside of self-adhesive letter scraps donated by a sign company. They then pulled off the paper backing and adhered the figures to their collages. Three periods.

Saturday Classes. Frank Wachowiak, Athens, GA. Bicentennial High School. Courtesy of Mary E. Swanson, Nashua, NH.

Having studied Matisse's cutouts, students can use cutouts in collage to gain an awareness of the power of positive and negative shape. Figures drawn in contour line and cutout depict a street fight at night. The abstractness of the collage medium makes it an excellent choice for such an emotional theme.

In contrast to a holistic, open, and less structured study, an artwork's features may be explored in a more or less sequential way. One sequence is listed below.

1. Identifying the content or subject matter of the art — What things do you see in this picture?

2. Recognizing the technique or art medium — What art materials did the artist use and how were they used?

3. Identifying the compositional or design factors in the art and recognizing their importance — How did the artist tie the picture together?

4. Recognizing the unique, individual style of the artist — Why do we think this other picture might be made by the same artist?

5. Searching for the meaning of the art and thinking about the artist's intent — What does the picture seem to be saying?

6. Learning about the context — What do you think might have been going on in the world at this time? Does it show up in any way in the picture?

We will explain these six approaches in more detail in the paragraphs that follow.

Identifying the content or subject matter of the art. Often this approach comes first and sets the stage for understanding a work of art. What does the viewer see: a woman, child, dog, house, tree, vase of flowers? What event is being depicted: a wedding, riot, sports event, fair, family reunion, rite of passage? Enthusiastic student participation usually develops when the subject matter is real or recognizable. Employing meticulous observation, the student is required to look beneath the surface to discover details. Try to complete a careful inventory of what is perceived before going on to interpretation.

While looking at a large art reproduction or projected slide, each student (either in the class as a whole or working in small groups) can take a turn naming something he or she sees in the artwork that no one else has brought up. In this exercise in perception and memory, the students should describe what they see as extensively as they can. The teacher can list on the chalkboard what students have seen.

A game to promote effective description is to have one student facing the class describe an art reproduction that is turned away from the class so that the rest of the class cannot see it. Students are instructed to close their eyes and imagine what the art looks like while the student who is "it" describes the artwork as thoroughly as possible. Then, the artwork is turned toward the class and the amazed students, who have envisioned

Espana, 1959 (color intaglio), Mauricio Lasansky (32 × 19). Collection of Frank Wachowiak, Athens, GA.

something completely different, can see it. A variation of this exercise is to use well-known artworks; when students in the class think they know which picture it is, they raise their hands.

Recognizing the technique or art medium. This approach to art criticism can give insight into how something is represented. Actual studio involvement by children with the media, techniques, and artist's materials helps them to appreciate the artist's solutions.

Identifying the compositional or design factors in the art and recognizing their importance. This approach is one of the most enlightening. Detect the basic line structure, the main thrust, the avenues into the composition, and the dominant and subordinant themes. Find the rhythms, balances, and contrasts of line, shape, value, color, pattern, and texture, and pinpoint those that unify the picture. Developing these skills can make for a fascinating game of search and discovery.

Recognizing the unique, individual style of the artist. This approach to art criticism is another intriguing and rewarding one. When students, guided by a knowledgeable and imaginative teacher, achieve the critical and perceptual skills to identify the artists' individual styles, they are on their way to a richer understanding and enjoyment of art's world of treasures.

Searching for the meaning of the art and thinking about the artist's intent. This approach is at the heart of art criticism. A teacher can easily influence and/or convince the students with his or her own judgments and prejudices about an artwork's meaning. Yet, if students merely parrot the teacher's views of art, they may not be able to relate the artwork to their own lives. Thus, avoid telling the students what you see in the art and what you feel about it until they have had a chance to tell you what they see and feel. Children will spontaneously put forth their explanations of the artwork's meaning. While you may not agree with their analysis and judgment, do not force your opinions on them. The meaning that a student finds may not be the artist's intent, but that does not invalidate the student's interpretive process. Provoke curiosity by pointing up a problem or conflict. "If that is the interpretation, then why do you suppose that this other thing is shown in this seemingly conflicting way?" Using a leading question such as this forces the child to defend and rethink his or her theories.

A good way to begin thinking about a picture is to have students first describe what they see in it. Seated on a tiny white-faced horse is a large human figure, hands anxiously cupped together, eyes open very wide, and lips tightly drawn. It wears an unusual white costume. Also seen is an adjacent figure, probably a woman, in a skirt and with a scarf on her head, with head in hands and perhaps weeping. At their feet is a 1-year-old baby, with two upraised hands, lying on the ground.

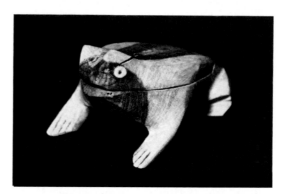

Discussing how the art medium is used is one way of understanding art. Students can compare how the theme of an animal is carried out in a variety of subtractive sculpture media. Clockwise, from top right, are a wood-pod monkey from Malaya; a cryptomeria rooster from Japan; an ivory elephant from India; a boxwood bird from Indonesia; a wood elephant from Africa; an ivory horse from China; and, in the center, a wooden frog from Mexico. Discuss how the carver achieved form. Did the medium present limitations, perhaps in the grain? How much detail is desirable or possible? Describe the main form from which the piece was carved ("like a barrel, like a rectangle with extra ears attached"). Discuss how shapes are repeated and varied to present a unified and charming representation. Also, consider its context—where it was made, and what that animal might mean in that society.

As in the inductive method of science, let the students come up with hypotheses based upon the evidence they have assembled. Hypothesizing requires a high tolerance for ambiguity. It depends upon curiosity and the ability to draw inferences. It requires both the courage to think independently and the ability to think metaphorically and hypothetically. Interpretations are not so much right as more or less reasonable, informative, inclusive, and coherent. Older students can conjecture about the metaphoric meanings in objects and how these meanings add to the artwork's interpretation. Rather than staying strictly within the confines of description, analysis, and then interpretation, you can mix these steps in with interpretive analysis.

Good interpretations tell more about the artwork than about the viewer. Although we must use our feelings as guides, we must realize that the feelings depicted in the artwork are most likely different from our own. We must be receptive to our personal feelings, yet willing to cast them aside to "hear" what the artwork is saying.

Allow the artists, craftspeople, and architects to speak for themselves through their art and their journals. For example, in a critique of the work of Vincent van Gogh, introduce the letters the artist wrote to his brother Theo. Help the students to gain a deeper understanding of how van Gogh's painting related to his creative highs and his frustrating, disappointing lows. Artworks—not the artist's life situation—are the object of interpretation. However, such biographical information can provide insight into the work by revealing the sociocultural milieu out of which the artwork developed. The general classroom teacher, who is charged with teaching interpretive writing, creative writing, and expressive writing, is in an even better position than the art specialist to have students write about artworks using metaphoric, expressive writing. What could be a better subject for such correlative writing than the most interesting visual objects on earth—artworks?

Learning about the context. This approach is an essential step in understanding an artwork. In examining the historical and social context of an artwork, students transfer learning from one discipline to another, from social studies to art. What was the artwork's function? What cultural concerns did it address? Was it made to signify status, territory, or kinship, to protect from natural disaster, to promote commerce, health, healing, or religion? What belief systems and economic forces were dominant in the world at that time? What was the social, religious, and economic nature of the artist's personal world? Students should learn that their perceptions and values, formed in their own culture, will likely differ from those held by people of other civilizations. The teacher can supply significant information, or, at this point, students might use materials either in an art-learning center, in the library, or—if older students—on the Web.

A new emphasis on cultural relevance and an openness to many different interpretations have come about in recent years, in part through developments in feminist art criticism and postmodern contemporary theories of art. This is in contrast to the past, when most art in the schools was presented in an apolitical manner. Conflict was minimized, and often historical-cultural value systems were ignored. Through today's art criticism, which emphasizes social-critical consciousness, students learn to deal rationally and fair-mindedly with conflicting points of view. They learn to support their opinions using facts, details, and information. Criticizing artworks requires the ability to identify problems, to examine and appreciate multiple perspectives, to take risks, and to develop the inner motivation to want to understand.

Two Perspectives on Art Criticism: Formalism and Contextualism

Two differing perspectives on art and art criticism are whether art should primarily be about art, or whether it should be about society. The first perspective leans more toward studio activities; the second focuses more on an intellectual understanding of meaning. These perspectives are referred to by the labels formalism and contextualism. Formalists emphasize the elements and principles, the manipulation of materials, handsome well-crafted objects, and originality. Individual creativity leads to idiosyncratic works that people have a hard time understanding. To Formalists, art *is* its form—how it looks, the materials it comprises, and the skills used to make it. In short, a formalist believes that art criticism should focus on the art itself.

Contextualists, in contrast, believe that art is a social communication system. An artwork's meaning is determined in the context in which it is made. A more extreme contextualist position, called instrumentalism, believes that art never is for its own sake; instead, the artwork should bring to mind some external purpose—some thought or action beyond itself. An even more confrontational instrumentalist view is that the action called for should *change* the existing social system. The contextual point of view downplays technical skills in favor of constructing and interpreting meaning and developing analytic aptitude. Because it demands signs and symbols that are plainly understood, contextualism deemphasizes idiosyncratic, personal self-expression.

The perspectives of formalism and contextualism are helpful to keep in mind when you teach in the art classroom, whether your focus is criticism, history, aesthetics, or art production. You can reach more students when you bring out both perspectives. On its own, neither a purely formalist aesthetic approach, with its emphasis on elements, principles, and media exploration, nor a contextualist approach, with its emphasis on a socially relevant subject matter, is adequate for a comprehensive art program. The two are not mutually exclusive concepts. Although at a given point an individual artist may emphasize one or the other perspective in his or her work, most art can be considered from both perspectives over time. Also, some art forms lend themselves to one or the other perspective—for example, the design of Persian rugs versus political posters. Fifty years ago, when abstract art was in its heyday, art in America emphasized formalism; however, today, in a society concerned with multiculturalism, the elements and principles of formalism may not be as relevant in discussing many forms of contemporary contextual art, such as conceptual art, feminist art, cooperative art, site art, and performance art.

Conducting Discussions of Aesthetics

Discussing aesthetics is the third way of learning about art in the four-part Discipline-Based Art Education model (The other three ways, you will recall, are art history, art criticism, and studio art learning.)

As teachers, we want our students to think about what makes objects and phenomena artistic; this is what constitutes aesthetics. Children love to ask "why" questions, and the questions "Why?" and "How do you know that?" are central to aesthetics. The most important teaching strategy in leading discussions of aesthetics is to encourage students to question. Likewise, essential to success is the ability to admit that there are things that we do not know. Most importantly, teachers of art must believe that students can gain something through being encouraged to examine and question art ideas. Thomas Ewens (1990) said:

> Wonder is something which comes upon us, overwhelms us and suggests a kind of transcendence, out of the ordinary, the wonder-full, the extra-ordinary. It is a combination of the intellectual, the emotional, and the sensuous. It is the not-taken-for-granted. Our task is to protect the wonder of the young. The disciplines of thinking and artmaking grow out of and are nourished by this soil. Their roots are in wonder.

Some "wonder-ful" educational goals that many teachers want their students to achieve for developing thinking ability are synonymous with the goals of aesthetics, such as the ability to do the following:

• Speculate
• See implications
• Handle abstract ideas
• Use language for clear thinking (about art)
• Raise questions and make statements (about aesthetics)

• Present reasons supporting their positions and thus justify their judgments
• Listen to others' points of view and ask questions about the other students' ideas

Aesthetics is not just about knowledge, however. It also is about feelings. Some objectives concerned with feelings, or affect, are that the students will be able to tolerate uncertainty, value questioning, be curious, and respect thoughtful disagreement.

Because aesthetics is so much a part of ordinary conversation, it can easily go unnoticed. Listen for students' questions and comments such as "Why is that weird thing supposed to be art?" and "Ugh, gross." Naturally occurring instances of art criticism need to be encouraged so that they can be transformed into significant discussions of aesthetics. On hearing students ask such questions and make such responses, we must learn to bite our tongues. We must not immediately answer, "Because the paint is so wonderfully thick, because it shows deep emotion, because it's in the museum." Instead, respond to the students' queries with your own questions. Let your interest in their comments guide the students to think more deeply.

For example, respond to students by asking them, "What makes you say that?" "Does everyone agree?" Model for the students the use of strategies in good reasoning. Help them to learn how to think logically about their statements: "If what you say is true, then how can [cave art] be explained?" Likewise, counterargument can be effective: "Is this *always* the case? Can anyone think of an instance in which this isn't true?" Keep in mind that the teacher's role is not to indoctrinate students with one "right" view or to inundate students with information. This would defeat the purpose of aesthetic inquiry and its concern with contested issues. Our challenge is to promote critical thinking.

Aesthetics and art criticism tend to blend, but a helpful distinction to keep in mind is that aesthetics focuses on the ideas behind the artwork and not on the artwork itself (which is the subject of art criticism). To start aesthetic discussions and to use as a reference, however, it is useful to have some art reproductions hung around the room or displayed over the chalkboard. Ask if any picture in particular has raised questions in a student's mind. The most obvious beginning is the open question, "What do you think about this picture?" Another good way to begin a discussion of aesthetics is by asking, "What's wrong with this picture?" because this presumes disputed ideas about right and wrong. Still another way of generating discussion is for students to select shocking or ugly art—anything out of the ordinary—and then to defend their selections. Have them examine boundary-breaking art, nonart, ugly art. Encourage students to defend a piece as art or non-art.

Topics and questions such as those in the following table can be brought up matter-of-factly to stimulate or extend classroom discussion.

Wonder comes into one's mind contemplating the tornado-tossed trees against a starry night. Also, what could be the meaning of the red hands against a sun? This painting is by New York neo-Expressionist painter Louisa Chase.

Photo courtesy of Deborah Lackey, Atlanta, GA.

Some questions in aesthetics can be "How important is originality to a work of art? Is it OK to copy somebody else's artwork? Is it valuable?"

Topic	Aesthetic Question
Accident in design	Can a picture that looks like the artist just threw paint around be called good art?
Advertising art	Should art be used to make people want to buy things they do not really need?
Anatomical accuracy	Is art better when figures depict muscles rather than sausage-looking arms? Are cave paintings with stick figures good art?

Private Collection.

Questions can be raised as to whether, in showing the figure, correct proportions and shading should be used to depict muscles. The direct expression of the African-American folk artist Mose Tolliver is shown here. His painting Black Jesus (20- × 12-inches) defies certain "expected" artistic conventions. Is realism always better? Is a balance between naiveté and realism desirable?

Topic	Aesthetic Question
Art's role in life	Is art work or play?
Artist's intention	If someone gets a different idea or meaning than you intended from your picture, does that mean your art is not as good? Is it better if the person knows exactly what you wanted to say?
Artist's involvement	Can art be made simply by calling up a factory and saying "make a red metal cube for me that is 6 feet square"? Must the artist have hands–on involvement in making it?
Art critics	If experts say something is good or bad, must we accept their evaluation as our own?
Art institutions	Does putting something into a museum make it art? If an artwork is not in a museum, does that mean it is not art?
Art support by government	Should our government give money for art that some people think is bad?
Clarity and metaphor	When you see an artwork and you cannot put into words exactly what the artist was saying, does that make the artwork better or worse?
Commercial design	Can objects such as bicycles, T-shirts, or fancy dress gowns be called art?
Disabilities	If a person is color-blind, uses colors nonrealistically, and makes a good piece of art, can it still be called art?
Economic validity	Because someone spends a lot of money for a piece of art, is it good art? If no one chooses to buy a given piece of art, is it still art?
Education	Are artists born or made? Does art that looks as though little children made it mean that it is not good art? Do people with many years of education usually make better art than people with less education?
Function	What good is art, after all? If art is used for bad purposes, is it still good art?
Gender	Why aren't there more famous women artists? Why are women usually represented as helpers?
Human art	Can monkeys make art?
Human endeavor	Why do people bother to make art when they could just relax and enjoy life instead of working hard to make something that most people probably will not like much anyway?
Individual authorship	Is it really art if several people make it instead of just one person?
Judgment	Does an artwork mean whatever anyone says it means, or are there absolute right and wrong answers?

Photo courtesy of Frank Wachowiak.

Discussions of aesthetics might concern whether the medium that is used should look like itself or whether it should look like things. Can beauty in painting be created by using tools other than paint brushes? Is beauty always desired? What is beauty? If realism is not most important, what is? Here, James Herbert, a professor of painting at the University of Georgia, employs rubberglove-encased hands to apply paint to his mural-sized canvas.

Topic	Aesthetic Question
Mental and emotional functioning	Can people who have mental or emotional problems make good art even if it shows an upset world? Do people have to be misfits in society to make art that has a special, weird quality?
Quality and intent	Can you name some things that are bad art? What is the difference between things that are bad art and things that are not supposed to be art at all?

Topic	Aesthetic Question
Realism	Can a piece of art still be called good art even if the objects in it are not drawn as they look in three dimensions?
Realistic depiction of nature	Can a picture be good if the sky does not touch the ground?
Scale	Are buildings or pictures that are big usually better art than those that are little?
Source and object	Are real rainbows art? Are wasps' nests art?
Spontaneity	Are pictures that took a long time to make usually better than pictures that were done quickly?
Technology	Can art made with machines be called art? If a camera or computer makes a work, can that work be called art?

Topic	Aesthetic Question
Text	Can art be just some words on a piece of paper, a canvas, or a light-emitting screen? Why or why not?
Time and effort	Can cluttered, carelessly made stuff that looks as though someone arranged a bunch of junk be called art?
Ugliness	Is art supposed to be only about beauty? Can it also be about ugliness?

Remember that discussions of aesthetics can use students' everyday language— special terminology is not needed. It is the discussion itself that is central to the curriculum in the exemplary art classroom.

Students might sort art reproductions into chronological order or match those of similar cultures and describe similarities and differences among them. **Left:** *Ashura, Buddhist deity, eighth century, dry lacquer, Kofukuji Temple, Nara, Japan.* **Right:** *The Calfbearer, ca. 560 BC, Greek, stone.*

Art Criticism at Home

Parents may be at a loss concerning how to respond to their child's artwork when he or she brings it home. Unfortunately, some parents feel compelled to criticize their child's art: "You're just like me—can't even draw a straight line." A brief letter to parents sent home with the first artworks of the year can suggest ways for talking with their child about his or her works. It can describe what will be taught in art history, art criticism, and aesthetics. Indeed, this is a good way to connect the student's art production and art criticism abilities. Suggest ways to display the works to build the child's confidence. Suggest ways that the child's art and his or her opinions about aesthetic issues can serve as a vehicle for generating family dinner-table discussions. Let the parents know what your art-program goals are so they can help to build their child's interest in art. The following is a sample letter:

Dear Parents and Guardians:

This letter is being sent home, along with one of your child's first art pieces done this year, to tell you something about our art program and to help you in talking with your child about his or her art learning.

This year we will be discussing what makes a good artwork. We will emphasize filling up the picture's space and capturing details. We will talk about whether looking real is the only thing that makes a picture good, and how friends and neighbors make art. In October, we will study mask-making in many cultures. In January, we will be studying art history masterpieces, especially Egyptian art.

One way you can help to foster your child's interest in art is to talk with the child about his or her art, artworks and sculptures you see in the community, and interesting things you find in nature. Post your child's art on the refrigerator door, refer to it from time to time, and remark on it when guests come. Another way to cultivate interest is by visiting museums and helping your child to participate in enrichment classes. Weekend art museum hours at the Quinlan Art Center (548–2314) are Saturdays, 9 A.M.– 3 P.M., and Sundays, 1 P.M.– 5 P.M.; Family Art Days are held on four Saturdays each year. In addition, the recreation department at Lyndon House Art Center (546–9968) offers children's art classes on weekdays, 3:30 P.M. to 5:00 P.M.

Research has shown that it is helpful for children to have a place for art materials at home and a quiet place in which to make art. Collections, artwork, and posters artistically arranged in a child's bedroom stimulate interest in art. Likewise, involving children in adults' artistic and cultural hobbies spurs their interest (the inconvenience will prove to be time well spent)

During the course of the year, we will be sending home with your child about six additional art projects that he or she has completed, including a still life, a group of figures in motion, a portrait of a classmate, an oil pastel of a farm scene, a computer art design, and a clay castle.

If you want to talk with me about your child's growth in art, or if you have access to human resources, art materials, or display facilities that could be used in our school art program, please call me at 546-9987 between 2:00 P.M. and 4:00 P.M. or at home at 543–7654. I hope that I will meet you soon at a PTO meeting (the last Wednesday of each month, 7:00 to 8:00 P.M.), where you will have the chance to see more of our students' artwork.

PART 6

TEACHING ART PRODUCTION

Photo A: Iowa City Elementary Laboratory School. Courtesy of Frank Wachowiak and David Hodge; ***Photo B–L:*** Saturday Children's Classes. Courtesy of Frank Wachowiak, Athens, GA, and Mary Sayer, Hammond, Athens, GA.

Chapter 22

DRAWING

Mounting evidence, exemplified and corroborated by contemporary child-art creations such as those illustrated in this book, suggests that we have been underestimating children's capabilities. In many instances, we have not even begun to tap their true potential for "thinking" and "problem solving" through art media. The ensuing pages describe a host of art projects and techniques in both two and three dimensions that are recommended for a qualitative art program in elementary and middle schools.

These chapters should be most helpful to those classroom teachers who themselves may be untaught in the basic art disciplines of drawing, painting, printmaking, collage, and sculpture. The lessons described also will help art specialists who are searching for new dimensions and challenges in school art programming. Both the projects and their documentation resulted from many years of in-depth teaching by dedicated and knowledgeable instructors of both elementary and middle school art. This has entailed continuing motivational experimentation, media exploration, process and product evaluation, and research in qualitative art practices in schools around the world.

The art program should be planned at all levels for in-depth involvement and sequential growth. Although an in-depth method may not be as popular as a smorgasbord of quick, unrelated projects in the long run it will produce greater gains as students come up with their own ideas and create art of the highest quality.

The following descriptions of art projects address motivational possibilities, clarify complex art techniques, offer solutions for organizational and supply problems, and suggest evaluation criteria. In no instance is the implication intended, nor is the reader to assume, that the projects and processes described are the only possible choices. The best lessons, of course, are those that come from the teacher's heart and soul. Informed by the needs of the class, in combination with recommended art education practices, the teacher's deep commitment results in the best lessons. However, the projects described in the following chapters have been found to be highly successful in situations typical of today's elementary and middle schools—in classrooms filled with eager, bright, boisterous, fidgety, dreamy, energetic, inquisitive, and sometimes apathetic students.

Three Kinds of Drawing

Elementary school children should draw every day. Drawing has been an important subject in American schools since 1870, when Massachusetts' first art superintendent, Walter Smith, led the state legislature to pass "An Act Relating to Free Instruction in Drawing; That the first section of Chapter 38 of the General Statutes be amended so as to include Drawing among the branches of learning which are by said section required to be taught in the public schools."

A drawing curriculum should address not just one way of drawing but all three families of the world of visual art objects: depictions, patterns and designs, and maps and diagrams. This chapter will mainly address the first family, that is, realistic depictions that usually are thought of as "children's art"—the creation of drawings and paintings from nature and life.

The second family—patterns and design—consists of creative play with shapes and spacing. This usually is thought of as design rather than drawing. Design receives more emphasis in later sections of this book, in discussions of architecture, mosaics, printmaking, clay, and sculpture. Designing patterns, however, also is important in making drawings and paintings. The doodles that one makes on a scratch pad while talking on the telephone represent this kind of play with shapes and spacing. A design

1 and 2, by Samantha Libman, 3 and 4 by Adam Levy, 5 and 6 by Staci Gruen, 7 by Jon Birnberg, and 8 by Elizabeth Siegel. Courtesy of Baiba Kuntz, Glencoe, IL.

One design approach using shapes is this wonderful block printing lesson for 7th- and 8th-graders. Students plan their blocks with two opposite corners being B and D, and the other two opposite corners as A and C. The block can then repeatedly be printed side-by-side and turned to make different arrangements, as these two alternative printing arrangements of the designs show.

approach using shapes, lines, and blocks was central in the Froebel kindergarten method, which influenced Frank Lloyd Wright's architecture so profoundly. It also was central in the teaching at a famous German design school, the Bauhaus. Because design is based on intuitive balance and measure, it lends itself well to correlational activities with mathematics, architecture, and engineering.

Maps and diagrams—visual representations of what one knows rather than what one sees—comprise the third family in the world of visual objects. Conception, not perception, is the focus. Communicating an idea through a map or diagram is not governed by the constraints of realism, however; maps and diagrams are means to promote visual literacy, ways to envision how something is or is to be built. During the Industrial

Courtesy of Gwenda Malnati, Athens Montessori School, Athens, GA.

A second kind of drawing (or design) is play with patterns. Here, primary student Dalton Tyler used a variety of colors and kinds of patterned lines. The teacher had talked about the patterning in Australian aboriginal art.

Encourage both ways of representation: what is conceived in the mind and how it appears. This beautifully detailed drawing of a tree was created by a second-grade youngster from Saga Prefecture, Japan.

Revolution, drawing was seen as an important way to represent and communicate technical understandings and inventions.

School assignments can be to map daily life events, how a pumpkin grows, how one's insides function, or where the food we eat comes from. A child can make a map of his or her neighborhood or show the cycle of evaporation and rain. Mapping helps students to conceptualize relationships in their minds. ("Using the international travel signs and symbols, show how you get home from school.") Students use graphic equivalents to represent objects and functions, and mapping lends itself to correlation with science. This type of "visual thinking" is embodied in such conceptual artworks as Alice Aycock's piece on cloud dispersion and Maria Merz's artwork based on Fibonacci series. Some other drawing activities that promote flexible visual thinking are drawing something from a nonhuman point of view, such as an ant's-eye or a bird's-eye view.

When preschool-age children draw their families, those drawings are like maps in that they draw what they know, not what they see. Similar visual representations of knowledge are found in works by folk artists as well as naive artists, who do not feel so constrained by demands for realism. Unfortunately, this kind of drawing is too often discouraged by some teachers who establish perceptual realism as a standard for artistic excellence. One example of a young child's "thought representation" that did not meet a teacher's criteria for perceptual realism occurred when the sculptor Henry Moore was in primary school. He felt crushed when his teacher criticized him for drawing feet pointing downward rather than realistically pointing sideways. The solution is not that teachers should be laissez-faire, but instead that they foster both ways of representation—perceptual and conceptual. This is especially important for teachers of young children. In a class, some children will draw what they know, others will draw what they see, and most will use a combination.

Concerning gender differences, research supports what can be seen by casual observation: the stereotypical tendency for boys to prefer drawing monsters, dinosaurs, vehicles, spaceships, and more supernatural and violent scenes, and for girls to tend to prefer drawing people and animals, landscapes, kings and queens, and domestic scenes of everyday experiences. A teaching implication of these different preferences is to frame topics so that the subject matter will interest both genders.

Figure Drawing

Which skills and techniques in figure drawing should be introduced and developed in elementary and middle school art programs? What should teachers say to their students regarding delineation of the figure? When, if ever, should the relative proportions of the human figure be identified and

Courtesy of David Hodge, Oshkosh, WI.

A middle school life drawing class in action. Notice that tables were arranged to make a unified drawing area where the model can be viewed easily by all the students. Paper size for sketching was 18 × 24 inches. Tools for drawing included sharpened dowel sticks and twigs dipped in India ink containers. If several drawings are planned, the model, as well as the position of the model, should be changed so that students are afforded a variety of views.

emphasized? The strategy most often proposed, unfortunately, is a laissez-faire placebo of "Leave the children alone. They will find their own solutions." This injunction admittedly provides the teacher with a face-saving excuse if results are less than satisfactory; however, it is hardly the kind of advice given by teachers of math, reading, and language. Through lack of guidance, students fail to meet their potential in drawing and painting the human figure. Instant art and gimmicky shortcuts, such as cutting and pasting photographs, keep students from developing the basic skills of creative self-expression.

If teachers want students to grow in their representation of the human figure, they must provide learning experiences and practice sessions for such growth. Direct the students' attention to details. Extend the child's frame of reference with statements such as, "Show us how your face looked when you were in the dentist's chair." Children want to be able to draw well. Students of all ages feel that the level of realistic representation is the most important criterion in determining the quality of each other's artworks.

Fortunately, there are some avenues a teacher can pursue to help children develop confidence in life drawing. Teachers can ensure a more intense awareness of the human figure and its characteristics by using posed models at every grade. The delineation of the figure in even the youngest child's drawings does not spring forth from a vacuum. It results from the varied encounters the learner has had in perceiving and conceptualizing the human figure, both in and out of school, through books, comics, television, and peers' art. Sadly, the drawings of most nonartistic and artistically untaught adults are no better than those of preadolescents: They draw a large head, ill-defined facial features, and a segmented body. Hands and feet often are not visible, and the picture shows an overall lack of organization. Given such results, too many students graduate from school with a sense of inferiority about how they draw. By offering instruction and guidance, however, teachers can help them to acquire or maintain confidence in their drawing ability.

Before the students actually begin drawing, a warm-up session is recommended. The teacher should propose motivating, leading questions: What action is the model performing? What is the model wearing? What portion of the model do you see from your drawing station? How large is the model's head in comparison with her body? How big are his hands? Ask each student to place one hand over his or her own face to realize its size. Likewise, how large are the model's feet? They must be

A motorcycle was brought to the middle school art room to make the drawing more true to life. After the making of a careful line drawing, vibrant colors of oil pastel were skillfully employed to enhance the composition.

Courtesy of Mary Sayer Hammond, Athens, GA.

Courtesy of Suzy McNiel, Iowa City, IA.

How marvelously observed are the details, such as eyelets, wristbands, folds in clothing, and cheekbones. See how the pattern changes in the falling socks. A first-grade child did this! Have high expectations and your students will rise to meet those expectations.

long enough and wide enough to keep the model balanced. At what point is the model's arm biggest—at the shoulders, elbows, or wrists? Where is the model's leg biggest—at the ankle, knee, or hips? At what places do the body, neck, leg, and arm bend? How far apart can the feet be from one another? How high can the arms reach above the model's head? How far can the torso of his body turn if his feet are planted in one position? How far down does the model's arm reach when she holds her arm at her side?

As the students draw, encourage them to look at the model constantly, carefully, and intently. Tell them to fill their eyes with the image. Caution them to avoid rushing through their drawing by scribbling or making hasty, random, meaningless lines. Remind them always to look first and then draw. Also, encourage them to make the figure large—to fill the page with it. In general, it is helpful for children to begin their drawing of a figure with the head at the top of the page.

In drawing figures, the size of the head generally determines the size of the figure. If students draw the figure's head too small, the body will not fill the page; however, if they draw the head too large, they will not be able to fit the whole body on the page. Children in the primary grades often draw a three-heads-high figure, like the *Peanuts* cartoon character Charlie Brown, and minimize the rest of the body to fit it on the page. Others will draw tiny heads and stretch the legs to reach the bottom of the page. In either case, the teacher should not discourage the results because the drawings capture the child's development at a moment of special charm.

Because many teachers believe they lack the expertise to guide children in drawing figures, they settle for what the students can accomplish on their own. Students need instruction, but the wrong kind of direction will not be helpful. Indeed, applying formulas such as stick or sausage figures and face proportions measured by rulers can create a stultifying dependence on stereotypes. The best instruction emphasizes heightened observation. Adult artists pay careful attention to contours and how planes are implied. While you teach your class, you can point out these features to your students. As children learn to draw, they first use outlines that do not suggest form. These are followed by strong interior contour lines that overlap each other. Later, there is some implying of form through planes, and still later, children begin to join interior lines with outlines. In upper grades, teach contour-line drawing by discussing how the line of an interior edge becomes visible and then joins the exterior silhouette. As it rounds the form, it becomes hidden. In the upper grades, talk about planes—the plane of the front of the body, the plane of the head, or the plane of a box. Show how the plane is revealed by its edges. By using this approach, you will be pleased at how well some of your students can suggest planes in space.

The contour-line technique is perhaps the most viable and successful drawing method for upper-elementary and middle-school children. Suggest that students draw slowly and deliberately with a soft-lead pencil. Urge them to look intently at the object they are drawing. This figure is by a middle school student.

Urge your students to heed their use of line by asking questions such as the following:

Are the lines varied from thick to thin to create interesting linear movement and subtle space-in-depth?

Is the line on opposite sides of a shape or object (body, tree, vase, fruit, and so on) drawn more heavily on one side and lighter on the other to create tension and space?

Do the lines drawn complete a shape instead of floating in space?

Figure drawing, like all drawing from life, teaches students to observe at many levels. Those who are perceptually aware very quickly will notice and draw the rich embellishing details, such as belts, ribbons, shoelaces, buttons, necklaces, earrings, bracelets, wristwatches, pockets, collars, cuffs, wrinkles, zippers, pleats, eyeglasses, teeth braces, hair combs, and clothing patterns such as stripes, checks, florals, and plaids.

In addition to drawing live models, students may draw from photos or other artworks. Here the translating from three- to two-dimensions has already occurred. The positive effect of encouraging children to do such drawing manifested itself in the career of the Norwegian expressionist artist Edvard Munch. He and his brother grew up in a family that advocated drawing as an activity. As a child, he drew elflike characters and animals in a variety of settings, such as castles and street scenes. Combining sequential images and text, he transformed one character into another and depicted stories with complex plots filled with humor, delight, and pleasure. His childhood drawings presaged the narrative impulse later seen in his adult work.

Still another approach to figure drawing does not use a model but instead relies on the representational devices of comics and TV cartoons. Some young people's interest in drawing is triggered by comic-book-illustration techniques: scenes in a series, thought balloons, speed lines, star-and-lightning-bolt symbols of violence, and strongly contrasting effects of light on muscles.

When children draw their classmates, be prepared for the occasional self-conscious titter or embarrassed laughter. Emphasize that we are all learning to see. Provide examples such as Jean Dubuffet's *art brut* drawings to show that realism is not the sole criterion of art. Be understanding when a student does not want to model for the class (perhaps because of embarrassment about appearance or clothing), because there always are other volunteers.

Students, especially in the upper grades, can later use their linear figure drawings in a painting, collage, print, or mural. The line drawings themselves, however, often have a validity, presence, and charm of their own. Subject-matter themes such as playing ball, riding a bike, flying a kite, brushing teeth, holding a pet, playing a musical instrument, holding

Rich visual stimulation is extremely important for students to create quality artwork. Many teachers build an ever changing still-life environment in their classrooms as a challenging and continuing motivational resource. Here, a young adolescent is attired in goggles, snowflake-patterned sweater, striped pants, and high boots while modeling against intriguing antique Americana artifacts.

Top: *In the center of the room, a standing girl and seated boy pose on a table. The table contains objects to break up space.* **Bottom:** *With stiff boards to back the drawing paper, peers draw each other in small groups.*

Courtesy of Baiba Kuntz, Glencoe, IL.

Self-portraits or portraits of classmates are wonderful subjects for expressive drawings. These drawings of classmates by eighth-graders show virtuosic handling in **Left:**. *the hair and blouse by Jennifer Buntman,* **Middle:** *the superb patterning of the shirt by Ashley Milne,* **Right:** *varied weights of blouse lines by Kasey Passen.*

a bouquet, cheerleading, skipping rope, ballet dancing, playing football or basketball or tennis, swinging on the swing, setting the table, twirling a Hula Hoop, and lifting barbells lend themselves to space-filling compositions. Some other figure-drawing strategies include the following:

- Pose a student in a colorful costume (clown, cowboy, dancer) or sports uniform on a table or a countertop so that everyone has a clear view. Or, pose the model in the center of a circle of sketching classmates, affording each child a different view. For an overlapping, multifigure composition, change both the action and the direction of the model in later poses.
- Introduce new drawing and sketching tools. Try free-flowing felt-tip markers, small watercolor brushes, Q-tips, eyedroppers, turkey feathers, twigs, and balsa woodsticks sharpened at one end as ink applicators, as well as charcoal and conté crayon.

- Pose the student model against a background sheet of cardboard, plywood, or Masonite approximately 4 × 8 feet—at minimum, slightly larger than the model. Use of a background will help the students to relate the posed figure to the boundaries of their paper. For additional interest, decorate the board with drapery, fishnet, or colorful posters.
- Consider having the model wear an ethnic costume and displaying ethnic patterned cloths in the background, thus opening up opportunities for social-studies integration.
- Demonstrate new techniques and directions for drawing the figure: contour, gesture, scribble, and mass methods. Following Henri Matisse's example in his famous paper cutouts, have students cut the figure from construction paper without making a preliminary drawing.
- Use a pose involving more than one student. The figures might be socially interacting, such as one handing something to the other or

*Left: Fifth-grader Alison Carey did her self-portrait in her winter coat holding her two cats and sitting on the front steps of her house. A classmate modeled for the legs. **Middle:** Fifth-grader Lauren Conway did her self-portrait with parakeet and brought in recalled imagery of* her horse stable. **Right:** Sixth grader Mark Sward used his balcony for a background. Note the details shown in the porch railing.

helping another to put on a coat. Stage the models in a related still-life and background.

• Challenge the students to use their imaginations. Let the action or stance of the model trigger a fantastic or legendary figure whom they can capture in line. Fill in the background with ideas from the imagination and remembered experiences.

• Assign different class members to take 5- or 10-minute turns posing in various sports actions. Urge the students to overlap the figures as they draw them.

• Vary the paper size and dimensions. Try a 9- × 18-inch or a 12- × 24-inch sheet for a standing figure, or use a long, wide sheet for a group of figures. Challenge students to fill the page.

• If your room has sufficient space, have the students use 24- × 36-inch paper with wide felt-nib markers, giant chunk crayons, or big brushes.

• Introduce a variety of papers: plain newsprint, cream or gray manila, recycled papers, assorted-color construction paper, computer-printout pages, and newspaper classified-ad pages. Newspapers may donate the ends of newspaper rolls, which are useful for large drawings.

• Older students might benefit from using resources such as a real skeleton, department-store mannequin, or life-size medical chart of the body's muscle structure.

• For action or gesture drawing that requires a looser, free approach, students should hold the crayon, pen, pencil, charcoal, or chalk horizontally as they sketch, rather than in the tight, upright manner used in writing.

• Inexpensive, lightweight drawing boards are excellent for field trips. Construct the boards using heavyweight chipboard, hardboard, or Masonite, cut to about 18 × 24 inches, with the edges protected with masking tape. During the drawing sessions, students can prop these boards against a table or desk, thus affording them a better working position from which to capture details.

- Upper elementary and middle school students can be encouraged to keep sketchbooks as a way to visually organize their perceptions of the world.

Portrait and Self-Portrait Drawings

The self-portrait or portrait of a classmate should be a part of every school art program curriculum. What more effective and immediate subjects are there for expressive drawings in all grades than the children themselves? Children of all ages like to draw the figure. While only a few 6-year-olds can draw reasonably correct proportions, the number increases to over half for 14-year-olds. A small number of 12-year-olds can draw true to appearance, as well.

If possible, discourage students from doing the typical portrait stereotype: the symmetrical frontal pose with arms hanging stiffly at the side. Instead, create contrasting directions of the arms and hands in unusual positions. Add interest and relevance with uniforms, costumes, a variety of headware, and assorted objects to hold. Encourage three-quarter or full-profile views. Some suggested poses include the following:

- Folding arms above the figure's head or positioning them akimbo
- Straddling a chair with the figure's chin resting on folded arms on top of the chair back
- Holding a musical instrument, sports equipment, a open umbrella, a bouquet of flowers, or a pet
- Putting on a hat, combing or brushing hair, applying make-up, or gazing into a hand mirror

The background adds immeasurably to the composition—a foliage arrangement, a multipaned window, a giant travel poster, a folding screen. Encourage students to add background elements that they remember or imagine, representing their interests or animals they love, for example.

Hasty, superficial observation usually results in stereotyped portraiture. Urge students to look intently at the model, whether it be their own image in a mirror or classmate posing, and to pay close attention to the individual's unique characteristics. To encourage self-acceptance in self-portraiture, show portraits of famous women and men, and discuss their widely dissimilar, far-from-perfect features and the different shapes of their heads. Call attention to the hairline, and how the hair follows the contour of the head. No thoughtless scribbles for hair should be allowed! Discuss the shape of the ears (tell them to feel their own ears) and their junction to the head. Discuss ways of delineating the nose, and show

drawings by Pablo Picasso and Ben Shahn. Use a rich motivation of color slides or reproductions depicting different portraiture styles from a variety of times and cultures. Show how to draw the lips as two subtly differing forms and the eyelids' structure as complementary features to the eyes. Bring out the astonishing fact that no two faces—or even two sides of the same person's face—are alike.

In upper elementary and middle school, *blind contour drawing* is a good way for students to capture the spirit of the subject rather than to strive for absolute realism. In blind contour drawing, a students looks intently at the subject—but not at his or her paper—as the student draws. If students become concerned that their drawings do not look like the posed model, tell them that the aim of expressive portraiture is not to achieve a photographic likeness. Remind them that the same model drawn by various artists will look different in each rendition.

Drawing the Landscape or Cityscape

Although very young children in the primary grades enjoy drawing simple themes and single objects, such as a butterfly, a bird, a pet, themselves, a classmate, or a house, maturing students will respond to the challenge of complex composition: the still life, the landscape, and the cityscape. In the upper elementary grades and middle school, they are interested in outdoor sketching and the excitement of field trips. The busy and infinitely varied world beckons and unfolds at their doorsteps. These students are fascinated by the following:

- Nearby building construction
- The colorful and crowded street of shops
- The county fair or park bandstand
- The boat marina or harbor with its ships
- The highway interchange
- The factories and foundries
- The bus, train, and airport terminals
- The challenging perspective down an alleyway
- The giant city skyscrapers
- The cluster of farm buildings on a country road
- The community's elaborate architecture
- The view from a bedroom or classroom window

These sites, as well as imagined cities of the future, can be the inspiration for sketches, compositions, paintings, prints, and collages. A variety of media can be used for field-trip sketching, including pencil, chalk (school chalk is recommended for sketches and preliminary drawings on colored construction paper backgrounds), charcoal, crayon, felt-nib or nylon-tip

The most important and architecturally distinguished building in town makes a good subject. It is valuable for the study of both drawing and architecture, as in this Colombian 13-year-old's drawing.

Because going on field trips can pose difficulties, the teacher may need to locate sketching sites from a school window or on the school grounds.

marker, conté crayon, and even a stick dipped in ink (depending on the maturity of the students).

Most children on a field trip draw with enthusiasm and confidence; however, some who are perplexed will besiege the teacher with questions: What should I draw first? Where should I start on the paper? Must I put everything in my picture? The complex view may overwhelm them, and the spatial and perspective problems often confuse them. Remind the students that they will be creating an entirely new aesthetic unity out of the vast conglomeration of visual stimuli. One recommendation for successful landscape and cityscape drawing is to use a light pencil or chalk sketch to

A motorcycle parked in the school lot will pique the imagination of students and afford lots of details to draw.

Brush, ink, and watercolors on white drawing paper, actual size. Grade 9, Dubuque, IA.

How sensitively observed, drawn, and delineated is this complex neighborhood scene viewed from a school window. Notice how the free-form preliminary washes tie the composition together and how the overlapping trees create a subtle depth in space. Notice, too, the variety employed in the lines, shapes, and positions of the buildings, windows, and roofs. Observe how the houses and trees terminating at the paper's edge create avenues leading the viewer into the composition.

establish the basic shapes and general outline. Values and details can be added later.

Another strategy—and one that is especially recommended for the complex view—is to have the students begin by drawing the shape in the center of the site (a doorway, window, telephone pole, tree) as completely as they can. Then have them proceed to draw the shape to the right and left of it, above and below it, and so on, until they fill their paper to the border. They will discover that incomplete shapes touching the paper's edge will create line avenues leading into their compositions. Encourage them to enrich their drawings with details, patterns, and textural effects.

Problems that students have defining distance in space often can be clarified by an understanding and use of the following guidelines. Objects or shapes in the foreground plane (those closer to the observer) usually are drawn larger, lower on the page, and in more detail. Objects farther away from the viewer (in the background plane) usually are drawn smaller, higher on the page, and with less observable detail. Effective space is created subtly by overlapping shapes and elements in the composition, such as a fence, tree, or telephone pole against a building.

Simple perspective principles based on employing the horizon line, vanishing points, and converging lines should be introduced when the students indicate a need for them. Some seventh- and eight-grade students will want to take up this challenge. Simple exercises in perspective may appeal to them, but remind them that mastery of perspective rules does not ensure that they will achieve compositional success.

The Sketching Field Trip

Sketching field trips should be undertaken only with adequate preparation by both the teacher and students. The teacher should scout out exciting subject matter beforehand. Avoid the barren view or monotonous vista that provides little opportunity for a varied breakup of compositional space. Note that permission to be away from school must be cleared with the principal's office and, when necessary, signed permission slips must be obtained from parents. Arrangements for using the school bus should be made well in advance.

A class discussion with visuals before the field trip should emphasize specific challenges. Tell the students to look for the architecturally significant character of the buildings, to see the value contrasts of windows in daylight, the foreground space allowed for steps and porches, and the receding of roads, sidewalks, and fences. Bring in aesthetic concepts. ("Will we see and depict nature as it is dominated and controlled by humans, or nature gaining control?")

On the day of the field trip, review rules of behavior and caution students to respect private property in the sketching vicinity. Directions for proceeding to and returning from the sketching site should be made clear, especially if it is within walking distance of the school. Keep the class in a line or group, bringing up stragglers when necessary. If roads are to be

Drawing landscapes or cityscapes directly at the site is recommended for upper elementary and middle school children. Sometimes, however, conditions make it inadvisable. The center and bottom illustrations show what can be accomplished when youngsters draw from a sequence of projected color slides. First, slides of towers, steeples, and chimneys were drawn high on the page. Then, storefront facades and signs were projected for the middle plane. Finally, street furniture, lamps, telephone poles, hydrants, traffic lights and signs, parked cars, motorcycles, and trucks were projected to complete the foreground.

Courtesy of Frank Wachowiak, Athens, GA.

crossed, stop signs that the teacher or monitors can hold up to warn and halt traffic are recommended.

In most instances, supplies for drawing should be distributed to the students before they leave the classroom. In some cases, however, the teacher may prefer to carry the drawing tools to the site and carry them back at the end of the field trip. If students walk to the site, they can be asked to carry their own drawing boards, however. When bus transportation is used, class monitors can bring the materials, drawing tools, sketchboards, extra paper, and thumbtacks to distribute at the site. Upon arrival at the sketching site, discourage students from sitting too closely together. Many a field trip can end up as a time-wasting social hour.

Remind the students that they may use the artist's prerogatives of changing, adding, deleting, or simplifying what they see as they draw. Explain that the criterion is not necessarily photographic reality or rigidly measured perspective. Students may add more trees, fences, telephone poles, fire escapes, air vents, chimneys, or windows. They may change a roof line or the cast of a shadow. They may delete a parked car or a trash dumpster. In the sky, they may add helicopters, birds, clouds, and fantasy creations. Each decision they make, however, should embody the dynamic rules of art: variety, unity, balance, emphasis, contrast, and repetition.

The most important responsibility of the teacher at the sketching site is to guide the students in a self-evaluation of their drawings, employing the perennial principles of composition and design. In the final analysis, if all the teachers have done is to bring the students to see something they have not really seen before, to notice something they have never noticed until that moment—a molding or cornice on a door or window frame, the shadow of a tree against a wall, the overlapping of shingles, the variety in tree bark, or the texture of a brick wall—then they have succeeded in enriching the lives of their students a thousandfold. In bringing a student to observe such details, the teacher may have started them on an exciting quest for shapes, patterns, textures, and color—an endless journey of visual discovery.

Drawing the Still Life

Whether as inspiration for drawing, painting, print, or collage, the still-life arrangement fosters an appreciation of commonly observed, everyday

Top: Courtesy of Frank Wachowiak, Athens, GA. *Middle:* Photo courtesy of W. Robert Nix, Athens, GA. *Bottom:* Courtesy of Joyce Vroon, Trinity School, Atlanta, GA.

Do you know someone who would be willing to lend your classes collectibles or antique objects? Perhaps the florist will donate flowers past their selling peak time.

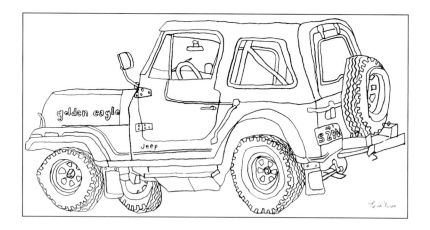

Top: Courtesy of Michael F. O'Brien, American Military Dependents School, Seoul, Korea.
Bottom: Courtesy of David Hodge, Oshkosh, WI.

Still-life arrangements need not be limited to the usual floral arrangements; they are all around us. Consider the bicycles, Jeeps, campers, and minivans parked behind the school. Consider the open car trunk, tool shed, cupboard, or closet. How about the piled-up desk, cluttered kitchen sink, box of playground equipment, and table set for dinner?

Courtesy of Joyce Vroon, Trinity School, Atlanta, GA.

Dolls, fancy chairs, musical instruments, and lunch boxes make good still life material.
Bottom: *Elizabeth Thackston, Fourth Grade.*

objects. It encourages keen observation and sensitivity to shapes, contours, and overlapping. Beginning in the third grade, children can be guided to see the limitless design possibilities in still-life compositions. When acquiring objects for still lifes, scavenge at secondhand stores, flea markets, attics, basements, and garage sales. Especially seek objects for their ability to tap into individuals' thinking and personal experiences.

Avoid the trite, such as miniature figurines or bud vases. Popular items are ballroom gowns, costumes borrowed from theater programs, athletic and military uniforms, as well as apparatus from army surplus stores. Objects from outdoor life and camping, as well as targets from archery ranges also will interest some students. Large art reproductions, posters from athletic wear stores and automobile dealerships, and unused billboard sheets make interesting backgrounds. Plant life can trigger nature discussions about why plant leaves have developed in shape and texture in the way that they have.

The placement of the various objects is critical to the success of the still-life composition or design. Have the students participate in the arranging process. Make construction of the still life a motivating, adventurous part of the lesson. For example, arrange the objects on an antique table, old sewing machine, rocker, stepladder, window ledge, desk top, or table in the middle of the room so that as they draw, students can be seated in a circle around the still life. Employ a variety of heights and levels (use cardboard cartons and plastic or wooden crates or storage units as supports). Create space by placing some objects behind others. Work for an informal rather than a formal balance in the arrangement. Use assorted fabrics, colorful beach towels, flags, banners, fishnets, bedspreads, quilts, or tablecloths to unify the separate elements and create visual movement. In most cases, the more objects that are used in the still-life group, the more opportunities students will have for selection and rejection. Indeed, the more objects the students include in their compositions, the more likely they are to achieve design success.

There are several ways to begin drawing a still life. Unless for class management reasons students must stay in assigned seats, encourage them to move around the still life and examine the objects. In this way, they can discover what to draw and from what vantage point, and they can make their own plans on how to go about doing the drawing. One successful strategy is to have students begin by drawing in the middle of their paper the central object in the still life, as seen from their individual point of view. They continue by drawing the objects next to it, left and right, above and below, until they have either filled the page or completed the still-life arrangement. Thus, the more varied and abundant the still life is, the more the students' compositions will fill the space.

Another tactic when drawing a still life is to have students select items from a general store of still-life material, choosing one object at a time to sketch at their desks or tables. They will build their compositions gradually, employing the principles of variety in size and shape of objects, overlapping, repetition, avenues into the composition, and informal balance. Talk with the children about how shapes are described by their edges and how an object's interior lines and outlines join together.

Visually appealing desserts might be donated by a caterer, for a lesson tied to Wayne Thibaud's dessert still-life paintings. Notice how third-grade students Sarah Nix and Ginny Gay used overlapping in the compositions. Also note the tables arranged around the still life, and the egg boxes and trays used for mixing the many tints and shades of tempera paint.

Courtesy of Joyce Vroon, Trinity School, Atlanta, GA.

Some teachers suggest that students they make a light, tentative sketch in pencil, charcoal, or chalk to indicate the general, overall arrangement. This preliminary drawing then is developed stage by stage, employing value (light and dark) and texture effects, pattern, shading, detail, and linear emphasis.

Drawing Animals

Most children respond enthusiastically to drawing pets and other animals. Students in the upper elementary and middle school often are especially interested in drawing horses. However, if the drawing of animals is to become a significant experience for the students, whenever possible have them observe live animals at zoos, aquariums, natural history museums, pet shops, farms, parks, and animal shelters. Likewise, pets brought to class provide a stimulating and immediate source of drawing inspiration.

Skill in drawing realistic animals develops slowly. Nearly all first-graders draw "just an animal"; by sixth grade, a third of students still do so. "Horselike" animals are drawn by 20 percent of second-graders and perhaps 50 percent of sixth-graders. Even by seventh grade, only 5 percent of students are able to make drawings that can be classified as "true to appearance."

Before an animal-drawing field trip, let the students look at celebrated animal drawings. Include Rembrandt van Rijn's lion and elephant;

Drawing of rabbits by a first-grade child, Japan.

Rosa Bonheur's horses and those by Chinese Han- and Sung-period artists; Albrecht Dürer's hare, squirrel, and rhinoceros; and Andrew Wyeth's birds. Discuss the animals' special characteristics: the textural pattern of the rhino's skin; the repeated yet ever varied spots of the leopard, the rhythmic rings of the armadillo's protective shell, the beautiful op-art variations of the zebra's stripes, the gracefully curved horns of the antelope, and the wrinkled and leathery face of the orangutan.

Discuss the animals' sociological and cultural significance, such as sacred tigers and cows, imperial dogs, and royal lions, symbolically representing the strength of the emperor. Encourage the students to think of similarities between people and animals in resting, eating, running, bathing, grooming, and caring for their young. As the educator John Dewey wrote, "The roots of art and beauty are in the basic vital functions, the biological commonplaces man shares with birds and beasts" (Dewey, 1934).

To stimulate kinesthetic awareness, students can dramatically reenact the animal's poses and actions using their own bodies. Older students can be challenged to capture the animal's peculiar stance, the swinging rhythm of the chimpanzee, the arching stretch of the giraffe, or the sway of the elephant's trunk.

Careful observation and sensitive variation of line are required in drawing animals. As the students draw, remind them to fill the page. The larger the drawing, the more opportunities the child will have to define special details, patterns, and textures. Pencils, sticks cut to a point and dipped in ink, and felt-nib or nylon-tipped pens are good for small sketches. Charcoal, conté crayon, chalk, crayon, oil pastel, Q-tips, eyedroppers filled with ink, and large-size blunt or square-tipped ink markers can be used for large works.

Limit the drawing activity to a single animal developed in depth rather than cursory attempts to draw several animals. Students also might be encouraged to draw detailed studies of an animal's eye, ear, snout, or horns. Because textural nuances can be added later, when the students return to class, on-the-site drawings might be limited to capturing significant form, that is, it might be a sketch showing the animal's spirit rather than an attempt to make a completed, detailed study.

When sketching a live animal is not possible or practical, color slides, films, filmstrips, and opaque projections of illustrations can provide supplemental motivation. In the primary grades, the visual material might be discussed and then posted for reference on the bulletin board. Photos and slides fulfill a definite need, but they should serve as an inspirational and informational reference only and should not be traced or rigidly copied.

Remind the students to consider the entire composition. In too many instances, the animal is isolated in the middle of the paper, floating in space without a hint of complementary foreground or background atmosphere. Encourage students to add compositional elements such as trees, shrubs, grasses, rocks, bushes, vines, hills, cliffs, clouds, and companion animals in

African-American folk artist Nellie Mae Rowe's family plowed many hours with a mule. She brought this knowledge to her rich colored-pencil drawing. In the background, imaginative patterns of checkerboards and circular, floral, and overlapping scallop designs create a thrilling feast for the eyes.

the foreground or background. Follow the example of Henri Rousseau, who used his own houseplants as models to create his jungles. Use plants, dried foliage, roots, rocks, and twigs from the immediate school vicinity drawn giant size to become ledges, mountains, and jungle trees for the animals' imagined habitats. Found materials such as these can serve to provide students with continuing opportunities to become aware of nature as an endless source of design inspiration.

Left: The animal world has always interested child artists. **Top:** *Rembrandt's use of wrinkle lines in the elephant's baggy skin indicate form and can give children ideas for their drawings.* **Middle:** *This first-grade student has drawn his elephant large to fill the space, and is now completing the filling in of the background.* **Bottom:** *A sixth-grade Iowa City youngster used oil pastel for this ant-eating aardvark at a natural history museum.*

Drawing Media, Especially Markers

Drawings can be strong and beautiful in just the drawn form, with no additional color added. Markers and bold, dark pencil drawings have produced many fine drawings in this book, such as those on pages 13, 83, 87, 139, and 143. However, in elementary school art programs, markers often are used for pictures that are subsequently to be colored. Alternately, another popular way to draw pictures that are ultimately to be colored is to use yellow chalk on white paper, white chalk on colored paper, or pencil. (Pastels and dark or black chalk are not popular since they can be messy for young children to use.)

Using white or light colored chalk for the initial sketching allows mistakes to be ignored, and allows lines to be readily redrawn with no permanent effect showing in the finished artwork. Bold marker lines are drawn over the lightly sketched chalk lines. Chalk's tentative quality makes it especially suited for drawing complex subjects, such as gardens.

Alternatively, on colored construction paper, rather than immediately covering the chalk lines with marker lines, students can do a preliminary sketch in chalk in other ways with other subsequent media. Watercolor, oil pastels, or tempera paint are frequently used to fill in the big, empty areas between the light chalk lines, *but the white chalk line is left showing.* The basis for this idea in color theory is that colors often look cleanest and brightest when separated from one another by a neutral or white or black line. This principle is shown in stained glass windows with their black lead lines between colors; since no colors touch, there is little problem of colors clashing.

A preliminary sketch in chalk also is used for "resist" techniques. For this technique, a gutter, or line, of plain paper on each side of the lightly sketched chalk line is left bare. This empty line or gutter should be from $1/16$ inch to $1/4$ inch in width. The subsequent oil pastel or tempera paint goes up to but does not touch the gutter. Thus, when a later overall application of black tempera or ink is used, the black paint or ink is absorbed by the blank paper but resisted by the greasy oil pastel or the heavy tempera paint. (Subsequent sections explain these techniques in greater detail.)

The drawn line can show in the finished product. Or it can be a preliminary step, to be gone over with another medium, such as marker. Likewise, it can be traced over, through another sheet of paper, with a white crayon. This technique will give a white outline to forms when the painting is gone over with watercolors. Some teachers have the children first make a drawing with bold marker; then, with a sheet of white paper covering it, they use a white crayon to trace over the bold lines, which can be seen dimly through the covering paper, pressing hard as they trace. These white lines serve as barriers to the subsequent addition

Courtesy of Frank Wachowiak.

On colored construction paper, a white chalk drawing was gone over with black marker and filled in with oil pastel. Observe the highly imaginative and free features that these upper elementary children invented for their bulletin boards full of construction paper masks. The teacher and the students discussed different ways to draw mouths, eyes, and noses. Everyone came up with a unique way to depict each feature. No two are alike. Marker drawings were enriched with oil pastel. Iowa City Laboratory School.

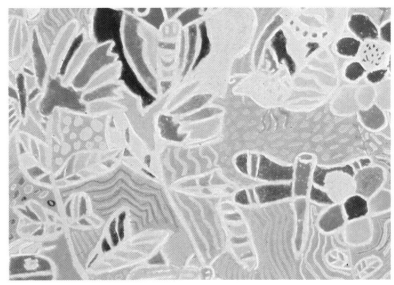

Frank Wachowiak often employed a different white line technique; after first being drawn on colored construction paper with chalk, these lines were then gone over with white oil pastel; then other colors of oil pastel were added. For this project, a collection of butterflies, as well as color photographs of butterflies in a garden, provided motivation. Notice how large and small butterflies in different shapes create variety and beauty. A host of patterns was used for the background: circles, dots, and wiggly as well as rippling lines.

Top: *The white line resist employs a black marker going over the lines of the initial pencil drawing. The highly visible heavy marker lines are then traced through another paper by using a white crayon. The third session, crayons, and the fourth, watercolor, were used by this second-grader to represent "The Butterfly Garden."* ***Bottom:*** *The white line resist was also used for this third-grade painting "I Can Fly," to which kids sang along with the CD.*

of watercolors. Their slightly ragged edge gives an organic quality to the artwork.

Much drawing in school today is done with markers. Whereas pencils leave a light line, markers leave a once-and-for-all dark line. Compared to pencils, markers are gaining increasing prominence, both because of their boldness, and because of their inexpensiveness. Compared to crayons, markers have a more bold and sure quality of line. One all-too-familiar disadvantage of markers, however, is that they will dry out if not tightly capped. A new product design, Capper®, remedies this problem by having all eight caps in one molded piece to help youngsters more readily keep track of the lids. (Also, Sanford's Colorific® markers have superior non-drying properties when inadvertently left uncapped.)

In the primary grades, teachers generally have the children draw directly with the bold markers. The children's naive way of drawing has much charm, which the worrisomeness of pencil drawing first would only diminish.

Peter Rabbit and His Sisters Playing in the Rain

Courtesy of Beverly Mallon, Chase Street Elementary School, Athens, GA.

An initial pencil drawing was gone over with watercolor and then markers. Kindergartners made up their own Peter Rabbit stories in this three-period lesson.

Courtesy of Baiba Kuntz, Glencoe, IL.

In order to preserve a freer quality to the drawing, no initial pencil drawing was done. Markers were used from the beginning for these carefully observed drawings of a bird still life.

In the upper grades, some teachers allow or encourage pencil drawing first, while other teachers strongly forbid it. Students, worried over making a mistake, much prefer to use pencil first. Teachers who eschew initial pencil drawings prior to using markers believe that the child's natural way of transcribing perceptions into marks has a distinct character that should be preserved. They believe that the belabored two-step process of first pencil and then marker obscures the drawing process's natural traces. These teachers are reluctant to give out a second sheet of paper (lest almost everyone ask for one) and, instead, tell their students, "No one messes up. The only way to mess up is to not make it your own way."

Drawings in which the pencil drawing is gone over with markers often have a "tighter" and less spontaneous quality. Paradoxically, teachers should encourage both careful observation but also a line quality "with life in it." "Look at Michelangelo's drawings; you will see lines that he did not feel were correct, yet he went on and drew them again where they should be. If he did not bother to fuss and erase, why should you?"

While marker drawing sometimes follows initial pencil drawing, another technique is that watercolors follow immediately after the pencil drawing is finished, with no intervening step of markers. Note, however, that if watercolor is to follow a marker drawing, then a waterproof marker, such as Sharpie®, must be used to prevent smearing.

Fifty years ago, the original markers were refillable, messy, and had a potent and harmful smell. Nowadays, many water-based markers, and even permanent markers, are odorless and nontoxic. Especially with permanent markers, look for the Art Products (AP) Nontoxic label. Fumes from a whole class of students using markers with a strong odor can be overpowering and cause headaches.

Any art supply catalog will present a vast array of alternatives to fit any budget: water-based, permanent, double-ended markers with one fine and one regular tip, brush pens, dual brush pens, markers with tips up to 2" wide, paint markers in 34 colors, Prismacolor® markers in 144 colors. While Pantone® makes three pointed markers in one pen, often the teacher wants just the normal fine point; that they are refillable cuts down on their expense. Markers can also be purchased at drugstores and discount stores. For writing on the markerboard (blackboard), use a low-odor, alcohol-based, dry-erase marker such as Sanford's Expo2®, as the odor from older types of dry-erase markers can be overwhelming.

Generally, avoid the ultra-fine tips, as the lines do not show up well when the artworks are viewed from a distance. Also, the tips often dull quickly. Regular tips are preferable, although chisel-tips can substitute if

Teacher Susan Whipple, Grace Christian School, Medford, OR.
Courtesy of the USSEA art collection of Dr. Ann Gregory, Los Angeles School District.

When marker strokes are applied parallel and just slightly overlapping, an ordered appearance in a solid color is achieved. Siobhan McDermott angel watching over the home and nation achieves its beauty in part through its two pairs of complementary colors, red and green, and yellow-orange and blue-violet.

used on a corner. Large areas of color can be beautifully and neatly applied when the chisel-tip markers are used in overlapping, perfectly parallel strokes.

Water-based markers are the least expensive by far. However, their relative slowness in drying can cause smearing if a protective shield of paper under the drawing hand is not used. Also there is the problem of smearing and bleeding if watercolor or tempera is subsequently used.

In middle schools, more unusual drawing methods such as scratchboard, silverpoint, conté crayon, and various ways of applying ink, such as by pen points, brushes, and even quill feathers, may find a place in the curriculum.

Top: Courtesy of Joyce Vroon, Trinity School, Atlanta, GA. *Bottom:* Courtesy of Baiba Kuntz, Glencoe, IL.

Scratchboard gives a sharp white line, set off against the velvety black of the board. **Top:** *Sixth-grader Sarah Hipp illustrated a poem by Langston Hughes about a broken heart.* **Bottom:** *Eighth-grader Joel Savitzsky drew a still life with pheasant. Note how entire areas can be removed to create white areas; also note how an etching type of shading can be done.*

Chapter 23

CRAYON AND OIL PASTELS

Crayon

At the turn of the century, crayons began to be manufactured for use in schools. Artists such as Henri de Toulouse-Lautrec, Georges Seurat, Henri

Courtesy of Shirley Lucas, Oshkosh, WI.

Crayon was richly used in this drawing of eight animals. Notice how the grassy terrain was outlined in a series of analogous colors.

Courtesy of the International Collection of Child Art, Illinois State University, Normal, IL.

Crayon alone was used to create the glowing rich colors in this 11-year-old Turkish student's illustration of the fable, "The Old Man, His Son, and Their Donkey." Four scenes are shown simultaneously, and a handsome texture is achieved in the straw-colored area by scratching in a texture. Tunceli, Turkey.

Matisse, and Kaethe Kollwitz used them. Today, they are available in over 64 colors. Resourceful teachers often combine crayon with other media to renew student interest in crayon's exciting potential. Some of these innovative techniques, which are described in the following pages, include crayon resist, crayon encaustic, crayon engraving, and multicrayon engraving.

Unfortunately, the rich possibilities of the wax crayon with its own singular merits as an expressive coloring agent, often are not fully investigated. Typical classroom projects in crayon usually are weak in color

Saturday Children's Classes. Courtesy of Frank Wachowiak, Athens, GA, and Mary Sayer Hammond, Athens, GA.

These crayon drawings of memories of a tree house began with a series of questions, such as "How will you climb into it? Who will come into it?" A preliminary drawing with white *chalk was made on 18- × 24-inch colored construction paper, which gives each drawing a suffused overall tone. Breaking up the background shape into varied colors adds interest.*

intensity, value contrast, and texture quality. In most instances, crayon is employed as a pallid, sketchy coloring agent instead of the glowing, vibrant, and excitingly expressive medium that it can and should be. If children are expected to grow in crayoning skills, the crayon's rich possibilities must be taught beginning from the first grade.

Whenever possible, request that the students or school supply agent obtain the large 48- or 64-color crayon boxes, with their beautiful range of tints and shades and their wide selection of neutralized hues. To bring out the deepest, richest color, prompt the students to apply the crayon with heavy pressure. ("Who can make the color sing?" "Who can make it shout?" as opposed to "Who is making it mumble?") Have students use a lot of newspaper padding under the paper to be crayoned. Point out the effects of using contrasting colors and of juxtaposing dark next to light colors, neutral next to high-intensity colors. Challenge the students to create patterns of stripes, checks, plaids, diamonds, stars, spirals, and dots. Use paintings by artists such as Vuillard, Bonnard, Ida Kohlmyer, Mariam Shapiro, van Gogh, and Gauguin as exemplars of vibrant color. Show them Picasso's crayon drawings.

The entire mood of crayon work changes when the crayon is applied to varicolored or varitextured surfaces. Work on backgrounds other than the commonly used cream manila or white drawing paper. Pleasing results come about when crayon is employed richly on pink, red, orange, purple, blue, green, and even black construction paper. Have the students allow some of the background to show between objects; the background paper color will unify their compositions. Color changes its appearance on different color papers: yellow changes to dull green on black construction paper; all of the warm colors are slightly neutralized when they are applied to green paper; and warm colors shimmer vibrantly when applied to red, pink, and orange surfaces.

Preliminary sketches for crayon pictures on colored paper may be made with school chalk or a light-colored crayon. Do not let students use a pencil, because they grow frustrated when they try to manipulate a blunt crayon to color in a pencil-sketch's tiny details. Encourage bold use of the crayon. Urge color repetition throughout the composition to achieve unity. Completed crayon pictures may be given a sheen by rubbing them with a facial tissue or a folded paper towel.

Wax-crayon still lifes created by university students. College students should discover in their teacher training classes the luminous beauty inherent in the common, everyday wax crayon.

Then, they will be more motivated and qualified to help children in their classes bring forth the rich potential of the crayon medium used by itself.

Some issues of aesthetics to discuss include: What does color add to a picture? Why should colors be intense? Should all colors be intense? Why should we push a medium to its limit?

One vexing problem that the teacher of art faces is children who rush through their crayoning, who quickly color in a few shapes and then claim they are finished. Some suggestions for dealing with this are given in Chapters 10 and 13. As always, the most successful strategies involve a teacher's well-planned, resourceful motivation that taps the students' concerns. This leads to a richly detailed drawing, which sets the stage for the crayon's expressive coloring.

Crayon Resist

For students of all ages, an exciting, creative art experience is the combination of vibrant, glowing wax crayon with translucent, flowing watercolors. For this technique, subjects that are rich in pattern and all-over design, such as fish, birds, reptiles, insects, and butterflies, are recommended. Students genuinely are excited by the variety of insects in their environment, and the teacher can stimulate further interest by having children col-

lect specimens to share with classmates. Illustrated books, wildlife periodicals, color slides, and films will broaden the students' awareness of nature's adaptational variety. Studying the appearance of insects' bodies increases general knowledge of design. For example, help the students to see and draw the filigree pattern of insects' wings, the rhythmlike segments of a grasshopper's abdomen, the symmetrical balance of a ladybug's body, and the grace of a praying mantis's legs.

The pattern, details, and designs of the subject are of utmost importance in the crayon-resist technique, adding as they do to the sparkling effect of the finished painting. Whatever the theme, the more detail that is incorporated and the more overlapping of shapes that is achieved, the richer the design becomes. When the design is rich and complex, the negative areas evolve into varied shapes as well. Background embellishment—adding flowers, weeds, trees, vines, webs, and rock and cloud formations—will tie the composition together.

A successful crayon resist requires the following:

The crayon must be applied with heavy pressure, so that it will resist the watercolor (or water-diluted tempera) in the final stage. A demonstration by the teacher of the results of light and heavy crayoning will make the point of how hard the students must press the crayon.

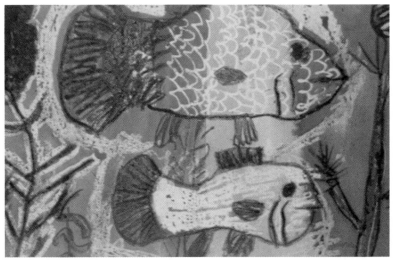

Underwater themes are particularly good for crayon-resist paintings. Here, the predominant use of a blue wash has one area of a highly effective contrast: the child chose a contrasting and off-center vertical band of pink water-diluted tempera going across both fish and background.

Putting several layers of newspaper padding under the paper facilitates heavy crayoning.

Leave some of the paper uncrayoned, such as between two solid shapes, two colors, and object and background color.

Negative space can be enriched with a pattern of radiating lines. These might include effects such as those formed around a pebble dropped in water together with dots, spirals, circles, hatching, and cross-hatching.

Encourage students to be imaginative in their choice of color. Reliance on natural or realistic colors should be minimized. Show the paintings of Raoul Dufy as examples of fantasy choices and use of washes. White crayon can be especially effective in this technique, providing a happy,

Iowa City Elementary Laboratory School, Iowa City, IA. Courtesy of Frank Wachowiak, Athens, GA.

Steps in a crayon-resist painting. Using white paper for the background, make a preliminary drawing in the first class session, with a light-colored crayon rather than a pencil. In a second class period add the crayon patterns, background details, and selected solid crayon areas. The children must be guided to apply the crayons with a strong pressure so that the wax will resist the subsequent watercolor. The watercoloring itself requires a final art class. Remind students to keep the watercolors transparent by adding sufficient water so that the paint does not obliterate the crayon design.

Courtesy of Donna Cummins, Brookview Elementary School, Atlanta, GA.

A heavy coat of crayon will resist the dark wash, which here has beaded up on the surface to create a texture enriching the crayon radiating flower design.

magical surprise when the paint is applied. If a final black tempera wash is not planned, black crayon provides strong contrast.

When the crayoning is completed and the student is given the teacher's go-ahead, either of two techniques of resist may be employed: the wet-paper process or the dry-paper process. In the dry-paper technique, students paint directly on their completed crayon work using watercolors or tempera. If tempera is being used, the teacher must first adjust the tempera's viscosity on a sample. Students may limit themselves to one color in painting the background or employ a variety of watercolors, as exemplified in the multileaf composition illustrated in this section. If the crayon has been applied heavily, paint can be applied directly over the crayoned area, producing an attractive texture.

In the wet-paper technique, the desks or tables first should be covered with newspapers. Because the paper is fragile when wet, students should put their piece on a solid surface such as a Masonite board and, at the sink, immerse both paper and board in water until soaked. Students then transport their pieces (still on the board) to the painting station and lift them off carefully. Next, students load their brushes with watercolor or diluted tempera and drop or float the paint onto the uncrayoned areas. They also may direct the paint-laden brush around the edges of the crayoned shapes and let the color flow freely. They may use one watercolor

Courtesy of Joyce Vroon, Trinity School, Atlanta, GA.

Second-grade student Emily Sharbaugh paints with different areas of color around the crayoned forms, being careful that the colors of wash do not run together.

wash (blue or blue-green is a favorite) or a variety of hues. They must be careful, however, that several bright colors do not flow together to make a dull, neutralized color. The wet-resist method is especially suited for undersea, aviary, and flying-insect themes. To add to the picture's charm, leave some white areas of the paper unpainted. For a large class, the teacher might prepare in advance several containers of water-diluted tempera. A large table or counterspace near the sink can be designated as a painting area, and students can take turns applying the wash over their

Crayon engraving is used boldly and directly to make a statement about flowers and insects. Children express their ideas in direct, inimitable ways. In the foreground butterfly and in the *huge, right-hand flower, the child's intuitive use of positive and negative pattern is brilliant. What youngsters depict so honestly and naively can be awe-inspiring.*

crayon composition while the rest of the class still is crayoning or other-wise engaged.

In addition to the subject ideas mentioned earlier, the following themes are recommended for crayon-resist projects: a flower garden, fire-works display, the circus, the fair, umbrellas in the rain, a Halloween parade, falling autumn leaves, kites in the sky, in the swimming pool, underwater explorers, and jungle birds with plumage.

Crayon Engraving

Crayon engraving, which sometimes is referred to as "crayon etching," is a fascinating technique. It involves the use of sturdy white drawing paper or manila file folders, wax crayons, black tempera paint, soap, brush, and engraving tools. It is a standard and popular school project, although its many possibilities seldom are carried to maximum expressiveness. If

Courtesy of Frank Wachowiak, Athens, GA, and
Mary Sayer Hammond, Athens, GA.

A youngster applies a heavy crayon undercoat for his crayon engraving.

teachers allow students to be satisfied with quick, superficial scribble designs and later with random scratches, students will never discover the new worlds of pattern and color overlay, or the rich enhancement that results when crayon engraving is combined with other media, such as oil pastel.

Crayon engraving uses a linear approach; therefore, materials that are rich in line, pattern, detail, and texture are ideal subject matter, and the natural sciences are a rich source. Some examples are animals such as the porcupine, anteater, armadillo, zebra, leopard, tiger, and rhino. Birds—especially those with exotic plumage—also are good subjects, as are reptiles such as turtles, iguanas, and horned toads and insects such as dragonflies, praying mantises, butterflies, grasshoppers, and beetles. Also of interest are crustaceans, such as crabs and crayfish; fish, shells, and coral of many species; and all varieties of plant life.

The preliminary drawing for a crayon engraving should be made in pencil on a separate piece of newsprint or manila paper that is the same size as the sturdy paper to be used for the final work. Because crayon engraving is a labor-intensive process, students with limited attention spans may come to appreciate using paper of a small size. Keeping sizes constant will prove to be beneficial for students retracing their drawings with dressmaker's white transfer paper.

The first step in a crayon engraving is to apply varied colors of crayon solidly to the sturdy paper's surface. The crayon should be applied evenly and with a strong pressure so that no part of the paper background shows. Coloring in two overlapping directions may help to ensure

a rich coat of crayon, as will newspaper padding under the paper. The children may begin the crayoning phase by first making scribble designs in a light-colored crayon all over the paper and then filling in the resulting shapes solidly with a variety of bright colors. Alternatively, they may apply swatches or patches of color or have their crayoned areas coincide with their compositions. Avoid black and metallic crayons; use the most brilliant colors.

After the crayoning has been completed, the surface crayon flecks should be brushed off with a cloth or paper towel. It is essential that students put their names on the backs of their crayoned sheets *before* the paint is applied. The black tempera paint should be about the consistency of thin cream. Lest the black tempera paint not thoroughly cover the waxy crayon, make it adhere better by adding liquid soap or detergent to the black tempera. Approximately 1 tablespoon of liquid soap per pint of tempera is needed. Or, the tempera-filled brush can be rubbed over a bar of soap before it is applied to the crayoned surface. The teacher should make a test swatch and, when it is dry, determine its engravability. If the paint is too thick, it will chip off during the engraving.

When the paint is thoroughly dry (overnight or longer), transfer the preliminary line drawing as follows:

1. Coat the drawing's reverse side with white crayon or chalk, or use dressmaker's white transfer paper.
2. Paper-clip the drawing (white crayon–surface down) to the black tempera–coated side of the sturdy paper, and, with a pencil or ballpoint pen, make the transfer. Engrave the lines through the tempera coating down to the crayon surface using a nail, scissors point, compass, or similar tool. (*Note:* Newspapers on the working surface are required, because the engraving phase can be messy.)
3. Add textures, patterns, and details with nut picks, forks, and pieces of old combs.

High contrast can be achieved by using a plastic, picnic-type disposable knife to scrape away some solid-shape areas down to the crayon surface. A recommended tool, if the school budget permits, is the Sloyd or Hyde knife. This sturdy, short-bladed knife can engrave a fine line with its point or scrape away a large surface with its flat edge.

After completing the engraving, students may enrich their compositions by applying oil pastel colors back over some of the black tempera

Facing page: *In these three crayon engravings, students wisely preserved certain dark areas intact to contrast with the light-colored areas from which they scraped away the crayon. Approximately half of the areas are light and half of the areas are dark. The dark areas are either plain black or remain dark even after having been gone over with crayon.*

Top left and right: Fish by middle school students. Courtesy of David Hodge, Oshkosh, WI. *Bottom:* Insects by a third-grade student. Saturday Children's Classes. Courtesy of Frank Wachowiak, Athens, GA, and Mary Sayer Hammond, Athens, GA.

Eighth-grade. Courtesy of Baiba Kuntz, Glencoe, IL.

Scratch board is a related technique that might be considered a variation of crayon engraving and is superb for capturing textures. Notice the shades of gray achieved in the radiating scalloped pattern of the chrysanthemum heads.

Athens Academy. Courtesy Mary McCutheon, Athens, GA.

Note the floral fine-art reproductions that are displayed, the live anenome bouquet, the newspaper-covered table, and the jars of melted crayon in the double boiler-type pan within a pan over a hot plate.

surfaces. Finally, the composition may be further enhanced by engraving details and texture through the newly oil-pasteled areas.

Crayon engraving is a challenging mixed-media technique. It opens up new avenues of discovery in line, color, contrast, pattern, and texture, especially for students at the upper elementary level and above (see page 271).

Crayon Encaustic

Crayon encaustic is a challenging painting medium to add to the upper elementary and middle school art repertoire. Many museums contain ancient Egyptian Fayumic mummy portraits that still glow with the inner light of wax. The Greeks used encaustic on marble, and early Christians mixed little glass pieces, called *tesserae,* into it. The encaustic process is the kind of creative adventure that is reserved for those teachers who are brave in spirit, eager to try something new, and persevering enough to collect a year's supply of broken crayons. Some teachers make encaustic paint-

These charming paintings were created by employing the melted crayon or encaustic method. The size of the cardboard is approximately 8 × 12 inches. Color reproductions of flower paintings by artists such as Odilon Redon, Vincent van Gogh, Paul Cézanne, and Paul Gauguin were displayed and discussed during the project. A bouquet of freshly picked, multihued anemones provided the immediate visual motivation.

ing an annual late-spring event, which the students eagerly anticipate. One teacher times the activity with the blossoming of colorful anemones, which become the visual motivation for the project.

The steps are as follows: Remove paper wrappings from the crayons, break the crayons into small pieces, and put them in glass babyfood jars or similar containers (not made of plastic or paper) or metal muffin tins. Each jar or compartment should contain a different color. If a muffin tin is used, make sure that it fits into a deeper and slightly larger baking tin. This slightly larger cake tin containing water, making a double-boiler arrangement to heat the containers of wax, is required to prevent fires. Because of space limitations, the number of colors may need to be limited to the primary and secondary colors plus white, black, and a few tints.

The most functional working station for encaustic painting is a large, sturdy, newspaper-covered table. Place one end of the table against a wall near an electrical outlet. Place one or two electric hot plates in the middle of the table. Put the crayon-filled containers or muffin tins in a 2- or 3-inch-deep metal baking pan. Fill the pan two-thirds full of water, and place it on the hot plate. When the crayons have melted, reduce the heat and place one or more Q-tips or watercolor brushes into each crayon container. These brushes should be old and reserved for this encaustic project only. Keep the water at the temperature of the melted crayon to maintain a consistent flow of crayon.

White or colored cardboard approximately 9 × 12 or 12 × 12 inches is recommended for the painting surface. Scrap mat board, chipboard, gift-box covers, and grocery carton cardboard coated with latex are other possibilities.

A preliminary sketch for a crayon-encaustic painting is recommended, unless the theme is purely nonobjective, in the manner of Jackson Pollock, Helen Frankenthaler, and Hans Hoffman. Subject-matter possibilities include a flower bouquet, butterflies, an exotic bird in foliage, a fantastic fish among shells and seaweed, an imaginary monster, and a clown.

The teacher must supervise encaustic painting carefully. Never crowd the working station. The group must be limited to four to six students, depending on the size of the table. To prevent wax fires, the water must never be permitted to boil out of the pan. The electrical current may need to be turned off and on periodically so that the melted crayon does not cool off. Additional pieces of crayon will need to be placed in the containers. Remind students that brushes or crayon applicators should *not* be switched from container to container; students must wait their turn for a color. *Caution:* The crayon containers are filled with molten wax and must not be taken out of the heated pan during painting.

Crayon encaustic cannot be rushed; sometimes, the beauty of encaustic does not materialize until several layers of melted crayon have been applied. If layers are built up, the finished work will take on an exciting, thick impasto quality. When one color is applied over another, there is the possibility of further embellishment. This can be done by incising lines with a nail through the top coat to reveal the crayon color underneath. To solve the problem of an insufficient number of old crayons when a large area must be covered, powdered tempera can be mixed with melted paraffin. Crayon encaustic produces paintings with color richness and glow that are unsurpassed (see also page 275).

Oil Pastel

The introduction of oil pastels in their rich and exciting array of hues has opened a whole new world of color exploration and expression in both elementary and middle schools. Oil pastels generally are within most

Top and middle: Saturday Children's Classes. Courtesy of Frank Wachowiak, Athens, GA, and Mary Sayer Hammond, Athens, GA. *Bottom:* Courtesy of Joyce Vroon, Trinity School, Atlanta, GA.

Top: *Oil pastel on black paper of birds in trees.* **Middle:** *Astronauts in their spaceship is the theme for this third-grade oil pastel.* **Bottom:** *Oil pastel is much more widely used in schools than regular pastel, shown here in this drawing of a pumpkin and corn on a crazy quilt by fourth grader Jay Bellman. Yet, as seen particularly in the foreground, regular pastel has distinct qualities unmatched by other media.*

schools' budget range. The only caution is that because of their oil content, they may stain clothing. The most attractive feature of oil pastels is the ease with which students can apply them to obtain shimmering, vivid, painterly color compositions. Thus, students can produce rich results without the pressure required for regular crayons. Oil pastels work especially well on deep-colored construction paper, in which the colored background serves as a unifying or complementary factor. Young students should be encouraged in their first efforts to apply the pastels boldly in solid-color areas, pressing hard to achieve a glowing surface, and to use color contrasts. Because the intensity of the pastel hues is affected by the paper color, students should note the effects of small color swatches on their paper's reverse side.

Recommendations for oil-pastel projects, especially when colored construction paper is used for the background, are as follows:

Make the preliminary drawing or sketch with white or light school chalk or crayon. Chalk is excellent, because it is easily erased. (Use a paper towel or facial tissue if the students want to make changes.)

Press for the richest effects. One suggestion for coloring in small or complex shapes is to apply the pastel in a line close to the chalk outline and then fill in the shape. Discourage haphazard, scribbled coloring.

Remind students that colors have many tints and shades, which are especially important for capturing leaves and grassy fields with their nuances of light and shade.

Black, white, and gray add to any color scheme.

Colors, both tints and shades, bright and dull, including the blacks and whites, should be repeated in different parts of the composition to create unity. This color repetition should employ differences of size, shape, and intensity. A hue that is repeated for unity should be differentiated in value so that the echo of the color is there without the monotony of pure repetition. Differentiation is especially important when the student is making a pattern such as bricks on a wall, tiles on a roof, or stones in a walk, where the repetition of the same color becomes static and lifeless unless sensitively varied. Remember that contrasting values are stronger than contrasting hues.

When it is desired that the colored paper background show through in a complementing way, apply the pastel impressionistically in strokes, lines, or dots. New colors can be created by applying pastel over pastel; however, a very light color cannot be totally darkened unless the light is first scraped off. A dark color can be lightened somewhat by the application of white, and colors can be dulled through application of their complements, such as red over green, orange over blue. To alter a color, first use soft pressure with varidirectional strokes, and then increase pressure.

Courtesy of Donna Cummins, Brookview Elementary School, Atlanta, GA.

A portrait was done in oil pastels on black paper following a study of Van Gogh and his post-Impressionistic manner of applying colors in small directional strokes.

Oil-Pastel Resist

Oil pastels alone can be beautifully employed as a final step in many techniques, such as tempera paintings, crayon engravings, and vegetable or found-object prints. However, they also can be used in the oil pastel-resist process with stunning results.

Teachers and students who are familiar with the crayon-resist technique will welcome oil pastel as another resist medium. It does not require the time or intense exertion on the part of the students that crayons demand.

Saturday Children's Classes. Courtesy of Frank Wachowiak, Athens, GA, and Mary Sayer Hammond, Athens. GA.

The same steps as outlined for the crayon-resist technique should be followed:

- Make a preliminary drawing in chalk.
- Vary the width of the chalk line, and emphasize thicker lines.
- Apply the oil pastel heavily so that it will resist the final coat of black paint.
- Leave the chalk lines uncovered.
- Use the brightest, most intense pastel hues.
- Avoid black.

Before applying paint, evaluate the final oil-pastel composition for a variation of repeated colors. Also, look for a variety of patterns: dots, circles, overlapping wiggly lines, radiating lines in circles or rays, ripple-in-a-stream lines, hatch and cross-hatch lines, stars, asterisks, diamonds, and spirals.

Before applying paint, also gently brush off the chalk lines. Place the composition on a newspaper-protected surface and apply a coat of black tempera paint. Applied with a soft brush, the paint must be of exactly the right consistency—not too thin, not too thick. Because paint formulas change, always do a test first (some tempera paints now contain an adhesive and cannot be used). If the paint covers the areas of oil pastel, it is too thick. The resisting oil in the oil pastels will dry out soon after it is applied to the paper, so do not wait too long to apply the black paint. Finally, oil pastel–resist compositions may be given a protective coat of gloss polymer medium to enhance their beauty.

Steps in the process of oil-pastel resist. **Top:** *Preliminary drawing in school chalk on colored construction paper.* **Middle:** *Oil pastel applied in solids and patterns up to but not covering the chalk lines.* **Bottom:** *Slightly water-diluted black tempera applied lightly with a soft-bristle brush.*

Oil-pastel resist takes oil pastel a step further. The resist color of wash goes into the lines left empty to create a stained-glass effect and also adds texture on the plain areas. Here, many shapes of different sizes and types help create beauty.

Chapter 24

PAINTING

Painting with Watercolors

Although tempera is the most common and popular painting medium in elementary and middle school art programs, many teachers use transparent watercolors. These come in semimoist cakes or tiny tubes packaged in metal or plastic containers, and they are available in primary and secondary colors as well as black. Transparent watercolor painting demands special technical skills; mature painters devote countless hours to its mastery, employing a wide range of beautiful colors available in tube form and costly sable-hair brushes.

The watercolor paintings on pages 196 and 281 are by Japanese elementary school children. These children are provided with a spectrum of watercolors in tubes and painting palettes beginning in the first grade. Most of their watercolor paintings begin with a preliminary sketch in pencil or pen. In some cases, children moisten the paper before beginning the coloring. As these paintings reveal, many persevere to produce rich, space-filled compositions that exhibit transparent watercolors' characteristic spontaneity.

Teachers often employ the semimoist watercolors to teach about the color properties of hue, value, and intensity. Mixing primary colors will produce secondary colors, and mixing secondary colors will produce tertiary colors. Diluting a color with water in gradual stages can produce a color-value chart. Color can be neutralized by mixing with complementary hues, and creating watercolor washes on moist paper achieves dark-to-light sky and water effects.

The following recommendations constitute a "primer" for watercolor projects:

White watercolor or construction paper is recommended.
Newspapers under paintings help to speed cleanup and also provide a practice surface.

What verve, what spontaneity is shown in this watercolor of daffodils! A free pencil sketch the previous period preceded Annabelle Barbe's watercoloring of this, the very essence of springtime.

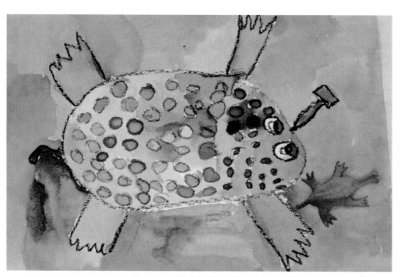

To illustrate a story, a kindergartner painted this frog, made delightful by multihued bumps and the breaking up of the body's form with a spectrum of colors.

Girls and boys use watercolors to color their marker drawings of toys and dolls. Notice the watercolor sets and the six-compartment plastic mixing trays for mixing colors.

Round, pointed, soft-bristle, camel-hair brushes are recommended. They should always be rinsed clean at the end of the period and stored either bristle-end-up or flat in a container.

Watercolor boxes containing the semimoist cakes of paint should be rinsed and wiped clean at the close of the period and then allowed to dry open.

Water containers should be changed when the water in them becomes muddy. Paper towels are handy for absorbing spills and blotting up excess paint on works in progress.

Preliminary sketches in pencil, felt-nib or nylon-tipped pen, or light watercolor applied with a small brush are recommended.

Areas that are to appear white or light in the final painting can be masked with masking tape before the paper is moistened or the painting begun. When the painting is completed and dry, the mask can be removed and a final touch-up made.

Watercolor washes of the same color in the same value applied over one another will darken the color. It is recommended that students begin a painting with light colors or values and build to darker colors for detail.

When painting is done on a wet surface, the paper may need to be remoistened by lightly sprinkling the surface with water from time to time.

This entrancing watercolor, My Friend and Me, *is the work of a first-grade child in Japan. Notice the variety of lines in the hairy, toothy main figure. Opposite colors, yellow and purple, along with mixtures of each color give the work power.*

Paintings appear vibrant and contrasting when moist but unfortunately lose their brilliance when dry. A second application of watercolor paint over a dried color may help.

While wet or moist, paintings should not be stored one on top of another. If no drying rack or counters are available, dry the paintings on the floor around the room's perimeter.

Some very successful watercolor projects are those in which watercolor is combined with colored crayons or oil pastels in a resist method (see Chapter 21).

Study art history exemplars: watercolors by Winslow Homer and John Singer Sargent, and brush paintings from China and Japan.

One aesthetic issue to be considered is the importance in art (and in life) of spontaneity, verve, and assuredness—a vibrant, fresh appearance versus a labored, fussy, muddled appearance.

Painting with Tempera

All children should have the opportunity to express their ideas with brush and paint. The best-quality tempera paints, whether in powder or liquid form, are rich in color and have excellent covering properties. Children who paint with tempera can apply color over color freely to achieve jewellike effects or repaint areas with which they are not pleased.

Although teachers are aware of the possibilities for colorful art expressions that tempera offers, they sometimes do not include it in their art programs because of its cost and the housekeeping chores involved. Tempera projects do require more preparation of materials, more careful storage, and more controlled cleanup procedures than watercolor or crayon projects; nonetheless, these factors should not prevent teachers from discovering how tempera painting can enrich children's art repertoire.

Even when classes are large and facilities limited, there are expeditious, time-saving methods for incorporating tempera into the art program. For example, cardboard soda-bottle containers and discarded glass-tumbler carryalls can be used as carrying cases. Likewise, discarded baby-food jars and half-pint milk cartons can serve as containers. To prevent the paint from drying out between sessions, the milk cartons can be resealed with spring clothespins.

Students can both perform a service and gain color knowledge by helping to prepare the tempera paint. They can mix various hues, tints, shades, and neutralized colors. For extra beauty in the paintings, consider restricting the color choices to, for example, only triadic colors, a narrow range of analogous colors, or all very light colors. For a class of 30 children, about 60 containers of varying colors should be prepared, as well as an additional six containers of white and four containers of black. Containers should only be partially filled, to keep paint from covering the brush's metal ferrule and the students' fingers.

Painting with tempera on large-paper surfaces gives children a real opportunity to express their ideas in paint. This bold portrait by a primary-grade student is on 24- × 36-inch paper. Newspapers covered the floor, and the child painted freely.

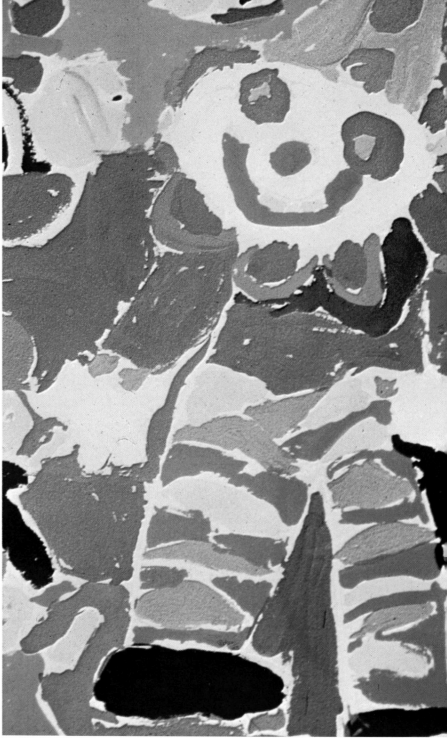

Courtesy of Frank Wachowiak and Ted Ramsay, University Elementary School, Iowa City, IA.

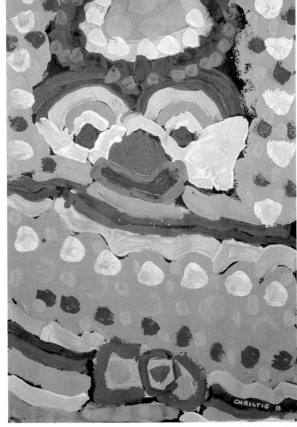

Courtesy of Joyce Vroon, Trinity School, Atlanta, GA.

Paint the large background shapes first. Then, when the color is dry, or on another day, add other colors to create patterns and textures, as third-grade student Christine Bunyan did in this clown painting. "Pass the Paint" was used; on the teacher's signal, students traded paint containers.

If class time is limited, the teacher may need to prepare the color assortment in advance. Those who object to this procedure because it does not give students the opportunity to learn about mixing colors should note that professional artists usually have a wealth of colors, tints, shades, and neutrals at their disposal to create paintings. Children deserve the same advantage. Thus, when the class is limited to a few basic colors because there is not enough time to mix a variety, the expressive output of the children suffers, and the joy in painting diminishes.

Individual containers of paint should be placed on a table or rolling cart that is accessible from all sides. It should be low enough so the various colors are visible. If possible, a separate brush should be available for every container. This procedure saves time, paint, and squabbles over brushes. The

Courtesy of Joyce Vroon, Trinity School, Atlanta, GA.

Tempera blocks are similar to watercolors in ease of use and cleanup, although the colors are more opaque. Elizabeth Crabtree painted this water scene from a calendar image.

Courtesy of Beverly Mallon, Chase Street Elementary School, Athens, GA, and Crayola® Dream-Makers®.

Tempera painting is enjoyed by young children for its boldness of representation. Using black paper, first-grader Tangenika Watson painted this elephant, inspired by a study of circus animals when the circus came to town. Look for the "E for elephant" hidden in the decorative circus blanket pattern. The background was sponge-painted on white paper, and the elephant was cut out and mounted on it.

children take turns choosing and using a container of color, and when they finish with it, they return it (with its brush inside) to the supply station. Children should use only one color at a time—and use it thoroughly throughout the painting. Some teachers have used a timed swap of colors among their students. To achieve unity and balance in their paintings, encourage students to repeat colors around the picture. While primarily aesthetic, this injunction also has the practical advantage of minimizing traffic around the supply station.

Adequate time should be allotted for cleanup. Because brushes left standing for long periods of time in paint lose their elasticity, they should be taken out of the paint containers and squeezed so that paint remaining in the brush flows back into the container. The brushes should then be placed in a large basin of soapy water to soak overnight. The next morning, they can be rinsed in clear water and stored either bristle-end-up or flat in a box. Brushes with wood handles must be washed and stored to dry immediately lest the wooden handle be damaged. Unless the baby-food jars of paint can be covered, store the jars in an airtight cupboard or drawer, or put the containers on a tray and seal the tray in a giant plastic bag. To prevent the lips and edges of containers from sticking, they should occasionally be wiped clean or waxed.

Some teachers use plastic egg cartons or ice-cube trays as tempera paint containers. In this method, each student has a brush, and he or she washes the brush before using another color. Preventing drying of leftover paint is more difficult with this method, but the cartons or trays can be sealed in plastic bags. To help prevent the unpleasant odor of aging tempera, a drop of wintergreen can be added to the big jars of tempera.

Semimoist cakes of opaque paint are now available in tubs or tins, and some teachers claim that these save time in cleanup and storage procedures. Others, however, say that paint in this form inhibits the free-flowing style that liquid tempera encourages in children. Indeed, during the primary grades, tempera painting is a hit. The very young child especially enjoys making bold, splashy designs in paint and needs only the materials and an invitation to start. Themes such as explosion in a paint factory, Fourth-of-July fireworks, butterflies in a flower garden, bunny rabbit's Easter party, a kite fight, and planets in outer space fire the imagination. Colored construction paper, including black, provides an excellent surface for tempera painting because the color of the paper can unify the composition. Also consider employing adventurous choices such as wallpaper samples and newspaper classified pages.

The following strategies have proved to be helpful in tempera painting projects:

Encourage students to make preliminary sketches on their paper in chalk or with a brush and light-colored paint.

Courtesy of Joyce Vroon, Trinity School, Atlanta, GA.

Wearing painting smocks of old white shirts to protect their clothing, second-grade students paint a large palette by mixing their own colors in little paint trays.

Minimize cleanup by using protective newspapers on paint supply stations and individual painting areas. Have moist towels available for accidental paint spills and use protective plastic on the carpet.

Develop preventive strategies for those likely to spill—for example, a minimal amount of paint in the containers, or special holders and containers.

Encourage children to wear protective clothing, such as an old shirt.

Remind students to wipe excess paint from their brushes back into the containers.

Lest the paint colors run together, caution children about painting next to a painted area that still is wet.

When making a color change, urge students to wait until a color is completely dry before painting over it.

If brushes must be cleaned during the painting session, tell students to squeeze out the excess water thoroughly before using the brush to paint again. Otherwise, the paint in the individual containers will become water-diluted and less intense.

During upper elementary and middle school, students can design with paint on moist, colored construction paper. They can use the dry-brush or pointillistic approach to achieve texture. They can explore mixed-media techniques, combining tempera and crayon, tempera and pastel, and tempera and India ink in a semibatik process.

Encourage older students to mix a greater variety of tints, shades, and neutralized hues to achieve a more individual and personal style. They can use discarded pie tins, TV-dinner trays, and plastic cafeteria trays for their palettes. They must be cautioned, however, to be economical and not to mix more paint than they need. For tints, they should add the hue a little at a time to the white paint rather than vice versa. Paint tins always should be rinsed out at the end of class.

Students cannot rush through a tempera painting project any more than they can hurry through any qualitative creative endeavor; therefore, sufficient time must be allotted for all phases of the undertaking. First comes the motivational time, then the preliminary sketching session. These are followed by the studio work, which involves choices of colors and then achievement of contrast, pattern, and detail. Throughout the studio activity, there should be evaluation of the work in its several stages. Finally, the completed paintings are exhibited. With so much to be gained from the experience, tempera painting should be included in every school art program!

Tempera Resist

For middle school students who have had many elementary school experiences painting with tempera, try tempera resist. Tempera resist employs a liquid tempera underpainting followed by a final coating of India ink. It is a challenging technique replete with hidden surprises. Although highly recommended as an exciting project in painting, tempera resist presents some materials problems, the high cost of India ink among them.

The tempera paint that is employed should be a good quality liquid tempera. Powdered tempera is not recommended, although some teachers claim that powdered tempera works when it is mixed with a small amount of liquid glue. Whether liquid or powder, the paint must be of a thick, creamy consistency—not watery—and should be applied heavily. Watery paint will absorb the final ink coating rather than resist it. Bright, intense hues of tempera should be employed for the highest contrast of black ink against color. Discourage the use of dark blue, dark purple, and brown, which will not show up. Subtle, lightly grayed hues, such as sienna, ochre, light umber, and light gray also are effective. White may be employed with discrimination but generally should be repeated, because a solitary white area often detracts from the rest of the composition. Recommended papers are construction paper in white or light colors and cardboard from store cartons.

Considerable time is needed for the various steps in the tempera resist process: the preliminary drawing, the tempera painting, the inking,

Fifth-grader Sarah Billington paints in the areas of her marker drawing of a bird. She chose an assortment of colors in low values to create a dramatic night effect.

The black resist line varies in width in the painting of the trees and the different background colors.

Tempera-resist painting by a middle school student shows a beautiful flowing division of shapes and a sophisticated series of analogous colors.

Bits of black attached to the solid-paint areas add interest to this painting of a dozen different flowers and a spider in its web.

the rinsing, and the optional coating with gloss polymer. The sketch or preliminary drawing should be made in chalk. Encourage students to vary the pressure of the chalk lines, making lines from thick to thin. The importance of this will be revealed in the second phase, when the ink is applied and soaks into the space left by the chalked lines. A relevant aesthetic consideration for this project is that the more the students break large shapes into small shapes, the more beautiful the finished result will be. As students paint with the tempera, urge them to paint up to, but not over, the chalked lines, leaving a gap from $\frac{1}{16}$ to $\frac{3}{16}$ of an inch wide. The more varied the chalk lines or the paper surface remaining between painted areas, the more successfully contrasting the composition will be.

Remind students not to paint the shapes, areas, and details they want to be black in the completed painting.

Caution students that a tempera color painted over another dry tempera area will wash off in the final rinse; therefore, they must plan their color scheme in advance. Patterns painted into wet tempera areas can be effective, however. Encourage students to be expressive in their color usage—for example, to employ varied kinds of green for grass and trees,

Saturday Children's Classes. Courtesy of Frank Wachowiak.

Top: *Steps in creating a tempera-India ink resist. The preliminary drawing is made in school chalk on white or light-colored construction paper.* **Middle:** *Paint is applied up to the chalk outline, but not covering it, and allowed to dry completely.* **Bottom:** *Undiluted India ink is applied generously over the tempera surface, allowed to dry thoroughly, and rinsed off at the sink.*

or many values and intensities of blue for skies. After all of the areas to be colored are painted, the work should be stored to dry completely. For the India inking phase, cover a work surface with newspapers. With a tissue, wipe off the chalk remaining in the lines. Place the painting on the newspapers and paint it with the India ink in random, circular strokes. Totally cover the painting, then store it overnight to dry completely.

Because wet paintings tear easily, for the final rinsing phase put the painting onto a protective backing, such as a Masonite board or old cafeteria tray. Place them into the sink and rinse with cold water, or take them outdoors and rinse them gently with a hose. Begin rinsing in the center of the work and move outward. Do not direct the water toward the same area for long, however, because too much paint will wash off or, even worse, the paper will disintegrate. A moist sponge or finger run may bring out the color where the ink stubbornly sticks. After rinsing, very carefully lift the painting onto a counter or the floor and blot it with paper towels. When the tempera-resist painting is completely dry, give it a protective and enhancing coat of liquid wax or glossy polymer medium.

Courtesy of David Hodge, Oshkosh, WI.

Before-and-after results in a tempera and India ink resist project by a middle school youngster. For successful results, be sure that the tempera paint is a quality-brand liquid type and the India ink is used undiluted.

An upper elementary student retouches the lines on the painted rhinoceros he contributed to a jungle-theme group mural. The preliminary drawings were made with school chalk on large cardboard sheets salvaged from mattress boxes. Then, chalk lines were gone over with brush and black tempera to provide unity of line quality throughout the mural. The children then colored up to, but did not cover, the black outlines. Finally, the murals were taken into the community to enliven a children's ward in a local hospital.

Mural Making

Mural projects help students to acquire not only art knowledge but also another kind of knowledge—what it means to work with others to plan and carry out a project. Collaborative art builds self-esteem and diminishes alienation. Group involvement in projects of large scale and scope—for example, decorating the classroom for a celebration, or presenting a series of works on a central theme—builds memories. With the teacher acting as facilitator, students can work as a group to generate ideas. Educational goals can be organized according to objectives, and strategies for assessing the project's effectiveness in addressing community concerns can be developed.

Some subjects have almost universal appeal to particular age groups, and certain themes are especially appropriate. For very young children, suggested topics are a butterfly dance, land of make-believe, fish in the sea, Noah's ark, and a flower garden. Intermediate and elementary school children favor the farm, birds in a tree, animals at the zoo or in the jungle, games on the playground, when dragons roamed the world, and fun at the beach. Upper elementary and middle school students react positively to astronauts in space, a kite-flying contest, aquanauts exploring the sea, rodeo, rock festival, block party, state fair, three-ring circus, winter carnival, world of the future, and where and how young people in our community play and relax. (See Chapters 14 and 18 for discussions regarding integration with other subjects.)

Before the class begins a mural, the teacher who is interested in integrating social studies with the project can ask, "What is the purpose of a mural?" "Who painted the first murals?" Show cave paintings from Altamira and Fonte de Gaume. Are there any murals in your community's public buildings, post offices, and schools? What was their original social, political, or educational intent? Through discussion of the artist who made the mural, children can gain knowledge of art history. Using art criticism methods, debate the relative merits of each mural. Discuss the aesthetic issues of realism and abstraction, and of colors muddied by aging.

The great Mexican murals were made to promote both social consciousness and aesthetic awareness, and older students can be involved in decisions about how to include real community concerns and goals in a mural. When murals are made in the community, a rich social setting comes into play and enriches the process. In mural-making projects, when aesthetic interests go along with other interests such as civic, commercial, health, or moral issues, the combination makes the experience doubly important to students.

Once a theme is selected, other questions follow: What medium or technique should be employed? How large should the mural be? Where

Courtesy of Frank Wachowiak and Ted Ramsay, University Elementary School, Iowa City, IA.

The group mural Fun at the Park *was painted by elementary school children on a 10- × 200-foot plywood construction barrier. The preliminary sketch on the previously primed barrier fence was made in chalk, then reinforced with black enamel applied with ½- and 1-inch-wide utility brushes. Parents donated leftover paints in a variety of colors for the project.*

Taking advantage of transmitted light for a stained-glass-window effect, fourth- and fifth-grade students stand atop the shelving to paint their jungle mural.

can we work on it? Where will it be displayed when completed? How shall each student's contribution to the mural be decided?

If, for example, a collage-type pin-up mural is agreed on, the following procedure is recommended: When all students have completed their individual contributions to the total mural, the teacher and students should devote at least one art session to composing the mural. Discuss the merits of the placement and design. Here, the teacher's tact and gentle persuasion play an important role. Bring to the children's attention that a mural in one sense is like a giant painting and requires the same compositional treatment. Urge students to strive for varied sizes of objects or figures, varied heights, and varied breakup of space in both foreground and background. Encourage overlapping of shapes, grouping of objects to achieve unity, and quiet areas to balance busy or detailed ones. Have students use larger shapes or figures at the bottom of the mural and smaller ones at the top to create an illusion of distance.

Children who complete their assigned segments early can enhance the compositions with space-filling elements, such as rainbows, clouds, and pets. They also might wish to add recreational and transportation equipment: balls, kites, cars, trucks, bicycles, motorcycles, frisbees, planes. Some can make street furniture—telephone poles, mailboxes, signs, fences, and benches—and landscape elements—trees, bushes, and rocks. When the separate segments finally are arranged in a composition that is pictorially unified, they are stapled or glued in place. If the mural is

attached to a separate piece of plywood or heavy carton cardboard, display it in the school's entrance foyer, hallway, or lunchroom for everyone to enjoy; exhibit it in a building out in the community; or exhibit it first in the school and then in the community.

For example, fun on the playground can be the theme for a collage (cut-and-paste) mural. Ask the following questions: What kinds of games or sports should be included? (List them on the markerboard or chalkboard.) How shall we decide which activity each student will portray? How many different areas of the playground will we include? What types of playground equipment will we show? Why shouldn't all children in the mural be the same size? Will they all be dressed alike? (Make a list on the chalkboard of the different kinds of clothing and uniforms the children in the mural might wear.) What patterns will we show on their clothes? (Wallpaper samples or fabric remnants may be used). What else can we include? (Make a list on the markerboard or chalkboard: trees, fences, airplanes, signs, and so on.)

A different method, using measuring and mathematical scaling, teaches students how to scale up a mural. For example, for a figurative mural such as "Playing on the Playground," begin by making a tag board

Hundreds of clay balls were flattened and stamped with designs. Some were stained. Then they were arranged by middle school students into a mural of lasting beauty. See Virginia Smithwick Robinson and Robert Clements, "Mosaic Panels," Arts & Activities, *May 1982.*

mannequin. Draw and cut from oak tag the parts of the bodies (a con-venient conversion is one foot = five feet, which is about the size of a child), then arrange the parts into an action pose. The more exuberant and active the pose the better: upside down, doing handstands, etc. Then put a paper over the loose, arranged pieces and rub over it with a dark crayon. In order to scale up the drawing to mural size, measure and draw 1-inch squares on the small sketch—called a "cartoon" in mural-making terminology. If the cartoon sketch was on 9- × 12-inch paper, and the final size is to be three times as large, then students will need papers 27- × 36-inch ruled into 3-inch squares. A length of newsprint from a discarded newsroll will give this size. Write tiny corresponding numbers on each square of both papers to help in copying lines in the correct square.

To paint the mural, tape down the drop cloth and erect the scaffold. To transfer the figure (now on large paper) to the wall, either cut it out and trace around it or hold the paper up to a window and put colorful chalk on the back side where the lines are. Next, place the paper right side up on the wall and go over the lines, leaving a faint chalk line on the wall. Then go over the lines and paint the figures. To minimize student crowd-ing at the mural, have students, working in small groups, paint throughout the day.

Other mural techniques and media also can be used. For example, for freestyle, expressive murals that are painted directly on surfaces such as oaktag, cardboard, poster board, and hardboard, use tempera or latex acrylic paint. Use a preliminary outline in black paint to spark the com-

Saturday Children's Classes. Courtesy of Frank Wachowiak, Athens, GA, and Mary Sayer Hammond, Athens, GA.

Fourth-graders used oil pastels to draw astronauts and spaceships. Students then cut out their drawings and transformed them into an exciting mural collage.

position and give it unity. Choose a design from among those submitted by individuals or small groups, or select several effective designs to be incorporated into one design. Then have small groups of students take turns painting.

Chapter 25

PAPER PROJECTS IN TWO DIMENSIONS

Collage

A popular form of visual expression in elementary and middle schools today is collage, with its related family of montage, decoupage, mosaic, collograph, and assemblage. Over 80 years ago, shocked dismay greeted the initial collages of Pablo Picasso, Georges Braque, Carlo Carra, and Kurt Schwitters, in which the artists dared to include cardboard and printed words. Today, their creations in paper, cardboard scraps, and paste (the word *collage* derives from the French *coller,* which means "to stick or to adhere") are priceless, and the collage technique has become standard in advertising art. The wellsprings from which contemporary artists such as Robert Rauschenberg and Alexis Smith now draw their materials are so bountiful that the technique is limitless in its possibilities.

The collage technique promotes design using overlapping of shapes and colors, positive and negative shapes, value contrast, pattern, and texture. Students have the unique opportunity of rearranging the elements in their work until they achieve a satisfying composition. Approaches to collage range from simple cutting, tearing, and pasting of paper to complex sewing, shearing, and gluing of fabric, plastics, posters, plywood, cardboard, Day-Glo paper, wallpaper and rug samples, paint chips, colored tissue paper, and colored magazine pages. (The artist Jean Dubuffet even used coffee grounds and butterfly wings!)

A preliminary sketch is recommended when the subject matter is a landscape, figure composition, or still-life arrangement. For themes from the imagination, for fantasy, or for purely nonobjective designs, direct cutting, tearing, and pasting are acceptable. In either approach, however, permanent adherence of the separate parts should be postponed until both student and teacher critique the work's strengths and weaknesses. Some other suggestions for making collages are as follows:

Saturday Children's Classes. Courtesy of Frank Wachowiak, Athens, GA.

A large drawing that bumps the edges is made with chalk on a piece of 12- × 18-inch colored paper. Then, the child cuts cloth scraps to fit the areas. Yarn, buttons, rickrack, and colored paper scraps embellish the artwork. Here, oil pastels were added on the face and hands.

Cut and arrange the large shapes or motifs first. If a colored background is being employed, include it in your design by allowing some of the background to show to unify the composition.

Small details and patterns can be pasted onto the large shapes before they are glued to the background surface. Overlapping of shapes is a major feature of collage making.

Eye-catching materials, such as aluminum foil, synthetic silver and gold foils, shiny plastic, and cellophane, fascinate children, who tend to overuse them. Guide the students to use such materials only as points of emphasis. Remove them if they detract from the whole.

Repetition of a color, shape, value, pattern, or texture adds unity to a collage; however, instead of repeating the element, color, or shape exactly, vary it somehow. Recommend using an uneven repetition of

elements; for example, repeat a certain shape or color three times rather than twice.

Encourage the use of informal (asymmetrical) rather than formal (symmetrical) balance.

Avoid a lot of "sticky" problems by using discarded magazines as paste applying surfaces. When a clean pasting area is needed, turn to another page.

Ambitious teachers may want to enlist both parents and children in making cloth banners from the students' paper designs. Army units in ancient Rome each had their own decorated standard. Cloth banners were first used in the Middle Ages during the Crusades, when each force had its own insignia. Artists such as Miriam Shapiro, Jim Dine, Henri Matisse, and Richard Lindner have had banners of their collage designs made.

Tissue-Paper Collage

On the first day of a tissue-paper-collage project, the teacher can surprise the class by unfolding a package of tissue papers of assorted colors. Students' excitement will grow as one color of tissue overlaps another on a white paper background or against the window. Students can tell the teacher which colors to overlap, and then they can invent a name for the resulting hue.

To encourage color awareness and exploration, a free-design, non-objective, colored-tissue collage is recommended for children in the third grade and older. Using a 12- × 18-inch sheet of oak tag, white drawing paper, or construction paper as a background surface, cut or tear different sizes and shapes of tissue. Adhere them to the background using undiluted liquid laundry starch as the adhesive, and overlap the various shapes. A ½-inch utility brush or a large watercolor brush makes an excellent starch applicator. Because it is difficult to change the value of a dark tissue by overlapping, begin with the lighter-colored tissues and proceed

---

Recycle scraps of colored construction paper into collage projects such as these. Primary-grade youngsters arranged paper scraps in assorted sizes, shapes, and colors for their compositions. Supplemental details, patterns, and motifs were added with crayons, oil pastels, markers, paper punches, and brush and paint. **Middle:** *After making a preliminary drawing, sixth-grader Kate Roberts used colored felts for her fish collage. Notice how the overlapping layers and the split-complementary colors of blue-green versus red-orange and yellow-orange add richness to the design.*

Pieced and appliquéd cotton embroidered with plain and metallic yarns, 69 × 105 inches. Bequest of Maxim Karolik. Courtesy of the Museum of Fine Arts, Boston, MA.

What could have more power and charm than the collagelike quilts made by African-American Harriet Powers (1837–1911), a former slave from Athens, Georgia? Her art-works now hang in our nation's most important museums. You can give your artwork strength by using her ideas. A large checkerboard pattern gives unity. Color is restrained to mostly white and very dark. Tints and shades of essentially only two complementary colors, orange and blue, are used. The almost abstract figures create bold positive and negative shapes. Most important, the artwork portrays biblical stories and personal anecdotes in her own words: for the lower left square, "Cold Thursday, 10 of Feb. 1895. A woman frozen while at prayer. A woman frozen at a gateway. A man with a sack of meal frozen. Icicles formed from the breath of a mule. All blue birds killed," Can you find the dead blue birds, woman praying, man with sack, and the mule with icicles?

Courtesy of Frank Wachowiak and Ted Ramsay, University Elementary School, Iowa City, IA.

The colored-tissue compositions illustrated here began as free-form collages. The children cut or tore the tissue and applied it on white construction paper in overlapping stages with liquid laundry starch. When it was dry, they used black and colored felt-nib markers to outline recognizable shapes. Some children used crayons and others paint and brush. Because a

dark-color tissue area is difficult to change to a light value, suggest that students begin pasting light values of tissue first and progress to darker values. One solution is to paste a sheet of white paper over the area and start again.

only gradually to darker values. Reserve the darker colors for the second phase of pasting.

First, apply a coating of starch to the area that is to be covered with tissue. Then, place the tissue carefully over the wet area and apply another coat of starch over it. If brushes pick up some of the color from the

moistened tissue, rinse them. Be sure that all loose tissue edges are glued down well. Empty half-pint milk cartons are economical and practical starch containers. Because tissue is expensive and wrinkles and crumples very easily, storage boxes should be used to store the tissue, one box for each hue.

Presbyterian Church School, Athens, GA. Frank Wachowiak. Saturday Classes.

This beautifully composed colored-tissue-paper collage is by a talented middle school student from Athens, Georgia. Photographs and color slides of matadors, toreadors, and "brave bulls" provided the visual stimulation. The preliminary drawing was made with a felt-nib pen (permanent black-ink type) on white construction paper. Before application of the colored tissue, the student chose certain shapes—matador's trousers, jacket, and so on—for a patterned embellishment and pasted colored sections from magazines onto those parts. The tissue was applied by first coating an area with liquid laundry starch and then placing the tissue over it. The area was coated again with the starch, making sure that all edges were smoothly secured. Light-colored tissue was applied first, progressing to the darker colors. Caution was employed in the final stages so that dark-value tissue did not obliterate the important, form-defining ink lines.

Although the abstract composition has an aesthetic validity of its own, it can be augmented as follows: After students have filled their compositions to the borders of the paper, challenge them to look for hidden shapes. These might be suggestive of animals, birds, insects, fish, or fantasy creatures. Once a form emerges, students can glue on additional torn pieces or strips of tissue in deeper colors to represent appendages, which give the shape character and individuality. Avoid outlining the revealed figure so boldly that it is isolated from the rest of the composition. Employ a variety of dark-colored tissues for this step rather than a single hue. Black tissue can be used, but only in a most restrained way. Similarly, if students outline only one figure with a black felt-nib marker, that one figure will be isolated, but if all emerging figures are outlined in black, a unity will be achieved.

In addition to black markers, students can use crayons, colored markers, and tempera paint in white, gray, or black to delineate desired shapes, such as bark on a tree, scales on a fish, feathers on a bird, and veins in a wing or leaf. Wait until the tissue surface is dry, especially if using water-soluble markers.

The free-design approach using colored tissue described earlier is only one of many avenues for creating with such tissue. Another approach uses a preliminary drawing made with black or dark-colored crayons on light-colored, heavy paper. After the drawing is completed, the cut or torn tissue paper is applied; as in the previous method, begin with the lighter hues. Cut or tear the tissue sheet slightly larger than the drawn shapes. Drawn lines sometimes are obscured by dark tissue overlays, but when the tissue layer is dry, these lines can be redrawn for emphasis. Using lettering from printed publications in conjunction with colored tissue adds a new dimension to the tissue collage, and this is one way to incorporate text concerning social issues into the artwork—an important consideration in contemporary art expression.

Mosaics

The multifaceted technique of mosaic art, with its colored pieces called *tesserae,* is a welcome, albeit challenging technique for children's art expression. It requires a generous time allotment, supplemental storage, and above all, students with both patience and persistence. Standard art materials (colored construction paper, paste, and scissors) are used.

A drawing with permanent marker of a seated boy with bird and bicycle wheel was made on 18- × 24-inch white paper. Then, a tissue shape was cut or torn and an area selected for it. Next, laundry starch was applied to that area and the shape was firmly pasted down. For extra interest, tissue shapes do not follow the figure's form.

Courtesy of David Hodge, Oshkosh, WI.

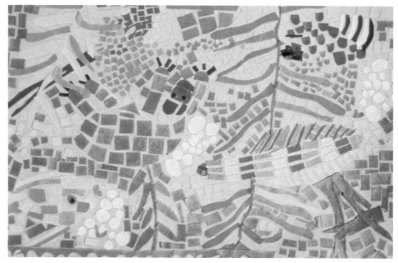

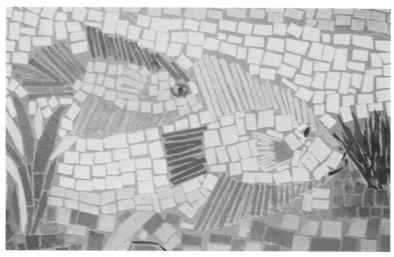

Courtesy of David Hodge, Oshkosh, WI.

Creating mosaics, a pleasantly repetitive and creative project, calls for much small-muscle, tactile activity. It teaches that wholes are made of parts, which is an important concept in mathematics, science, and social studies.

Motivation for the project might include visits to mosaics in the community. If available, show color films and slides of mosaic art, both past and present. This can include San Vitale in Rome, Gaudi's Cathedral in Barcelona, Simon Rodia's Watts Towers in Los Angeles, and the mosaic-paved avenues of Rio de Janeiro. Subject matter for paper mosaics that is manageable yet exciting includes birds, fish, and animals in their habitats; flower bouquets; butterflies in a garden; dragons; and clowns.

In mosaic design, as with most two-dimensional art expression, an important initial step is the preliminary sketch. Make it from life and nature, from visits to museums, or from references to photographs and color slides. The preliminary sketches then are developed into a linear composition the size of the actual mosaic that is desired. The background surface may be colored construction paper, chip-board, or salvaged gift-box container.

Critical to the project's success is an adequate supply of tesserae. Cut narrow strips of colored construction paper, not necessarily the same width, and store them according to color in shoe boxes. Students then cut these strips as needed into individual tesserae. They need not cut all of the strips into perfect squares; some can be rectangular or triangular. Some adventurous teachers have used vinyl, tile scraps, linoleum, and even colored glass (with caution) instead of construction paper.

During a mosaic project, students should take turns selecting the desired color strips or tesserae from the supply-table boxes. Apply school paste or white glue to the background paper and press the tesserae firmly into the adhesive. Usually, it is best to begin on the outer edge of a shape and work inward toward the center. To achieve the mosaic effect, tesserae should not touch or overlap each other. The students should be reminded that in professional mosaic work, a grout is mortared between tesserae. Avoid a rigid, bricklaying technique—the minute, open spaces between tesserae should vary somewhat for best effect.

Students may create excitement with their mosaic compositions through a contrast of colors in specified areas. Contrast the wing of a bird against the body, the stamen against a flower petal, an insect against a leaf.

Underwater themes are especially effective for mosaics, because of the variety of shapes, details, and patterns that are found in fish, shells, coral, and seaweed. These beautifully space-filled compositions are by upper elementary students, who used a variety of sizes and shapes of the tesserae.

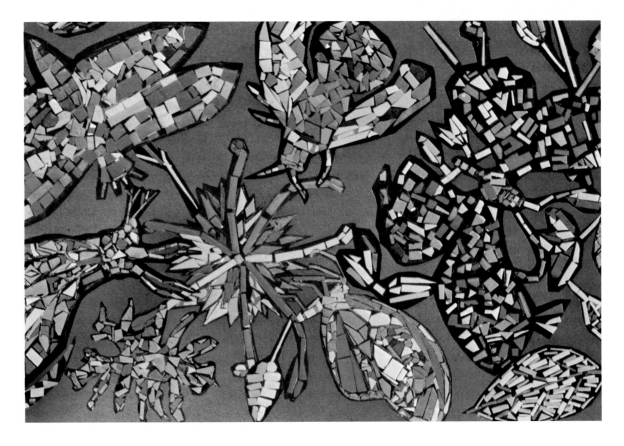

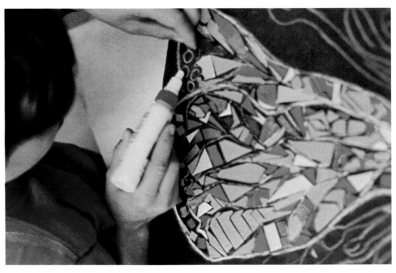

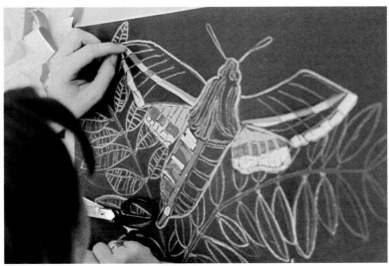

Saturday Children's Classes. Courtesy of Frank Wachowiak, Athens, GA, and Mary Sayer Hammond, Athens, GA.

A group mural in which each student's mosaic insect on black paper was cut out, with border preserved, and then mounted onto a large piece of brown cardboard.

Recommended background surfaces for paper mosaic projects include construction paper in assorted colors, railroad board, chip-board, oak tag, or discarded gift-box covers. Suggested adhesives include school paste, white glue, or glue sticks.

One important strategy in achieving expressive mosaic quality is to employ several values of a color in the larger areas: for example, use two or three values of blue in the sky, and two or three values of green in the grass and leaves. Use several kinds of brown ochre, umber, and sienna colors for earth and tree trunks. The brightest, most intense colors may be reserved for sharp contrast or emphasis—on the beak or claws of a bird, the eyes of a tiger, the stamen of a lily, or the horns of a bull.

The bird mosaic employed vinyl and linoleum tesserae glued to Masonite® board with tinted grout used as a filler.

Chapter 26

PRINTMAKING

Printmaking with Found Objects

Printmaking projects should range from simple processes during the primary grades to complex techniques in upper elementary and middle school. Some of the most colorful and successful prints can be made by very young children employing vegetables and fruit. Found objects, such as buttons, flat or round wooden clothespins, wooden spools, bottle caps, mailing tubes, corks, sponges, and erasers, also can be used for making prints. In addition, cord can be glued in a free design to the smooth metal top of a condiment container to produce a printing shape. Still another technique is to cut shapes from stiff sponge; for a handle, use hot melt glue to glue a discarded film canister to it.

A science-correlated study of nature's form and function can use assorted vegetables (okra, cabbage, mushrooms, peppers, carrots, artichokes) that are cut in half or in pieces, painted, and printed. The excitement quickens when students gain awareness of the hidden design in these natural forms. (However, in classes where children are poor and hungry, the use of food for painting is problematic.) The halved or quartered vegetables are painted on the cut side with colored tempera of a creamy consistency, or they are pressed on a tempera-coated, folded paper towel. Water-soluble printing ink also can be used. Then, they are printed repeatedly on colored construction paper or tissue paper to form an all-over or repeat design.

For best results, the vegetables must be fresh, crisp, and solid. They should be kept refrigerated between printmaking sessions. The most popular vegetable for this project is the potato. Cut in half, its flat, open surface is incised to create a relief. Children must be reminded to exercise caution when using sharp tools, however. Recommended tools include small scissors, fingernail files, nut picks, dental tools, and assorted nails. Melon-ball

scoops are excellent for creating circular designs. In upper elementary and middle school, paring knives, Sloyd knives, or Hyde knives may be employed if they are used with extreme care.

Students should strive for a simple, bold breakup of space in their cutout or incised designs. Suggest the use of cross-cuts, wedges as in a pie, assorted-size holes, and star, asterisk, cogwheel, sunburst, and spider's web effects. Students can use large potatoes to print monogram motifs, but letters must be reversed to print correctly. Students should begin by making a preliminary drawing on paper of the shape of the cut potato to guide them in their cutting. It is possible to reverse the design at the window and then copy it onto the potato surface.

Construction paper in assorted colors is, perhaps, the most popular and serviceable surface for vegetable printing, although colored tissue, wallpaper, and fabrics have been used. Generous newspaper padding should be placed under the paper to be printed to ensure a good impression. In addition, students should stand in order to exert firm pressure. Also, if a potato is being used, cutting wedges out of the holding end can improve the student's grasp.

We recommend making a few practice applications of the vegetable stamp on scrap paper before beginning. In planning their printmaking, students might be encouraged to develop a repeat pattern in several places on their paper (this does not have to be a measured, mathematical repeat), thus allowing some prints to go off the page to create an all-over effect. Discourage restamping without reinking and rushing to finish, which result in sloppy printing. Often, however, the imperfection of a child's effort lends a fresh, spontaneous quality to the product. By sharing their stamps, children can produce exciting variations.

For a project correlated with writing, have the students use vegetable and found-object prints as covers for their creative-writing notebooks.

Saturday Children's Classes. Courtesy of Frank Wachowiak, Athens, GA, and Mary Sayer Hammond, Athens, GA.

Top right: *A potato, with the pattern cut into it, is inked or painted before making the print. Do not insist on a measured, rigidly controlled design. Because caution must be exercised in cutting the designs, use nails, plastic knives, and melon scoops for this process.* **Top left:** *Vegetable prints are enhanced by the application of oil pastels. A youngster applies the pastel colors between the printed motifs, allowing some of the background paper to show.* **Middle left:** *Notice in this example how the light-blue pastel complements the yellow-*

orange paper color. **Bottom left:** *Notice how the jagged edges of the oil pastel areas add a contrasting element against the round forms of the potatoes.* **Bottom right:** *Vegetable-print, all-over repeat designs make excellent covers for notebooks, pencil holders (recycle a soup or coffee can), and household dispensers. To protect the surface and make it shine, apply a coat of gloss polymer medium.*

The prints also can be used for pencil containers (glue the printed paper to a discarded box or can). In both cases, students can coat the surface with gloss polymer medium.

Vegetable and found-object prints, which are artistic in their simplest form, also can be embellished for added richness. One or more crayon or oil-pastel colors can be added in the negative spaces between the printed shapes. For unity, let some of the background surface between the pasteled or crayoned areas and the printed motifs remain uncolored.

Glue Line–Relief Prints

A printmaking process that is remarkably successful with students in all grades is the glue-line-on-cardboard print. It is a relatively simple technique, but it requires at least two class sessions. Time is needed both for the glue to dry overnight before printing and because students must take turns at the inking stations.

In addition to pencils, other required materials for making glue line-relief prints include the following:

- Printing plates—use a smooth-surfaced cardboard (discarded, glossy-surfaced gift-box covers are excellent) or tagboard; recommended plate sizes are 9- × 9-inch, 9- × 12-inch, 12- × 12-inch, or 12- × 18-inch
- Small plastic containers with a nozzle of white liquid glue or, even better, the new thick line variety
- Water-soluble printing ink (black is recommended)

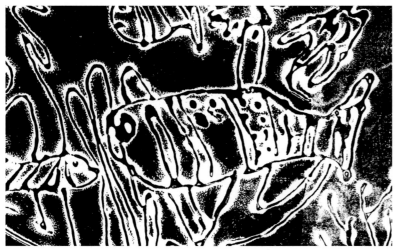

Saturday Children's Classes. Courtesy of Frank Wachowiak, Athens, GA.

Glue-line technique produces beautiful flowing lines.

Courtesy of David Hodge, Oshkosh, WI.

Glue-line relief print by a sixth-grade student based on a drawing from a posed model. Because of the pressure applied by the soft-rubber brayer, the printing ink covers parts of the background as well as the glue lines.

- A soft-rubber brayer or roller for inking
- An inking surface, such as a discarded cafeteria tray or metal cookie sheet
- Protective newspapers
- Newsprint, tissue paper, or classified-ad pages on which to print

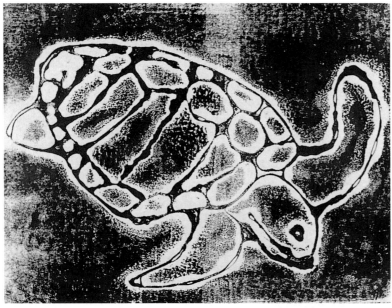

The flowing glue-line technique adapts well to portraying the swimming of this determined sea turtle.

Appealing subject-matter choices for young children are butterflies, birds, fish, flowers, and animals. Students in upper elementary and middle school may choose more complex themes: historical legends, space and science explorations, still life, cityscape compositions, portraits, and figure studies.

A preliminary drawing definitely is recommended. Because intricate details will blend together in the glue line and get lost, make the initial drawing with chalk for boldness and simplicity. Limit the composition to one large motif (bird, insect, fish, animal) with its complementary foliage or seaweed rather than using several smaller motifs. With only one large figure, there will be room to clearly delineate details, such as eye, beak, whiskers, antenna, claw, feather, and fish scales. Evaluate the compositions with the student for space-filling design, shape variation, and pattern.

The cardboard printing plate with its linear composition now is ready for the glue application. Gently squeeze the container, trailing the glue over the drawn line. A linear variety is achieved naturally, because it is difficult to manage an even, steady flow of glue. Dots of glue will produce sunburst effects in the final printing. The glue must be allowed to dry thoroughly overnight before inking; when dry, the glue will be transparent and free of white ridges and welts.

See the section later in this chapter on printing for specific recommendations. The most successful prints are those that capture both the raised glue lines as well as the background inked areas. This will require pressure with palm and fingers into the smaller background areas. Uninked areas between glue lines and background provide the necessary light and dark contrast. For the demonstration, the teacher might use white tissue so that students can actually see the ink absorbing into the paper and detect areas requiring more pressure. Several prints can be made from the same plate. Trim borders, if necessary, and mount the print on colored construction paper for an exciting display.

Collographs

Students in intermediate and upper elementary as well as in middle school are interested in and challenged by more complex approaches to printmaking. Cardboard prints sometimes are referred to as *collographs* (a word combination of *collage* and *graph*), and collographs can be created with commonly available materials and nonhazardous tools. The final results, however, often are comparable to those of woodblocks and lino prints. An especially welcome advantage of this technique is the flexibility it allows in rearranging or deleting compositional elements before the final gluing.

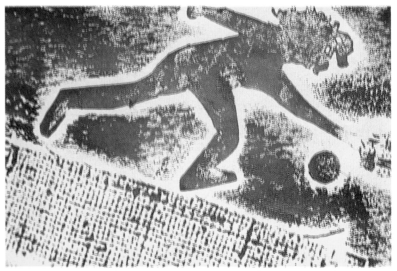

Collographs can be made from common materials. In fourth-grader Graham Grubb's tennis collograph, burlap represents the net.

Courtesy of Frank Wachowiak and Ted Ramsay, Iowa City Elementary Laboratory School, Iowa City, IA.

The Jungle, 18 × 36 inches. Group project collograph by intermediate elementary grade children. The students used a paper punch to create pattern in the leopard and on the bushes. Pinking shears cut the palm tree leaves. Additional cutout holes, as well as little squares and triangles of paper, were pasted down onto the cardboard plate. See especially the gorilla's exciting background at left. The plate was then printed.

The following tools and materials are required: a sheet of sturdy cardboard (such as the lid or bottom of a gift box), chip-board, discarded scraps of illustration board (tagboard is not recommended), glue, scissors, assorted-weight papers (smooth or textured), assorted-size paper punches, a soft-rubber brayer, water-soluble printing ink in black or dark colors, newsprint, gloss polymer medium, a utility brush, and lots of protective newspapers.

The animal world is a favorite theme for collographs because it provides so many options for creating a strong, lively design. Especially important is using a variety of cut-out shapes to fill the space. While helpful, an overall preliminary drawing is not required. Separate motifs or shapes may be drawn first before cutting. Large printing plates may create a management problem in crowded classrooms, however; therefore, a recommended plate size for students in the intermediate and upper-elementary grades is a sheet that is 9- × 9-inches, 9- × 12-inches, or 12- × 12-inches.

Students draw and cut out the individual shapes from tagboard (oak tag), construction paper, brown wrapping tape, and other assorted-weight papers. Then they create open patterns in some of these shapes, employing paper punches and utility knives, and arrange these elements on the background cardboard until they achieve a satisfactory composition. Some shapes may overlap for unity, spatial effects, and interest. Students can add a variety of found materials to create textural qualities, using gummed reinforcements, textured wallpaper samples, masking tape, fabric, string, yarn, confetti, liquid glue, and flat, found objects. If the relief is too high, however, such as from thick cord or buttons, the print will

Steps in making a collograph print. **Top left:** *Gluing down the paper-punched birds. Caution: If water-based printing ink is employed, the teacher must give the plate a protective, water-resistant coating.* **Left middle:** *Inking the collograph.* **Top right:** *A middle school student peels back the print from the plate while checking that areas have been sufficiently inked and pressed.* **Bottom left:** *The finished print with attractive tree shapes.*

not be successful. When the students, with the teacher's guidance, achieve a satisfying, space-filling design, they carefully glue down the pieces. Use a discarded magazine as a gluing surface, and turn to a clean page for each application. All edges must be glued securely.

The whole composition then is sealed with a coat of polymer medium to further prevent the separate pieces from coming loose during the printing and cleaning phases. A separate table or counter that is protected by newspapers should be designated as the sealing area. Allow the plates to dry overnight before inking. (See the section in this chapter on inking and printing.) Collograph plates do not need to be washed between printing sessions. Finished prints can be attractively mounted for display, and students may want to exchange prints. Also, the plate itself can be painted and mounted. In addition, it can be covered with heavy-duty aluminum foil and further embellished, as described later in this chapter in the section on aluminum-foil relief.

Linoleum Prints and Styrofoam® Prints

In the primary grades, Styrofoam® prints are recommended as a way to make relief prints. Everyone is familiar with this material in its common use as trays on which meats, vegetables, and fruits are sold in the super-market. (Some store managers, if asked, will donate these trays.) If trays are to be used for printmaking, the raised rim must first be cut off. Alternately, large flat sheets of half-inch-thick, polystyrene foam, sold for insulation in 3- × 8-foot sheets (or ¼-inch thick, sold in rolls) at builder supply stores such as Home Depot, can be purchased and cut to the desired size.

The obvious advantage of foam over linoleum is that no cutting by the children is required. After the pencil sketch is transferred to the foam, the design is incised by firmly going over it with a pencil or pen. Patterns of dots, circles, and squares can be made by using pencil points and hollow ¼" circular and square tubes.

A technically demanding form of relief printmaking recommended for students in the upper elementary and middle school is linoleum ("lino") block printing. A new product, flexible printing block, is gaining in usage over linoleum. Students are challenged by using diverse tools and by manipulating, if available, a heavy roller press. Because of these built-in attractions, teachers will have little trouble introducing lino prints into the art program.

The unmounted, gray, pliable "battleship" linoleum suggested for this project may be obtained from art-supply companies. Cut the linoleum plates large enough to give the students ample opportunity for a rich composition. A minimum size of 9- × 9-inches, 9- × 12-inches, or 12- × 12-inches is recommended. A 4" x 9" size is good for cards as it conveniently fits into a standard size business envelope. For middle school students who want to make very large prints, luan plywood is suitable. The basic materials and tools needed include sets of lino-cutting gouges

Courtesy of Frank Wachowiak, Athens, GA, and Ted Ramsay, Iowa City Elementary Laboratory School, Iowa City, IA.

Linoleum prints with bold designs by fourth- and fifth-grade children. The left picture of monkeys uses a series of monkeys—big, small, and smallest—to set up a rhythm. The right

kangaroo picture has an interesting feature—a positive and negative cactus.

This fifth-grade student's linoleum print began with a sketching trip drawing animals at the natural history museum. Notice how the leftover linoleum lines in the sky were cut in an attractive movement to give a feeling of unity to the composition. Note how some birds in the sky were black on white and others white on black.

for the students to share, rubber brayers, inking surfaces of cookie tins or old cafeteria trays, and water-soluble printing ink.

Effective subject-matter themes for lino and foam prints are those that promise a strong light- and dark-value composition, with a variety of shapes, pattern, and detail. Some possibilities are birds, jungle animals and their young, insects, fish, shells, old houses, legendary or mythological figures, portraits, and still-life arrangements composed of musical instruments, antiques, plants, household utensils, and sports equipment. A field trip to a natural-history museum will provide a wealth of motivational material.

A preliminary drawing on paper with black crayon, felt-nib pen, brush and ink, or white crayon on black paper is an important requisite for a successful lino-print project. It usually determines the final composition and establishes the dark and light pattern, variety of textural exploitation, points of emphasis, and lines of motion. Remind students that letters and numerals must be reversed in the sketch.

After preliminary drawings have been made and evaluated for design potential, the students may use them as a reference for their drawing on the lino plate. Or, the students may transfer the design to the lino plate with carbon paper or dressmaker's white transfer paper. If the lino surface is dark and no white transfer paper is available, paint the lino block with white tempera paint first. To reverse a sketch before transferring it to the block, hold it against the window, and trace lines on the back of the sheet. Another technique sometimes used is to transfer the design by placing the drawing pencil-side-down onto the block, taping it down securely, and rubbing over it with a metal spoon.

After the drawing has been made but before the cutting begins, check that there are enough sharpened gouges in various sizes for the entire class to use. Students should be introduced to the potential of the many gouges through a teacher demonstration emphasizing the correct way to hold and manipulate the gouge. Never put a supporting hand in front of a cutting tool. To make lino cutting safer, a wooden bench hook can be anchored against the table edge to provide a supportive ridge to hold the block. Each lino gouge makes its own particular cut, and although gouges are not as easily controlled as pencils or pens, they often produce lines that are more dynamic. The richest print effects are achieved by using a range of gouges, from veiners to scoops and shovels. Number 1 and 2 veiners or V-shaped gouges are suggested for making the initial outlines. Another approach is to use the scoop or shovel gouges, working from inside the shapes and thus minimizing tightly outlined compositions.

To prevent mistakes in cutting, students can mark an X on those areas to be gouged. Use directional gouge cuts to follow the object's contours, like ripples around a pebble tossed in a stream. Instruct students not to make their cuts too deep, however, because the low ridges that remain in the lino will produce an attractive texture. If students have difficulty cutting because the linoleum is too hard, heat it on a cookie

These woodblock prints of a bird and its hungry babies, cows at milking time, and three hens are by Japanese children, Grades 4 and 5. Notice how much was observed and recorded in these space-filled compositions. Printmaking that incorporates woodblock cutting tools is introduced in the third grade in Japanese schools. Note in the top design the skillfully cut pattern of positive and negative shapes in the leaves and branches.

Actual size woodblock print. This seventh-grade student found and created strong patterns in the tree branches and feathers. The block was painted with colored tempera and printed in several stages to achieve the color overlays.

tin over an electrical hot plate turned to a low setting. (See the following section for information on inking and printing.)

Wooden scraps, which often can be secured from building sites or lumber yards, are an alternative to linoleum for printmaking. Especially with small blocks, a bench hook is required for safety, however. Also, before inking, seal the wood's porous surface with diluted white glue.

Proofing, Inking, and Printing

This section applies to glue line, collograph, linoleum, Styrofoam,® and aluminum-foil relief prints. Proofs of the work-in-progress can be made by placing paper over the design and, with the side of a black crayon or oil pastel, rubbing over the paper with a steady and even pressure. The

A woodblock print by Käthe Kollwitz (1867–1945) was the motivation for the three self-portrait prints by upper-grade Japanese youngsters.

*Two examples of linoleum blocks printed over colored-tissue collages. **Right:** White printing ink was employed over a dark tissue design. **Left:** black printing ink was used over a lighter valued tissue underlay. Which of these middle school designs do you like better? Before pulling the print, be sure that the tissue is glued down firmly and smoothly and is thoroughly dry.*

resulting proof will reveal to the students how the print design is progressing. To avoid the need to give individual instructions, demonstrate the inking, printing, and wet-print storage procedures step-by-step one time for the entire class.

Inking and printing are very exciting, but without careful planning, this stage can develop into a chaotic bedlam. Designated inking and printing tables, covered with newspapers, should be positioned so that several students can stand and work comfortably. You will need to provide several inking surfaces and soft-rubber brayers that are 3 or more inches wide (do not use the gelatin type) as well as black water-soluble ink. At the inking station, squeeze out a brayer-width ribbon of ink onto the inking surface. With the brayer, roll out the ink until it is tacky—you will hear a snapping, hissing sound—and then apply the ink to the plate in both directions. Standing up to get more pressure, evenly ink every part of the plate, especially its edges and corners. Then, carefully and quickly, lift and carry the inked plate to the printing station.

Make the print immediately, because water-soluble ink dries rapidly. Use newsprint, brown wrapping paper, colored construction paper, colored tissue paper, wallpaper samples, fabric remnants, classified-ad pages, or colored pages from magazines. Carefully place the slightly larger-sized sheet of paper over the inked surface, and pat it down with the palm of the hand. Beginning in the center, smooth out to the edges, being careful that the paper does not shift. Standing up, exert stronger pressure with a rubber brayer, heel of a hand, jar cover, spoon, or commercially available baren; go over the entire surface, especially borders and corners and between shapes. Where the print is to be darker, press harder. To check the impression, lift the paper partially off the block from various sides. If not satisfied, apply more pressure.

Caution: Do not wait too long to carefully remove the newsprint from the plate. The water-soluble ink dries quickly, and it may cause the paper to stick to the plate. Therefore, pull the paper off the block carefully. So that all students may have a turn to print, the number of initial prints a student pulls must be limited. Remind the children that additional prints always can be made later.

Aluminum-Foil Reliefs

The aluminum-foil relief over collograph plate, collage, or glue line-relief plate is an exciting and novel technique to which students in upper elementary and middle school will respond enthusiastically. The process is not technically a printmaking process; rather, it is a subsequent process that follows the making of a glue-line or a collograph print.

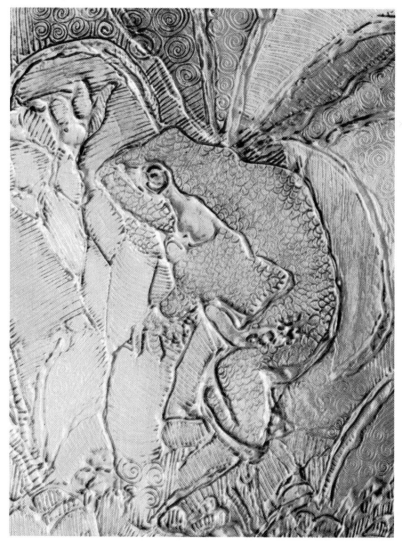

Saturday Children's Classes. Courtesy of Frank Wachowiak, Athens, GA, and Mary Sayer Hammond, Athens, GA.

The final richness of the aluminum-foil relief transcends the readily available materials from which it was made: household heavy-duty foil instead of expensive copper sheeting, cardboard, white glue, blunt pencils, and water-based printing ink. The glowing finished product makes a gift that often is preserved by families for decades.

Materials needed include heavy-duty aluminum foil, blunt-point pencils, soft-rubber brayer or inking roller, white glue (check for consistency—glue should not be watery), gold patina, masking tape, water-soluble printing ink (black or dark hue), and protective newspapers.

If students have been pulling prints from a collograph or a glue-line plate, they can reink the plate and, while the ink still is sticky, cover it with a sheet of foil (shiny side up) that is cut slightly larger than the printing plate. Then, stretching the foil with the heel of a hand toward the edges of the plate, overlap the foil on the back of the plate. Secure the excess foil on the other side with masking tape. To keep the corners as flat as possible, carefully fold them.

On an uninked collage, be sure the pieces of the collage are secured. With glue-line prints, be sure the glue-relief lines are thoroughly dry. Then give the plate a coat of white glue and, while wet, apply the foil.

Next, using a blunt-pointed pencil, press into the foil along both edges of the glue lines and also along the edges of collage shapes to emphasize the relief. Avoid puncturing the foil. Teacher and student each should check to see that all of the relief edges have been sufficiently emphasized. To enrich the relief, indent the foil with the pencil point to create additional details, patterns, and textures. These can be leaves on a bush, veins in the leaves, grass, feathers on a bird, scales on a fish, bark on a tree, or ripples in a stream. Incorporate a variety of invented patterns, such as hatching and cross-hatching; dots, circles, and dots within circles; triangular and diamond shapes; wiggly, jigsaw, and radiating lines; asterisks; stars; and spirals. The more detail, pattern, and texture that are employed, the more effective the result.

To ink the aluminum plate, apply water-soluble black printing ink to the surface with a soft-rubber brayer so that the whole plate is covered except for the deep pencil indentations. To be sure that ink gets into all the crevices, some teachers recommend applying ink with a dauber, made by rolling several paper towels into a tight cylinder and taping them together. See the previous section for directions on making the print.

After making a print, make the foil relief from the plate itself. While the ink is still moist on the plate, use newspapers to remove the excess. Using a hand or a brayer, press one sheet at a time over the moist plate. When no impression is visible, take a folded flat (never bunched or crushed), moistened paper towel and wipe the plate gently to remove excess ink from all areas except the indented ones. When one side of the towel gets inky, unfold and fold it again to provide a clean surface. When the moist towel no longer shows an ink residue, use folded, dry paper towels to burnish the plate, being careful to allow ink to remain in the indented lines. This can be the completed foil relief, or you can enrich the raised surfaces of the plate by the slightest application of gold patina. Aluminum-foil reliefs can be attractively mounted and displayed, and they make excellent gifts.

Saturday Children's Classes, student Cal Clements. Courtesy of Frank Wachowiak, Athens, GA, and Mary Sayer Hammond, Athens, GA.

Aluminum-foil relief is an exciting adventure in bas relief and embossing that has untold possibilities for exploration in the art program. Here, a frog looks this way and that, half-submerged in the pond and awaiting the next morsel. The project also affords an ideal medium for learning about ways to create texture and pattern.

Chapter 27

VISUAL TECHNOLOGY: COMPUTER ART, PHOTOGRAPHY, AND VIDEO

What should one call a chapter touching on photography, video, and computers? One must wonder about calling over-a-century-old photographic processes new media. Let us suggest visual technology. Even discussing computer art, photography, and video as separate subjects seems old-fashioned. With digital cameras, scanners, video capture, animation software, downloading from the Web, and photocopying, the media interpenetrate each other and assume new powerful hybrid forms.

Whereas much school curricula tend to be fragmented, by its very nature visual technology is multidisciplinary and intercultural. Cultural and personal meanings can be shared through highly interactive viewing modes, such as slide shows, videos, and projected movies and multimedia projects. Words and images can interpenetrate; students can develop scripts and images by chatting together on their home computers. Indeed, students interact with visual technology in a new way—one less focused on formalist concerns and more focused on expressivist concerns. And this linking, interconnectedness, and openness are also characteristics shared by both the Web and by postmodern art in general.

The electronic media encourage the constructivist view of education, as students redefine their personal knowledge bases and engage in active learning. While photos, videos, and multimedia presentations can be made of formalistic arrangements focusing on arrangements of the art elements, the new media lend themselves especially well to personally and socially relevant subject matter (see section on formalism and contextualism in chapter 21). The students' lives, individuals' clothing styles, and their interactions with peers, for example, are powerful topics for personal statements. Likewise, the school itself, nearby food kitchens, child care centers, and construction projects can present socially relevant subject matter.

Experiences with visual technology can bring out valuable social studies integration. Yet there is a caveat: with power comes responsibility. Especially with socially relevant photo and video projects, balance the

Courtesy of Carol Case, Argyle Elementary School, Smyrna, GA.

Second-grade student Erika Pshsniak's computer painting of water lilies show blending in the flowers and leaves and a textured paper effect in the background.

obligation to use photographic documentation to critically highlight society's problems with the obligation to build the school art program's good standing. Teach about individuals' rights to privacy and the need to get photo permissions from subjects. Before undertaking a potentially controversial documentation project, check first with relevant authorities, for in our very interdependent society many officials unfortunately view schools as agencies whose purpose is to reinforce the existing social order. Certainly, visual images can be a minefield, bringing with them value-

314

An elementary child created a marathon-race effect by multiplying images using the computer's cut and copy or drag functions.

Fourth-grade student Malory Brock made these triangular tessellation patterns filled with colored circular motif and printed her work on a dot matrix printer.

laden assumptions that are esteemed by social reconstructivist teachers, but may be eschewed by others.

Computer Art

There are a number of advantages to including computer-art activities in the overall art program. For example, computers already have an established importance as central elements in education. Thus, use of computers in the art program can lend prestige to the program as a whole and help youths gain valuable career skills. In addition, through using desktop-publishing programs, art students and teachers can help the school to create school publications with top-quality design and graphics. Student artworks can be scanned onto the school's Website. Computer graphics, banners, calendars, and announcements can not only serve as vehicles for teaching design, they can help the school disseminate information.

Another advantage to teaching computer art skills is a practical one: Sometimes it is possible to obtain costly computer resources on a scale far beyond that of traditional art-teaching budgets. In fact, computer equipment is available now in a growing number of elementary and middle schools. Teachers of traditional academic subjects, however, may be fearful of integrating computers into their curricula. Their hesitancy may prove beneficial to adventuresome art teachers wishing to use the computers, however. The art teachers may find they have the equipment virtually to themselves, in such situations.

Finally, early computer-art experiences can help to overcome students' fear of using computers. Early exposure to computer art techniques can become a bridge to skills and experiences that will spur students' interest in the "careers of tomorrow," many of which require high-level computer literacy. Rather than finding hesitant students, however, most likely the teacher will find that many students in the class have home computers and are eager to serve as teaching assistants.

The Computer as a Design Tool

The computer, even more than most art media, focuses attention not so much on the product but on the process. Computers permit students to save progressive stages of a work and to create an infinite number of variations. Students are excited about the "trial and error" capability for "seriation," producing a series of images from a single image. They can test out colors, move shapes around, and recycle pictures quickly and easily while leaving the original intact. Morphing can show the interspaced steps between two images, for example, a person's head changes into the head of the school mascot. The multiple levels of storing an original image and changing it or mixing others with it blurs individual authorship. Thus, it is important that each step or decision be recorded so that it can be studied, analyzed, and redirected. Using the computer as a design tool enables learners to "see" design operations that involve repeating and varying images:

cut	paste	duplicate	rotate
shrink	mirror	enlarge	texturize
fragment	blur	trace edges	twirl
make transparent	superimpose	magnify	ripple
distort	introduce bilateral symmetry	introduce four-way symmetry	pixelate

The computer allows students to manipulate scale—they can look at a work at normal size, then zoom in for close-up work. Pixel size can be manipulated as well, creating analogies to weaving and mosaics. Sophisticated visual effects can be achieved by using a range of special tools; for example, putting one image over another using different transparency functions, making forms grow according to predetermined patterns (fractalizing), or making forms appear as if they were in a reflecting orb (spherizing).

Children learn computer skills as well working in small groups as they do working individually. This painting was made in tempera resist, a technique discussed earlier.

Computers also offer sophisticated ways to combine letter forms and words with graphic elements. Students can "publish," either electronically or in hard copy, their own stories set in type and with the pages graphically designed. In this way, computer art can perform a valuable educational role in integrating school art programs with writing programs.

Implementing a Computer-Art Program

A main barrier to implementing a computer-art program in the past has been the art teacher's ignorance and fear: fear that the equipment will get broken through use and perhaps even the fear that some students will know more about the subject than the teacher does. Just push aside such groundless fears, however, because all can learn together. Another problem arises when there is not enough computer equipment to serve a whole class, or significant portion thereof. When there are too few computers in the classroom, children seldom have individual time at the machine.

Fortunately, research indicates that students can learn computer skills as effectively in small groups as they can individually. Computer art can be taught to small groups of children, one group at a time. Of course, when this is done, it may be difficult for the teacher to keep students who are not at computers working on some other task. If the teacher focuses his or her attention on those students who are engaged in noncomputer activities, the problem then becomes one of providing effective instruction in the qualitative production of computer artwork.

One solution in such circumstances may be to have students do computer artwork only after they finish other assignments, or to have them come in either before or after class to use the computer. Another approach is to have traditional methods of drawing and painting included as a part of computer-generated projects. For example, story boards illustrating story concepts need to be drawn. Sound effects need to be recorded. One group of students can begin a design on the computer and have a copy printed out for each student in the group. Then, those students can go to their desks to do the hand coloring, while other students, who have been generating design sketches by hand, render their work on the computer.

Still another way to deal with the shortage or absence of computers is to approach computer art as an activity in art criticism. Class discussion can focus on the computer-art imagery that students see daily—for example, in movies' special effects, in animated titles and images opening television programs, in newspaper graphic layouts and special effects of lettering. Art criticism can deal with these mass communication images, both addressing their formal design elements and how they reinforce content. A bulletin board in the classroom can serve as a center of this collection and analysis.

To develop interest in computer art during elementary school, have students with computers at home bring their own computer designs to be

When the rope ladder is pulled up, no girls are able to come into this tree house.

mounted in an exhibit. Such an exhibit may spur school administrators to support a school computer-art program that would be available to all children. Those who have used computer-art programs at home then can use the school computers to teach those who have not had access to these machines. Also the teacher can arrange a virtual exhibition of student art on the Internet. Likewise, a teacher and her students in Japan can converse by e-mail with a class in Mississippi and view each other's artwork on the Websites.

The ideal solution, of course, is that the teacher convinces the school administration that computers should be an integral part of the program—that using computers for art expression is just as essential for students' educational development as is using computers for programming, mathematical operations, and word processing.

Art and Art History on the Web

Art historical resources abound on the Web, readily accessible to students who want to use them to adapt their own reports and their own artworks and educational products. For example, for the Japanese artist Hokusai, there are 2,800 Web page listings in the search engine Altavista. Altavista lists 18,000 Web pages on Asian art, 400,000 on Near Eastern Art, and 700,000 on ancient African art. Students as young as age 9 or 10 can make their own art history Hypercard stacks and add multimedia resources. Through computer art, art teachers can take on new, challenging

roles as instructional designers, managers, and facilitators of art content. Computer images from Websites can be jumping-off points toward generating other images. Art education lesson plans and art historical visuals for art from around the world are at artsednet.getty/edu/ArtsEdNet. It is easy to use a one-stop interface to Internet guides; just type Dogpile, or Topclick, or Hot bot into your search engine's browser line. This will take you to the main search engines or portals, such as Yahoo, Excite, Altavista, Askjeeves, Snap, and Lycos. Then type in Art history or Art museums. For example, about.com has an area: artforkids and an area: arthistory. The prefix http:// has been omitted, since browsers nowadays insert it automatically. Although individual Websites often change and become inactive, these resources can provide an excellent start. Just log onto the Web and go exploring!

Some nations currently ban the Web, believing it is an evil method of Westernizing the world; ironically, it seems rather to be a way to internationalize the world.

Artists

A virtual museum of Diego Rivera's art can be seen at:
  www.diegorivera.com.
A virtual museum and historical information on the life of Frida Kahlo can be found at: www.cascade.net/kahlo.html.
Find artists' biographies at: biography.com and at arthistory.net.
Learn about European historical artists at: euroweb.hu/art
  and also at: www.ocaiw.com.
View Vermeer's paintings at: www.ccsf.caltech.edu/~roy/vermeer.

Topics and Periods

African art is at
  http://viva.lib.virginia.edu/dic/exhibit/93.ray.aa/African.html.
Native American art can be found at: hanksville.org/NAresources
  and at www.powersource.com/powersource/gallery/default.html.
Information on Latin American art can be found at: latinoweb.
Egyptian art may be viewed at: pharos.bu.edu/Egypt/Cairo.
Art from India can be found at: www.lavanya-indology.com.
Impressionistic art in the Musem d'Orsay is at:
  meteora.ucsd.edu:80/~norman/paris/Musees/Orsay/Collections.
Medieval art is at: www.georgetown.edu/labyrinth.

American Museums

The Detroit Institute of Arts is at: www.dia.org.
The Metropolitan Museum in New York City is at:
  www.metmuseum.org.
Visit the National Gallery of Art in Washington, D. C.at: www.nga.gov.
The Museum of Modern Art is at: www.moma.org.
The Smithsonian Institutions are at: www.si.edu.

Museums both on and off the Web are at:
   archive.comlab.ox.ac.uk/archive/other/museums.html.

Museums Abroad

Museums in Paris, including the Louvre, are at:
   www.paris.org.:80/Musees.

The Louvre Museum is also at: www.atlcom.net/~psmith/Louvre.

View art at the Uffizi Gallery in Florence, Italy—one of the oldest
   museums in the world—at: www.televisual.it/uffizi.

General

Art history Websites and bibliographies are at:
   www.ilpi.com/artsource/general.html.

The art history research center is at:
   http://art-history.concordia.ca/AHRC.index.htm.

Artists' quotes and links are at: www.art.net.

The Kennedy Center, Washington, D.C., is at: kennedy-center.org.

Photography

Blueprint paper acquired from a local blueprint company or light-sensitive
photographic paper obtainable from a photo store can be used by elementary school children for beginning photographic experiences.

Courtesy of Nancy Eliott, Athens, GA

*These photograms are of objects as simple as keys, religious medals, pins, and paper clips.
They helped teach middle school students concepts of overall pattern and positive and negative shape.*

Exhibited at the School Art Symposium, Georgia Museum of Art, Athens, GA.
Courtesy of Molly Chase and teacher George Mitchell, Atlanta, GA.

*Student Molly Chase of Atlanta, Georgia, studying photography at school, captured a special
moment of children at the neighborhood store. Probably only a young photographer could elicit
the charming expressions of these children caring for children. The photograph is given structure by the geometry, repetition, and perspective in the mammoth shortening display.*

Through this medium, they can create designs and learn concepts such as
geometric, organic, sinusoidal, pierced, undulating, and lacy.

Before you begin, find a totally dark closet somewhere in the school
building. Then, with your students, collect an array of opaque, translucent,
and transparent objects of varying color values that have interesting shapes,

patterns, and textures. Suitable items are fern leaves, grasses, confetti, flowers, ribbon, lace, torn paper shapes, tissue, acetate, window screen, crumpled plastic wrap, shapes of figures and animals cut from paper, checkers, shoelaces, paper doilies, drawings on acetate or translucent tracing paper, and three-dimensional objects, such as coins and keys.

Children should first plan their designs. Next, they will arrange an assortment of these objects on a stiff sheet of clear acrylic plastic, acetate, or overhead transparency plastic. Properly supervised older students can use a piece of glass with its edges taped. Emphasize consideration of the negative shapes (the empty spaces). Also, urge students to think about repetition, unity, and variation. While the children are waiting for their turn in the darkroom, have them write a list of the objects they collected and the design concepts they embody; this will build the students' art vocabulary.

For the printmaking stage, have a student monitor govern when the darkroom door may be opened. Students take turns carrying their designs into the darkroom. In the dark—by feel or with a red safelight on—they position their designs on top of same-size pieces of blueprint paper. Then, the design of shapes (*on* the clear plastic *on* the blueprint paper) is taken outside and exposed to sunlight for about 15 minutes (or until the yellow paper turns white).

The print is then developed. Soak some cotton in a teaspoon of household ammonia and place the cotton in the bottom of a large jar with a fitted lid, such as a gallon mayonnaise jar from the school cafeteria. Roll the print tightly enough to fit it into the jar, insert it, and recap the jar. The ammonia fumes will turn the paper blue in a few minutes.

If light-sensitive photo paper is available, the design transfer can be done in a darkroom, using a flashlight to expose the film, and then developed as you would a photograph. With either method, after the print is made, the designs may be left as they are, or students may use oil pastels and markers to add color. Another variation of this lesson, and one that is especially suitable following a contour line–drawing lesson, is to have the students go into the darkroom, and, using a tiny pocket penlight, draw the figure as they remember it on the light-sensitive photo paper. Picasso's drawings with this technique may be studied. Another variation is for students to draw on a sheet of translucent paper with a black marker and then make a reverse print in the darkroom; the results will be similar to the cliché verre process used by Corot.

Class discussion afterward should build art vocabulary through listing on the chalkboard or markerboard names for the shapes, patterns, and textures that the children have created with light. Discuss similarities between their works and those of Fox Talbot and Man Ray. Beginning in the fifth grade, students can use pin-hole cameras to make their own photographs. Load the camera in a darkroom with slow-emulsion, plastic resin–coated paper. Have the children look around the school grounds and point the camera at what interests them—for example, a bicycle wheel, a friend's

Courtesy of Nancy Elliott, Athens, GA.

Middle school students constructed pinhole cameras. Then, they went into the schoolyard to capture light on the forms of sports cars, gravel, walkways, and buildings.

face, a tree silhouetted against the sky, patterns of bicycle shadows on the ground. Likewise, students might choose to document activities on the playground, an architecture field trip, the class garden, or vehicles used to travel to school. Tell students not to worry about composition or whether the subject moves. An impression is what is sought. Have the children develop the image inside the darkroom; a negative image can be contact-printed back for a positive. This lesson can be correlated with a study of such artists as Corot, Delacroix, Courbet, the impressionists, and the futurists, who were fascinated by photography. Discuss what kind of day and light were captured. Was the light direct, soft, or diffuse? Look at the shadows and describe them.

Still another approach is to use Polaroid or 35-mm print film in a camera. One roll of 36 pictures will allow each child to make one picture. A local photo lab may donate out-of-date film. If the supply of film is limited, have the children work in pairs to plan out the subject of their photo and take the picture. If slide film is used, students can discuss and share each others' work easily and effectively. A language arts–correlated lesson is to have the children make up a story using the slides, then put on a slide show complete with narration and sound effects and the children playing the roles. Digital cameras present opportunities for students to take photos at no cost, once the camera and computer are available. The children's photos then can serve as visual resources for art projects using other art media.

Teach children the vocabulary of photography. Terms and concepts about light include: light and shadow, direct light and reflected light, contrast, value, low contrast, high contrast, direction of light, high-key delicate lighting containing nothing darker than middle grey, low-key somber lighting containing nothing lighter than middle grey, sharp and diffuse shadows, point of view, low angle, distant shot, foreground, near ground,

Courtesy of Joyce Vroon, Trinity School, Atlanta, GA.

After studying David Hockney's photo collages, a sixth-grade student made this photo collage of the construction at his home.

Courtesy of Joyce Vroon, Trinity School, Atlanta, GA.

Surreal wave reflections, mountain ridges, and a bold value pattern characterize this photo by sixth-grade student Mandy Freel.

middle ground, and background. Terms about the technical process include: positive, negative, camera, shutter, lens, diaphragm, f-stop, focus, film speed (ISO), stop bath, and fixer. Historical terms include: daguerreotype, Talbot-type or Calotype, ambrotype, tintype, and cartes de visite (visiting cards with a photograph).

Photography and social studies can easily be integrated through art criticism using historic photos: Matthew Hines's photos of child labor abuses in New England spinning mills, Edward S. Curtis's photos of Native Americans, and Matthew Brady's photos of the Civil War are some examples. Photography and science can be integrated with a unit on the science of light, replicating the 1830s sun drawings of Henry Fox Talbot. Photos of scientific phenomena, close-up microscopic views, and macrocosmic views of outer space can be studied as works of art using the photographic vocabulary described earlier. Art criticism can be taught using a collection of photographic masterpieces. For example, clip photographs from an issue of *Life* magazine on the history of photography; with these photos, students can engage in some of the educational game-like activities discussed in Chapter 17. Digital cameras are becoming available in some middle schools and some students may have access to their families' digital camera. These are especially useful in creating Web pages and electronic reports.

Video

Video—the art medium of our time—is transforming the nature of art and of our lives. The famous video artist Nam June Paik said, "Information has to be recognized as an alternative energy source. Information changes our lifestyle" (1987). Video's power to capture the affect in human interactions, its accessibility, its spontaneity, and the ease with which it is disseminated are awesome. Unfortunately, and perhaps because of a fear of technology, too much video equipment stays locked in school closets, gathering dust and becoming obsolete.

Video can provide valuable educational experiences to students. Most homes now have videocassette recorders (VCRs), and families with cameras shoot their own home videos. Teachers of art should put this technology into the hands of their students. Videos also can be converted into pictures and movies for multimedia presentations. Further, it can be used to document events in the classroom, school, and community. Art concepts of light, space, movement, and time become real to the students as they make films, watch, and analyze videos and films.

Some instructional objectives for a video program are as follows: In the area of art creation, the students will be able to use the video camera to apply spatial concepts involving close-ups and long shots and to manage the art elements of light and space. In the area of art criticism, students will analyze techniques used in art-history videos as well as those made by famous artists. Students will learn the vocabulary of motion film. They will identify instances of backlighting, soft focus, freeze frame, establishing zoom shots, slow disclosure shots, low-angle shots, long shots, and panning shots.

Family of Robot: Aunt, 1986 (video sculpture, 86-½ × 21 inches). Courtesy of Carl Solway Gallery, Cincinnati, OH.

Pioneering video artist Nam June Paik (born in Korea in 1932) uses hundreds of television monitors to create video walls of information. He wants them to humanize and demystify television technology, as does the figurative piece shown here that is constructed from TV sets.

An elementary school child videotapes a guest speaker discussing his passion, raising horses. Children also can video field trips to sketching sites and peers in the process of making art.

Further, students can discuss how artists have humanized technology—for example, the installations and performances of Nam June Paik and Laurie Anderson. To extend their learning, students can carry home the videos they make and view them on their home VCR. With their families, they can discuss how they made their shots and how they used light, space, and action. Finally, videos of students creating in another art media can be used as a tool to help them critique their performance in achieving video-related art objectives.

Videos also serve a documentary function in the teaching of art. For example, art displays in elementary school hallways can be videotaped as a

way of documenting the quality of the work. This video can be shared with the students whose work is depicted as a way to give them feedback. It also can be shared with future classes when they embark on the same kind of project. Likewise, videos documenting the community's artists can be used as part of an art history/social studies curriculum. Videos of senior citizens sharing their arts and crafts heritage become historical records of knowledge that can be passed on to future generations.

A student can video his or her classmates making art, then take the videotape home and write a critique of the result. Students depicted in the video can take the tape home and watch it, then write a review of their

Courtesy of Melody Milbrandt, State University of West Georgia, Carrollton, GA.

A student gives a video-recorded demonstration in the classroom while another student does the recording.

art-making process, telling what they would like to do better or differently. If the museum permits, videos can document students' museum field trips; this visual documentation then can be used to review the experience and give the students the opportunity to share their responses. Later, these videos can be shared with evaluators as well as at parent–teacher meetings and programs to underscore a program's effectiveness.

Students who have received training in camera use can apply their skills by documenting school functions, game days, and seasonal festivities. The videos can then be played in the school halls or in classes to provide feedback to the participants. Art-club members can videotape the musical, dramatic, and dance performances of the other arts programs. In many middle schools, where art competes with orchestra, band, and chorus for enrollment, videos of the art program in action can be used as a way of recruiting students and building a program of quality.

Video also can bring the art program into the community. School-produced videos can be shown at the local library as part of a humanities program. Gain valuable community support for your art-education program by documenting the historical contributions of community groups. Document your students' reactions to social and political events in the community, such as older siblings going off to serve in the military and the impact of their departure on younger siblings at home. Videos documenting community life can be shown at town festivals; for example, a video of making sorghum syrup might be shown at a local fall festival. For social studies projects, students might make a video in a nearby senior citizens' center, documenting the seniors' memories of fires, riots, wars, and floods. Teachers are amazed at the time and energy that children put into their involvement in video projects. This medium gives students a way to create their own reality.

Chapter 28

THREE-DIMENSIONAL DESIGN: ADDITIVE AND SUBTRACTIVE SCULPTURE

Courtesy of Frank Wachowiak and Ted Ramsay, University Elementary School, Iowa City, IA.

In box sculpture, allow the shape of the box itself to trigger the student's imagination. Square and rectangular boxes are much easier for young children to assemble.

Many challenging sculptural techniques, both additive and subtractive, await those upper elementary and middle school students and their teachers who are willing to make a serious, time-consuming commitment to a painstaking yet adventurous task. Too often, sculpture in the elementary school has been presented as a therapeutic activity, with minor emphasis on its expressive potential. If sufficient time cannot be allotted for students to become thoroughly involved in the sculptural process, postpone it until the middle school years, when more time is budgeted for art and the students' perseverance and constructive skills are more developed. If the elementary school teacher of art understands the sculptural media and can motivate the students to carry projects through to culmination, however, the sculpture experience can be one of the most fulfilling in the upper-elementary grades art program.

The major consideration often is not so much of student motivation as of material resources, preliminary planning, special techniques, cleanup, and storage. A class of 25 or more students working on additive or subtractive sculpture poses several organizational problems. Teachers must decide beforehand whether they want the entire class to use the same medium or whether they will allow students to work with materials of their choosing. Skilled instructors may be able to control a large class in which some students are working on toothpick or balsa-wood construction, some on plaster block carving, and some on wire or metal sculpture. The resulting products, however, must show evidence of the students' growth in sculptural design. If, as often is the case, the teacher becomes merely the dispenser of various materials and tools and has little time to evaluate work in progress with the students, it is much wiser to limit the offering and have the entire class use only one sculptural medium. In such instances, the teacher can organize the materials, tools, and storage space more effectively. A rich motivational plan and evaluation plan can be developed over the several days necessary for the project.

This chapter will first discuss box sculpture and constructions in space, then masks, and, finally, subtractive sculpture in plaster.

After the boxes have been taped together, the sculpture is allowed to dry and become sturdy. Then, the sculpture can be painted.

In view of today's widespread ecological concerns about our planet's vanishing resources, sculptures from recycled materials take on added significance. Some soldering skills were necessary for this metal construction by a middle school student. It is another example of the adage "The whole is greater than the sum of its parts."

Box Sculpture and Constructions in Space

Older and more mature children often need a change of pace. New challenges, materials, and techniques can spark a growing interest in art. Using cardboard boxes, mailing tubes, and assorted found objects gives upper elementary and middle school students a rare opportunity to express their individual ideas in a unique, three-dimensional form. They find value in recycling discarded materials at the same time they struggle with a complex construction problem. They come to appreciate in a creative way the adage "the whole is greater than the sum of its parts."

An exciting new world of additive sculpture has opened up with the burgeoning exploitation of found materials. These include applicator sticks, drinking straws, thin dowels, assorted toothpicks, reeds, discarded game parts (for example, Tinkertoy pieces), pick-up sticks, scrap lumber, and plastic packing materials. The resulting constructions have many labels: stabiles, mobiles, space modulators, combine art, scrap sculpture, or assemblage. Constructions definitely will add an adventurous dimension to art programs and hold the interest of today's students.

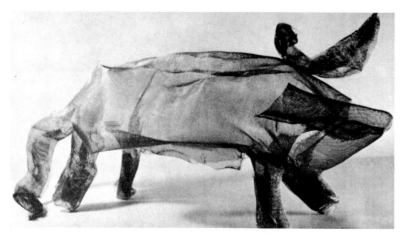

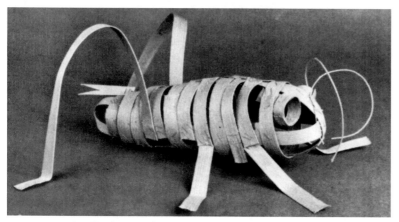

In many instances, students will be eager to create nonobjective, abstract, and geometrically oriented constructions, allowing the materials to dictate the form. This is particularly true when straws, applicator sticks, toothpicks, and reeds are the building elements. The design grows stick by stick, straw by straw, dowel by dowel. Unless the construction itself is stable, an auxiliary support or separate base of wood, plywood, or Masonite is needed. Determine the placement of supports that are required, then drill or hammer holes into the base at these points. Begin the structure by securely inserting and gluing the initial supports into these holes.

A host of materials can embellish stick or straw constructions. Experiment, for example, with bottle corks, thread spools, beads, cord, Ping-Pong balls, small rubber balls, pegboard pegs, construction paper, mailing tubes, colored cardboard, cardboard spools from tape dispensers, miniature cardboard boxes, plastic pieces, wood or plastic buttons, and tiny film canisters. Outdoors, the teacher can give completed constructions a coat of black or white spray paint, which contributes to a striking unifying visual impact.

Additive sculpture also can be made using more challenging materials and techniques. Wire can be combined with found metal pieces. Toothpick and applicator-stick constructions can be dipped into melted crayon, wet plaster, or liquid metal. Corrugated cardboard can be cut into various shapes that are then slotted, joined, and glued together to form a stabile. Cardboard mailing tubes can be cut into multisized cylinders and rings, then assembled into animals, insects, and figures. Exacto knives, Sloyd knives, or utility knives are necessary to cut cardboard boxes, but they must be used only under a teacher's strict supervision. A coping saw or a small vibrating-table jigsaw is useful for cutting heavy cardboard, chipboard, Masonite, and heavyweight cardboard tubes.

At least 2 to 4 weeks before the project begins, students should start collecting discarded cardboard boxes. A letter to their parents listing materials that are needed will help to build a necessary store of discards, scraps, and remnants. This early, personal involvement on the part of the students builds interest in the expressive adventure ahead. Store the accumulated boxes and objects until needed in a giant cardboard carton, or have students store their personal collections in a grocery sack labeled with their name.

Useful fastening materials include straight pins, masking tape, paper clips, string, double-faced tape, rubber bands, gummed tape, white liquid glue, school paste, scissors, paper punch, nails, and wire. Plan ahead so

Wood scraps, rope and yarn remnants, dried corn husks, discarded metal screen, and spools from thread can be recycled in today's school art programs. This lion, elephant, and grasshopper are successful examples. Let the childrens' imaginations soar.

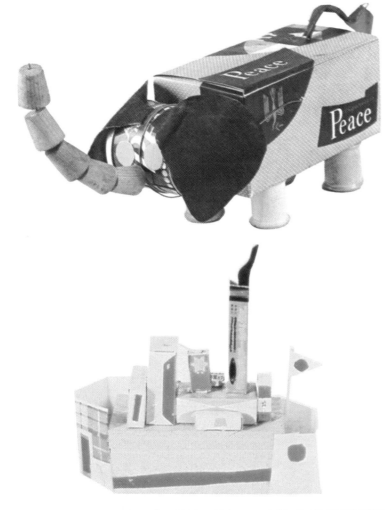

Iowa City Elementary Laboratory School, IA. *Top and middle:* Courtesy of Frank Wachowiak, Athens, GA.
Bottom: Courtesy of Frank Wachowiak and Ted Ramsay.

Courtesy of Barbara Thomas, Whit Davis School, Athens, GA.

With the use of a piece of ³/₄-inch Styrofoam insulation for a base, the structure grows with shish-kebab skewers, Popsicle sticks, and golf tees.

there are adequate storage facilities for the found objects, for the supply of fastening devices and materials, and for the constructions in progress.

Imaginative box-sculpture themes are almost limitless: astronauts, spaceships, space stations, robots, creatures from another planet, engines, planes, toys, rockets, homes, vehicles and computers of the future, fantastic designs for playground equipment, masks, nonobjective space modulators, and imaginative animals, bugs, birds, and fish.

One way to start the project is to invite students to select three or four different-size boxes and a set of cardboard mailing tubes (for small

---

Top: As is the case with this elephant, it is not always necessary to paint box sculpture. Some boxes already have colorful printed designs. ***Middle:*** This cruise ship ingeniously employs box sculptural forms. ***Bottom:*** This construction of reeds and construction paper by a sixth-grade student shows a good use of restraint. It employs only triangular shapes, which create a unified design.

Courtesy of Beverly Mallon, Chase Street Elementary School, Athens, GA.

A two-foot-high giraffe was made over a foundation of wire, sticks, and newspaper, held together with brown paper tape. To strengthen it, it was then covered with newspaper strips soaked in wallpaper paste, prior to being painted.

Top: *A sixth-grade student created this space modulator with construction paper strips and school paste.* **Bottom:** *Perhaps such a project will inspire one of your students to become a sculptor and to create pieces, not 30 inches high, but rather 30 feet high. In any event, because of the school experience that you provide, all students will be able to appreciate more intensely the rhythm, repetition, and construction in such works as Alice Aycock's 1987 sculpture.*

Top: Milwaukee, WI. *Bottom: Three-Fold Manifestation II* (steel painted white, 32 feet high). Alice Aycock. Storm King Art Center, Mountainville, NY. Gift of the artist. Photo: Jerry L. Thompson.

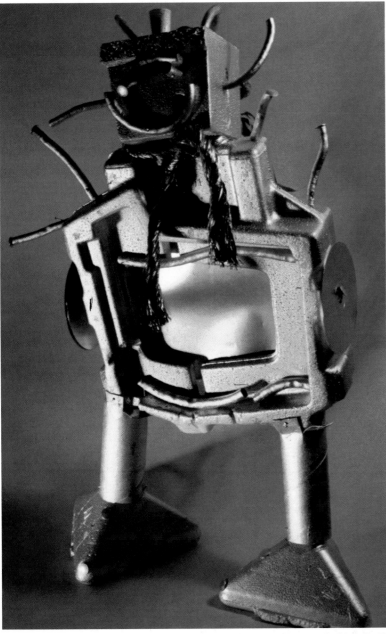

Courtesy of Ted Ramsay, University Elementary School, Iowa City, IA.

A sixth-grade student combined plastic discards to produce this imaginatively constructed robot. Then, after working surfaces had been protected with newspapers, the entire sculpture was sprayed with metal paint. Only the teacher, not the students, should use spray paint; even then, spray outdoors.

constructions, use toilet-tissue tubes), then juxtapose these in various configurations until an idea is triggered. Another approach is to have a theme in mind and select boxes to form this preconception. After students decide on a basic shape for their creations, making sketches will help them to plan. The excitement builds as students see the creation grow. Sometimes, an unusual box turns up that is just right for the head of a monster and triggers the design for the rest of the construction. Often, a box can be partially opened and hinged to become the mouth and jaws of a voracious, mythical lion or dragon. What began as a dream car might easily emerge in the final stages as a space station.

The most challenging part is fastening the separate boxes together and securing the appendages. The recommended method includes first gluing and then tying, pinning, paper-clipping, and/or taping the boxes together until the glue dries overnight. Finding an adhesive with ideal properties can be problematic, however, because many adhesives have some, but not all, of the desired properties. For example, white glue (such as Elmer's glue) is safe, available in most schools, and reasonably effective, although its tackiness and drying time are not ideal. A new product, Elmer's Tacky Glue, has more tackiness and therefore is superior for box and wood-scrap sculptures. Glues such as airplane glue and Duco Cement should *not* be used in classrooms because these glues contain the harmful solvents xylene or toluene. A teacher might use a hot-melt glue gun for difficult attachments. (See safety section in Appendix A).

Working on a stiff base, such as a 1-foot-square piece of cardboard or Masonite, gives increased stability to the piece-in-progress and facilitates its rotating so that all sides can be studied. In constructing standing figures, students must decide how to make the figure stand upright. If necessary, a stabilizing third leg or support can be created. A tail can be added, or the figure can hold gear, such as a spear or banner standard, that touches the ground. Heightened interest, decoration, and texture can be added by using egg cartons, corrugated and embossed cardboard, paper drinking straws, plastic packing noodles, clothespins, toothpicks, paste sticks, dowels, corks, pipe cleaners, reeds, beads, Tinkertoy pieces, Ping-Pong balls, and game parts.

Sometimes, the containers themselves with their printed designs and logos are so exciting that painting them would only mask their bold design qualities. Rather than painting boxes that already contain graphics or lettering, another possibility is to camouflage them with colored paper, comic-book and magazine pages, tissue paper, wallpaper samples, cloth, or gift-wrapping papers. If the sculpture is to be painted, the features that give it individuality must be emphasized, especially the eyes, mouth, nose, ears, and horns. If the boxes' glossy surfaces resist water-based paint, make it adhere by adding soap to the paint. Spray paints are not considered to be safe for student use, and any spray painting must be done by the teacher outdoors. Silver, copper, or gold paints may be employed for a robot, knight in armor, or astronaut. Clearly, there are endless possibilities in box and found-object sculpture. The teacher and students who are resourceful, persistent, and patient enough to try this project have a real art adventure awaiting them.

Masks

Multicultural education certainly will include the study of masks. Rather than tying maskmaking to overworked Halloween motifs, the activity is on a firmer academic base when integrated with a social-studies cultural unit: In Africa, likenesses of departed chiefs are used in memorial services. Native Americans use masks in rainmaking and agricultural ceremonies. Judges in New Guinea wear masks to heighten their authority. The masks worn by medieval mummers might signify one of the seven deadly sins, biblical characters, or forces of nature. In China, Burma, and Ceylon, masks were worn to prevent illness and cure diseases. Thieves wear them to conceal their identity. Police officers, firefighters, hospital personnel, and football players wear masks for personal protection.

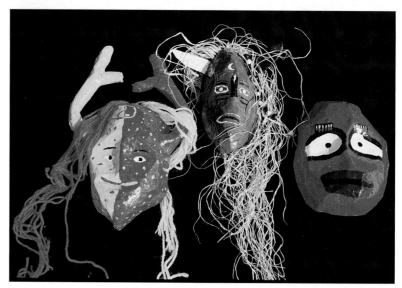

Courtesy of Nancy Eliott, Burney-Harris Middle School, Athens, GA.

Middle school students made these papier-mâché masks and decorated them imaginatively with straw and fiber hair, one mask with a half-yellow, half-red face with antlers and another dark mask with white and black horns.

Courtesy of Julie Daniell Phlegar, Upper Tammany County Elementary School, Slidell, LA.

This second-grade student loved making his dramatic mask headdress of blue waves and four patterned water snakes. From tagboard, the bottom 6 inches of the paper are cut in partway to form a headband, and the lower three inches are cut away even more to leave just a mask, which was colored with markers.

Always a popular undertaking, maskmaking in the elementary and middle schools has, unfortunately, been one in which design considerations seldom have been effectively implemented. Too often, basic compositional factors have been minimized and raw colors applied in a random, slapdash, form-negating manner. On occasion, very young children can create colorful, expressively naive masks when richly motivated. Because of the cultural and symbolic connotations of maskmaking and the often complex techniques required for implementation, however, maskmaking is best postponed until students reach upper elementary and middle school.

The most inspired and evocative masks of past centuries and cultures almost always have been based on an abstract, stylized concept rather than on natural appearance. To emphasize certain features, maskmakers often abstracted the face, whether human or animal, into combinations of ovals, squares, and circles. A study of masks such as those by tribal Africans and Native Americans reveals recurring aspects. Whereas facial features that capture the mood or spirit usually are exaggerated, they seldom are distorted to the extent that they appear to be something so alien and trite as star-shaped eyes. The most expressive masks are imbued with the essence and vitality of a particular mood or emotion: astonishment, serenity, power, anger, dignity, joy, fury, frenzy, benevolence, or wonder. Another recurring characteristic is continuity of facial forms and features, as exemplified by the linear flow of the nose structure into the eyebrow contour.

Decoration is used to heighten the mask's visual appeal. Taking a cue from maskmakers of the past, students should use lines or shapes to reinforce and emphasize the dominant features. They should create pattern and texture on the face, delineate hair and beard, and emphasize eyes by using highly contrasting colors and values. Color must be used judiciously, however, lest it jeopardize the mask's impact or appeal. Color must be integrated with the features—not superficially applied—and it must complement rather than detract. Subtle, limited color harmonies should be encouraged, and primary colors should be used with discretion (generally only to provide a necessary contrast).

Papier-mâché over a clay foundation still is the most popular and effectively controlled technique, allowing for highly individualized interpretations and detailed facial modeling. Also recommended is papier-mâché or plaster-impregnated gauze applied over a mixing or salad bowl,

Kindergarten children created their own Halloween costumes by recycling paper garment bags. If such bags are not available, fasten together with glue or masking tape two large-size grocery bags, one with the bottom cut off.

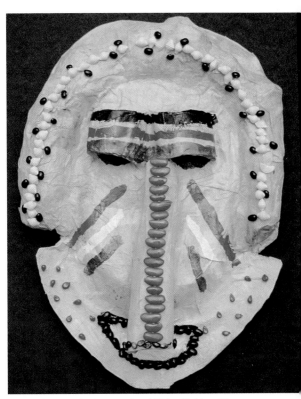

Right: Courtesy of Barbara Thomas, Whit Davis School, Athens, GA. Others: Courtesy of Frank Wachowiak, Athens, GA.

Varied approaches to maskmaking. **Far left:** *Boxes, spools, paper cups, and yarn create a face by varying conical forms.* **Center:** *Construction paper is bent into a canoelike shape and raffia added. Feathers could also be incorporated.* **Right:** *Beth Pearson used red, white, and black*

beans to create repeated patterns and lines. Basic mask forms also may be achieved by applying newspaper strips with wheat paste or liquid starch over a balloon or mixing bowl.

Courtesy of Frank Wachowiak and Ted Ramsay, University Elementary School, Iowa City, IA.

Colored construction-paper masks. A three-dimensional effect was achieved by cutting short slits into the borders of a square or rectangular sheet of paper and then overlapping the resulting tabs and stapling them together. Masks make highly decorative artifacts to brighten up the classroom.

Courtesy of Frank Wachowiak, Athens, GA.

Posing on the jungle gym with their scary outstretched clawlike hands, first-grade students loved making these giant colored construction-paper masks and scaring each other with them.

small dishpan, balloon, or beach ball. As the pasted form develops, it can be embellished with additional pieces of plastic foam, bent cardboard, and found objects to create nose, eyes, mouth, and ear shapes. String, yarn, raffia, and plastic packing material may be used for hair, beard, and other textures. These details are covered with a final layer of gauze or glue-moistened paper toweling. When dry, the mask can be painted.

A popular maskmaking technique is the paper- or cardboard-construction process. This generally requires intricate cutting and scoring of the paper to achieve an effective, three-dimensional quality. It has many possibilities, however, and because of the availability of materials and tools, it can be pursued in the ordinary classroom. Unlike papier-mâché projects that involve a lengthy cleanup period and abundant storage space, paper-sculpture masks are simpler to manage and store. For children in the primary grades, creation of a paper-plate, paper-sack, or plastic meat-tray mask is the most practical and successful technique, because it does not involve a complex, three-dimensional process.

Totem Poles

A study of early Pacific Coast Native-American life provides rich motivation for several art projects, including the group construction of a totem pole; however, the culture of the Northwest Native Americans must be genuinely examined. Cross-cultural comparisons can be made about the role of art in their culture and their beliefs about nature, death, religion, and the roles of men, women, and children. For the Native-American carvers, art is empty when it omits the spiritual dimension of life. As was the custom of the totem carvers, encourage students to identify with some other living entity or with an animal or bird school symbol.

Use a sheet of colored construction paper 12 × 18 inches as the background for each totem mask. With the paper placed horizontally on the desk and the 18-inch border at the bottom, students draw with chalk the outline of their mask in the center of the paper. The top and bottom of their mask should touch the edge of the paper. The larger they draw it, the better, but they should leave some of the paper plain at each side to wrap around the pole. When the drawing is complete, the mask may be painted with tempera paint or colored with crayon or oil pastels. Students should be encouraged to exploit unusual color combinations in their masks, including the use of black and white; to repeat colors for unity; to create contrast by juxtaposing light and dark colors; and to emphasize important parts of their masks through a selection of vivid, dominant colors.

After the mask is colored, make parts of it three-dimensional by cutting slits with scissors around an ear or nose and either folding these pieces outward from the main mask or bending them back. A backing sheet of a contrasting color, 12 × 18 inches, may be added when assembling the several masks into the totem form. Students also may add supplementary shapes of multicolored construction paper for teeth, fangs, horns, ears, earrings, and eyebrows.

There are several ways to construct totem poles from the separate masks. One way is to obtain an empty gallon food tin from the school cafeteria for a base foundation, and fill it with sand or clay. Then, wrap a 24 × 36-inch sheet of tagboard around the can, and secure it with masking tape, creating a 36-inch-tall cylinder. Build another cylinder above the first, if desired. Secure it again with tape, and with the tagboard cylinder as a steady foundation, fasten the masks around it with glue, masking tape, or staple-gun tacker. Another type of pole can be made from a cardboard cylinder from a carpet showroom.

Courtesy of Frank Wachowiak, Iowa City Elementary Laboratory School, Iowa City, IA.

Masks created for a totem-pole project. Colored construction paper, 12 x 18 inches, and oil pastels were used. Noses, teeth, ears, and cheeks were made by cutting slits in the mask. These portions then were bent out to create three-dimensional forms. Completed masks were secured to discarded food tins from the school cafeteria.

Once the basic totem pole is sturdily constructed, embellish it with supplemental wings, feet, and arms made of cardboard. Display the completed totem poles at a cultural celebration or in the school foyer as a way of sharing the multicultural learning experience with the school at large.

Top left: Iowa City Elementary Laboratory School, courtesy of Frank Wachowiak, Athens, GA. *Bottom left:* Barrow Elementary School, Athens, GA. *Others:* Courtesy of Alice Ballard Munn, Anchorage, AK, and Diane Rives, Athens, GA.

Totems usually are made in conjunction with a study of Native-American culture. **Top right:** *In a second-grade class, each child selected an animal thought to have special powers and made a northwest Native-American totem dedicated to it.* **Bottom right:** *Northwest Haida women's hats were made and the women's stories told.* **Top left:** *Cylindrical forms were made by stacking a column of school cafeteria cans and taping them together.* **Bottom left:** *A tree was used for the vertical column, and masks by upper-elementary school children were attached to the column.*

Subtractive Sculpture in Plaster

Subtractive sculpture (carving) has appealed to artists of all cultures throughout history. Wood probably has been the most popular medium for sculptors, but exquisite creations have been carved in a host of materials, including jade, ivory, bone, marble, soapstone, and alabaster. Many of these art materials are, of course, unsuitable for the usual art class. They may be banned (such as ivory), too costly (such as jade), or too dangerous (such as soapstone, which may contain asbestos). For school use, ideal materials must be safe, economical, relatively easy to carve, and allow quick cleanup. Recommended and readily obtainable materials for subtractive sculpture include plaster-of-Paris, leather-hard clay, balsa wood,

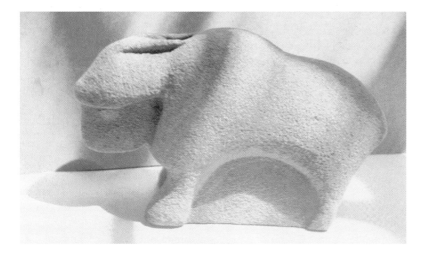

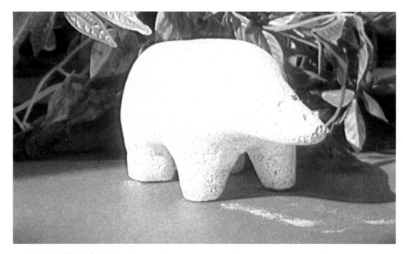

Courtesy of Frank Wachowiak and Ted Ramsay, Iowa City Elementary Laboratory School, Iowa City, IA.

Subtractive sculptures. **Top left:** *Sandcore, a by-product from metal casting, and porous firebrick can be carved. Notice how cleverly this child has solved the problem of thin legs breaking off by keeping a central band intact between the legs.* **Top right and bottom left and right:** *Teachers usually add vermiculite to plaster of Paris so it can be carved more easily. The vermiculite also gives a rough texture. Observe in this bear, mountain goat, and rhinoceros how these sixth-grade artists have solved the problem of delicate parts breaking off by using volumetric compact forms.*

porous firebrick, and large bars of soap. A metal-casting byproduct, sand core, which consists of sand held together with binders, may be available free from a local metal foundry.

Plaster usually is the material chosen for subtractive sculpture in school programs because it is cheap and easy to get. Plaster should be mixed with additives such as white sand or fine-grain zonolite to give it a texture and make it easier to carve. Approximately one-part additive to one-part dry plaster will produce a fairly porous and workable carving block. A half-gallon or quart-size milk or juice carton made of waxed cardboard makes a sturdy, leak-proof container.

Subjects that students can handle successfully include fish, nesting birds, animals (especially those in repose, to prevent thin legs from breaking off), and portrait heads. Organic or nonobjective free forms can be developed from motifs based on rocks, shells, nuts, pods, and other natural or biomorphic forms.

Students begin by making preliminary front-, side-, and back-view sketches for their sculptures on paper cut to the size of their plaster block. While the class is sketching, the teacher can help two or three students at a time to make their plaster molds. All necessary materials and tools should be on a newspaper-protected table or counter and near a water source (if possible). Have ready the molding plaster, vermiculite or sand, scoops or cups, milk cartons opened wide at the top, water, small-size rubber or plastic dishpan, wood stock or paddle, dry tempera colors (if desired), and lots of newspapers to line the nearby wastebaskets and both cover and recover the counter and floor around the plaster-mixing area.

Fill a milk carton three-fourths full with water, and pour the water into the dishpan. Sift plaster into the water slowly, using a hand, cup, or scoop. When islands of plaster appear above the water, add zonolite or sand. Stir the mix gently yet swiftly by hand, squeezing out the lumps until thoroughly mixed. As the mixture thickens very quickly, be ready to pour it immediately into the milk carton. After pouring it into the carton, tap the carton on the table to remove trapped bubbles, or stir it quickly with a stick or paddle.

Caution: Never pour plaster down the sink, or even rinse plaster-coated tools there. Instead, scrape excess plaster left in the dishpan, on hands, and on tools into the newspaper-lined wastebasket. Then, rinse hands and tools in another pail of water, but do not pour this rinsing water down the sink either.

Allow the plaster mold or block to dry overnight. If color is desired in the plaster block, mix tempera powder into the dry plaster before it is combined with water. Neutral colors such as umber, ochre, sienna, and earth-green are recommended.

Students may transfer preliminary pencil sketches to the block using carbon paper, or, using their sketches as a reference, they may draw directly on the block with a pencil or ink marker. The sculpture should make fullest use of the block. Remind students that no amount of texture, detail, or pattern will redeem the work if the basic form is weak. Caution them not to choose a subject that is too intricate and complex or that might be expressed more easily in wood, wire, metal, or clay.

The recommended tools for the carving process are a Sloyd or Hyde knife with a 2-inch blade, a utility knife (a knife with a metal handle encasing a replaceable blade), or a small plaster rasp. Students should cut, file, rasp, or chisel away the excess plaster to delineate the dominant profile or outline view. Next, they may refer to their top, front, and rear sketches and carve away to define those contours. They should proceed cautiously as they remove the plaster, turning the block around to define all forms consistently. As they carve, encourage them to think about how each part flows freely and naturally into the next.

Tables and floors in the working areas should be covered with newspapers or plastic dropcloths to expedite cleanup. Cleanup also may be minimized by having the students hold the plaster block inside a large, shallow cardboard box as they carve. In fair weather, minimize mess by having the class carve outdoors, working on drop cloths away from high-public-visibility areas such as building entrances.

When sculpting animals, heads, or human figures, keep the base part undefined during most of the carving process. This way, the piece does not become top-heavy, topple over, and break. Help the students to evaluate their in-process sculpture: to be aware of large masses contrasting with small forms; to capture the characteristic stance or action; to emphasize a feature, such as the beak or claws of a bird; and to enrich the surface of their creation through texture and pattern. Delicate appendages such as hands, ears, horns, tusks, beaks, tails, and other jutting forms should be kept undefined until the basic shape is well established. During the final stages, carve textural and decorative details with nails, discarded dental tools, or nut picks.

The finished sculpture may be stained, glazed, waxed, or metalized. To provide a sealed undercoat for the stain or patina, coat the sculpture with slightly diluted white glue, and allow it to dry thoroughly. A paint stain in subtle shades can be applied freely and allowed to penetrate into the incised areas. After letting the stain set briefly, judiciously wipe the raised areas to bring out highlights. A complementary sculpture base of driftwood, stained blocks of wood, and sections of tree trunks with the bark left intact can help to give the carving distinction.

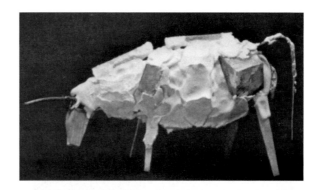

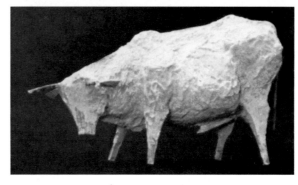

Often, plaster is used both additively and subtractively on the same sculpture. Shown here is a sturdy interior form called an armature, which is then covered with plaster. For larger projects, bend and weld reinforcing bars together. Then fill out the form with thinner wire, mesh, string, wood, and paper. Finally, add plaster and carve away the excess.

Chapter 29

ARCHITECTURE

Architecture has been called the mother of the arts, because it contains all other art forms. Architectural education conducted in elementary school can introduce future citizens not only to the delights of studying architecture but also to the importance of wise community design decisions. Unfortunately, architecture has not been a well-established component in the crowded elementary school art curriculum. Nevertheless, teachers with an interest in architecture should bring their passion about the field to their students through an architecture learning experience.

Courtesy of Lawrence Stueck, *The Design of Learning Environments,* Ph.D. dissertation, 1991, University of Georgia, Athens, GA.

Children can gain awareness of architectural form by helping to build a playscape.

Architecture is an art form that is readily comprehended and is essential to the visual essence of our communities. Architecture lends itself readily to integration with environmental education, history, and social studies. For example, the architecture of Monticello illustrates Thomas Jefferson's rejection of English colonialism and his commitment to the rationalistic ideals of French enlightenment thought. (However, the slave quarters behind his home show other social realities).

One recommended activity is to construct a model of architecturally interesting buildings in a town. This activity can also integrate ideas of engineering structure and math with art. Some instructional objectives include the following:

- Students will create a model of an existing building incorporating the design qualities of repetition, pattern, and texture.
- Students will discuss the reasons particular buildings have certain architectural character. An objective might be that they will be able to identify examples of neo-Classical, Victorian, and Prairie-style. Intermediate grade students will be able to find examples to show that the design of buildings changes over time.
- Students will arrange their model buildings to replicate an actual section of a town.

Design sources can be photographs, slides, or drawings of the actual buildings. Small boxes, such as hand-appliance, cereal, shoe, and drugstore gift boxes, can be used for the basic structure. These can be covered with construction paper, or they can be painted. Signs and architectural features can be cut from paper, decorated, and attached. Temporarily arrange the buildings onto a large piece of cardboard, such as from a major appliance. Then, the streets and grounds can be sketched in, the background painted, and models of vehicles, street signs, and street fur-

In this sixth-grade marker drawing of a Victorian house, the structure is clearly delineated, and decorative moldings, columns, and stonework are shown. Even the shutters, lamps, and cat in the windows are included.

niture, such as benches and stop signs, added. The project might be given a public display, and publicity, at the meeting of a community development group, such as at the Chamber of Commerce or downtown development authority.

Models of local architecture can be constructed in other media as well. Designs of individual building facades can be rendered in clay and labeled. Then, these can be attached with construction adhesive to plywood to make a mural for long-term educational display and appreciation.

Three-dimensional clay models of historic buildings may become prize community possessions. Pen-and-ink drawings of buildings can be assembled for a community calendar, or a cloth quilt based on historic community buildings can be made for public display.

Sketching fantasy houses is another architecture lesson. Sketches of one's dream house might include exotic architectural features, such as moats, drawbridges, and crenelated towers. Students of a more practical mindset may want to design something for actual use, such as a design for the interior of their bedroom or a corner of a garden. Students enjoy expressing their personalities through the choice of artwork, interior design, furniture arrangements, color schemes, plants, and bushes. A scrapbook of components can be put together from department-store newspaper advertising sections, home and garden design magazines, and postcards and photocopies of historical exemplars, and the collection can be used by students as the basis for a color, overall design plan. A follow-up activity is to have students take before-and-after photos of places where aspects of their designs actually implemented.

Young primary-level children can enrich their architectural imagings about castles and fortresses through use of a sandbox. Using their bodies, they can enact architectural forms, such as arches, tunnels, and

A series of house facades drawn on accordion-folded tagboard comprise Josephine Allen's street-front scene.

Top: *Fifth-grade student Lisa Molinaro's sketch of an imaginary house shows arched second-story windows in groups of two and four.* **Bottom:** *Good clay-working tools are essential for the careful work that is entailed in making a clay house bas-relief.* **Above right:** *Lisa's finished house showing the series of arched windows, a bay window, and an arched front door, along with landscaping.*

Ceramic low-fire underglaze colors and clear glass glaze enhance the finished quality of the clay house bas relief by sixth-grade student Whitney Brown.

The architecture of Antonio Gaudi and other fantastic architecture can be shown to children to motivate their construction of imaginative structures, such as these sea castles by young Japanese schoolchildren. In most instances constructions like this are assigned as group table projects.

tiny spaces, and imagine what it feels like to be a building. With string or rope, several students in a group can make geometric shapes. Students can experience the architectural element of "forms in space" by developing design criteria and temporarily rearranging the classroom chairs and tables. Primary grade children can learn the idea that engineers and designers figure out how to make things that people need.

Middle school students can study the role of a designer: part engineer, architect, drafter, sculptor, graphic designer, and salesperson. They can learn that design uses a team approach; that ergonomics is how the human interacts with the object, and that form often follows function. Students can play the role of an architectural historian detective and figure out "How did the community come to be this way?"

On a walk around the school, have students sketch the architectural elements they see—for example, triangular pediments, quoins at corners, columns, arches, fan windows, foyers, and courtyards. In art criticism and art history, teams of students can critique their classroom, school, and community buildings: How do the parts work together? What messages about society are conveyed by the forms? How do you feel about the different spatial arrangements in our school building? How does it show its functions? How would you characterize it, as heavy, serene, or lively? Does the size suggest power or influence? If we could redo it, how would we change it? Students can critique the design of their school as to whether the building's materials and forms connote what occurs inside or say something else.

A local architect can be invited to share building plans with a class, and students can do sketches for the visitor to critique. During a follow-up group discussion, students can share their reasons for preferring modern or traditional styles, classical or romantic designs. Students can go on a sketching tour of their community's most illustrious buildings and list their architectural features.

Informed citizens should be able to interpret architectural plans before buildings are actually constructed. As one way to develop such a skill, students can analyze and critique plans that were used for existing structures or areas, such as their school or a nearby recreation center, park,

Courtesy of Faye Brassie, Athens, GA.

A drawing of a local historic home by a middle school student is an excellent way to foster architectural awareness.

Saturday Children's Classes. Courtesy of Frank Wachowiak, Athens, GA, and Mary Sayer Hammond, Athens, GA.

Children who are challenged to be aware of their environment and encouraged to be "noticers" draw their homes in a personal, individual way. They emphasize those features that make each house unique. Third-grade student David Nix worked 2 hours on his felt-nib pen drawing.

Courtesy of the National Building Museum, photo by Jack Boucher, HABS.

It was determined that it would be in the nation's best interests to set aside a building dedicated to the study of architecture. The National Building Museum, Washington, DC, was established by Congress in 1980 to encourage the nation's aesthetic sensitivity to architecture. It is in the National Pension Building, built in 1881 in the Italian Renaissance style. Its Great Hall, shown here, is considered to be one of America's most architecturally thrilling interior spaces. Outstanding architectural education materials for schoolchildren are available there.

neighborhood, or subdivision. They can judge whether design strengths and shortcomings found in the built structures were foreshadowed in the plans.

Nelson Goodman believed that a building is a work of art only insofar as it signifies, means, refers, or symbolizes in some way. Students can discuss the "meanings" of buildings—the messages that buildings send out. Some other aesthetic issues might be addressed by asking such questions as: How does the visual complexity of patterns affect the "interest quotient" of a building? Can a building have too much regularity? Do size and cost determine the quality of a building?

Students can debate what qualities should be considered when ranking buildings ("What is more important, complexity or orderliness?"), and then do a class poll to determine whether preference relates to personality. Because architecture is so public an art form and so open to community response, aesthetics and art criticism activities in which learners learn to look critically at their own environment are especially valuable.

Chapter 30

CRAFTS

Saturday Children's Classes. Courtesy of Frank Wachowiak, Athens, GA, and Mary Sayer Hammond, Athens. GA.

Metal repoussé can begin with preliminary drawings on paper taped to a sheet of copper or aluminum of a limited size such as 6- × 9-inches or 9- × 12-inches. Using a blunt pencil, transfer the design through the paper to the metal. Then work directly on the metal, adding details. To show off the embossing further, apply black shoe polish and then wipe it off.

The term *crafts* covers a very broad area. Some materials and techniques that it almost always includes are works in cloth and fiber, as well as jewelry and metalwork. Examples of these are shown in this chapter. Also, note that other crafts are mentioned elsewhere in this book; for example, cloth banners and quilts are described in the section on collage. The aluminum-foil relief process (described in the section on printmaking) is a variation of repoussé metalwork. Also usually considered as crafts are ceramics and sculpture. Sculpture is discussed in Chapter 28, and ceramics is covered in Chapter 31. For hundreds of other crafts ideas on the Web, see: craftsforkids.

Although the initial designing may take only a short time or be done even as the project is made, most crafts require considerable labor-intensive handwork during the execution phase. This results from the repetitive, cumulative nature of many craft activities and handicrafts, such as spool weaving, bead work, shag pillows, and metal work. Teachers often decry students' avoiding activities requiring focused, long-term attention and their seeking seemingly instantaneous rewards. Crafts can play a role in building a student's attention span. The lesson that is learned from attending to criteria over a considerable period of time to produce something of significance is valuable—and one that crafts can teach. This attending to goals and applying principles over a period of time is at the heart of the qualitative method espoused in this book. Also central to the qualitative method is the student's receiving expert guidance and evaluation, which point out the student's accomplishments as well as areas in which he or she could profit by additional effort. Craft activities can help to promote the habits of careful craftsmanship and the taste for and love of things that are well executed.

The relationship between the craftsperson's effort and the response of the material that he or she works with is central to the African concept of "Mana," which means being sensitive to the spirit within the object one is

343

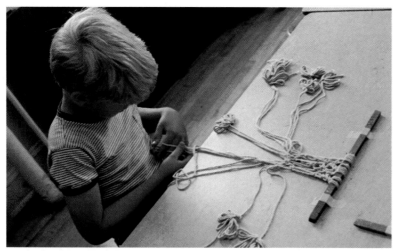

Courtesy of David Hodge, Oshkosh, WI.

With his macramé frame taped to his desk and his lengths of yarn in neat pull-out bows, this student can clearly see which yarns go over and under.

Courtesy of Claire Clements, Athens, GA.

Hooking is done with a crochet hook through burlap. A shag-rug technique is used to create a wall hanging of a yellow-and-black bee.

Courtesy of Claire Clements, Athens, GA.

Macramé is made with square knots and double half-hitches. Used by sailors and ancient Egyptians, the variety of knots in macramé makes it a challenging craft and one that produces a beautiful and sophisticated product.

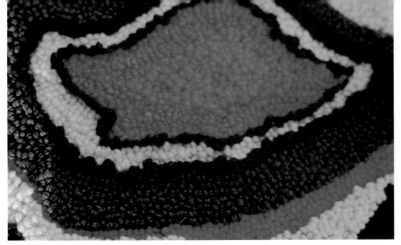

Rug hooking makes an excellent group project; individuals can make burlap pillow covers or wall hangings. Here, an attractive islandlike design with radiating surrounding forms will be used for a pillow cover.

making. For example, the Hausa people urge those making their subtractive embroidered robes to have "an ear for what the cloth wants to say." To Africans, shaping material with one's hands involves both a giving out and a taking in; it entails sensing the reciprocating spiritual force between the hand of the maker and the material being made.

Because crafts often require a special love and special skill, as well as specialized tools, it is desirable that a teacher with real interest in the activity conduct it. Let the activity be that teacher's forte—something for students to look forward to as they proceed through the years; let it be a quality, in-depth experience driven by the motivation from within the teacher's heart.

Techniques must be taught. The teacher must create the vessel in which self-expression can occur. The initial work almost always requires specific directions made quite clear. Consider Friedrich Froebel's instructional pattern: from structured activities to semi-structured and on to free activity. This conceptual model for craft technical instruction offers a way

Metalwork repoussé, done with heavy gold embossing foil, can be related to the study of African masks.

Yarn pictures can be stitched by children. The effect is best when the children take the time to solidly fill in areas with color. Notice the variety in the directions of the stitching of this red-headed figure.

Children love to make porcelain medallions using their initials, then hang them from their own macraméd necklaces.

In this elementary student's stitchery, the columns of pink stitching seem akin to the folds on the face of a heavy-set person.

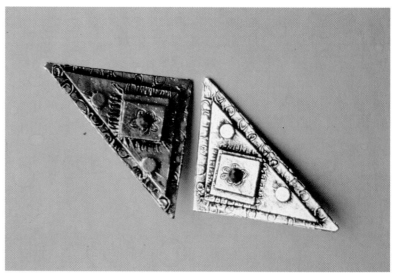

Earrings can be made by building up layers of thin cardboard and using an aluminum foil repoussé process.

to bring in both the structured beginning as well as the later, imaginative opportunity.

While the structured beginning is important, so is the last phase—the individually creative and personally meaningful ending. ("Does anyone have an idea how they can make it in their own unique way?") Always work to personalize and give added meaning to the project. ("Who will you give it to?" "What colors do you associate with that person, maybe the yellow and red of a campfire you sat around together?") Urge students to come up with their own meanings for their designs. Help them to learn to think symbolically as a way of giving depth to personal experiences and developing abstract thinking skills.

A class of students totally involved in a craft activity is a joy to behold; eyes, brains, and hands are in synchronicity with each other, producing an aesthetic experience. Crafts also are excellent for students who come to school early or have idle time around lunch or recess. Some crafts can even be done while riding the bus to and from school. Some students with special needs may find crafts to be an especially satisfying avenue for achievement, perhaps because of the calming, repetitive activity.

There may be certain special-needs students who will require additional help in the psychomotor operations that crafts require. Team up these students ahead of time with those who can perform the operations easily. Using peer teaching can prevent students' frustration as well as afford the other child an opportunity to teach. Also, the teacher can avoid frustration—for example, being asked to tie knots for 30 students in a brief time. For gifted students, have craft examples by more mature artists available to motivate and extend the gifted students' efforts and abilities.

Involve the community's craft practitioners with your instructional unit. Through a display in the school of community craftspeoples' work, give students a vision of the craft form carried out at a more elaborate and mature level. Conversely, have the students' productions exhibited in the adult members' venues, such as at a fibercrafts guild meeting or a community art fair. Seek the involvement of industries in the community. For example, a carpet mill might donate yarn for shag rugs, or a store's drapery department might donate discontinued sample books to use for making banners.

Crafts can readily be integrated with other academic areas. Develop a social-studies unit on how famous individuals have related to the craft form. For example, Paul Revere and his silversmithing might be tied to a repoussé lesson on aluminum-foil relief. In social studies, examine how the economy and governmental policies interfaced with the craft—for example, nontraceable purchases of indigenous Southeast ceramic jugs during Prohibition. For history, point out how the technique has been used in other cultures and for other purposes, perhaps for utilitarian, secular, and governmental articles of apparel and display. Reading can be brought in through stories about people practicing the craft—for example, *Silas*

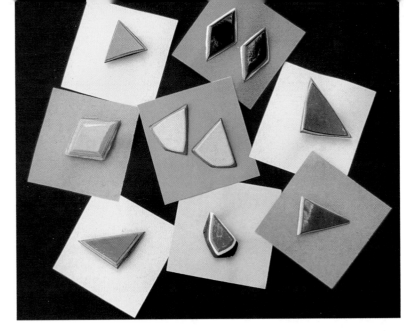

Courtesy of Barbara Thomas, Whit Davis School, Athens, GA.

Gluing together several layers of colored papers and cardboard, and then sanding the edges to reveal a series of colored parallel lines surrounding the shape, is a way to make attractive earrings.

Courtesy of Barbara Thomas, Whit Davis School, Athens, GA.

Bracelets can be made by gluing cut-out shapes punched from thin cardboard to a strip of oak tag, then gluing the strip into a circular bracelet shape, wrapping it with aluminum foil, and engraving with a pencil.

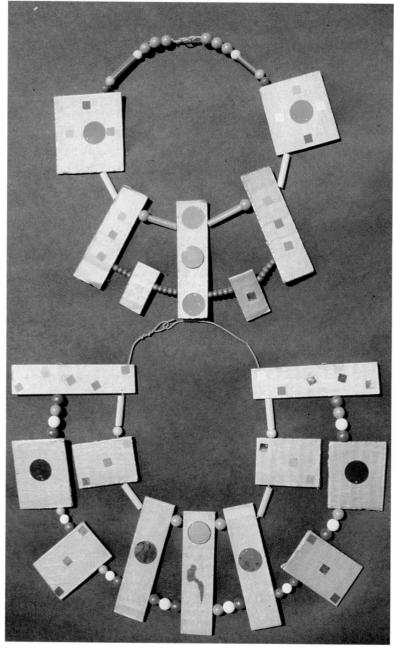

Third-grade students made these Egyptian-style necklaces from rectangular shapes of cardboard, gummed stick-ons, beads, and telephone wire.

Use people in your community for resources. Here, Gary Carroll, a computer salesman, shows his hobby. He practices the Western Ukrainian art of the Hutzel people called pysanki—eggs decorated with colors and symbols. First, either hard boil or blow out the eggs.

Mexican Huichol Indians made nearikas—yarn art pictures—by pressing bits of scrap yarn into softened wax. Here, third-grade students imitated the technique. Using white glue instead of beeswax, they pasted small scraps of yarn to a hard backing to make a jungle mural of lions, elephants, giraffes, zebras, parrots, and monkeys.

Marner and weaving. Mathematics can be integrated through studying the units of measurement required, such as lengths of yarn required for fiber crafts. Finally, bring in economics by discussing how entire cultures flourished through trade in certain crafts, such as East Asian silks during the sixteenth and seventeenth centuries.

Weaving

Weaving is the interlacing and crossing of threads to form cloth. The warp threads run lengthwise and form the skeleton of the fabric. Putting the warp threads on the loom is called *warping the loom*. The weft threads run at right angles and bind the warp threads together. The weaver alternates threads, lifting alternate ones up and going underneath the others. To simplify the task, there are varieties of heddles—devices for lifting alternating rows of threads. Other variations of weaving include plaiting or braiding as well as looping, which includes knitting and crocheting.

One way to introduce weaving to kindergartners is to have several students stand in a row, side by side, in front of the room. Then, have a volunteer take the end of a long piece of rope and go in front of the first student, behind the second, and so on. When the volunteer reaches the end of the row, he or she then comes back to the beginning in the same

Comer Elementary School. Courtesy of Claire Clements and Jo Nan Tanner, Athens, GA.

Elementary students did these weavings on cardboard box looms. The loom can be made from a sturdy shoe box. The box is cut diagonally on its two long sides and the upper material is removed, along with the one short end. The top and bottom cardboard edges are measured at one-half-inch intervals and cut one-half-inch deep. The warp threads are put on, and then the horizontal weaving of the colorful weft begins.

Courtesy of David Hodge, Oshkosh, WI.

A primary grade girl weaves on a cardboard loom. Notice how her black marker drawing on the cardboard beneath guides her as she fills in the areas with her weaving.

Courtesy of Deborah Lackey, Fulton County Schools, Atlanta, GA.

Weaving equipment can be simple or elaborate. In this well-equipped art classroom, a boy works on his woven hanging. He uses a floor loom that alternates his warp threads up and down to facilitate his weaving through of the weft threads.

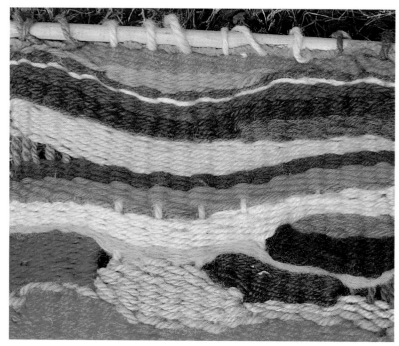

The primary-grade child who made this weaving showed an intuitive mastery of color and undulating shapes.

The thin black warp threads are woven partially together in discrete areas of heavy yarn, and areas are filled in with sticks to create a distinctive wallhanging. The heavy stick across the top gives structure to the hanging, and the grouping of the top warp threads into two clusters makes a unique method of hanging.

fashion. This is a good way to refresh the children's concepts of "in front of," "behind," "over," and "under" as they relate to weaving. Early weaving activities usually include paper weaving, in which the warp is cut on a folded piece of paper (but not so far as to cut through the edge). Pre-cut lengths of rug yarn and regular yarn, along with lengths of natural fibers such as weeds, often are woven through these papers, along with strips cut from colorful photos and foils.

Weaving's rhythm of over and under also can be taught through the ever-popular *Ojo de Dios* (Eye of God). Crossed sticks, or tongue depressors, are used for the warp structure of decorative weavings made in Central American countries and hung above doorways to protect and bring good luck.

A really easy and convenient loom is made from plastic soda straws. They can be used full length or cut in half for little hands. Four or six is about the limit that one can hold between thumb and forefinger. A little half-inch slit is made in the top of each straw, the lengths of warp yarn are sucked through the straw, and the top is firmly taped in the slit. Then, holding the pack in one's left hand, the over-and-under wrapping pro-

ceeds, always adding the new row on the top. Eventually the weaving fills up the straws, causing the weaving to be pushed off onto the loose warp threads. Varicolored yarn can be used, or just tie on a different yarn when a change in color or texture is desired.

Cardboard purse looms are a good early weaving activity. The top and bottom of a stiff piece of cardboard are slit a half-inch deep at half-inch intervals and the warp thread is wrapped around the cardboard. For a cylindrical variation rather than a rectangular shape, weaving can be done on an oatmeal box. A cardboard-box loom can be easily made from a sturdy shoe box or other sturdy cardboard box cut diagonally on its two long sides and the upper material removed along with the one short end.

Top: Here, a purse is shown still on the cardboard loom. Notice how the student has made landscapelike forms by weaving in irregular-shaped areas. Bottom: Some purses made by a class of elementary children.

First, the top and bottom cardboard edges are measured off in half-inch intervals, cut a half-inch deep, and the warp threads put in place. The horizontal weaving of the colorful weft then begins. The advantage of

These purses seem to be just the right size for these proud first-grade boys to use to hold their valuables.

this diagonally cut box is that a large, open area beneath the weaving is provided for manipulating the over-and-under threading. Simple wood-strip looms also can be made. Just drive finishing nails at half-inch intervals slanted outward on the top and bottom boards, and then string or "warp" the loom. Alternately, old picture frames or unused stretcher strips can be used.

Courtesy of David Hodge, Oshkosh, WI.

Students can weave on stretcher strip frames, such as those used for canvas paintings.

Finger weaving (really knitting) using a skein of varicolored yarn is a pleasant introductory activity guaranteed to keep any active child occupied. Wrap yarn over and under around the fingers of one's left hand (assuming one is right-handed) and then back again, then use the fingers of the right hand to pick up the bottom layers and cast them over the top. Proceed to wrap the fingers with another course of yarn, over and under, and then cast what is now the new lower course once again over the top. Eventually, a long knitted rope will fall off the back of the hand. A similar knitting activity uses an empty spool and fine metal wire. On a large, empty spool from the sewing box, five tiny headless brads are pounded around the hole. Fine metal wire is then woven around them and cast off, with a pointed object such as a large nail, down the hole in the middle of the spool. The cords that are formed can then be used to make jewelry.

From time to time, embroidered jackets and jeans become a fad that sweeps a school. Students may use embroidery as a way to celebrate and comment upon one's own culture. This interest can afford a good opening for the teacher to develop a unit on embroidery and to bring out its design constraints and opportunities for expressing in fresh ways the values of the young people. Exploring ways to decorate wearing apparel can also bring in related fibercraft methods, such as batik, appliqué, and molas. One strong feature of applique and related techniques is that it is appropriate for all ages and costs practically nothing.

Starch-Resist Batik

Batik originated in ancient Egypt and is very popular in modern India and Java. For cloth batik, first wash the cloth to remove sizing. The process can be as easy as making a simple paste of flour and cold water. Slightly over one cup of flour is gradually added to one cup of water, and this mixture is brushed on or squeezed through a plastic condiment bottle and/or spread with a fork or stick. Dry overnight, and then, rather than dipping, brush or sponge on the dye color.

For a higher-quality recipe, follow the "adire eleko" starch-resist paste cloth pattern design technique of the Yoruba people of Nigeria. They used cassava tubers, and the cloth was subsequently dyed with indigo (which grows in the southern United States). The starch paste first was

Courtesy of Claire Clements, Athens, GA.

This batik in a radiating design was dyed in successive yellow, red, and brown dyes. Before each successive dyeing, a larger area of the cloth was masked out and the cloth was crinkled to create an attractive network of fine lines. For natural dyeing, boiled onion skins will give a gold color, and sumac berries will give an orange-brown.

Courtesy of Joyce Vroon, Trinity School, Atlanta, GA.

Colorful wax batiks hang outside on the line to dry.

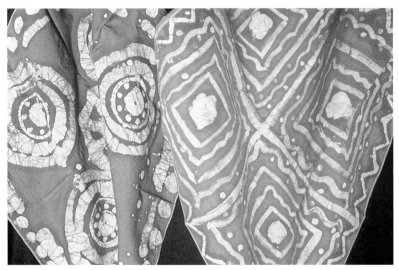

Courtesy of Joyce Vroon, Trinity School, Atlanta, GA., 4th grade.

Designing for batiks often requires a knowledge of geometric pattern. Here, an understanding of how geometric shapes are repeated to create patterns can be seen in these fourth-graders' batik bandanas.

tinted with rust to make it easier to see and then applied with a chicken feather. A paste is made of ¾-cup pearl tapioca and an equal amount of water, cooked in a double-boiler pot until smooth. In a ½-cup of cold water, dissolve 6 tablespoons of gluten flour and cornstarch, and blend into the tapioca mixture in ½-cup portions. Cook uncovered in a double

Courtesy of Joyce Vroon, Trinity School, Atlanta, GA.

Here, children use rubber gloves and tongs to make certain that dye reaches all areas of the cloths.

boiler until thickened, add ½ teaspoon of alum, and refrigerate. For best results in using the paste, spread the starch on thickly with a tongue depressor, and scratch lines in it before it dries. After the starch is thoroughly dry, dye the cloth, and then remove the starch by peeling, scraping, or soaking. The Yoruba women used indigo and avocado leaves, which they chopped and boiled for their blue and rust colors of dye. In our elementary schools, starch resist avoids the hazards of hot wax.

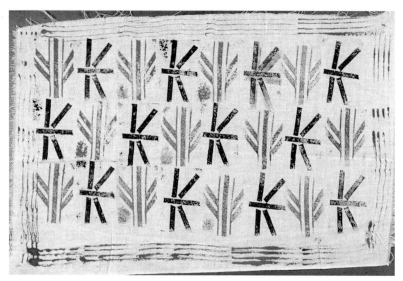

Adinkira is a patterned fabric made by the Ashantis from the African Ivory Coast. It is made by stamping designs on the cloth's surface with calabash (potatolike) prints combined with lines made with a wooden comb dipped in dye. For his adinkira rubber stamp design, a fourth-grade student used strips of rubber innertube glued to blocks of wood and printed in rows and columns.

Fibercrafts are particularly appropriate to integrate with the study of other cultures, because a culture's clothing and other fiber articles may be quite distinctive. For example, the Crow Indians of the American Plains had distinctive parfleches (leather storage bags adorned with geometric designs). Likewise, the Inca people of South America's west coast are famous for their patterned tapestry weaving and feather work. Finally, the artistic designs used in Panamanian appliqués and the molas of the Cuna Indians convey to us something of the values and unique traditions of their civilizations.

On the Web, find hundreds of crafts projects for children at: craftsforkids.about.com. Also browse: weaving.about.com and jewelrymaking.about.com and the names of other crafts activities—basketry, beadwork, and so on—followed by .about.com.

Fifth-grade student Phyliss Helwig's weaving shows a judicious use of grays that make the red, white, and black stand out.

The intricate beauty of a batik design of plant leaves is seen in this fifth-grader's project done on tableau paper.

Sixth-grade student T. J. Meyerholtz made his weaving after studying bold geometric Native-American designs. Among the Hopi Indians, it is the men who weave; among the Navajo, it is women.

Chapter 31

CLAY MODELING

All children, both in elementary and middle school, should have the opportunity to create and express their ideas in clay. Clay is a hands-on wonder—sensuous, malleable, unpredictable, and on occasion, messy. Some students respond to clay more enthusiastically than others, but all children benefit from the unique challenges provided by this gift from Mother Earth.

Clay in the Primary Grades

Young children work with clay in several ways. Most add clay pieces to the basic form. A few will pat clay into a pancake and draw into it, and a very few will pull out features from a ball or lump of clay. The teacher's main responsibility in the early stage is to provide the children with an adequate supply of workable clay. Check the plasticity of the clay at least a day or two before the project takes place. Clay should be as soft as possible without being sticky. If the clay is too sticky or wet, put it on cloth- or canvas-covered boards, layers of newspaper, an absorbent surface such as Celotex®, or a plaster bat to dry.

If the opposite problem occurs, that is, if the clay is too dry to easily work with one's hands, flatten it to a 1½–inch thickness, poke holes in it, and fill the holes with water. Let it set, and then pour off the excess water. If clay is rock hard, have children break it into small chunks with a hammer and a screwdriver as wedge; put the clay pieces in a bucket and cover them with water. When the clay becomes soupy, pour it onto a plaster bat so that the excess water may be absorbed.

If powdered clay is used, mix it several days (or months or even years) ahead, as its plasticity improves with age. Indeed, the older it is, the better.

For brave teachers only (with excellent housekeeping skills), an experience students remember forever is using their bare feet to mix powdered clay with water.

If clay is stored in plastic bags, double bag it in case of a tear in one of the bags. The bag itself can be first dipped in water to add moisture. Keep clay in a lidded airtight pail. To create a moist climate in the airtight pail, damp sponges or similar materials can also be put in.

A ball of clay the size of a baseball is recommended for each child, along with extra clay to be used for additions. Use newspapers or plastic sheeting to protect desks or tabletops.

A period of experimentation with the clay should precede every project. Before students can express a particular idea, they first need to acquire the feel of the clay. During these orientation sessions, call the students' attention to the desired plasticity. Discuss keeping excess clay moist by rolling the pieces and crumbs into a single ball, and explain the mechanics of cleanup.

Emphasize how touch experiences help to give shape to objects. One way of introducing students to the exciting tactile potential of clay is to play the clay-in-a-paper-sack game. A student puts a ball of clay about the size of an orange into a sturdy paper sack and, without looking, manipulates it until it has an interesting form. Encourage the children to think

Courtesy of *London Sunday Mirror,* London, England.

Facing page: Terra-cotta clay sculpture by a middle school adolescent, London, England. Notice how the textural quality of the clay has been retained to give the work a spontaneous naturalness.

357

Japan

with their hands—to stretch, squeeze, and poke the clay. They must not peek inside the sack at any time during the process, however. When the exercise is complete, display the finished pieces. Ask the students if anyone sees a real form hidden in the clay creations—an animal, a bird, a fish? How did playing the game help the students learn about clay?

Introduce just enough stimulating subject-matter motivation, such as animals and their young, to get the class started. The animal kingdom provides a wealth of inspiration for the young clay manipulator. Four-legged mammals, such as cows, horses, pigs, hippos, elephants, rhinos, and bears, are especially suitable, because the child can model sturdy legs to make the figures stand. Other popular animals are cats, dogs, rabbits, turtles, frogs, squirrels, whales, porpoises, and alligators. Group projects, such as Noah's ark, a three-ring circus, the zoo, the farm, and the jungle, are very popular with young children as well. Standing human figures can be difficult, however, and children must be guided to provide additional supports or to model thick, sturdy legs and bases to hold the figure erect.

Primary school children especially love clay's plastic changeability as they poke, squeeze, pound, stretch, and roll it. They may describe a sequence of action with one figure, such as a clown or an acrobat, manipulating it to create various postures—standing on its head, bending backward and forward, and falling down. The clay manipulating and modeling seems to fulfill a therapeutic and a storytelling need.

Some students will pat and pound their clay into a flat, cookie shape. More advanced students will hold the clay ball in their hands to model their animal's body in three dimensions. They will pull out or add legs, tails, trunks, horns, beaks, and wings. Because figures made in pieces often come apart during drying and firing, many teachers strongly advocate that students be taught to pull out appendages from the body rather than to add them on. Encourage students who insist on adding the appendages to make holes in the body with a stick or fingers and then insert the appendages into those holes to strengthen the joint. Older students can learn to score and join clay with slip (a paste made of clay and water). To prevent the sagging of a form, use temporary clay or cardboard supports,

such as a "fifth leg" under the animal's body, until the clay is leather-hard. Always emphasize the importance of a sturdy basic form.

Although many children in the primary grades are not concerned with detailing, some will enjoy experimenting with textures and pattern on their creations. A collection of found objects (which should be washed at the close of the project) such as plastic forks, popsicle sticks, bottle caps,

Japan

Facing page: **Top:** *Three stages in the construction of a clay hippopotamus are illustrated. First, a basic body with legs and tail added. Second, a tongue depressor can be used to create the open mouth. Third, addition of characteristic details: ears, eyes, teeth.* **Bottom:** *The directness of clay manipulation holds a universal fascination for children. The delightful clay figure illustrated at right possesses a mobility that only the clay medium captures so well. Youngsters can first take a variety of poses themselves and feel the kinesthetic awareness in their own bodies before making a figure in clay perform similar action-packed feats. Children might strut, twist, dance, juggle, bend, and even stand on their heads.*

Left: *This elephant's head, neck, ears, and front legs were pulled out from the clay rather than being added onto; encourage children to hold the clay in their hands when modeling small sculptural pieces, especially in the beginning stages. This promotes sturdiness. Michelangelo said that a good sculpture should be capable of being rolled down a hill without parts breaking off.* *Right:* *The kangaroo's large tail provides support to the burden of the adolescent contentedly sitting in its pouch. The theme of an animal and its young is a surefire hit—one with which all children can identify.*

Courtesy of David Hodge, Oshkosh, WI.

This sturdily constructed clay elephant was made by pulling out forms. Then the elephant was decorated with pattern and texture. Youngsters can employ objects such as tubes, pencil erasers, bottle caps, bark, wire mesh, and pinecones to add imaginative texture and pattern to their clay creations.

Saturday Children's Classes. Courtesy of Frank Wachowiak.

Young children often pound their clay into cookie shapes. Here, two projects suitable for students at this stage are shown. One is a bas-relief face to which features have been added. For the decorated mirror frame project, the teacher breaks up a mirror into little pieces and traces around them on paper. These paper shapes are then cut out and given to the children, who form a donut-shaped or squarish frame suitable to cover the mirror scrap. These pieces then are glazed, and the teacher tapes in the mirror scrap. Prior to firing, remember to put in a hole, by which the piece can be hung.

nails, screws, toothbrushes, dowels, and wire mesh will spark their interest and entice them to experiment.

Clay Alternatives

Children enjoy making small figures not only of clay but also from a variety of other moldable, plastic materials. Teachers also appreciate not having to be concerned with firing a kiln. These alternatives to clay are especially useful if real clay cannot be obtained. Homemade mixtures contain varying proportions of material, binder, and water. Here are few "formulas" for such mixtures:

- Everyone is familiar with mixing flour and water in equal parts to make modeling mixtures for relief maps. A firmer mixture can be used to model objects.
- Also easy to make is salt ceramic, made from 1 cup of salt, $\frac{1}{2}$ cup of cornstarch, and $\frac{3}{4}$ cup of water.
- Another popular mixture, often used for seasonal ornaments, is baker's clay, for which 4 cups of flour, 1 cup of salt, and $1\frac{1}{2}$ cups of water are mixed, shaped, and then baked at 350 degrees for 1 hour until hard.
- For a sawdust–wheat paste mixture, use 2 parts sawdust, 1 part flour or wheat paste, and hot water. (Optionally, $\frac{1}{2}$ part of plaster can be added.) This is good for tennis-ball-size puppet heads and will withstand a lot of bumping. For the puppet's neck, roll a cylinder of oaktag paper around one's index finger, tape the edges of the tube together, and, for sturdiness, tear or cut and flare out the tube's top edge to facilitate embedding it into the mixture. Then pack more mixture around the tube to make the head.

Supply budget permitting, water-set clay, such as Wet-Set Clay®, is suitable for young children and requires no firing. It will not harden in air, so students can work on their forms for a period of days. Unbelievably, it hardens when placed in water for at least 3 hours. Since it is relatively heavy, it is also good for sculpture bases for sculptures of all kinds, and it can be painted with acrylic paints.

Somewhat more expensive are the commercially made polymer clays, such as Sculpey® and Fimo®, which come premixed in 30 colors. Because of the cost, these clays may be more suitable for upper grades, where permanence is a greater concern. Polymer clays stay permanently pliable at room temperature. Using clays in the numerous colors solves the problem of painting in fine details. With polymer clays, each part is completed in full detail at the time it is modeled (for example, beginning with the head baked in an ordinary oven at 275° to preserve it), and then the next part is added. Since it does not shrink at all as it dries, these figures can be built

The white animal at top is made of WetSet Clay®. The in-process figure at bottom is made of Sculpey®. As Sculpey® is somewhat expensive, give the children tiny squares of the various colors. Eighth graders worked for weeks on their Sculpey® figures.

over sticks and wires for stability. Polymer clays can also be used for jewelry projects and made into millefiori.

Clay in the Upper Grades

Older students are more successful in mastering the complexities of advanced clay modeling, but they may ask for help with specific problems. For example, figures and appendages may sag or come apart, and students may need assistance with balance and proportion, or with the intricate delineation of eyes, mouth, nose, and ears.

The handsome branch pots made by seventh-graders started as basic coil, slab, and pinch-pot forms. Through the addition of complementary clay and feet and the elegant decoration of surface forms, they emerged as distinctive, one-of-a-kind ceramic containers. Decoration enhances rather than disguises or destroys the fundamental ceramic form. After staining, if the stains appear to be too intense, earth can be rubbed into the surface to subdue the effect. Further embellishment can be achieved by inscribing designs through stained surfaces, and liquid wax can provide a subtle sheen as well as a protective surface.

At this stage, effective motivations include the following: field trips to sketch animals at a farm, zoo, animal shelter, pet shop, or natural-history museum; family pets brought to class to model; and photographs and art reproductions. As a subject, prehistoric creatures fire students' imaginations. Dinosaurs are uniquely adapted to interpretation in clay. Their ponderous mass, protective armor, and wrinkled, scaly skin evoke the quality of the ancient earth itself.

Emphasize structural elements that can give the piece character. Talk about the sway of the body, stance of the legs, swing of the tail, tilt of the head, action of the jaws, flow of the mane, or flare of the wings. An imaginatively expressive creature also may combine the characteristics of several different animals. In upper elementary and middle school, a preliminary drawing of figures to be modeled in clay often helps students to clarify their ideas. The polymer clays mentioned above are excellent for fine detail work.

Extra clay may be needed, especially for reinforcing junctures. To prevent cracking and exploding when the clay is dried and fired, avoid using armatures, such as sticks, inside the structure. To develop the form three-dimensionally, the sculpture should be viewed from all sides. Use a 12- or 16-inch-square Masonite sheet or a turntable as a working base to facilitate rotation.

Whether on a clay pot, figure, animal, or tile, there are almost no limits to clay-relief pattern and textural exploitation. To make scaly, armor-like dinosaur hide, students might roll out balls, coils, and ribbons of clay, then apply them to the body of the creature. Slip can be used as an adhesive to secure the pellets and coils of clay to the main surface. Discarded broken saw blades and combs can be used for linear effects. Squeezing moist clay through window screen produces masses of clay strings for manes or tails.

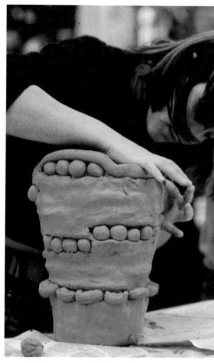

Right: Courtesy of Baiba Kuntz, Glencoe, IL.

Hand-building in clay holds students' interest. **Left:** *A boy studying ancient cultures constructs a model of a cliff dweller's home.* **Right:** *This tall pot is being constructed from coils. The coils are then smoothed together for strength. Rows of bold balls and loops give contrast.*

Construction Techniques

Hand-Building

In overcrowded middle school classes, the beleaguered art teacher would find it difficult, if not impossible, to instruct everyone in the sophisticated, highly technical, and time-consuming craft of throwing pottery on a wheel. Do not frustrate a majority of students by demanding skills that college ceramics majors work long hours to attain. Instead, concentrate on teaching hand-building techniques that all students can master.

Students must be guided to avoid trite bud vases and ashtrays. Show films and photos of contemporary ceramic and hand-building techniques. Introduce students to the exciting work of contemporary potters, such as Mary Engel, Andy Nassisse, and Shoji Hamada, and to the beautiful, functional clay vessels of the pre-Columbian craftspeople of Mexico, Guatemala, Colombia, and Peru. Encourage students to collect an assortment of stones, shells, seedpods, nuts, and driftwood to trigger ideas.

The basic form must be the first critical concern. No amount of additional embellishment or decoration can redeem a piece that is weak in formal concept or structure. Critiques of clay work-in-progress should be standard procedure during every studio session, and students should share their discoveries with their classmates.

Variety in the basic sculptural form should also be emphasized, however. Because students are accustomed to symmetrically styled ceramics,

Collection of Frank Wachowiak, Athens, GA.

An ancient ceramic Haniwa horse from the pre-Jomon period, Japan. Hollow clay cylinders form the animal's basic shape. Notice how clay coils were flattened to add characteristic reins and saddle.

Clay-Slab Construction

Slabs of approximately 12- × 18- × ½-inch should be prepared in advance. Moist clay, a rolling pin, a burlap- or linen-covered board, guiding strips of wood ½-inch thick, and plastic covering to keep slabs moist during storage also are needed. Additional slabs can be made as the project progresses. Impress fired clay-relief stamps and found objects into the moist slab to enrich the surface before beginning construction of the container. Divide the large slab into the number of slabs that will be needed for the sides and bottom (and sometimes top) of the container. The junctures where two slabs are to be joined should be scored (roughened) and covered with water or slip before attaching the slabs. When slabs are joined, use a wooden paddle to secure them and form the container's shape. Two or more clay-slab constructions in different sizes may be joined to make a larger, more complex structure.

Pinch-Pot Sculpture

For pinch-pot sculpture, approximately 5 pounds of moist clay per student is recommended. First, a large portion of the clay is shaped into a large ball and cut in half. Then, each half is formed into a pinch-pot shape, keeping the walls fairly thick and each pot similar in size. Students then join together the two pinch pots (scoring and moistening the junctures) and pinch the seams tightly to form a hollow ball. Holding the hollow ball of clay in one hand, the student paddles it until the pinched seams disappear. To create a decorative surface effect, use a piece of wood, approximately 1 × 2 × 15 inches and wrapped at one end generously with cord. Students must rotate the clay ball as they paddle so that the entire ball will be paddled evenly. This action packs the clay and seals in enough air to support the walls. During paddling, students can change the shape of the ball to resemble a pod, nut, or gourd. Although a cord-wrapped paddle produces an attractive texture, additional decoration may be done by using stamped, incised, and bas-relief motifs.

For unusual effects, students may apply clay pellets, straight and undulating clay ribbons or snakes, and clay coils to the surface. Be sure the surface clay is sufficiently moist for the adhesion of any additions. If not, moisten it, or use slip. Feet, handles, bases, legs, animal necks, and heads may be added, but to preserve strength, the sealed ball should not be opened until the whole container is complete. Once opened, spouts and vase necks may be added. Many exciting forms result when students combine two or more pinch-pot balls of various sizes and shapes into one unified structure.

the teacher must guide them to see the beauty of asymmetry. Variety can be achieved through contrasting the forms of the appendages, spouts, necks, and feet. It also can be achieved through exploitation of the positive and negative spaces created by the vessel's openings, by its handles and lids, and by its delineation of incised and relief areas to create dark and light pattern.

Unity also is vital to the total impact of the clay structure. There should be a natural flow from one plane or contour to another. Appendages should grow naturally from the basic body structure and be in scale with it; they should complement, not detract from, the whole. The same is true of decorations: designs should go with the form, not compete with it or ignore it.

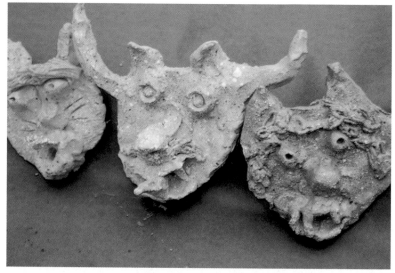

*Ceramics can play a role in a multidisciplinary approach correlating art with science and social studies. **Left:** Intermediate-elementary children studying ocean life made clay fish. They cut fish shapes out of clay slabs and attached them to the ocean-floor bases. The pieces then were bisque-fired and painted with acrylic paint. The two fish on the left are kissing; the top left*

*fish is dining on another fish. **Right:** Second-grade children studied the role of monsters in medieval culture and saw how cathedrals used grotesque gargoyle waterspouts. The children then made these clay monster plaques and painted them with simulated-stone spatter paint.*

Drying, Firing, Glazing, and Staining

If a kiln is available, clay sculptures should be allowed to dry evenly and slowly in a cabinet or under a sheet of plastic before firing. If the finished object is to be kept and fired, and the "body" is larger than your fist, hollow out the bottom before it is leather-hard so the walls won't be much thicker than ¾ inch. Another way of allowing air to escape during firing is to poke pin holes in the leather-hard piece. Trapped air can cause an explosion, and one exploding piece can destroy a kilnful of other pieces! Other precautions are proper wedging of the clay to remove air bubbles, and adding grog to increase the clay's strength. Of course, the kiln should be off-limits to curious children and prying hands. The kiln should ventilate to the outdoors.

It is relatively easy to fire greenware. Raw-clay pieces may be stacked closely inside of or on top of one another, rest against one another in the kiln, and even rest against the kiln's sides (taking care they do not touch the heating elements). Engobe-decorated pieces, in which a clay slip is applied before the first firing and scratched through for graffito designs, can be fired

Face mugs allow a study of caricature and create memorable objects. Students have adorned their face mug characters with features such as mustaches, beards, and a monocle.

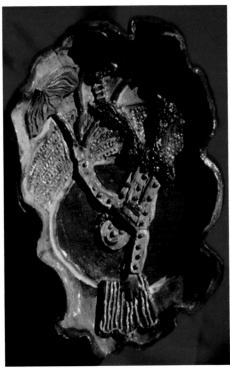

Ceramic glazes add beauty to this ceramic slab dish. The piece's undulating sides make it unique. Many glazed pieces of children's art stay in families for decades as heirlooms.

in a similar manner; however, do not let the clay get too dry before applying slip decoration, lest peeling and cracking occur during firing.

Keep the kiln lid cracked open for an hour or more with the temperature on Low. A precaution to avoid a kilnful of exploded pieces is to fire almost a whole day at lowest temperature. The slower the raising of the initial heating, the better. (Pieces even 2 inches thick can survive firing if the heat is raised very slowly over a period of days.) Then fire several hours at medium, and a few hours or more at high. In cooling the kiln, do not rush; leave it untouched at least overnight to cool with the lid closed. Resist the urge to look inside. In the morning, prop up the kiln lid an inch with a tiny block for a few hours, then more later before finally opening it all the way.

Glaze firing requires more care. Kiln glazing of bisque-fired clay pieces (those that already have been fired once) is a way for ambitious teachers to bring the ceramic process to a rich culmination. Children

create beautiful pieces, which frequently become family treasures. (Because old glazes found at the back of a supply closet may contain dangerous elements, such as lead and arsenic, use only glazes certified as being safe, especially for food containers.) The glazed pieces must be stacked carefully so that no piece touches another or the wall of the firing chamber. Because molten glaze will adhere the piece to the kiln's floor, a protective kiln wash is useful. The bottom and lower ¼- to ½-inch of the piece should be wiped free of glaze, and/or supports such as stilts or pins should be used. Weeks of firing may be necessary, especially if many students have created large clay structures. The large student populations of elementary schools, limited budgets, and limited kiln size frequently make it impractical to glaze large pieces.

An alternate way to beautify fired clay is to rub neutral colors of pigment, moist dirt, or soil of another shade into the incised areas. Before the dirt or applied stain dries, the raised surfaces may be partially wiped with a moist rag to create contrasting effects. In most cases in which staining or coloring (try gluing on torn pieces of colored tissue paper) is applied to bisque-fired clay, adding a final coat of liquid wax or clear gloss polymer is advised.

Clay Plaster Reliefs

Students in upper elementary and middle school often are self-critical concerning their drawing ability and need the satisfaction and challenge of creating in an art medium more dependent on design skills. Creating plaster reliefs, which involves manipulative skills with special tools, materials, and surprise effects, is one such challenging adventure. (Other art projects in this general category are metal repoussé, ceramics, papiermâché, stitchery, weaving, and mobiles.)

For a plaster-relief project, you will need moist clay, plaster, a plastic or rubber dishpan, and a container for the clay mold (shoe box, cigar box, or half-gallon or gallon waxed-cardboard milk carton). Also needed are an assortment of found objects (spools, nails, wire, cogwheels, lath, screws, keys, clothespins, buckles, rope, bolts, cord, reed, dowel sticks, bottle caps, jar lids, coins, printer's letters, combs, plastic forks and spoons, and natural objects, such as twigs, pinecones, acorns, nuts, seashells, and bark). To finish the piece, you will need a plaster-sealing medium, such as white glue or polymer medium, a 1- or 2-inch utility brush, and stains.

The first step is to reinforce the box sides with masking or strapping tape. Use the lid under the box to reinforce the bottom, and line the inside of the box with wax paper. Milk cartons requiring no protective lining can be cut in half lengthwise and the open end resealed. If the separate reliefs are to be assembled later into one large group mural design, uniformity of sizes may be desirable. A free-form relief shape can be made

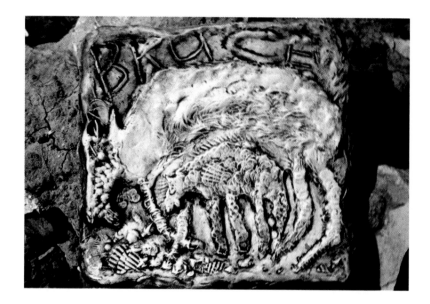

Two attractive plaster reliefs by middle school youngsters. Notice especially how composition fills the space and the metal patina brings out the relief highlights. "Animals and their young" is a popular theme chosen by many students for this challenging, three-dimensional | *project. Suggest that students limit the stains to neutral colors at first to achieve unity. Be sure to apply one or two coats of white glue to the plaster relief before staining it. Allow the stain to flow into the incised lines.*

by using a sheet of tempered Masonite as the working surface and building a clay wall around the slab of clay.

There are two methods for making the basic slab of clay. The simplest is to roll out the clay into a slab approximately ½- to 1-inch thick, cut the slab to the size of the box, and place the slab in the bottom of the box, ready for the next stage of the process. In the second method, the clay is placed pellet by pellet into the box until the bottom is filled with a clay layer ½- to 1-inch thick. If a very flat surface is desired, the clay may be stamped down with the end of a 2- to 4-inch woodblock.

Before students begin their relief designs, incisions, and textural impressions in the clay slab, they should practice on a sample slab. Demonstrate that impressions made in the clay will be reversed in the plaster cast. Designs that are pressed or incised in the clay will bulge out in the plaster version. Show students examples of relief sculpture throughout art history. For example, the Greek Parthenon frieze, coin designs, and sculptures by the modern artist Marino Marini can be used in discussions about the beauty of high and low relief. Letters and numbers must be imprinted backward in the clay to read correctly in the final product. Once the teacher makes these basic principles clear, students are free to be expressive and innovative.

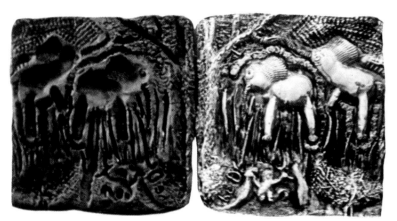

A clay negative mold and the completed plaster relief. Letters and numerals must be impressed backward into the clay mold to read correctly in the final relief; shapes pressed into the clay bulge out in the plaster version. A seashell was used to make the elephant's ears. Other effective imprinting objects include beads and discarded costume jewelry, plastic forks and spoons, crumpled heavy-duty aluminum foil, heavy cord, reed, and wire.

There are several ways to model in the slab. A very free and natural approach involves the use of hands and fingers. Commercial ceramic tools also may be employed. Coils, pellets, and ribbons of clay cut from a thin slab may be applied with water or slip.

With younger children, it might be wise to limit designs to those that can be achieved by pressing into the clay, because it is more difficult to dig lines out of the clay. (In addition, the digging approach often produces sharp, hazardous edges in the final plaster cast.) For straight lines, use applicator sticks, popsicle sticks, or the edge of a thick piece of cardboard. For curved lines, use bent reed, cord, or the edges of round containers.

Recommended subject-matter themes for plaster reliefs include the following: birds with plumage, fish, insects (butterflies), animals in their habitat, flowers, theater or clown faces, heraldic devices, personal insignia, monograms, and abstract, imaginative, and nonobjective designs. By combining individual efforts into one large "mural" composition, a project of significant scope can be achieved.

When the impressed and incised designs are completed, liquid plaster-of-Paris is poured over the clay to a $\frac{1}{2}$- to 1-inch thickness. (Plaster-mixing procedures are described in Chapter 28 in the section on subtractive sculpture.) Before the plaster sets, insert wire, twisted at the ends, for a hanger. The hardening capabilities of plaster vary widely; semihard pieces are easily broken, and the teacher should allow time for the plaster to harden. Hardening takes at least 1 to 2 hours; plaster should be allowed to set overnight.

If your class does a sand-plaster project at a beach, care must be taken to form the mold far enough up the beach so that the plaster will not be affected by dampness at the water's edge. If there is too much moisture in the sand, the plaster will not harden. If you are at a saltwater beach, use fresh water, because salt can weaken the plaster's strength. Sand will not hold nearly as much detail as clay, so the outer edges of sand-plaster reliefs usually form the shape of the object. Sand-plaster reliefs often require coat hangers, wire, or sticks added quickly after the plaster is poured for added strength.

When the plaster is quite hard, the student pries open the cardboard container and separates the plaster from the clay. If the separation is done carefully, most of the moist clay in the mold can be salvaged for a future project. (*Note:* If the clay contains bits of plaster, do not reuse it for a clay project that is to be fired; the plaster may cause the clay to explode.)

To prepare the plaster relief for staining, students should file or sandpaper away the excess edges and any sharp, abrasive points. The relief then should be washed with water, using a discarded toothbrush or

Courtesy of Julie Daniell Phlegar, Upper St. Tammany School District, Slidell, LA.

In this clay/plaster bas-relief pond scene by a sixth-grade student, frogs, a toad, and flowers teem with life.

nail to clean away the clay from narrow recesses. Before staining, give it a generous coat of slightly water-diluted white glue, and allow it to dry thoroughly. Then apply stain, and wipe the raised areas to bring out highlights.

Plaster reliefs are a good project for upper elementary and middle school teachers and students. The project's appeal comes from its being not totally dependent on drawing skill, from its sophisticated, finished appearance, and from the unusual inverse bas relief three-dimensional carving experience.

Chapter 32

ASSESSMENT OF ART LEARNING

The assessment of a student's art learning obviously involves much more than just written tests. In terms of art production, it includes examining the student's artworks both in progress and after completion and talking with the student about those assessments. It involves the ongoing monitoring of the learner's progress, which might include examining a portfolio of the student's projects. It includes assessing learning in art criticism, art history, and aesthetics through informal journals, in-class written assignments and tests, and contributions in class discussions. Assessment can also be made of the student's attitudes in the classroom. In summary, assessment includes all of the procedures used to make decisions about a student's progress.

Courtesy of Joyce Vroon, Trinity School, Atlanta, GA.

Studying Marisol's sculpture, Zibby Stokes did this "Celebrity Sculpture" of an Olympic runner.

Courtesy of Joyce Vroon, Trinity School, Atlanta, GA.

Students can be helped through in-process evaluation to assess if they have attained their goals. Here, sixth-grade student Zibby Stokes deliberates on her next course of action for her Celebrity Collage Sculpture.

Evaluation is even more comprehensive than assessment. Evaluation necessitates obtaining information so that educational assessment decisions can be made. It includes value judgments about the effectiveness of lessons and curricula. It reviews the entire teaching/learning process, including the environment, program, practices, methods, organizational procedures, and outcomes.

Although some authors differentiate sharply between assessment and evaluation, in common parlance, the terms frequently are used interchangeably.

The Need for Open Objectives and Evaluational Criteria

Evaluation can be done by the teacher's asking open questions of students: "How do you like your picture?" "Is there some part of your picture you like best?" "Is there something that bothers you about it?" "What could you do to fix the part you don't like?" Open questions do not have a specific, expected answer.

Today, some school systems require clearly stated, unambiguous, sequential educational objectives along with clearly spelled-out standards

From Robert Clements and Lawrence Stueck, "Earthworks: A Two-Hundred Ton Art Media," *Art Education*, July 1983.

Artistic activity can occur in a state of openness, when the objective is unclear even to the creator. Allow for meditation. A mound of loose clay can provide an exciting medium for the unplanned, the unexpected, and that which is full of wonder.

for evaluation. However, as teachers of art, which is a personal, poetic subject filled with wonder and uncertainty, we also must value that which is open, indeterminant, and imaginative.

One example of a teacher's statement identifying and reinforcing imagination and poetic interpretation is: "Makeela's picture has a sense of mystery in it—the feeling that we can't quite tell what is going to happen when the figures in the picture meet." The teacher thus reinforces the child's use of imagination and exploration of the unknown. People learn about art through continually coming back to main concepts in a holistic, contextually sensitive way. Proponents of one-dimensional curriculum goals may need to be reminded of that learning process.

Much quality art production by artists of all ages occurs in a state of nondirectional "play." It appears as if the artist is fiddling around—that the objective is unclear even to the creator. A teacher of art must allow for this "water gazing." Art education has been criticized for trying to force students into a curriculum with predetermined contents and goals. Thus, even though school systems may require goals and objectives to be spelled out, where else but in art class will encouragement be given for the irrational and the quirky? Where else will the mysterious, the subversive, and the unexpected—elements necessary for our society's continuing renewal—be nurtured?

The Need for Defined Objectives and Evaluational Criteria

In contrast to an open, free-form way of evaluating students, many feel that clarity of education is greatly promoted when objectives and evaluational criteria are clearly spelled out both in the teacher's mind and in the minds of the students. In education, the principle of *expectancy* emphasizes the need to inform the learners in advance about the objectives of any task they are to perform (Gagné, 1975). Objectives and evaluation are two components of the same learning process, with the former coming early and the latter coming later in the process.

To do well in the critical first year of teaching and to keep their enthusiasm and dedication high, new teachers must grow in confidence and pride in their work. One key way to develop this confidence is by being *fully* prepared for each class. Write out the vocabulary words and ideas to be presented, and do not rely on last-minute inspiration. Prepare a written outline of objectives and refer to it during class and during the evaluation in order to give emphasis to important aspects. Continually review the project's long-range evaluational goals and make the students aware of them in advance.

Goals as Contrasted with Objectives

State or local systems often set broad goals. It then is up to the individual teacher to focus on the specific objectives that will allow students to achieve those goals. For example, a system-mandated goal might be: "Students will appreciate the art of diverse cultures." One of the objectives through which an individual teacher believes a class can attain this goal might be: "Students will be able to differentiate photos of pre-Columbian, Mississippian Native-American, and Greek Cycladic sculptures." By setting clear, attainable objectives, teachers and students can readily evaluate their success.

Perhaps your school system has developed a set of goals. Your task then is to determine how, given your skills, interests, and beliefs (and those of your students, the school, and the community), you can develop objectives to meet those goals. Writing objectives requires more specificity than stating goals. You must carefully examine each goal and determine the specific outcomes that you will accept as evidence of mastery.

Note, however, that this two-part way of thinking about goals and objectives is not universally accepted. Some professors instead prefer a three-part way of thinking about the issue. To the two terms "goals and objectives," they feel a third term "outcomes" is necessary as the final, most specific step. In this alternate system, the term "objective" is used for an intermediate step. Using the example above, the objective might read, "Students will know and understand stylistic characteristics of Prehistoric and ancient civilizations' art." In this system, the sentence, "Students will be able to differentiate photos of pre-Columbian, Mississippian Native-American, and Greek Cycladic sculptures" would be called an outcome.

Other professors, more in sympathy with the idea of open objectives, as previously discussed, believe that art learning has, at its core, learnings of a subtle, cerebral, inner, intangible, even spiritual nature. They believe strongly that art learning defies behavioral measurement. Their evaluational methods instead emphasize looking and talking with students about their artworks and portfolios and reading student journals.

Yet, writing lesson plans in terms of objectives is a skill required in many teacher-education programs and even, in an increasing number of states, to receive teacher certification. Two-thirds of our nation's school districts and their elementary schools have art-curriculum guides that specify instructional goals and student outcomes. In over a third of elementary-level art programs, there exist sets of required or recommended student classroom textbooks that often are written in instructional objectives.

One of many ways to write instructional objectives is the highly structured (and some would say overly structured) ABCD method (Mager, 1975). *ABCD* stands for Audience (who), Behavior (what), Conditions (how), and Degree (to what extent or standard):

Courtesy of Joyce Vroon, Trinity School, Atlanta, GA.

One goal was that the students appreciate the art of modern masters. An objective was that fourth-grade students apply Matisse's concepts of shape and pattern to their own artmaking. ***Top:*** *Here, Tricia Clineburg used pattern in the striped tablecloth and floral drapes to set off the strong shapes of her goldfish artwork.* ***Bottom:*** *Lindsay Garfield depicted pattern in a floral wallpaper, plaid curtains, and blue tablecloth. A distant seaside fishing scene out the window is added to elaborate upon the fish theme.*

A. The *subject* of the sentence is the student or the learner or audience. It is not what the teacher will do.
B. The *verb* should indicate some demonstrable behavior, such as to identify, list, match, or depict. It should not be a broad, vague, or difficult-to-assess goal, such as "to understand" or "to appreciate." Goals typically cover a whole curriculum or course, whereas instructional objectives most often deal with one lesson.
C. *Conditions* are the supplies and motivational resources available and the time allotted for each phase of an art project.
D. *Standards* of quantity or degree of quality should be spelled out. (Some examples are: "Must meet at least four out of the eight criteria listed on the chalkboard." "Must bump the edges of the paper." "Must show several very large objects and many very small objects.")

An example of these four features in an objective is as follows: The student (or students) will sketch the main shapes of the model in the still life, using chalk on colored paper, in 20 minutes, showing the floor plane, the ceiling plane, the figure's general shape, and the background's spatial breakup. A. The subject is "the student"; B. the behavior or verb is "will sketch"; C. the conditions are "using chalk on colored paper, in 20 minutes"; and D. the standards or degree of satisfactory achievement are "showing the floor plane, the ceiling plane, the figure's general shape, and the background's spatial breakup."

The goal that is much broader, more vague, and may carry over several years is that students will develop the ability to represent the human figure in its environment. (Note, however, some educators object strongly to such things as "understandings" being "reduced" to demonstrable behaviors and some object to such a highly structured approach).

Categories of Art Objectives and Assessment

Just as there are many ways to teach, there are many different ways to evaluate lessons. From myriad objectives and evaluative methods, teachers choose to emphasize those that are at the core of their personal values

Courtesy of Joyce Vroon, Trinity School, Atlanta, GA.

The general goal was to increase perceptual skill and drawing skill. The specific objective was that students depict in their drawings the forms, folds, and patterns of three-dimensional objects, specifically in the old dolls, as seen in fifth-grader Erica Silverstein's drawing.

Stress only a few objectives each lesson. During the first lesson in this Japanese classroom, line was used to delineate every part of the bicycle. Filling this picture plane also was stressed. Later lessons focused on using color to set off the bicycle background.

about art and education. Major factors concerning which methods are appropriate for you are your own teaching style and beliefs as well as the ages, ability levels, and learning styles of your students. A few school administrators and supervisors, however, may require that certain types of goals and objectives be used in plans to have on file in the school's central office.

With many means of assessment planned to convey to your students the importance and purpose of the art activity, you can pick and choose among these means to meet an individual student's needs. Students with differing ability levels and learning modes, as well as those with developmental disabilities, will require that you emphasize different objectives. For example, gifted students may already know the concept, and some students with significant mental challenges might master it to their level of ability. The experienced art teacher has the insight to know what specific skills are within the general grasp of a given class of students and can customize the general objectives to address special needs. By using several categories of objectives, you will create powerful motivations that will sustain the learning activity of all your students. It is better to have extra plans, which might be carried out if time permits or perhaps with only a few of the students, than to exhaust the plans for a lesson early and try to "fill up time."

To keep *art* itself the central focus, five types of art objectives and areas to evaluate are discussed in this chapter: They are the cognitive, affective,

and psychomotor. But for now, let us consider the five types of objectives specifically about art:

1. Art production
2. Artistic perception
3. Art criticism
4. Aesthetics
5. Art history

Remember that these categories are not totally separate entities. Instead, like ingredients in a well-cooked stew, they blend. When writing an objective, determine which of the several categories into which the objective may fit.

Objectives and Evaluation of Art Production

As art teachers, we must teach first about art. In too many instances, we find art teachers apologizing for making suggestions to children, initiating projects, and emphasizing art fundamentals. Let the truth be known! Where promising, sequential, imaginative, and qualitative elementary and middle school art programs exist, the classroom or special art teacher is on the job organizing, coaching, motivating, questioning, demonstrating, evaluating, approving, and advising—in other words, teaching. The importance of actively helping students learn to apply art concepts in their creation of art cannot be overemphasized.

We believe that specific objectives are best. It is not enough simply to write, "Students will draw the still life" or "Students will use colors with good design." The vagueness of these statements helps neither the teacher nor the students to assess whether the students have met a specific objective. Without specific standards, the verbs "draw" and "use" are too general. An educationally more helpful phrasing would be "Students will draw the table plane, suggesting depth by overlapping and creating avenues in depth," or "Students will show how at least seven objects and forms overlap," or "Students will compose the design so at least three of the objects go off the edges."

In carrying out a project, stress only a few art objectives each class period. Do not confuse students with too many directions at once. In a drawing project, for example, emphasize the quality of line and the full use of the picture plane during the first session. During the second session, guide the students in identifying and evaluating the variety of shapes and overlapping planes in their drawing. During the third session, challenge the students to enrich their drawings with detail, texture, and pattern.

Courtesy of Beverly Mallon, Chase Street Elementary School, Athens, GA.

Too many directions all at one time can confuse students—better to give a few directions in one period. The motivation for this first-grade project, covering four 35-minute periods, was, "If I were a king or queen." The first period the students were to draw in pencil their figures with heads, torsos, arms, and legs, and fill the picture space. The second period they watercolored their figures' clothes and background and foreground objects. The third period they used marker for additional details in the background, figures, and foreground, The fourth period they enriched their pictures, using sequins and glitter for jewels, fireworks, and patterns in clothing. Following this long project, they did an immediate gratification project.

Formative Objectives: In-Process Evaluation of Student Work

Among the many questions that teachers of art seek to answer, the most commonly repeated is: "How can I help those students who rush through their projects, who so often exclaim, 'I'm finished!' when they have barely begun to tap their expressive potential?" No doubt the quality and promise of a school's art program depend in great measure on how teachers meet this particular challenge. There is no miracle formula—no surefire panacea—for dealing with those students with a short interest span, deficient school preparation in art, and minimal self-motivation. Every teaching strategy and stimulative approach will meet with varying success, depending on the students' backgrounds, personalities, and readiness. Some students simply need personal encouragement, some demand specific help, and others require only a clue. All students, however, are entitled to more than vague generalizations. They are entitled to assessment of their learning. The best evaluative criticism provides the students with guidance they can understand, store, and use over and over in later art pro-

Courtesy of David Hodge, Oshkosh, WI.

Here, in these works by intermediate-elementary-grade children, the human figure is interpreted through crayon, collage, and paint. The teacher can help students to evaluate their work in terms of the lesson's instructional objectives. The instructional objectives for the painting of the girl may have been use of analogous and complementary color. Her green lips and orange and purple eyes are absolutely superb!

jects. These are called *formative objectives* since they assist the students as they form the artwork.

One highly productive one-on-one evaluational procedure is for the teacher to sit down with a student and discuss the student's work at various stages, perhaps using a framing mat to set off the work. The most positive evaluations always take into consideration the personalities of the

Courtesy of David Hodge, Oshkosh, WI.

Instructional objectives to break up the space into small areas, to leave the space of the chalk line unpainted between forms, and to imaginatively use colors helped the sixth-grade artist of *this tempera-India ink resist to create this "bouquet with owl."*

children themselves. Considering the children's individual personalities is increasingly necessary in today's diverse classrooms with students with a wide range of cognitive abilities. Children at all stages have individual styles in art expression and diverse imaginative and inventive capacities. Thus, the teacher might say that one rambunctious student's piece shows his or her "energetic personality through the dynamic shapes and way the colors fly out of the shape borders." The teacher may comment on a contrasting piece by a quiet, calm student by saying that the work shows "a calm, determined, and thoughtful way of working by the way each shape is carefully drawn all the way around."

The subtle strategies of high-caliber teaching are evident in the words, action, sincerity, and confidence that teachers exhibit when they

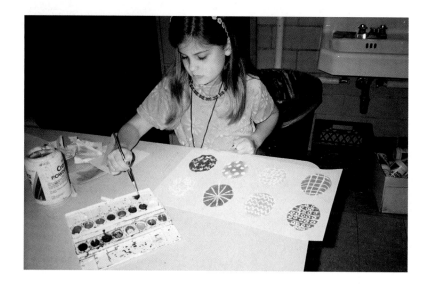

Second-grade students were instructed to use their knowledge of pattern to create as many different patterns as they could think of. Using a white crayon, they decorated holiday eggs with patterns of stars, stripes, radiating designs, and plaids. Watercolor resist technique on top *revealed the patterns. A patterned basket and grassy background were painted and the eggs were inserted at various places through slits in the paper.*

help students to evaluate their art efforts. What instructors say, how they say it, how much they say, and what they leave unsaid are vitally important.

If the students are engaged in a multilesson crayon-engraving project, for example, the following self-evaluative questions, either written on the chalkboard, or photocopied on slips of paper to be given out on the successive days, will provide working criteria for each stage:

1. Did I use enough pressure in applying the crayon so that the paper is completely and solidly covered? With padding under my paper, did I apply the crayon heavily and smoothly? Did I vary the sizes and shapes of the many crayoned areas?
2. After coating the drawing with black paint and transferring the sketch to it, ask: Does my preliminary line-drawing composition for my engraving fill the space effectively? Have I employed a variety of lines, shapes, and sizes? Have I emphasized detail, pattern, and textures that are especially effective in the engraving process?
3. During the engraving process (the main part of the lesson), did I engrave the basic outlines of the shapes in my composition first? Did I make variations of lines—thick, wavy, jagged? Did I take time to engrave details, vary patterns, and create textural effects as contrasts against plain black areas? Did I create some bold contrasts by scratch-

ing away solid areas of black to reveal the crayoned surface underneath? Have I fully used all three methods: engraved line only; detailed and patterned areas; and scraped-out, solid crayon shapes?
4. During the final enrichment lesson, did I enrich the composition by applying oil pastel over some of the remaining black areas and repeat the oil pastel colors in different parts of my composition to achieve unity? Did I engrave lines, details, or patterns through the oil pastelled areas for even more subtle embellishment?

Thus, the very clear, published list of criteria on the students' desktops helps to heighten the student's own evaluative questioning and bring it directly into the student's creative actions. Furthermore, the list helps the teacher to assess the lesson's ongoing effectiveness, and the teacher can point to a phrase on the list to assist in discussing that feature with a student.

Ask one or more of these questions to evaluate design and composition:

Are the sizes and shapes of objects (people, buildings, cars, trees, and so on) varied?

Do they produce interesting negative spaces?

Is informal balance employed (as opposed to formal balance) to create a varied, more flexible composition?

Courtesy of Barbara Thomas, Whit Davis School, Athens, GA.

This third-grade boy's gesture appears to indicate that he believes he has met the criteria of dividing the space.

Are the shapes or objects drawn at different levels to create varied space breakup in the foreground and background?

Do objects or shapes overlap each other to create unity and depth?

Do some lines converge to create space-in-depth?

Do some lines or shapes touch or intersect the borders of the picture plane to create movement in depth into the composition?

Is contrast achieved by juxtaposing light areas and dark ones, and patterned or detailed areas and plain ones?

Depending on the students' ages, one or more of the following color evaluational criteria may be used by the teacher and students:

Are colors repeated throughout to achieve movement and unity?

Has pressure been used in coloring to achieve rich, glowing colors?

Does the picture lack excitement because of too rigid a dependence on the use of local color?

Are bright, high-intensity colors employed for emphasis wherever such emphasis is needed?

Are the intensities of the colors varied for diversity and subtlety?

Is the color scheme limited or monochromatic to achieve unity?

Are the tints and shades of the colors varied for interest and contrast?

Courtesy of Beverly Mallon, Chase Street Elementary School, Athens, GA.

Make your picture fill the page. Make it interesting to look at all over. What is on the ground in front? What can be seen in the sky—butterflies, birds, rainbows, the sun? A first-grader drew this action-packed picture of Peter Rabbit's family playing outside on a sunny spring day.

Is the color employed based on one of the color-wheel schemes: complementary, split-complementary, analogous, or triad?

Are the neutralized colors in the palette (umber, ochre, sienna, and so on) employed for their special, subtle effects?

Are colors used to achieve a feeling or mood: warm and cool colors, colors with psychological impact?

Courtesy of Joyce Vroon, Trinity School, Atlanta, GA.

Are colors repeated to achieve movement and unity? Notice how the spectrum of colors is repeated in this hex design by Katherine Vickers.

Courtesy of Joyce Vroon, Trinity School, Atlanta, GA.

Top: *Bright, high-intensity colors at the center of a picture are set off against muted colors in the background—a sure way to achieve glowing colors in a picture. Fourth-grader Elizabeth Beilman's collage, after Picasso, shows this color principle.* ***Bottom:*** *Color can be used to create a mood. Here the luscious pink tones suggest the delightful flavor of watermelon. Hilary White, Grade 2.*

For average and slower students and those who lack assurance, assessment can be used as a way to give praise and encouragement. Give these students personal, encouraging comments on their work, rather than just a grade. As an example, using one of the criteria from the above list, write, "I like the rich, glowing colors you made with the crayons." This will give that student a boost and motivate him or her to try harder in the future. Individual assessments and IEP's can assist in helping slower, unsure students. After an assignment, try to give feedback as soon as possible.

Portfolios provide an accurate picture of the student's ability and seriousness of effort. Not only can they help teachers assess the effectiveness of their teaching, they serve as a focal point for discussions with parents about the student's progress. Also, they are convenient for getting together works for display. In addition to portfolios, teacher observations and anecdotal records can also play a useful role in assessment.

Objectives and Assessment of Artistic Perception

While art production is one area to evaluate, artistic perception is another. Artistic perception helps students to identify elements of beauty and interest in their daily lives. If teachers can bring children to notice something

Courtesy of Barbara Thomas, Whit Davis School, Athens, GA.

A student intently paints the sunflower petals observed in the still life.

they have never noticed before, to see with the inner eye, they will have started them on an endless, exciting, and rewarding journey toward a thousand discoveries. Three sources for perceptual objectives are: the classroom, artworks, and the students' daily life experiences.

- The classroom: Examples of perceptual objectives based on what can be seen in the classroom are: "The student will identify at least three triangular shapes in the classroom" or "The student will describe analogous color schemes from among the colors seen in classmates' shirts."
- Artworks: An example of a perceptual objective based on what can be seen in artworks presented and created is: "From the artwork of a group of classmates, the student will be able to point out instances demonstrating (1) exaggeration and (2) swinging design." (Note that a perception objective about artworks becomes the same as a type of art criticism objective.)
- Daily life experiences outside the classroom: Perceptual objectives also can be based on what the students have seen outside the classroom. ("The students will be able to recall the order of the colors in a rainbow." "The students will be able to describe and depict the design of insects' homes that they have seen.") Perceptual objectives and evaluation about nature state that the students "will describe verbally using metaphors" or "show in their artwork" that they have perceived such phenomena.

Much evaluation of artistic perception is done of the class's discussion as a whole. Skill in perception also is very clearly shown when its results are evident in students' artwork. Yet, it can also be evaluated through an individual paper and pencil questionnaire, as follows:

A Perceptual Exercise

If you were to describe these sights to a person without sight, tell in your own words what they are like:

1. The intricate pattern of a spider's web
   like squares
2. Cracked shapes in mudflats and ice
   like hexagons
3. The blue shadows on fallen snow
   never saw
4. The variety of grain pattern in wood
   like creepy lines
5. The varied textures and patterns of tree bark
   Bumpy
6. The shadows of tree branches on building walls
   scary
7. The lines and patterns of bridge girders and cables
   beams
8. The pattern in leaf veins
   lines
9. The pattern in insect wings
   beauTfil
10. The pattern of frost on a windowpane
    never saw
11. The changing formations of clouds
    like T rex dinosaurs
12. The dew on early morning spider webs
    like gum drops
13. The undulation of reflections in water
    zig zag lines
14. The moody, misty colors of a foggy or rainy day
    foggy lines
15. The flashing colors of stoplights, neon signs, and beacons in the rain
    bulleTs
16. The tracks of animals in the snow
    holes
17. Peeling paint on old wood and metal
    peeling bark

Top row and middle row right: Courtesy of Frank Wachowiak; *Middle row left and center:* Courtesy of David Hodge, Oshkosh, WI.; *Bottom row:* Courtesy of W. Robert Nix, Athens, GA.

As a way to assess students' perceptual abilities, have them write about their perceptions of nature. Urge students to notice the subtle variations in the leaves and petals of flowers and in the feathers of birds. Lead them to examine the spaces in a spider's web and the scales of a fish.

Dropped Bowl with Scattered Slices and Peels, 1989, Claes Oldenburg and Coosje van Bruggen, Art in Public Places Program, Miami, FL.

This picture in Chapter 1 began this book, and now it ends it. In art criticism, students should demonstrate their knowledge of art by describing an artwork.

Objectives and Evaluation of Art Criticism

Objectives in art history, criticism, and aesthetics are described in Chapters 20 and 21. One way to state an art criticism objective is: "Students will use the language of art to describe qualities in an artwork." (Our example for evaluation of an individual student's writing uses the sculpture shown on page 3 of this book; alternately, the class's discussion as a whole can be evaluated.)

Dropped Bowl with Scattered Slices and Peels
by Claes Oldenberg and Coosje Van Bruggen, 12- × 50- × 50-feet, 1989, Miami, Florida

Describe this artwork.

What colors are used?
How are shapes used?
How do you think it was made?
What does it mean?
Why is it in Miami?

Art criticism interpreting feelings could be assessed through the objective: "Students will describe how the artworks displayed or artwork by peers in the class have used artistic devices to show different kinds of feelings." Students might say that the dark lines around Joe's eyes make the guy look tough, that the light lines in Maria's picture make the person look gentle and kind.

For assessment of an art criticism objective to analyze an art element, for example, depth, an objective might be: "Using classmates' artworks, describe three ways to indicate that an object appears to go back in space." Using as an example the Turkish student's artwork shown on page 17, the students might write or say: "1. The figures in front are bigger. 2. The figures in front overlap, and 3. The figures in back are up higher on the page."

The case study method can also be used. For example, a newspaper clipping dealing with a new piece of public art sculpture might be headed, "Sculpture Detracts, Says Neighborhood" and can be debated by a table of students, while other tables debate other contemporary or historic articles, such as the French art critics debunking the Impressionist painters' exhibition. Assessment of learning is facilitated by each student taking notes on the points raised, using two sides of a vertically folded sheet of paper, labeled "For" and "Against."

FOR	AGAINST
good	(dumb)
	ugly
nice	
	sTupid
cuTe	
	makes iT look bad
preTTy	
figurisTic	
makes someThing beTTer	junky

Objectives and Assessment in Aesthetics

Aesthetics is about ideas of beauty or the nature of art. Examples of aesthetics objectives are: "Students will discuss varying ideas of what makes a good picture," "Students will debate whether art that does not realistically

Courtesy of Joyce Vroon, Trinity School, Atlanta, GA.

represent objects and figures can be considered good art," "Students will debate whether ugly subject matter can make good art." (See Chapter 21.)

Much evaluation of aesthetic discourse and thought is done based upon the class's discussion as a whole. While there is no one right answer to such thought questions, nevertheless, the teacher can assess the class's ability from the quality of the discourse and the sophistication of the language and thought. Assessment of small groups in discussion can also effectively occur: a table of students, given one or two art reproductions to start the conversation, can explore both sides of an issue (such as the relationship of form and feeling and innovation) by debating "Is it true that, in art, anything goes?"

Objectives and Evaluation of Art History Learning

Objectives and evaluation can focus on many of the important educational roles of art history, which are described in more detail in Chapter 18. Lower-level art history objectives (such as to identify or match) lend themselves to evaluation by paper and pencil tests. The teacher holds up a series of reproductions (or shows slides) and students write the name of the artist, the style or the historic period, or the historic event from a list of choices written on the board. Upper-level skills, such as of synthesis, can best be assessed by written paragraphs in the higher grades. Objectives include the following:

Study of art history concepts: "In class discussion, working in pairs or small groups, or on individual tests, students will identify different art styles."

Analysis of famous historical artworks to gain a perspective into the overall development of culture and history: "Students will describe how and why a theme has been shown differently throughout several centuries."

Aesthetics concerns ideas of beauty and the nature of art. Fifty years ago there was much debate about whether splatters, such as those used in Jackson Pollock's paintings, could be considered art. Abstract expressionism espoused the idea that accidental effects enhance an artwork. Here, a student and artwork illustrate a way to make this awareness real. If a brave teacher wishes to do this activity, it needs careful supervision, outside, with water based paints, and students should wear old clothes.

Gwenda Malnati, Athens Montessori School, Athens, GA.

From a study of Van Gogh's sunflowers, primary student Dalton Tyler drew in pencil and then used sponges to paint these sunflowers.

Use of historic artworks to give students ideas for their own art: "From examples of Persian and Medieval art, students will analyze and apply the concept of overlapping to their own artwork."

1. As the six pictures are displayed, hold up the correct number of fingers on your hand to identify the piece's style: 1. Medieval, 2. Persian, 3. Impressionism, 4. Realism, 5. Twentieth-Century Abstraction.
2. Comparing the mysterious Peruvian Nazca lines in Peru to Robert Smithson's *Spiral Jetty* (1970), how do you think the cultures might differ?
3. After studying the Persian and Medieval art examples, make a thumbnail sketch below showing how overlapping occurred in those pictures.

Another goal of art history is for the student to be able to locate and use information to write a report. This is in line with the goal of discovery learning or inquiry learning: that the student can develop strategies to manipulate and process information. The essential criterion is that the learner organizes into final form the material to be learned. To collect material, the student can use the resources at a learning center in the classroom, in the library, or on the Web.

Reporting Art Progress to Parents

We shall now turn from the evaluation of art learning in five (more or less) separate ways, and take up how to share assessments with parents. Most likely the school system will have a standardized report card you are to use. Reporting of students' art progress varies from school to school, from primary and intermediate through upper elementary to the middle school grades. In early grades, S for satisfactory or U for unsatisfactory may be used. Some systems also add E for excellent and substitute NI for needs improvement rather than the more harsh sounding U grade.

By the time of middle school, most systems use the letter-grade system. Some schools employ separate evaluations for behavior and subject mastery. One example of a behavior scale is the following:

(4) Accepts assignments willingly;
(3) Accepts assignments, but requires some encouragement;
(2) Accepts assignments with reluctance and requires more than three prompts;
(1) Does not accept assignments.

When letter or numerical grades for art are given, teachers often take into account the students' classroom working habits and behavior as a factor in their evaluation. Forewarn the students that their seriousness of effort, behavior, and conduct will affect their grades, because in almost

Art history knowledge can be applied by making one's artwork in the style of famous artists' works. **Left:** *Following a study of early American portraits, a first-grader did her own portrait, with toy and pet, in a decorated frame.* **Middle and Right:** *Following a study of* Grant Wood's American Gothic, *fourth-graders Sarah Simmons and Beth Aitcheson did their versions using adult figures familiar to them. Rather than just copying the outer form of the art historical work, the couple was selected to represent the contemporary American scene.*

every instance, the student's prudent use of class time will result in higher-quality work. For reporting to parents, the main goals of the program are listed, as on the report below. Or, your school likely will mandate the use of a standard reporting form by the art, music, and physical education teachers.

An elementary school art specialist teacher may work with from 300 to 1000 students. For art teachers with so many students, reporting should be streamlined so that it is both a fair and accomplishable task. With this many students, the art specialist teacher may find it helpful to photocopy a progress report that describes the goals and abilities assessed, along with multiple choice checks (for satisfactory or needs improvement) to be completed in evaluating the individual student's achievement. Then the teacher is free to write in specific comments, such as "Outstanding" or "Off task behavior" describing the child's achievement or problems.

Art Progress Report, Spring

Ability	Satisfactory	Needs Improvement
Drawing ability		
Design ability (ability to use repetition and variation of shapes, lines, colors, patterns, and textures)		
Interest and ability in looking at and talking about art and art ideas		
Enjoyment of a positive experience in class		
Seriousness of effort		

Courtesy of Joyce Vroon, Trinity School, Atlanta, GA.

With 500 to 1000 students to evaluate, a simplified method is recommended. It is readily apparent that second-grader Henry Baird would receive high marks for the bold composition and sure painting of his red rooster.

Another evaluational system, more suitable for upper grades, assesses generic abilities used in daily living:

Art Report

Satisfactory	Exceptional	Needs Improvement	
			Discovery (seeing possibilities, finding alternatives)
			Pursuit (taking initiative, staying on task, developing works over time)
			Perception (visualizing, showing attention to details)
			Expressing feelings and communicating though arts media (emotions shown in art and captions, using symbols)
			Self- and social awareness (tapping into personal feelings, sharing discoveries, tolerating frustration, cooperating, negotiating, appreciating others' contributions)
			Skill use (muscle coordination, demonstrating a sense of standards)
			Creativity (responding flexibly to different situations, crossing artistic domains)
			Analysis (describing to others what is seen, imagined or done, showing an interest in using arts vocabulary, giving opinions)
			Critique (talking about their own works and those of peers, accepting and incorporating suggestions, using others' works for inspiration)

An excellent type of evaluation occurs as teachers send home the child's artwork throughout the year. Parents themselves can assess whether in their minds the child is learning and achieving. Their review of the work with the child and subsequent mentioning of the concepts can also help the child to continue learning the objectives. A sheet accompanying the return of the work describing the art program and the units' objectives

Courtesy of Baiba Kuntz, Glencoe, IL.

and giving other information about upcoming art units and exhibitions is particularly helpful to parents.

January–May Art Report, Fourth Grade

In April of this year in art, the 4th-graders studied and drew insects, using newly emerged real insects and photos. Notice particularly the variety of pattern and texture used in the details in wings, mandibles, and legs. Thanks, parents, for your contribution of insects and insect collections to draw. The project was ultimately executed using analogous colors in a crayon resist technique, and the project accompanies this report. Our study of repetition in pattern and texture was preceded in March with the built-up bas-relief bracelets covered in aluminum foil and antiqued, which were sent home in time for Mother's Day. In January, in connection with a social studies unit on 19th-century America, we did a unit on still life drawing of Americana agricultural equipment and antiques using markers for direct line observation of interior and outside edges and emphasizing the depictions of overlapping forms to give depth. These pictures have been on display in the school and at the U. S. Department of Agriculture Building on Broad Street. Following up on this, in February we studied cultural history and art history, particularly of the Industrial Revolution.

Next fall we will begin by studying architecture and community planning, so on your travels this summer, keep an eye out for interesting buildings and architectural features. For this project we need boxes, so please save shoe boxes, and cereal boxes, and any other smaller boxes.

Eight pieces of 4th-grade art will be on display at the new El Dorado Restaurant during June. Hope you saw the article on our November dinosaur project in the *Daily News,* January 14, section B, page 12.

The Recreation Department is having Art Camp this summer, phone 489-1221. This summer, draw with your child and do fun art activities. Next fall, I'd like to see what you did.

Sue Varanco, art teacher,
West Adams Elementary School
e-mail: lvaranco@westadams.foxtwnshpschls.sunnet.edu
School assignments phone number 548-0033, box 1444.

Left: Sixth grade student Ali Schier did this multiperiod marker drawing with no initial pencil drawing, from a posed model; captured the turning on the hat's every straw strand and the myriad patterned and folded cloth designs. *Right:* Laura Towbin added a background, envisioning the sophisticated individual sitting on a balcony in a big city. *Bottom:* The teacher laminated the drawings to prevent the marker color from fading. Nine 20- × 40-inch frames were grouped in this four-way hallway intersection to create a wonderful display.

Left and middle: Courtesy of Joyce Vroon, Trinity School, Atlanta, GA. *Right:* Courtesy of Beverly Mallon, Chase Street Elementary School, Athens, GA.

Left: *Careful perception and thorough representation are shown in fourth-grader Katie Calhoun's drawing of a doll.* **Middle:** *Third-grader Wade Askew showed exceptional expression of feelings in his pastel drawing of the skull-like red mask.* **Right:** *Social awareness, self awareness, creativity in combining related arts, and expression of a love of music and dancing are shown in this first-grade Hispanic child's picture of salsa dancing. The school had received a state education grant to develop a dance program in the schools. Students danced and also looked at video snippets of different kinds of dances.*

Courtesy of Joyce Vroon, Trinity School, Atlanta, GA.

It isn't easy to reduce a fluffy formless stuffed animal with few visible edges to a hard pencil line drawing, yet the subject matter is so appealing to elementary grade students that they work diligently at the task.

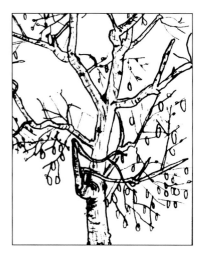  

In evaluating children's art, be alert for children's work showing a unique and personal artistic vision. Here, the teacher fostered individuality of expression by challenging students to represent in their own ways the trunk, bark, knots, branches, leaves, roots, twigs, buds, blossoms, *and fruit. Let them touch the trees, perhaps climb them, and pretend to be a tree swaying in the wind, feeling the rain, the snow, and the warm sunlight.*

Summative Evaluation

Summative evaluation summarizes both the students' learning and the teacher's effectiveness. It is differentiated from formative evaluation used to help the student in the process of making the artwork. Summative evaluation is used to diagnose, to revise curricula, and to determine if objectives have been met. Usually it is done at the end of the academic year, or when artwork portfolios are returned. Save the students' work in portfolios, and periodically go over them to determine if your goals are being met. Through photos and video, document three-dimensional work and exciting art events. Older students might keep journals to document what they are learning. Ask the students to help you, either through questionnaires or class discussion, to determine whether the program is leading students to understand art, whether the students are finding satisfaction in the process, and whether the language the students use in discussing aesthetics and writing about art is becoming more advanced.

Evaluating Our Year in Art

Did you learn any new words or art ideas this year? What?

What was good about art this year?

What was not so good about it this year?

If anything did not work out for you, how would you handle it in the future?

What did you learn this year about how to make art?

Did we do anything in art that helped you to learn about science or social studies or other subjects? What?

How is art different from other subjects?

How could the teacher make art class better and be better to the students?

What could the other kids do to make art class better?

When you are older, how will you use anything you did in art this year?

How would you change what we did this year?

Do you have any ideas about how we could make art more real and not just like school?

Do you have any ideas for ways to make art class better?

How did you like it when the class talked about art and thought together about art?

Outside of school and on your own, did you do any things that were like art? What? Did you do it by yourself or with someone?

Outside of school, did you talk with anybody about art ideas? What was the discussion about?

Did anything good about art happen in the community?

Why do you think students should study art in school?

From the following list of what we did in art this year, mark those activities that you really liked, or from which you learned a lot. Write if there was anything about the activity that made it especially good.

This questionnaire should be followed by a list of the projects done during the academic year.

Courtesy of Baiba Kuntz, Glencoe, IL. Students Megan Munitz; Joel Savitzsky; Rana Brizgys.

Sixth-grade students enjoyed the novel experience of creating a collage picture out of colored felt. First, students looked at undersea pictures; then, with no drawing ahead of time, they directly cut the fish out of the felt and decorated it, using white glue to attach pieces. They carefully selected a 22- × 24-inch background color, which the teacher glued to a piece of cardboard with rubber cement (a process requiring skill and speed). Then students made and added other elements and unique border designs, gluing them down with white glue.

Concluding Statement

Wherever art programs of quality and promise exist, there is an enthusiastic, resourceful, knowledgeable, imaginative, and gifted teacher, unselfishly dedicated and enthusiastically involved. We hope that this teacher is you, helping students to open their eyes and hearts to the design, color, form, rhythm, texture, and pattern in the world about them. Students learn a new language, a language with which to give form to and make meaning from their personal experience, and learn to share something of this with others. The teacher knows that art has the capacity to transform and reorganize our conceptions of the world, the capacity to make ordinary experiences extraordinary. In this happy, charged environment of children's searching, discovering, and creating, art reveals its unique, spirit-enhancing, and rejuvenating power. Our hope is that you have partaken of and, in the future, will partake increasingly in this emphasis on art—art as an adventure; a flowering; a celebration; and a discipline with its own singular demands, unique core of learning, and incomparable rewards.

Courtesy of Baiba Kuntz, Glencoe, IL.

To achieve a chromatic unity, the color scheme is limited to analogous colors, yellow through green. What concentration the fifth-grade girl displays as she colors her sunflowers! She is using oil pastel on black construction paper. A preliminary sketch was made in silver.

Appendix A

ART MATERIALS, SAFETY CONCERNS, MODELING FORMULAS, AND FACILITIES PLANNING

Multiarts exhibits can combine an art display with students' musical or dramatic performances; students may demonstrate special art skills in the hall or foyer. School arts festivals can be made more special by having students wear costumes and bring special theme-related food to be served at the opening, or by including a joint exhibition of parent and child art.

Materials and Supplies

To develop the confidence that will help them teach art successfully, teachers must be familiar with the art materials and equipment available for their classes. They should discover the art potential of these materials through actual involvement with them. The following art materials and tools are frequently found in elementary and middle schools today, furnished by either the school or the students. Teachers should learn to use the supplies creatively, know available sources, order them in economy lots and sizes, and store them properly.

Expendable Materials

Pencils	School paste
Wax crayons	Clay
Craypas	Manila paper
Colored chalk	Newsprint
School chalk	Construction paper
Fingerpaint	White drawing paper
Tempera paint	Oaktag (tagboard)
Watercolors	Fingerpaint paper

Nonexpendable Supplies and Equipment

Art slides and slide projector	Paper cutter
Art reproductions	Overhead projector and
Scissors	projection screen
Watercolor brushes	Rulers, compasses
Easel brushes	Hammer, saw, stapler

Generous Budget Supplies and Equipment

Video player, TV, art videos, and VCR	Computers
Felt-nib or nylon-tip pens	Art gum erasers
Printing inks (water, oil-base)	White liquid glue
India ink	Felt-nib watercolor markers
Brayers (rubber rollers for print-making)	Linoleum and tools for block cutting
Clay kiln	Clay glazes
Poster board (for mats)	Tissue paper (assorted colors)
	Gloss polymer medium

Toxic Materials and Inhalants

Toxic art materials are particularly harmful to children. Their nervous systems, internal organs, and reproductive systems are more at risk because their cells are still dividing. In 1990, Congress passed a law requiring that all toxic art materials have labels warning of their toxicity. However, many toxic materials still do not have such labels. Also, old materials purchased before the law went into effect may still be on the shelves, and these materials should be discarded. School shelves may hold pigments containing lead (lead white or flake white), cadmium, mercury, chromates, manganese, and cobalt. All of these are toxic. The main risk is ingestion while working through eating and nail biting.

One in six U.S. children—3.5 million youths—have harmful levels of lead in their blood. Elevated blood lead is linked to learning disabilities, lower IQs, and dropout rates. Toxic ceramic glaze chemicals may be especially dangerous if used on ceramics that are then used for food or drink. Wheat paste contains toxic preservatives, yet it is used in over half of the schools. The use of all toxic materials should be banned in elementary schools.

Other health hazards are as follows:

Carbon monoxide, sulphur dioxide, and nitrogen oxide from unvented kilns. School kilns should be vented through a canopy hood. Dusts from carving can cause lung irritation, so work outside or use fans that do not pull the contaminated air past one's face.

Turpentine and other solvents. Over a 3-hour period, one-fourth to one-half of a small cup of turpentine can evaporate. Inhaling high concentrations of fumes from turpentine or mineral spirits can cause narcosis, dizziness, nausea, fatigue, and respiratory irritation. Drinking 6 ounces of turpentine is fatal. Nowadays some elementary schools ban oil paints because turpentine might be used in the cleanup. (Odorless mineral spirits are less hazardous.) Prolonged exposure to all solvents containing aromatic hydrocarbons can cause skin allergies. Ingestion of benzene, toluene, and xylene can be fatal. For this reason, references to varnish and shellac, which require mineral spirits, turpentine, and alcohol as solvents, have been deleted from this book. Teachers are urged to use gloss polymer medium when a sealant or a high sheen is desired. At this time, alternatives to mineral spirits, akin to baby oil and vegetable oils, are in the developmental stage.

Adhesives. Building supply adhesives and household cements, such as model cement and Duco cement, contain hydrocarbons, which are harmful when inhaled.

Markers. Permanent felt-tip markers contain aromatic hydrocarbons, can be very toxic, and should never be used in elementary classrooms.

Aerosol spray paint contains chemical compounds that can be extremely harmful when inhaled by students who use this "legal drug" for a cheap, brief, and intense high. The student first sprays paint into a plastic bag. Then the student blows the bag up the rest of the way and puts the narrow opening to the mouth and inhales. Some students spray paint into a soda can and then innocently appear to be drinking. Some children paint their nails with typewriter correction fluid repeatedly throughout the day.

Inhalants are particularly prevalent in the eighth, ninth, and tenth grades. Paradoxically, as drug use declines nationally, inhalant use is increasing. Telltale signs are loss of interest in appearance, food, and family activities. Spaced-out behavior, lack of coordination, sores on the nose and mouth, frequent coughing, dried spray paint on clothes, and empty aerosol cans, from hair spray to Scotchguard to Reddi Whip, may be indications of inhalant use. Long-term effects of sniffing are mood swings, depression, hallucinations, memory loss, and impaired judgment. Brain, kidney, and liver damage, damage to the central nervous system, and heart failure may also result.

Practical Suggestions

Keep all tools and materials in order. Store them in cigar boxes, shoe boxes, freezer containers, coffee or vegetable-shortening tins, commercially available tote trays. Label the containers. Paint tool handles with an identifying color.

Keep all tools clean. Do not let metal tools get rusty. Wipe them dry if they get wet, and oil them if they are to be stored. Do not use scissors for clay or plaster projects. Never pour plaster in any form down a sink drain.

Mount motivational resource photographs on oaktag (tagboard). Store them in labeled accordion folders or flat drawers, or put them in plastic looseleaf protectors and keep them in notebook binders.

Wash brushes clean (use detergent if necessary) and store them with bristle ends up in a jar or tall coffee can. Be sure students rinse and clean watercolor tins. Leave them open and stack them to dry overnight. Order semimoist cakes of watercolor in bulk to refill empty tins.

Store scrap construction and tissue paper flat in drawers or discarded blanket cartons to prevent the paper from being crushed.

When placing orders for tempera paint, always order more white paint, because a great deal is used to mix tints of colors. You can also order crayons or oil pastels in colors needed in bulk.

Hardboard in 4- × 8-foot pieces in ¼-inch thickness is excellent for drawing boards and working surfaces on desks or tables. For drawing boards, have the lumber dealer cut the hardboard into either 18- × 24-inch or 12- × 18-inch rectangles, depending on which size works best in your situation. For longer wear, mask the edges of the boards with tape.

Yarn purchased on skeins should be rewound on balls or spools for ready use. A closed cardboard carton with holes punched in it for the yarn to pass through may be used as a dispenser.

Keep school paste in jars until ready to use; then dispense it on small squares of cardboard. Scrape off the unused paste back into the jar at

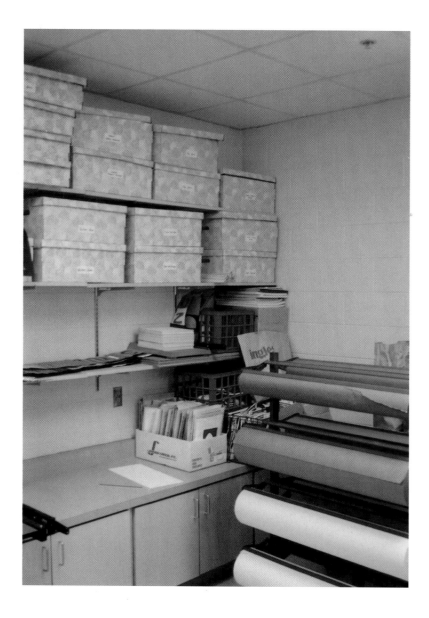

Left: Organized materials not only make things go better but also teach children that order facilitates learning. The wall has adjustable shelves, and matched boxes have been attractively covered in wallpaper and labeled. The colored-paper display dispenser facilitates putting up bulletin-board displays. ***Above:*** Open bins make collecting, sorting, and distributing tools and supplies easy. Bins hold fine and broad markers, crayons, bottles of white glue, and palettes.

the close of class; moisten it slightly with a few drops of water and cap tightly.

When crayons break and do not fit easily into the original carton, store them in discarded cigar boxes, coffee or vegetable-shortening tins, or freezer containers.

Powder tempera is much easier to store than the liquid kind, but liquid tempera has definite advantages. It is always ready to use if sealed properly, and it usually has a smoother texture. The most vexing problem in tempera projects is what to do with the liquid tempera remaining in multicompartment muffin tins, plastic egg cartons, or ice-cube trays. It can't be poured back into the original containers. That is why paint should be doled out a little at a time, with refills as needed. To minimize spills, the teacher should, if possible, be in charge of paint distribution. Before closing covers on tempera jars, check the plasticity of the paint. If the paint is too dry, add a little water to ensure moistness and then cap the jar tightly. To prevent liquid tempera lids from becoming difficult to open, wipe the jar rim before closing, or put a little petroleum jelly on the rim. To prevent liquid tempera from becoming sour, add a few drops of wintergreen or oil of cloves to each container.

Recycling Materials

Recycled materials not only enrich artworks, their use conveys a valuable lesson about conservation of the earth's limited resources. In America's productive and wasteful society, there are vast resources that teachers of art can tap for nontraditional art materials. Using imagination and skill, discarded items, empty containers, scraps, and remnants ordinarily thought of as worthless can be recycled into artworks. Care must be taken, however, to keep the students from regarding the use of interesting materials as an end in itself. The artwork must transcend the materials to be a whole that is truly more than the sum of its parts.

Interesting sizes of cut-off paper can be secured for free from printing companies, and newsroll ends often are donated by newspapers. Other paper sources are computer printouts from institutions and businesses, cardboard boxes from appliance stores, and unused printed billboard papers from outdoor advertising companies. Virtually every company that produces objects has some discarded materials that may be useful in sculptures, collage, weavings, etc. The company might even underwrite an exhibition crediting their contribution. Most teachers of art are not shy about requesting materials for such a societally worthy cause as children's art expression. Children and their parents can help build a store of materials such as the following:

Acorns	Bottle caps
Baby-food jars	Bottles
Balls (rubber, polystyrene, Ping-Pong)	Boxes
	Bracelets
Bark (tree)	Buckles
Beads	Burlap remnants
Blades (saw, broken)	Buttons
Blinds (matchstick, plastic)	Cardboard
Blotters	Carpet samples
Bolts and nuts	Cartons
Bones	Cellophane

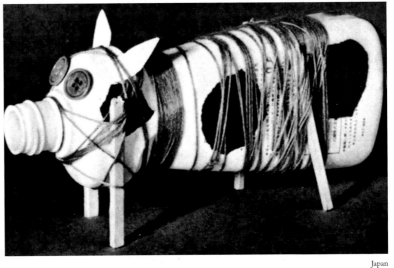

Japan

Recycling material conveys an important ecological lesson. Wood scraps, which usually would be carelessly burned or buried, can be made into imaginative animal sculptures. Care must be exercised when cutting into plastic. It may be prudent to reserve such constructions for upper elementary and middle school. Plastic containers, yarn, sticks, and old buttons usually end up in landfills; instead, such materials can gain a reprieve as animal sculptures and serve a higher purpose, to build the minds and imaginations of tomorrow's creative, adaptive, inventive leaders.

Celotex
Checkers
Clock parts
Clothespins
Coat hangers
Confetti
Cord
Corks
Cotton
Dowels
Driftwood
Earrings
Fabric remnants
Feathers
Felt
Foam rubber (scraps)
Foil (aluminum)
Greeting cards
Gourds
Leather remnants
Linoleum scraps
Magazines
Marbles
Masonite scraps
Meat trays (plastic foam)
Mirrors
Nails
Necklaces
Newspapers
Nuts
Paper bags
Paper cups and plates
Paper tubes (toilet tissue, mailing)

Paper towels
Paper (shelf, gift wrap, crepe, tissue, plain, colored)
Pebbles
Pie plates
Pinecones
Pins
Pipe cleaners
Polish (shoe)
Q-Tips
Reed
Ribbon
Rope
Rubber (innertube)
Rubber bands
Sand
Sandpaper
Sawdust
Screening
Screws
Seashells
Shades (window)
Spools
Sticks (applicator)
Straws
String
Tile (acoustic, vinyl)
Tongue depressors
Toothpicks
TV dinner trays
Wallpaper samples
Wood scraps
Yarn remnants

Special Materials and Tools

Hardboard—For drawing or sketching board, as protective coverage for desks or worktables, and for mural projects.

Brayer (rubber roller)—For inking plate in printmaking. Get the sturdy, soft, black rubber kind for longer wear (not the gelatin type).

Celluclay—Commercially available dry mixture for use in papier-mâché-type projects.

Dextrin (powdered)—Add to dry or moist clay (5 to 10 percent) to harden completed work without firing.

Drywall joint cement—For creating relief effects on a two-dimensional surface; can be painted when dry.

Firebrick (porous, insulation type)—For upper-elementary-grade and middle-school three-dimensional and relief-carving projects.

Grog—Aggregate for plaster molds, clay conditioner.

Masonite (tempered)—For clay modeling boards, inking surface in printmaking projects, and rinsing board in tempera or crayon resists; also practical as a portable sketching board.

Pariscraft—Plaster-impregnated gauze in varied widths for additive sculpture projects.

Plaster of Paris (molding plaster)—For plaster sculpture and reliefs.

Polystyrene—For printmaking plates, collage and craft projects, and printmaking stamps.

Posterboard (railroad board)—For multicrayon engraving project; available in several colors.

Sloyd knife (Hyde knife is similar)—All-purpose utility knife with a semisharp blade; excellent for carving in plaster and for delineating details and pattern in crayon-engraving projects.

Dressmaker's transfer paper—A white carbon paper useful in crayon engraving projects.

X-acto knife—Craft knife with sharp interchangeable blades for paper and cardboard sculpture. *Caution:* To be used by the teacher only.

Formulas for Modeling Mixtures

As many, many materials can be used for modeling and thus substituting is quite feasible, it is helpful to consider the three basic elements in modeling mixtures.

• One is a material to give bulk and substance to the material; this may be something like sawdust, or clay, or plaster, or gardener's Vermicullite®, or flour.

• Two is the glue or binder; it may be white glue such as Elmer's glue, or carpenter's glue, or wallpaper wheat paste (*caution:* wallper wheat paste nowadays often has poison added to it to discourage rodents). Flour (or plaster) acts both as a binder and a source of bulk or substance.

• Three is a liquid to make the material plastic so it can be modeled. This is almost always water in sufficient quantity to create a plastic substance.

• Of course, a fourth element is most important, willpower and the desire to form, create, or recreate. Students love to make recreations of things familiar to them, such as dogs, birds, and human figures and motivation is rarely a problem. Occasionally, students, often very young children, may be tactile resistant to slimy or mucky materials, but this can be minimized by the material's being just the perfect consistency of plasticity, not too mucky, not too hard or too stiff.

Sawdust and glue (or wheatpaste) is a tough material useful for puppet heads and small models which get bumped together. Acquire fie sawdust from a building supply store, lumberyard or parent's woodshop and dampen it. Add white glue such as Elmer's or wallpaper wheat paste.

A Playdough®-like mixture can be made of 4 cups flour, 2 cups salt, and about 2 cups of water. A variation of the formula calls for 2 or 3 cups flour, 1 cup salt, a spoon of salad oil to alleviate stickiness, and just enough water to cook until it releases from the sides of the pan, cool and knead to a consistency that won't stick to hands. It will take two or three days to dry.

For a salt and cornstarch dough, heat 1 part water and 3 parts salt, slowly add 1 part cornstarch, stir well and knead. Coloring the dough is optional, as is adding oil of peppermint and cream of tarter which help the mixture to keep for several months. After being modeled, the mixture can just be let set to dry, or alternately it can be baked 1 hour on low heat for additional hardness. This is called Baker's clay, and is often used for seasonal ornaments. For ornaments, give each child a golf-ball-sized piece.

Saturday Children's Classes, courtesy of Frank Wachowiak, Athens, GA.

Collages such as this fantasy environment can be made from wallpaper sample books, and patterned paper.

Planning Facilities for Art

The elementary classroom or the art room can be the child's first and often most enduring art lesson. It is there, through exciting displays and eye-catching exhibits, that teachers can provide the example for good design through creative, inspiring, and stimulating surroundings. Students should be involved in projects to make the classroom attractive and colorfully stimulating. Bulletin boards and displays should be changed frequently to provide evaluative and appreciatory opportunities for completed projects and to whet interest for further art endeavors. Still-life arrangements should be on view for sketching. Students should be encouraged to contribute to the store of found objects and nature's treasures on display.

Most elementary art projects take place in the self-contained classroom. A few schools boast a multipurpose art room. To make rooms function better for art teaching, the changes that need to be made are in the strategic areas of storage, display, and cleanup. If a multipurpose art room is planned, it should be on the first or ground floor, adjacent to the auditorium stage or to the cafeteria, and near a service entrance. An outdoor court, easily accessible from the art room, can provide excellent auxiliary space for sketching, mural making, ceramics, and plaster sculpture projects in favorable weather.

Sufficient space should be provided to allow students to work on individual projects with some flexibility of movement. Easy rearrangement of furniture for group projects should be planned. An easy flow of student traffic to the teacher's desk and storage and cleanup areas or stations is desirable. In the elementary art room a space of 55 square feet per student is recommended; there should also be a vented kiln, a separate storage area, and a sink. The self-contained classroom should provide adequate space at the rear of the room and along one or two walls for storage, a cleanup (sink) facility, and counter work space. There should be sufficient room at the rear of the class for one or two large, sturdy tables suitable for craft activities and group projects.

Tables and desks should be easily movable for special projects. Counter surfaces of nonglare, waterproof, and scratch-resistant materials are recommended. Light-colored laminated plastic working surfaces must be protected during projects involving linoleum or wood-block cutting, carving in semihard substances, or sawing and hammering on wood constructions. In the special art room, stools that can be recessed under tables during cleanup can ease the traffic problem. In the primary grades freestanding easels can effectively augment the limited desk space.

Sufficient storage for art supplies, tools, visual aids, work in progress, and completed art projects held over for future display is helpful. Adjustable shelves and tote trays are convenient for storing various-size art papers and art materials. Yarn, wood scraps, and found materials can be collected in large cardboard cartons painted in bright colors. Sturdy galvanized or plastic waste containers, water-tight and air-tight, are necessary for clay, and can be used for plaster, zonolite, and sand.

A cabinet or movable cart with shelves and pegboard panels is suggested for storage of small tools. Pegboard secured to a wall and the accompanying hardware can alleviate the most pressing tool-storage problems. Painting an identifying shape or outline of each tool on the pegboard expedites storage and inventory. A hollow box made of Masonite with holes drilled in the top provides an excellent scissors container and inventory device.

Because so much of children's art revolves around painting, there should be adequate horizontal storage spaces for paintings in process. The need for horizontal storage space is especially true in the special art room, where one class quickly follows another. A clothesline and spring clothespins can be used as a drying facility for prints, but not for tempera paintings, which will drip.

To minimize traffic problems, sinks should not be located in a closet or in a corner. They should be large enough to allow two or three persons to use them at once. They should be low enough so children can reach faucets with ease; if not, students should be provided with step-up platforms.

Generous amounts of space should be allotted for display purposes and instructional bulletin boards. Display-panel backgrounds should be neutral in color: subtle, nonglare whites, grays, umbers, and blacks are recommended. Surfaces, in most instances, should be matte finish in cork or Celotex; this affords easy pinning, stapling, or tacking of artwork. Acoustic tile can be glued directly to wall surfaces or to Masonite or hardboard panels to provide a display facility. Cork-surfaced doors on cupboards, closet doors, and storage cabinets will augment display space.

Floors should be of nonskid materials that are easily cleaned. Ceilings should be acoustically treated and provide maximum light reflection. A projection screen and room-darkening shades or blinds are required for projection of color slides, videos, and films.

Electric outlets should be positioned at frequent intervals around the room, though not near sink areas. For a ceramic kiln, 220-voltage wiring is almost always required. The ventilator fan in the kiln hood also requires wiring.

Courtesy of Ted Ramsay and Frank Wachowiak, *Emphasis Art*, Second Edition.

Illustrations on this page show easily constructed, plywood storage facilities for both two- and three-dimensional art projects. Notice in the background of the left picture the rack for art magazines and books and the file cabinets for storage of motivational reproductions. At right, sturdy plastic trays, available commercially, slide in and out on wooden runners tacked to the sides of the cubby holes. Ceramics and reed sculptures with wooden bases are attractively displayed on a background of varied colored papers.

Information and resources on accessible classrooms for persons with disabilities can be obtained from the following Websites:

www.adaptenv.org/Index.htm
www.adaptenv.org/udep.htm
www.cuv@ncsu.edu

Special furniture and equipment can promote a qualitative program. The following items are recommended: clay bin or cart, vibrating jigsaw, color slide projector, projection screen, workbench with vises, large-size paper cutter, electric heating plate, utility cart, ceramic kiln, drying rack for flat work in progress, gun tacker, stapler, large scissors, yardstick, and several wastebaskets or large-sized trash containers.

A BRIEF CHRONOLOGY OF ART EDUCATION IN THE UNITED STATES

Attendant with the Industrial Revolution, between 1790 and 1853 drawing was increasingly used to represent and communicate technical understandings and inventions.

1870—To train artists for industry, the Industrial Drawing Act passed by the Massachusetts legislature required that drawing be taught to all students over fifteen years of age in communities of over 20,000.

The Oswego Movement emphasized the study of geometric solids in kindergartens.

1871—The Metropolitan Museum of Art in New York City was established.

1873—Massachusetts Normal Art School was established—the first training school in the United States for the preparation of teachers of industrial drawing. Walter Smith was the founder and first principal. As the Boston schools' art instructor, he wrote *Teachers' Manual of Free-hand Drawing Designing.* He later organized Massachusetts Art Teachers Association, the first professional art-teachers group, and published a series of graded art lessons to teach geometrical drawing. Copying was encouraged to train the eye and hand.

1875—Art Students' League, New York City, was founded. William Merritt Chase was one of the first instructors.

1876—Thomas Eakins began teaching at the Pennsylvania Academy of Arts, Philadelphia. He relied little on cast models and instead stressed anatomical studies.

1883—The Department of Art Education was established as an integral part of the National Education Association.

1895—Colonel Francis Wayland Parker, a Chicago leader in the child-centered movement (or progressive education), opened up the curriculum to include art: modeling, drawing, and painting.

1896—John Dewey started the University of Chicago Laboratory School.

1898—Arthur Wesley Dow became art instructor at Teachers College, Columbia University, New York City. Dow subsequently wrote the textbook *Composition,* which stressed design and influenced many art teachers.

Late 19th and early 20th century, students were taught the elements and principles in order to produce good designs.

1901—First publication of *The Applied Arts Book,* which later became *School Arts,* with H. T. Bailey as editor. The book employed picture-study units that emphasized the storytelling aspects of paintings and the design content.

1904—John Dewey, author of *Art as Experience,* joined the faculty of Columbia University.

Franz Cizek, called the Father of Child Art, began his influential children's art classes (Kunstgewerbeschule) in Vienna, emphasizing drawing from memory rather than from life.

1912—Paintings by children exhibited in Steiglitz Gallery, New York City.

1913—A. H. Munsell introduced *A Color Notation,* which established a structure by which color theories can be taught. Provided color wheel, color terminology, and color harmonies.

The Armory Show opened in New York City, introducing the paintings of the fauvists ("wild beasts"), futurists, cubists, and post-impressionists to the United States art community.

Clive Bell wrote *Art,* a treatise that emphasized formal elements.

1919—Western Arts Association, the largest of the regional art-education associations, was founded. Drawings from nature sources were emphasized.

1920—Pedro J. Lemos, who served as editor of *School Arts Magazine,* wrote *Applied Art,* emphasizing multicultural contributions.

1923—Robert Henri wrote *The Art Spirit.*

1924—Margaret Mathias, art teacher in Cleveland, Ohio, wrote *The Beginning of Art in the Public Schools.*

Belle Boas wrote *Art in the School.*

From 1900 to 1930, the progressive education movement emphasized the child's process of learning, stressed the importance of subjects' correlation, and decried copying.

1928—Leon L. Winslow wrote *Organization and Teaching of Art.* Sallie Tannahill wrote *Fine Arts for Public School Administrators.*

During the twenties, the picture study movement was responsible for bringing art reproductions, especially those emphasizing patriotic and family values, into the schools.

1933—With the Carnegie Corporation as sponsor and Edwin Ziegfeld as director, the Owatonna, Minnesota, Community Home Art Project began, emphasizing the role of art in daily life; the project continued through 1938.

Joseph Albers, author of *Interaction of Color,* introduced the German Bauhaus design philosophy and techniques at Black Mountain College, North Carolina.

1934—Works Progress Administration (WPA) provided employment for many artists. Scores of murals in state and federal buildings resulted. John Dewey wrote *Art as Experience.*

1938—Leon L. Winslow wrote *The Integrated School Art Program.*

1940—Natalie R. Cole wrote the inspirational book *The Arts in the Classroom.* It describes how painting, drawing, printmaking, and lettering were creatively taught by an elementary classroom teacher.

Art for personal adjustment, emotional release, and leisure-time activity was especially emphasized during this period.

The Progressive Education Association, chaired by Victor D'Amico, published *The Visual Arts in General Education.*

1941—Kimon Nicolaides wrote *The Natural Way to Draw,* which emphasized contour and gesture drawing.

Ray Faulkner, Edwin Ziegfeld, and Gerald Hill wrote *Art Today,* an art appreciation textbook emphasizing art and design in daily life, for example, furniture design.

1942—Victor D'Amico, educational director at the Museum of Modern Art, New York City, wrote *Creative Teaching in Art.*

Wilhelm Viola wrote *Child Art,* documenting the teaching methods of Franz Cizek.

During the war years, art for social responsibility and individual freedom received special emphasis.

1943—Herbert Read wrote *Education through Art.*

The National Committee on Art Education was formed, with Victor D'Amico as chairperson. The committee urged teachers to seek closer ties with practicing artists.

1947—Viktor Lowenfeld, professor at Pennsylvania State University, wrote *Creative and Mental Growth,* which emphasized art for self-expression and creativity.

Rose H. Alschuler and LaBerta Hattwick wrote *Painting and Personality,* a psychological approach to understanding the visual expressions of young children.

1948—National Art Education Association (NAEA) was established and gradually assumed the administrative functions heretofore held by the four regional art associations.

Henry Schaefer-Simmern wrote *The Unfolding of Artistic Creativity,* which emphasized matching the individual's stage of conceptualization, and documented the role of art in helping people who have disabilities.

1951—Florence Cane wrote *The Artist in Each of Us.*

Herbert Read helped found the International Society for Education through the Arts (INSEA).

1952—Charles and Margaret Gaitskell of Ontario, Canada, wrote *Art Education in the Kindergarten.*

Olive L. Riley wrote *Your Art Heritage,* an art-appreciation text for secondary schools.

1955—Rudolph Arnheim wrote *Art and Visual Perception.*

1957—The National Endowment for the Arts and Humanities was established.

1958—Charles D. Gaitskell wrote *Children and Their Art: Methods for the Elementary School.*

Italo DeFrancesco wrote *Art Education: Its Means and Ends.*

1961—Louis F. Hoover wrote *Art Activities for the Very Young.*

June King McFee wrote *Preparation for Art,* giving new emphasis to perceptual, sociological, and environmental issues in art education.

1965—Title V of the Elementary and Secondary Education Act (ESEA) was enacted. Federal funds strengthened state departments of education and made it possible for 36 states to hire a state art director.

The Pennsylvania State University Seminar for Research in Art Education became one of the first federally supported conferences to bring together experts from many fields to discuss content in art education.

Essentialism emphasized the intrinsic value of art study as a discipline itself.

Frank Wachowiak and Theodore Ramsay, both teaching at the University of Iowa, wrote *Emphasis Art: A Qualitative Program for the Elementary School.*

During this period, a movement called "visual literacy" emphasized drawing for perceptual and cognitive development. Newer media such as film and TV began to be studied.

1969—As a part of an assessment of the quality of education in many subjects in the United States, the U.S. Office of Education funded a National Assessment Program in Art, directed by Brent Wilson.

The National Endowment for the Arts established Artists in the Schools programs.

1970—Edmund B. Feldman, professor of art, University of Georgia, wrote *Becoming Human through Art, Aesthetic Experience in the School.* Frank Wachowiak, University of Georgia, and David Hodge, University of Wisconsin, wrote *Art in Depth: A Qualitative Program of Art for the Young Adolescent.*

1972—Central Midwest Regional Educational Laboratory, directed by Stanley Madeja, developed multiarts aesthetic educational materials.

1975—Public Law 94-142 mandated that students with disabilities were to receive the full range of educational services.

1976—Art educators of New Jersey wrote *Insights, Art in Special Education, Educating the Handicapped through Art.*

NAEA begins sponsoring a National Art Honor Society for 12,000 students.

1978—Francis Anderson wrote *Art for All the Children: A Creative Sourcebook for the Impaired Child.*

Rawley Silver wrote *Developing Cognitive and Creative Skills through Art.*

1980—Vincent Lanier focused on "Aesthetic Literacy," a dialogue curriculum like that in an English or literature class, focusing on responses to artworks. Multicultural emphases brought an awareness of sociology, along with popular, folk, and commercial arts into classrooms.

1982—The Getty Center for Education in the Arts, directed by Lani Lattin Duke, was established. The Center supported the establishment of discipline-based art education programs in schools.

Museum education was increasingly seen as a supplement to art classroom instruction.

1984—Claire and Robert Clements wrote *Art and Mainstreaming: Art Instruction for Exceptional Children in Regular School Classes.*

1988—The National Endowment for the Arts published *Toward Civilization: A Report on Arts Education* (first draft written by Brent Wilson). Ros Ragans wrote *Art Talk,* a student text incorporating art criticism with studio activities.

1989—NAEA began sponsoring a National Junior Art Honor Society.

1990—The National Governors Council adopts the National Education Goals.

1992—Claire Golomb wrote *The Child's Creation of a Pictorial World.*

1993—Getty Center publishes *Discipline-Based Art Education and Cultural Diversity.*

1994—Congress enacts the Goals 2000: Educate America Act, containing Visual Arts Standards.

1995—Artsednet@getty.edu, an electronic on-line service over the Internet for K–12 art teachers was established by the Getty Center for Education. The NAEA establishes an electronic media interest group. In response to conservative political forces, National Endowment for the Arts and National Endowment for the Humanities programs were cut or restructured. NAEA develops a five-point plan based on the Goals 2000: Educate America Act for the National Visual Arts Standards, a Professional Development Initiative.

1997—The arts in the schools were assessed by the National Assessment of Educational Progress (NAEP); results were published in the December 1998 *NAEA News* and at www.ed.gov/NCES/naep.

1998—Davis/Getty Units of Study were published by Davis Publications and Getty Educational Institute for the Arts.

1998—George Szekely publishes *The Art of Teaching Art.*

2000—NAEA publishes *Standards for Art Teacher Preparation,* Carole Henry, chair (draft in *NAEA News,* Feb 1999). Mary Erickson and Bernard Young co-edit "ArtWorks in Transtion," NAEA.

Appendix C

RECOMMENDED READINGS

Abrahamson, Roy E. 1980. "The Teaching Approach of Henry Schaefer-Simmern." *Studies in Art Education* 22(1):42–50.

Alexander, Kay, and Day, Michael, Eds. 1991. *Discipline-Based Art Education: A Curriculum Sampler.* Los Angeles: Getty Center for Education in the Arts.

Amdur, D. "Art and Cultural Context, A Curriculum Integrating Discipline-Based Art Education with Other Humanities Subjects at the Secondary Level." *Art Education* 46(May 1993):12–19.

Anderson, T., and McRorie, S. "A Role for Aesthetics in Centering the K–12 Art Curriculum." *Art Education* 50(May 1997):6–13.

Anderson, Tom. 1988. "A Structure for Pedagogical Art Criticism." *Studies in Art Education* 30(1):28–38.

———. 1995. "Toward a Cross-Cultural Approach to Art Criticism." *Studies in Art Education* 36(4):198–209.

Armstrong, Carmen. 1993. "Effect of Training in an Art Production Questioning Method on Teacher Questioning and Student Responses." *Studies in Art Education* 34(4):209–221.

———. 1994. *Designing Assessment in Art.* Reston, VA: NAEA.

Arnheim, Rudolf. 1966. *Art and Visual Perception: A Psychology of the Creative Eye.* Berkeley: University of California Press.

Baker, David W. 1990. "Git Real": On Art Education and Community Needs." *Art Education* 43(6):41–49.

Barrett, Terry. 1994. *Criticizing Art: Understanding the Contemporary.* Mountain View, CA: Mayfield Publishing Co.

Barrett, Terry. "Interpreting Art." *Art Education,* September 1994, 9–13.

Batain, Margaret. 1994. "Cases for Kids: Using Puzzles to Teach Aesthetics to Children." *Journal of Aesthetic Education* 28(3):89–104.

Beittel, Kenneth R., Edward L. Mattil, et al. 1961. "The Effect of a 'Depth' vs. a 'Breadth' Method of Art Instruction at the Ninth-Grade Level." *Studies in Art Education* 3(1):75–87.

Berrson, Ron. 1983. "For Cultural Democracy: A Critique of Elitism in Art Education." *Art Education* 39(4):41–45.

Bickley-Green, Cynthia. 1995. "Mathematics and Art Curriculum Integration: A Postmodern Foundation." *Studies in Art Education* 37(1):6–18.

Billings, Mary-Michael. 1995. "Issues vs. Trends: Two Approaches to a Multicultural Art Curriculum." *Art Education* 48(1):21–24, 53–56.

Blandy, Doug, and Kristin Congdon. 1990. *Culture and Democracy.* New York: Teachers College Press.

——— and ———. eds. 1991. *Pluralistic Approaches to Art Criticism.* Bowling Green, OH: Bowling Green University Press.

Blandy, Doug, E. Pancsofar, and Tom Mockensturm. 1988. "Guidelines for Teaching Art to Children and Youth Experiencing Significant Mental/Physical Challenges." *Art Education* 41(1):60–67.

Blandy, Doug. 1988. "A Multicultural Symposium on Appreciating and Understanding Art." *Art Education* 41:20–24.

———. 1994. "Assuming Responsibility: Disability Rights and the Preparation of Art Educators." *Studies in Art Education* 35(3):179–187.

Bloom, Benjamin S. 1984. *Taxonomy of Educational Objectives: The Classification of Educational Goals.* New York: Longman.

Bowers, C. A. 1990. "Implications of Gregory Bateson's Ideas for a Semiotic of Art Education." *Studies in Art Education* 31(2):66–77.

Brouch, Virginia, and Fanchon Funk, eds. 1987. *Appleseeds.* Reston, VA: NAEA.

Broudy, Harry S. 1972. *Enlightened Cherishing: An Essay on Aesthetic Education.* Urbana: University of Illinois Press.

Brown, Eleese V. 1984. "Developmental Characteristics of Clay Figure Modeling by Children: 1970–1981." *Studies in Art Education* 26(1):56–60.

Catterall, J. "Does Experience in the Arts Boost Academic Achievement? A Response to Eisner." *Art Education,* July 1998, 6–11.

Chalmers, F. G. (1996). Celebrating Pluralism: Art, Education, and Cultural Diversity. Los Angeles, CA: Getty Education Institute.

Chandra, Jacqueline. 1993. "A Theoretical Basis for Non-Western Art Historical Instruction." *Journal of Aesthetic Education* 27(3):73–84.

Chapman, Laura H. 1982. *Instant Art, Instant Culture: The Unspoken Policy for American Schools.* New York: Teachers College Press.

Cherry, Claire., *Creative Art for the Developing Child*. Columbus, OH: Merrill Publishing Co, 1990.

Chijiiwa, Hideaki. 1987. *Color Harmony: A Guide to Creative Color Combinations*. Gloucester, MA: Rockport Publishers.

Churchill, Angiola. 1970. *Art for Preadolescents*. New York: McGraw-Hill.

Clahassey, Patricia. 1986. "Modernism, Post Modernism, and Art Education." *Art Education 39*(2):44–48.

Clark, Gil, and Enid Zimmerman. 1987. *Educating Artistically Talented Students*. Syracuse, NY: Syracuse University Press.

Clark, Gil, Michael Day, and Dwaine Greer. 1987. "Discipline-Based Art Education: Becoming Students of Art." *Journal of Aesthetic Education 21*(2):130–193.

Clements, Claire, and Robert Clements. 1984. *Art and Mainstreaming: Art Instruction for Exceptional Children in Regular School Classes*. Springfield, IL.: Charles C. Thomas.

Clements, Robert D. 1975. "A Case for Art Education: The Influence of Froebel Training on Frank Lloyd Wright." *Art Education 28*(3):2–7.

———. 1975. "Instructional Objectives or Objectionable Instructions." *Journal of Aesthetic Education 10*:107–118.

———. 1978. "Art Teacher Appeals: A Way to Motivate and Discipline." *Art Education 31*:15–17.

———. 1979. "The Inductive Method of Teaching Visual Art Criticism." *Journal of Aesthetic Education 13*(3):67–78.

Cohen, Elaine, and Ruth S. Gainer. 1984. *Art: Another Language for Learning*. New York: Schocken.

Colbert, Cynthia, and M. Taunton. 1987. "Problems of Representation: Preschool and Third-Grade Children's Observational Drawings of a Three-Dimensional Model." *Studies in Art Education 29*:103–114.

Cole, Natalie R. 1940. *The Arts in the Classroom*. New York: John Day.

Collins, Georgia, and Rene Sandell. *Women, Art, and Education*. Reston, VA: NAEA.

Congdon, Kristin. "Multicultural Approaches to Art Education." *Studies in Art Education 30*(3):176–184.

Corwin, Sylvia, and Ruth Perlin. 1995. "A Videodisc Resource for Interdisciplinary Learning: American Art from the National Gallery of Art." *Art Education 48*(3):17–24.

Cromer, Jim. 1991. *History, Theory, and Practice of Art Criticism*. Reston, VA: NAEA.

Csikszentmihalyi, M. 1975. "Play and Intrinsic Rewards." *Journal of Humanistic Psychology 15*(3):41–63.

Csikszentmihalyi, M. (1996). *Creativity: Flow and the Psychology of Discovery and Invention*. New York: HarperCollins.

Dalton, Kimberly, and David Burton. 1995. "Children's Use of Baselines: Influence of A Circular Format." *Studies in Art Education 36*(4):105–113.

Davis, Don Jack. 1990. *Behavioral Emphasis in Art Education*. Reston, VA: NAEA.

Degge, Rogena M. 1985. "A Model for Aesthetic Inquiry in Television." *Journal of Aesthetic Education 19*(4):85–102.

Delacruz, E. M., and P.C. Dunn, 1995. "DBAE: The Next Generation." *Art Education. 48*(6):46–53.

Delacruz, Elizabeth. 1995. "Multiculturalism and Art Education: Myth, Misconceptions, and Misdirections." *Art Education 48*(3):57–61.

Dewey, John. 1934. *Art as Experience*. New York: Minton Balch.

DiBlasio, Margaret. 1987. "Reflections on the Theory of Discipline-Based Art Education." *Studies in Art Education 28*(4):221–226.

Dissanayake, Ellen. 1988. *What Is Art For?* Seattle: University of Washington Press.

Dobbs, Stephen. 1992. *The DBAE Handbook: An Overview of Discipline-Based Art Education*. Los Angeles: Getty Trust.

Donougho, Martin. 1987. "The Language of Architecture." *Journal of Aesthetic Education 22*(3).

Douglas, Nancy, and Julia B. Schwartz. 1967. "Increasing Awareness of Art Ideas of Young Children through Guided Experiences with Ceramics." *Studies in Art Education 8*(2):2–9.

Dunn, Phil. 1988. *Promoting School Art: A Practical Approach*. Reston, VA: NAEA.

Dunnahoo, D. E. "Re-thinking Creativity: A Discipline-Based Perspective." *Art Education 46*(July 93):53–60.

Eaton, Marcia. 1994. "Philosophical Aesthetics: A Way of Knowing and Its Limits." *Journal of Aesthetic Education 28*(3):19–32.

Edwards, Betty. 1979. *Drawing from the Right Side of the Brain*. Los Angeles: J. Tarcher.

Edwards, L. C. 1990. *Affective Development and the Creative Arts; A Process Approach to Early Childhood Education*. Columbus, OH: Merrill Publishing Co.

Edwards, Linda Carol. 1997. *The Creative Arts, A Process Approach for Teachers and Children*. Englewood Cliffs, NJ: Prentice Hall, Inc.

Efland, A., P. Stuhr, and K. Freeman, 1996. *Postmodern Art Education; An Approach to Curriculum*. Reston, VA: NAEA.

Efland, Arthur. 1990. *A History of Art Education: Intellectual and Social Currents in Teaching the Visual Arts*. New York: Teachers College Press.

Eisner, Elliot. 1979. *The Educational Imagination: On the Design and Evaluation of School Programs*. New York: Macmillan.

———. 1987. *The Role of Discipline Based Education in America's Schools*. Los Angeles: The Getty Center for Education in the Arts.

Erickson, Erik. 1963. *Childhood and Society*. New York: Norton.

———. 1968. *Youth, Identity, and Crisis*. New York: Norton.

Erickson, Mary. 1988. "*Teaching Aesthetics K–12.*" In Steven Dobbs (ed.), *Research Readings for Discipline-Based Art Education*. Reston, VA: NAEA.

———. 1995. "A Sequence of Developing Art Historical Understandings: Merging Teaching, Service, Research, and Curriculum Development." *Art Education 48*(6):23–24, 33–37.

———. 1995. "Second-Grade Students' Developing Art Historical Understanding." *Visual Arts Research 21*(1):15–24.

Ewens, Thomas. 1990. "On Discipline: Its Roots in Wonder." *Art Education 43*(1):6–11.

———. 1990. "Flawed Understandings: On Getty, Eisner, and DBAE." In London. *Beyond DBAE*: The Case for Multiple Versions of Art Education. North Dartmouth, MA: Southeastern Massachusetts University.

———. 1994. "Rethinking the Question of Quality in Art." *Arts Education Policy Review 96*(2):2–15.

Feldman, David H. 1986. *Nature's Gambit*. New York: Basic Books.

———. 1987. "Developmental Psychology and Art Education: Two Fields at the Crossroads." *Journal of Aesthetic Education 21*(2):243–59.

Feldman, D. H., M. Csikszentmihalyi, and H. Gardner, (1994). *Changing the World; A Framework for the Study of Creativity*. Westport, CT: Praeger Publishers.

Feldman, Edmund. 1970. *Becoming Human through Art*. New York: Prentice Hall.

———. 1996. *Philosophy of Art Education*. Upper Saddle River, NJ: Prentice Hall.

———. 1993. "Best Advice and Counsel to Art Teachers." *Art Education* 46(5):58–59.

Fitzpatrick, Virginia. 1992. *Art History: A Contextual Inquiry Course*. Reston, VA: NAEA.

Flannery, Merle. 1986. "Art as a Neotenizing Influence on Human Development," *Visual Arts Research* 12(2):34–40.

Freeman, Kerry. 1994. "Interpreting Gender and Visual Culture in Art Classrooms." *Studies in Art Education* 35(3):157–170.

Freeman, Kerry. 1991. "Possibilities of Interactive Computer Graphics for Art Instruction: A Summary of Research." *Art Education*, 44(3):41–47.

Freeman, Nancy. 1991. "The Theory of Art that Underpins Children's Naive Realism." *Visual Arts Research*, Spring:70–71.

Freeman, Nancy H., and M.V. Cox. (eds.). 1985. *Visual Order*. Cambridge, England: Cambridge University Press.

Freeman, Nancy. 1980. *Strategies of Children's Drawings*. New York: Academic.

Froebel, F. (1974). *The Education of Man*. W. N. Hailman, trans. Clifton, NJ: Augustus M. Kelley. (Original work published 1826, published in English 1887.)

Funk, Farley, and Ron Neperud. 1988. *The Foundations of Aesthetics, Art, and Art Education*. Westport, CT: Greenwood.

Gagné, Robert. 1975. *Essentials of Learning*. New York: Dryden.

Charles D. and Margaret R. Gaitskell. *Art Education in the Kindergarten*. Peoria, IL: C.A.Bennett.

Galvin, S. "Scent Memories; Crossing the Curriculum with Writing and Painting." *Art Education* March 1997, 7–12.

Garber, Elizabeth. 1995. "Teaching Art in the Context of Culture: A Study in Borderlands." *Studies in Art Education* 36(4):218–232.

Gardner, Howard, Ellen Winner, and M. Kirchner. 1975. "Children's Conceptions about the Arts." *Journal of Aesthetic Education* 9:60–77.

Gardner, Howard. 1973. *The Arts and Human Development*. New York: Wiley.

———. 1980. *Artful Scribbles, The Significance of Children's Drawings*. New York: Basic Books.

———. 1982. *Art, Mind, and Brain: A Cognitive Approach to Creating*. New York: Basic Books.

———. 1983. *Frames of Mind*. New York: Basic Books.

———. 1989. "Arts Propel." *Studies in Art Education* 30(2):71–83.

———. 1990. *Art Education and Human Development*. Los Angeles: Getty Center for Education in the Arts.

Gates, Eugene. 1988. "The Female Voice." *Journal of Aesthetic Education* 22(4):59–68.

Geahigan, George. 1983. "Art Criticism: An Analysis of the Concept." *Visual Arts Research* 9(1):10–22.

Getty Center for Education in the Arts. 1986. *Beyond Creating: The Place for Art in America's Schools*. Los Angeles.

Getty Center for Education in the Arts. 1993. *Discipline-Based Art Education and Cultural Diversity*. Los Angeles.

Getzels, J., and P. Jackson, 1963. "The Highly Intelligent and Highly Creative Adolescent. A Summary of Some Research Findings." In C.W. Taylor and F. Barron (eds.), *Scientific Creativity; Its Recognition and Development*. NY: Wiley, 166–172.

Getzels, Jacob, and Mihalyi Csikszentmihalyi. 1976. *The Creative Vision: A Longitudinal Study of Problem Finding in Art*. New York: Wiley.

Goldsmith, Lynn T., and David H. Feldman. 1988. "Aesthetic Judgment: Changes in People and Changes in Domains," *Journal of Aesthetic Education* 22(4):83–93.

Goldstein, Ernest, Theodore Katz, Jo D. Kowalchuk, and Robert Saunders. 1986. *Understanding and Creating Art*. Dallas: Garrard.

Golomb, Claire, and Maureen McCormick. 1995. "Sculpture: The Development of Three-Dimensional Representation in Clay." *Visual Arts Research* 21(1):35–50.

Golomb, Claire, and D. Farmer. 1983. "Children's Graphic Planning Strategies and Early Principles of Spatial Organization in Drawing." *Studies in Art Education* 24(2):86–100.

Golomb, Claire. 1974. *Young Children's Sculpture and Drawing: A Study in Representational Development*. Cambridge, MA: Harvard University Press.

———. 1992. *The Child's Creation of a Pictorial World*. Los Angeles: University of California Press.

Goodlad, John. 1984. *A Place Called School: Promise for the Future*. New York: McGraw-Hill.

Goodwin, MacArthur. 1993. *Design Standards for School Art Facilities*. Reston, VA: NAEA.

Greene, Maxine. 1987. "Creating, Experiencing, Sensemaking: Art Worlds in Schools." *Journal of Aesthetic Education* 21(4):22.

———. 1994. "The Arts and National Standards." *Educational Forum* 58(4):391–400.

———. 1995. "Art and Imagination: Reclaiming the Sense of Possiblity." *Phi Delta Kappan* 76(5):378–82.

Guay, Doris. 1994. "Students with Disabilities in the Art Classroom: How Prepared Are We?" *Studies in Art Education* 36(1):44–56.

Guhin, Paula. 1995. "Photograms, Compliments of the Sun." *Arts and Activities* 118(5):28–29.

Hamblen, Karen. 1984. "An Art Criticism Questioning Strategy within the Framework of Bloom's Taxonomy." *Studies in Art Education* 26(1):41–50.

———. 1984. "Don't You Think Some Brighter Colors Would Improve Your Painting?' Or Constructing Questions for Art Dialogues." *Art Education* 37(1):12–14.

———. 1985. "Developing Aesthetic Literacy Through Contested Concepts." *Art Education* 38(5):19–24.

———. 1986. "Artistic Commonalities and Differences: Educational Occasions for Universal-Relative Dialectics." *Visual Arts Research* 12:2.

———. 1986. "Exploring Contested Concepts for Aesthetic Literacy." *Journal of Aesthetic Education* 20(2):67–76.

————. 1987. "Approaches to Aesthetics in Art Education: A Critical Theory Perspective." *Studies in Art Education* 29(2):81–90.

————. 1989. "'An Elaboration on Meanings and Motives, Negative Aspects of DBAE." *Art Education* 42(4):6–7.

————. 1991. "In the Quest for Art Criticism Equity: A Tentative Model." *Studies in Art Education* 17(1):33.

————. 1993. "The Emergence of Neo-DBAE." Paper presented at the American Educational Research Association Conference in Atlanta.

———— and Camille Galanes. 1991. "Instructional Options for Aesthetics: Exploring the Possibilities." *Art Education* 44:12–25.

Hamblen, K., and Galanes, C. "Instructional Options for Aesthetics: Exploring the Possibilities." *Art Education,* January 1997, 75–83.

Harris, Dale. 1963. *Children's Drawings as Measurements of Intellectual Maturity.* New York: Harcourt, Brace and World.

Hausman, Jerome. 1990. *"Editorial: Art Education and 'All that Jazz.'"* *Art Education* 43(5):4–6.

————. 1990. "Unity and Diversity in Art Education." In London, et al. *Beyond DBAE.*

Haynes, Deborah. 1995. "Teaching Postmodernism." *Art Education* 48(5):23–24, 45–50.

Heberholz, Donald, and Barbara Heberholz. 1990. *Developing Artistic and Perceptual Awareness,* Dubuque, IA: Wm. C. Brown.

Henry, Carole. 1995. "Migrant Mother." *Art Education* 48(3):25–28, 37–40.

————. 1995. "Parallels between Student Responses to Works of Art and Existing Aesthetic Theory." *Studies in Art Education* 37(1):47–54.

Hewett, G. C., and Jean C. Rush. "Finding Buried Treasures: Aesthetic Scanning with Children." *Art Education* 40(1):41–43.

Holmes Group Executive Board. 1986. *Tomorrow's Teachers: A Report of the Holmes Group.* East Lansing, MI.

Holt, David. 1990. "Post Modernism vs. High Modernism: Relationship to D.B.A.E. and Its Critics." *Art Education* 43(2):42–46.

————. 1995. "Postmodernism: Anomaly in Art-Critical Theory." *Journal of Aesthetic Education* 29(1):85–94.

Hubbard, R. 1989. Authors of pictures, draughtsmen of words. Portsmouth, NH: Heinemann.

Hurwitz, Al, and Michael Day. 1994. *Children and Their Art.* New York: Harcourt Brace Jovanovich.

Hurwitz, Al, and Stanley Madeja. 1977. *The Joyous Vision: A Source Book for Elementary Art Appreciation.* Englewood Cliffs, NJ: Prentice-Hall.

Hurwitz, Al. 1983. *The Gifted and Talented in Art: A Guide to Program Planning.* Worcester, MA: Davis.

————. 1993. *Collaboration in Art Education.* Reston, VA: NAEA.

Jenkins, P. D., 1980. *Art for the Fun of it; A Guide for Teaching Young Children.* Englewood Cliffs, NJ: Prentice Hall, Inc.

Johnson, M. "Orientations to Curriculum in Computer Art Education." *Art Education,* May 1997, 43–47.

Johnson, P., 1997. *Pictures and Words Together; Children Writing and Illustrating Their Own Books.* Portsmouth, NH: Heinemann.

Johnson, Andra. 1992. *Elementary Art Education Anthology.* Reston, VA: NAEA.

Kaelin, Eugene. 1989. *An Aesthetics for Art Educators.* New York: Teachers College Press.

————. 1990. "The Construction of a Syllabus for Aesthetics in Art Education." *Art Education* 43(2):22–34.

Katter, Eldon. 1995. Multicultural Connections: Craft Community." *Art Education* 48(1):8–13.

Kauppinen, Heta, and Read Diket (eds.). 1995. *Trends in Art Education from Diverse Cultures.* Reston, VA: NAEA.

Kellogg, Rhoda. 1970. *Analyzing Children's Art.* Palo Alto, CA: National Press.

Kinder, A. 1987. "A Review of Rationales for Integrated Arts Programs." *Studies in Art Education* 29(1):52–60.

Kindler, A. M. (Ed.) (1997) *Child Development in Art.* Reston, VA: NAEA.

Krathwohl, David, Benjamin Bloom, and Bertram Masia. 1984. *Taxonomy of Educational Objectives, Handbook 2: The Affective Domain.* New York: New Directions.

LaLiberte, Norman, and Alex Mogelon. 1967. *Painting with Crayons: History and Modern Techniques.* New York: Reinhold.

————. 1966. *Masks, Face Coverings, and Headgear.* New York: Reinhold.

LaLiberte, Norman, and Shirley McIlhany. 1966. *Banners and Hangings: Design and Construction.* New York: Reinhold.

Lark-Horowitz, Betty, Hilda Lewis, and Mark Luca. 1973. *Understanding Children's Art for Better Teaching.* Columbus, OH: Merrill.

Linderman, Marlene. 1990. *Art in the Elementary School: Drawing, Painting, and Creativity for the Classroom.* Dubuque, IA: Wm. C. Brown.

Lippard, Lucy. 1984. *Get the Message? A Decade of Art for Social Change.* New York: Dutton.

Lommel, Andreas. 1981. *Masks: Their Meanings and Function.* London: Ferndale.

London, Peter, Judith Burton, and Arlene Linderman (eds.). 1990. *Beyond DBAE: The Case for Multiple Visions of Art Education.* North Dartmouth, Mass.: Southeastern Massachusetts University.

Lowenfeld, Viktor. 1947. *Creative and Mental Growth.* New York: Macmillan.

Mager, Robert F. 1975. *Preparing Instructional Objectives.* Belmont, CA: Fearon.

Marcia, J. E. 1980. "Ego identity development" in J. Adelman, ed., *The Handbook of Adolescent Psychology.* New York: Wiley.

Markowitz, Sally. 1994. "The Distinction between Art and Craft." *Journal of Aesthetic Education* 28(1):55–70.

Martinello, M. and G. Cook. 1994. *Interdisciplinary Inquiry in Teaching and Learning.* New York: Macmillan.

Mattil, Edward, and Betty Marzan. 1981. *Meaning in Children's Art: Projects for Teachers.* New York: Prentice-Hall.

McCann, Michael. 1985. *Health Hazards Manual for Artists.* New York: Nick Lyons Books.

————. 1991. "Oil Painting Hazards in Classrooms." *Art Hazards News* 14:2.

McFee, June K. 1988. "Art and Society." In Getty Foundation for Education in the Arts. *Issues in Discipline-Based Art Education: Strengthening the Stance, Extending the Horizons.* Los Angeles: The Getty Center for Education in the Arts.

McFee, June, and Rogena Degge. *Art, Culture, and Environment: A Catalyst for Teaching.* Belmont, CA: Wadsworth.

Michael, John. 1983. *Art and Adolescence, Teaching Art at the Secondary Level.* New York: Teachers College Press.

Moody, Larrie. 1992. "An Analysis of Drawing Programs for Early Adolescents." *Studies in Art Education* 34(1):39–47.

Moore, Michael. 1995. "Towards a New Liberal Learning in Art." *Art Education* 48(6):6–13.

Morman, Jean. 1989. *One- Two- Three Murals: Simple Murals to Make Using Children's Open-Ended Art.* Everett, WA: Frank Schaeffer Publishers.

National Art Education Association. *Position Paper: The Essentials of a Quality School Art Program.* Reston, VA: NAEA.

National Commission on Excellence in Education. 1983. *A Nation at Risk.* Washington, D.C.: GPO.

National Endowment for the Arts. 1988. "Overview, Toward Civilization." *NAEA News* 30(3):3–7.

Neperud, Ron. (ed.).1995. *Context, Content, and Community in Art Education.* New York: Teachers College Press.

Nicolaides, Kimon. 1941. *The Natural Way to Draw.* Boston: Houghton-Mifflin.

Nyman, Andra. (ed.). *Instructional Methods in the Artroom.* Reston, VA: NAEA.

O'Brien, Bernadette C. 1978. *Tapestry: Interrelationship of the Arts in Reading and Language Development.* New York: New York City Board of Education.

Olson, J. L. 1992. *Envisioning Writing: Towards an Integration of Drawing and Writing.* Portsmouth, NH: Heinemann Educational Books.

Paik, Nam June, cited in Beverly J. Jones. "Toward Democratic Direction of Technology." In Blandy and Congdon. *Art in a Democracy,* New York: Teachers College Press pp. 64–73.

Parsons, M. J. 1987. *How We Understand Art: A Cognitive Development Account of Aesthetic Experience.* Cambridge, England: Cambridge University Press.

Perkins, David. 1994. *The Intelligent Eye: Learning to Think by Looking at Art.* Champaign: University of Illinois Press.

Pariser, David. 1995. "Not Under the Lamppost: Piagetian and Non-Piagetian Research in the Arts: A Review and Critique." *Journal of Aesthetic Education* 29(3):93–108.

Parsons, Michael, and H. Gene Blocker. 1993. *Aesthetics and Education.* Urbana and Champaign: University of Illinois Press.

Parsons, Michael. 1987. *How We Understand Art: A Cognitive Development Account of Aesthetic Experience.* Cambridge, England: Cambridge University Press.

———. 1994. "Can Children Do Aesthetics? A Developmental Account." *Journal of Aesthetic Education* 28(3):33–46.

Peterson, Charles R. 1993. "Visual Art and the Physically Challenged Person," Videotape, Bloomington, IN: Agency for Instructional Technology.

Piaget, J. 1982. "Creativity." In J. M. Gallagher and D. K. Reid (eds.). *The Learning Theory of Piaget and Inhelder.* Monterey, CA: Brooks/Cole.(Originally published in 1972.)

Piaget, J. 1959. *The Language and Thought of the Child,* 3rd ed. London: Routledge and Kegan Paul.

Pile, Naomi F.1973. *Art Experiences for Young Children.* New York: Macmillan Co.

Primm, J. 1990. The need for new criteria in selecting art reproductions to develop children's art learning sequentially. Unpublished manuscript, California State University, Long Beach.

Purser, R. E., and Montouri, A. 1999. *Social Creativity.* Cresskill, NJ: Hampton Press, Inc.

Qualley, Charles A. 1986. *Safety in the Artroom.* Worcester, MA: Davis.

Read, Herbert. 1955. *Icon and Idea: The Function of Art in the Development of Human Consciousness.* Cambridge: Harvard University Press.

———. 1973. *Education Through Art,* 3d ed. New York: Pantheon.

Reiff, J. 1991. *Learning Styles.* Reston, VA: NAEA.

Rossol, Monona. 1990. *The Artist's Complete Health and Safety Guide.* New York: Allworth.

Rottger, Ernst. 1961. *Surfaces in Creative Design.* London: Batsford.

———. 1963. *Creative Clay Design.* New York: Reinhold.

———. 1969. *Creative Wood Design.* New York: Reinhold.

———. 1970. *Creative Paper Design.* New York: Reinhold.

Runco, M. A. 1997. *The Creativity Research Handbook.* Vol 1. Cresskill, NJ: Hampton Press, Inc.

Rush, Jean C. 1984. "Bridging the Gap Between Developmental Psychology and Art Education: The View from an Artist's Perspective." *Visual Arts Research* 10(2):9–14.

Russ, S. W. 1993. *Affect and Creativity, The Role of Affect and Play in the Creative Process.* Hillsdale, NJ: Lawrence Erlbaum Associates.

Russell, R. L. 1991. "Teaching Students to Inquire About Art Philosophically." *Studies in Art Education* 32(2):94–104.

Sacca, Elizabeth J. 1989. "Invisible Women: Questioning Recognition and Status in Art Education." *Studies in Art Education* 30(1):122–127.

Sacccardi, M. 1997. *Art in Story: Teaching Art History to Elementary School Children.* North Haven, CT: Linnet Professional Publications.

Sarason, Seymour. 1991. *The Challenge of Art to Psychology.* New Haven, Conn.: Yale University Press.

Saunders, Robert J. 1977. *Relating Art and Humanities to the Classroom.* Dubuque, IA: Wm. C. Brown.

———. 1982. "The Lowenfeld Motivation." *Art Education* 11:30.

Schaefer-Simmern, Henry. 1948. *The Unfolding of Artistic Activity.* Berkeley: University of California Press.

Schapiro, Meyer. 1953. "Style." *Anthropology Today,* ed. A. L. Kroeber. Chicago: University of Chicago Press, 81–113.

Schiller, Marjorie. 1995. "The Importance of Conversations about Art with Young Children." *Visual Arts Research* 21(1):25–34.

Sharff, Stefan. 1982. *The Elements of Cinema.* New York: Columbia University Press.

Smith, Nancy R. 1982. *Experience and Art: Teaching Children to Paint.* New York: Teachers College Press.

Smith, Nancy, and C. Fucigna. 1988. "Drawing Systems in Children's Pictures: Contour and Form." *Visual Arts Research* 14(1):66–76.

Smith, Ralph A. (ed.). 1986. *Excellence in Art Education.* Reston, VA: NAEA.

Smith, Ralph, and W. Levi. 1991. *Art Education: A Critical Necessity.* Urbana, IL: University of Illinois Press.

Sorri, Mari. 1994. "The Body Has Reasons: Tacit Knowing in Thinking and Making." *Journal of Aesthetic Education* 28(2):15–26.

Stokrocki, Mary. 1990. "A Cross Site Analysis: Problems in Teaching Art to Preadolescents." *Studies in Art Education* 31(2):106–107.

Strommen, Erik. 1988. "A Century of Children Drawing: The Evolution of Theory and Research Concerning the Drawings of Children." *Visual Arts Research* 14:13–24.

"Symposium: Blocker on 'Primitive' Art." 1995. *Journal of Aesthetic Education* 29(3).

"Symposium: On Marcia Eaton's Philosophy of Art." 1995. *Journal of Aesthetic Education* 29(2).

"Symposium: On the Child's Pictorial World." 1994. *Journal of Aesthetic Education* 28(2):51–70.

Szekely, George. 1988. *Encouraging Creativity in Art Lessons.* New York: Teachers College Press.

———. 1995. "Circus." *Art Education* 48(4):44–50.

Thorne, J. H. 1990. "Mainstreaming Procedures: Support Services and Training." *NAEA Advisory.*

Tolley, Kimberly. 1994. *The Art and Science Connection.* Reading, MA: Addison-Wesley.

Torrance, E. Paul. 1966. "Torrance Test of Creative Thinking." Bensenville, IL: Scholastic Testing Service.

Vallance, Elizabeth. 1988. "Art Criticism as Subject Matter in Schools and Art Museums." *Journal of Aesthetic Education* 22(4):69–82.

Vonderman, Carol. (1999). *How Math Works.* Pleasantville, NY: Readers Digest Association.

Vygotsky, Lev S. 1962. *Thought and Language.* Cambridge, MA: MIT Press. (Originally published 1934.)

Vygotsky, Lev S. 1978. "Mind in Society: The Development of Psychological Processes." M. Cole, V. John, S. Steiner, and E. Souberman, eds. Cambridge, MA: Harvard University Press.

Wasson, Stuhr, and L. Petrovich-Mwaniki. 1990. "Teaching Art in the Multicultural Classroom: Six Position Statements." *Studies in Art Education* 31(4):234–246.

Wilson, B., and Rubin, B. 1997. "DBAE and educational change." *Visual Arts Research* 23(2), 89–97.

Wilson, Brent, Al Hurwitz, and Marjorie Wilson. 1987. *Teaching Drawing from Art.* Worcester, MA.: Davis Publications.

Wilson, Brent, and Harlan Hoffa (eds.). 1988. *History of Art Education: Proceedings from the Penn State Conference.* Reston, VA: NAEA.

Wilson, Brent, and Marjorie Wilson. 1981. "The Use and Uselessness of Developmental Stages." *Art Education* 34(5):4–5.

——— and ———. 1982. *Teaching Children to Draw.* Englewood Cliffs, NJ: Prentice-Hall.

Winfrey, Anita. 1995. "Adinkra Prints." *Arts and Activities* 118(3):24.

Winner, Ellie. 1982. *Invented Worlds: The Psychology of the Arts.* Cambridge, MA: Harvard University Press.

Wolf, Dennie, and M. D. Perry. 1988. "From Endpoints to Repertoires: New Conclusions about Drawing Development." *Journal of Aesthetic Education* 29(3):13–35.

Wygant, Foster. 1993. *School Art in American Culture.* Cincinnati: Interwood Press.

Young, Bernard. 1991. *Art, Culture, and Ethnicity.* Reston, VA: NAEA.

Zakia, Richard. 1993. "Photography and Visual Perception." *Journal of Aesthetic Education* 27(4):67–82.

Zimmerman, Enid. 1990. "Issues Related to Teaching Art from a Feminist Point of View." *Visual Arts Research* 16(2):1–9.

———. 1990. "Questions About My Culture and Art Education or 'I'll Never Forget the Day M'Blawi Stumbled on the Work of the Post-Impressionists.'" *Art Education* 43(6):8–24.

Zurmuehlen, Marilyn. 1989. "Serious Pursuit of Cultural Trivialization." *Art Education* 42(6):46–49.

———. 1990. *Studio Art, Praxis, Symbol, Presence.* Reston, VA: NAEA.

Appendix D

ADDRESSES OF PROFESSIONAL ASSOCIATIONS, ART MATERIALS SUPPLIERS, AUDIOVISUAL SOURCES, COMPUTER WEBSITES, AND ELECTRONIC LESSON PLAN DATABASES

Although these lists are by no means complete, they can serve as starting points to obtain further information.

Professional Art Education Associations

National Art Education Association, 1916 Association Drive, Reston, VA 22091 (www.naea-reston.org)

The Association also has interest groups. Some of them are:

The Women's Caucus, The Electronic Media Interest Group (http://www.cedarnet.org/emig) and The Social Theory Caucus, which has as its goal for art education to go beyond a formalist, modernist, studio orientation. (email: ghowenstein@artic.edu or dfehr@ttu.edu).

Also, each state has a state art education association.

International Society for Education through Art, c/o Prof. Kit Grauer, University of British Columbia, Dept. of Art Education, Vancouver, B.C. V6T 1Z5 Canada.

United States Society for Education through Art (USSEA), c/o Dr. Mary Stokrocki, School of Art, Arizona State University, Tempe, AZ 85287.

Art and Craft Materials Suppliers

A few addresses of representative arts and crafts suppliers. Many also have regional distribution headquarters throughout the country.

Dick Blick Art Materials, P.O. Box 1267, Galesburg, IL 61402-1267
Nasco Arts and Crafts, 901 Janesville Ave., P.O. Box 901, Fort Atkinson, WI 53538-0901 1-800-558-9595

Pyramid Art Supply, 923 Hickory Lane, Mansfield, OH 44901-8104
R. B. Walter Art and Craft Materials, P.O. Box 62331, Arlington, TX 76005
Sax Arts and Crafts, P.O. Box 51710, New Berlin, WI 53151
Triarco Arts and Crafts, 14650 28th Ave. No, Plymouth, MN 55447

Sources for Audio-Visuals: Reproductions, Slides, Cassettes, Viseodiscs

The National Gallery of Art, Constitution Avenue and 6th Street, N.W., Washington, D.C. 20001, offers a program of semi-permanent loan of their video and slide resources, called the Extended Loan Program. Materials, 36-slide sets and 22 videos, are lent for a year with an automatic renewal; the only provision is that the borrower is asked to file a semiannual report of use. E-mail: www.nga.gov

"The Art Education Video Series," color videos on the several areas of DBAE, are available from Getty Trust Publications, P.O. Box 2112, Santa Monica, CA 90407.

A CD-ROM for the Macintosh computer, entitled "Your Own Art Teacher," is available from Art Instruction Software, 38 Balsam Dr., Medford, NY.

A CD-ROM for children to use to make their own tesselations, "MECC Tessel Mania;" is available from Macromedia, 1-800-68-MECC, ext. 529.

The Shorewood Art Program for Elementary Education has art by many cultures and topics for each grade: grade 1–2, seasons; 3–4, early transportation; grades 5–6, how do I feel. Twelve reproductions are in each of 16 sets. Shorewood Reproductions, Inc., 475 Tenth Avenue, New York, NY 10018.

American Library Color Slide Co., 222 West 23rd Street, New York, NY 10011.
Art Education, Inc., Blauveldt, NY 10913.
BFA Educational Media, 11559 Santa Monica Boulevard, Los Angeles, CA 90025.
Communacad, The Communications Academy, Box 541, Wilton, CT 06897.

Crystal Productions, Box 2159, Glenview, IL 60025. 1-800-255-8629, fax: 1-800-657-8149.

Encyclopaedia Britannica Films, 425 North Michigan Avenue, Chicago, IL 60604.

Films for the Humanities and Sciences, P.O. Box 2053, Princeton, NJ 08543-2053. 1-800-257-5126.

Films Incorporated Video, 5547 Ravenswood Avenue, Chicago, IL 60640-1199.

Gould Media, 44 Parkway West, Mt. Vernon, NY 10552.

International Film Bureau, 332 South Michigan Avenue, Chicago, IL 60604.

Life Filmstrips, Time and Life Building, New York, NY 10021.

Media for the Arts, P.O. Box 1011, Newport, RI 02840.

Reinhold Publishing Co., 600 Summer Street, Stamford, CT 06901.

Society for Visual Education, 1345 Diversey Parkway, Chicago, IL 60614.

The Roland Collection, 22-D Hollywood Ave., Ho-Ho-Kus, NJ 07423. 1-800 59 ROLAND.

Universal Color Slide, 8450 South Tamiami Trail, Sarasota, FL 34238.

Van Nostrand Reinhold, 450 West 33rd Street, New York, NY 10001.

Art reproductions and slides also can be acquired inexpensively from most art museums, including the following:

Metropolitan Museum of Art, Fifth Avenue and 82nd Street, New York, NY 10028. Email: www.metmuseum.org

Museum of Modern Art, 11 West 53rd Street, New York, NY 10019. E-mail: www.moma.org

Computer Websites and Electronic Lesson Plan Databases

A lengthy list of art history resource Websites is included in Chapter 29 , Computer Art. Two important art education web sites are ArtsEdNet and ArtsEdge:

The Getty Center for Education in the Arts has established ArtsEdNet@GETTY.EDU, an electronic on-line information resource over the Internet for K–12 arts teachers, classroom teachers, academics, and advocates. http://www.artsednet@getty.edu or http://www.getty.edu

ArtsEdge. Kennedy-Center.org is a collaboration between the John F. Kennedy Center for Performing Arts, the Department of Education, and the National Endowment for the Arts.

"Becoming an art teacher" is available at http://www.arts.UFL,edu.art/Forum/forum.html

ARTS USA is created by the American Council for the Arts.

The Southeast Center for Education in the Arts provides teaching resources in art, music, and theater for K–12.

ARTnet is sponsored by the Nebraska Department of Education.

Several states have gateways, including the Florida Institute for Art Education, the Minnesota Center for Arts Education, the North Texas Institute for Educators in the Visual Arts, and the Ohio Partnership for the Visual Arts.

Glossary

Abstract. In art, objects or figures that are depicted in a simplified or stylized way (in which nonessential aspects are discarded) yet remain recognizable. Similar to nonrepresentational.

Aesthetic. Dealing with art theory or issues of appreciation in art; the beautiful as related or contrasted to the good, the true, or the useful.

Analogous colors. Closely related colors; neighbors on the color wheel.

Applique. Decorative design made by cutting pieces of one fabric and applying them by gluing or stitching to the surface of another fabric.

Armature. Framework (of wood, wire, and so on) employed to support constructions of clay, papier-maché, or plaster.

Assemblage. A sculptural form using found materials, often being three-dimensional.

Balance. A principle in art. May be formal or informal, symmetrical or asymmetrical.

Balsa. A strong, lightweight wood used for model building and stabiles.

Baren. A device made of cardboard and bamboo leaf that is used as a hand press in taking a print (of Japanese derivation).

Bas relief. In sculpture, when the objects or figures remain attached to the background plane or project only slightly from it.

Bat. A plaster block used to hasten drying of moist clay.

Batik. A method of designing on fabric by sealing with melted wax those areas not to be dyed.

Bench hook. A wood device secured to a desk or table to stabilize the linoleum block during the gouging process.

Bisque. Clay in its fired or baked state (unglazed).

Brayer. A rubber roller used for inking in printmaking processes.

Burnish. To make smooth or glossy by a rubbing or polishing action.

Calligraphy. The art of fine writing often done with a brush or pen.

Ceramic. A word used to describe clay constructions and products thereof.

Charcoal. A drawing stick or pencil made from charred wood.

Chipboard. Sturdy cardboard, usually gray, of varying thicknesses, used for collage, collograph, sketching boards, and in construction projects.

Classical. The art of ancient Greece or Rome, or more broadly, any art based on a regular, clear, rational structure, emphasizing proportion and balance.

Clay. A natural, moist earth substance used in making bricks, tile, pottery, and ceramic sculpture.

Collage. A composition or design made by arranging and gluing materials to a background surface.

Collograph. A print made from a collage. Relief plate created with an assortment of pasted or glued items such as pieces of paper, cardboard, cord, string, and other found objects.

Color. An element of art. Also referred to as *hue*.

Color, analogous. Closely related color; neighbors on the color wheel: green, blue-green, yellow-green, for example.

Color, monochromatic. All of the tints and shades of a single color plus its neutralized possibilities.

Colors, complementary. Colors found opposite one another on the color wheel: red and green, for example.

Colors, primary. Red, yellow, blue; three basic hues.

Colors, secondary. Green, orange, violet; achieved by mixing primary colors.

Construction paper. A strong, absorbent, semitextured paper available in a wealth of colors and used for paintings in tempera, drawings in crayon, and oil pastel, printmaking, collage, and paper sculpture. A staple item in the school art program.

Content. In a work of art, the meaning or message in or conveyed by the artwork.

Contour drawing. A line drawing delineating the outer and inner contours of a posed model, still life, landscape, or other selected subject matter.

Domination. A principle in art. Opposite term is "subordination." These principles complement each other.

Easel. A wood or metal frame to support an artist's canvas during painting. A simple version is found in many kindergartens for use in tempera painting.

Embossing. Creating a raised or relief design on metal or leather by tooling or indenting the surface.

Emphasis. A principle in art. Important elements in a composition are emphasized.

Encaustic. A painting process employing hot beeswax mixed with color pigment. Sometimes used to describe melted-crayon creations.

Engobe. Clay slip, colored or white, used to decorate greenware before firing.

Engraving. A process of incising or scratching into a hard surface to produce a printed image, as in copper engraving or crayon engraving.

Expressive. Artwork that seems to spring directly and honestly from the artist's feelings.

Findings. Metal clasps, hooks, loops, and so on used in jewelry making.

Firing. In ceramics, the baking of clay in a kiln or an outdoor banked fire; also see Raku.

Form. The physical characteristics of an object.

Found objects. Discards, remnants, samples, leftovers, and throwaways that are exploited in collages, junk sculpture, assemblages, and as stamps in printmaking projects.

Frieze. A decorated, horizontal band in paint or in relief along the upper part of a building or a room.

Glaze. A transparent or semitransparent coating of a color stain over a plain surface or another color used in oil painting, plaster sculpture, or ceramicware.

Gradient. A gradual shift from distinct to blended together, as in a textural gradient, or from one color to another, as in a color gradient (or graduated color blending).

Greenware. Unfired clay in leather-hard stage, firm but not completely dry.

Ground The background or empty space between objects in a two-dimensional artwork.

Grout. A crevice filler such as the conditioned plaster sealed between clay, glass, or vinyl tesserae in a mosaic.

Gum eraser. A soft eraser used in drawing. Available in cube or rectangle form.

Harmony. A combination of objects or design motifs that pleases an individual, contrasted to a clashing or unharmonious arrangement.

Hue. Another name for *color.*

Impasto. In painting, heavy thick paint applied like butter to a surface.

India ink. A waterproof ink made from lampblack. Used for drawing, designing, and in tempera resists.

Intensity. The level of richness or saturation or, conversely, dullness or subtlety of a color.

Intermediate colors. A color between a primary hue (red, blue, or yellow) and a secondary hue (orange, green, violet); for example, blue-green is between blue and green.

Kiln. An oven used for drying, firing, and glazing clay creations.

Kneaded eraser. A gray eraser made of unvulcanized rubber that must be stretched and kneaded to be effective. Used most often in charcoal drawing.

Line. An element in art. The basic skeletal foundation of a design or composition.

Loom. The supporting framework for the criss-crossing threads and yarn in weaving.

Macramé. Lacework made by tying, knotting, and weaving cord in a pattern.

Manila paper. A general-purpose drawing or coloring paper, usually cream color.

Masonite. A pressed board made of wood fibers. Used for clay-modeling boards, inking surfaces in printmaking, and rinsing boards in tempera and crayon resists.

Mat board. A heavy poster board, available in many colors and textures, used for mounting or matting artwork.

Mobile. A free-moving hanging sculptural construction in space; Alexander Calder's innovation to the art world.

Monoprint. One-of-a-kind print, usually made by incising or marking on an inked glass plate and taking an impression.

Mosaic. A design or composition made by arranging and gluing tesserae or geometric pieces of material next to one another, but not touching, on a background surface.

Motif. A recurring pattern (or figure, symbol, or artistic device) in an artwork.

Mural. A monumental artwork on the inside or outside walls of a building. Executed in paint, mosaic, metal repoussé, or a combination of materials.

Negative space or shape. A background shape as seen in relationship to the foreground objects.

Newsprint. Newspaper stock used for sketches, preliminary drawings, and prints.

Oil pastel. A popular coloring medium consisting of a combination of chalk and oil; available in a host of exciting colors.

Papier-mâché. Name given to paper crafts that use newspaper moistened with wallpaper paste or laundry starch. Also called *paper pulp constructions.*

Patina. Originally the color produced by corrosion on metal—the antique sheen of old age—now artificially obtained through use of patinalike wax pastes.

Pattern. Design made by repeating a motif or symbol (all-over pattern).

Perspective. The creation of a three-dimensional space illusion on a two-dimensional surface by means of vanishing points, converging lines, and diminishing sizes of objects.

Plaster. A white, powdery substance that, when mixed with water, forms a quick-setting molding or casting material (sometimes referred to as *plaster of Paris*).

Positive-negative. Positive shapes in a composition are the solid objects—the people, trees, animals, buildings. Negative shapes are the unoccupied empty spaces between positive shapes. Atmosphere, sky, and earth considered negative space are sometimes designated as "foreground" and "background" space.

Prime. In painting, to put down a first coat of paint, usually white, to seal the surface and onto which the actual painting is done.

Radiation. Lines, shapes, or colors emanating from a central core. Sun rays, fan leaf, ripples around a pebble thrown into a stream.

Raku. A ceramic firing process using a primitive kiln and producing smoky and iridescent effects.

Representational. Resembling in appearance the known likenesses of objects in nature.

Relief. A projection from a surface. Low relief as in a coin is called bas relief.

Repetition (rhythm). A principle of art. Repetition of lines, shapes, colors, and values in a composition creates unity.

Repoussé. A design in metal art in which tooling and hammering are employed to achieve relief effects.

Resist. An art technique wherein a material such as wax or starch is used to mask out areas that are to remain temporarily of a different color or value.

Rhythm. The way that repeating, varying, and spacing elements create the equivalent of notes and pulses in music.

Scoring (clay). To make rough indentations in clay with a nail or similar tool as a step in cementing two pieces of clay together. Also used to describe the guiding indentation in paper-sculpture curved-line folding.

Selvage. The edge of a fabric where the weft returns to weave its way to the opposite edge.

Shade. Refers to the darker values of a color or hue. Maroon is a shade of red; navy blue is a shade of blue.

Shape. A two-dimensional area defined by lines, colors, or values.

Sketch. Usually a preliminary drawing made with pencil, pen, crayon, charcoal, brush, pastel, or similar tool.

Slip. Clay diluted with water to a creamy consistency. Used as a binder to join two pieces of clay in ceramic construction.

Space. In art, the area and/or air occupied by, activated by, or implied to be in an artwork.

Stabile. A sculptural construction in space resting on the ground, akin to a mobile, which hangs.

Still life. An arrangement of objects, usually on a table, as a subject for drawing, painting, collage, and so on.

Stipple. A pattern of closely spaced dots or small marks used in drawing and printmaking that may suggest modeling.

Storyboard. A series of drawings or sketches to visualize the movement of a movie or video, done before the actual shooting.

Subordination. A principle of art in which parts of the composition are subordinated so that others may dominate and be emphasized.

Tactile. Pertaining to the sense of touch, such as the use of textured materials and surfaces, often for an aesthetic purpose.

Tagboard. Sometimes referred to as *oaktag*. A glossy-surfaced, pliable cardboard used in collage, collographs, glue-line prints, and paper constructions.

Tempera paint. An opaque, water-soluble paint available in liquid or powder form. Also referred to as *showcard* or *poster paint*.

Tessera. A small segment of paper, cardboard, vinyl, ceramic, and so on (usually in geometric shape, such as a square or rectangle) that is fitted and glued to a background surface to produce a mosaic (plural: *tesserae*).

Texture. The actual or visual feel of a surface—bark on a tree, fur on an animal, sand on a beach.

Tint. The lighter values of a color or hue. Pink is a tint of red.

Unity. A principle of art. When everything in a composition falls into place through use of fundamental principles of art, unity is achieved.

Value. In color terminology, the lightness or darkness of a hue.

Warp. The thread or yarn that supports the weft in weaving.

Watercolors. Water-soluble colors, generally transparent or semitransparent. Can be employed thickly to become opaque. Available in semimoist cakes or tubes.

Wedging. A method of preparing moist clay by kneading and squeezing to expel the air pockets and make it more plastic.

Weft. The thread that goes across the warp from side to side in weaving; also refers to the yarn used as weft.

Photo Credits

Athens Academy, GA, 348

Aycock, Alice, 328

Bell South Advertising and Publishing Corporation, 316

Boucher, Jack, 342

Brassie, Fay, Athens, GA, 103, 116, 342

Burns-Knutson, Sharon, IA, 82, 87, 92, 96, 105, 143, 189, 195, 206, 345, 354, 355

Carl Solway Gallery, Cincinnati, OH, 321

Case, Carol, Smyrna, GA, 314

Charles C. Thomas Publishers, Springfield, IL, 126

Chase, Molly, Atlanta, GA, 318

Clements, Claire, Athens, GA, 49, 122, 126, 158, 185, 344, 345, 346, 349, 350, 351, 352

Clements, Robert, Athens, GA, 126, 151, 372

Collection of Gladys Nillson and Jim Nutt, 133

Crayola® Dream-Makers®, 54, 201, 283

Crosby, Jessica, Port Gibson, MS, 199

Cummins, Donna, Atlanta, GA, 270, 277

Davis Publications, Worcester, MA, 4, 115

Ellett, Jackie, Lawrenceville, GA, 18, 70, 95, 104, 153, 162, 169, 172, 176, 192, 195, 304, 315, 354

Elliot, Nancy, Athens, GA, 16, 286, 318, 319, 330, 364

Fein, Sylvia, 52

Finster, Rev. Howard, 217

Georgia Museum of Art, 115, 318

Hamilton, Eric, Athens, GA, 216

Hammond, Mary Sayer, Fairfax, VA, 10, 21, 27, 53, 162, 168, 208, 241, 247, 263, 267, 272, 273, 276, 278, 279, 286, 291, 299, 302, 312, 313, 342, 343

Harvell, David, Athens, GA, 36, 62–63, 175

Henry, Carole, Athens, GA, 107

Hirshhorn Museum and Sculpture Garden, Washington, DC, 224

Hodge, David, Oshkosh, WI, 8, 19, 31, 39, 47, 56, 75, 94, 112, 114, 118, 123, 173, 179, 181, 241, 246, 249, 250, 258, 273, 286, 287, 297, 298, 303, 344, 349, 350, 352, 360, 361, 365, 366, 376, 377, 382

Holly Solomon Gallery, New York, 118

Horne, Jenni, Tyrone, GA, 76

Hyde, Alma, Savannah, GA, 317

International Collection of Child Art, Illinois State University, Normal, IL, 11, 17, 18, 24, 41, 102, 110, 120, 161, 176, 254, 266

Kuntz, Baiba, Glencoe, IL, 14, 15, 16, 19, 20, 26, 30, 42, 47, 55, 61, 62–63, 99, 100, 108, 111, 136, 139, 145, 160, 169, 178, 244, 251, 252, 264, 265, 274, 285, 293, 340, 369, 388, 391

Lackey, Deborah, Atlanta, GA, 103, 180, 237, 349, 361, 362

Lazzari, Mary, Athens, GA, 183, 364

Lucas, Shirley, Oshkosh, WI, 15, 266

Mallett, Marla, Atlanta, GA, 41

Mallon, Beverly, Athens, GA, 6, 23, 57, 60, 64, 65, 66, 67, 68, 72, 73, 77, 124, 125, 131, 132, 138, 147, 151, 152, 154, 165, 192, 193, 196, 197, 202, 204, 205, 206, 208, 209, 211, 231, 263, 264, 280, 283, 328, 376, 379, 386, 389

Malnati, Gwenda, Athens, GA, 216, 245, 385

Matisse, Henri, 230

McCutheon, Mary, Athens, GA, 274, 275

McNeil, Susan, Iowa City, IA, 101, 248

Milbrandt, Melody, GA, 1, 37, 70, 71, 73, 78, 82, 83, 90, 91, 100, 174, 177, 191, 194, 200, 201, 280, 290, 323

Mitchell, George, Atlanta, GA, 318

Moore, Mary Ruth, 9

Munn, Alice Ballard, Anchorage, AK, 5, 175, 334

Museum of Fine Arts, Boston, MA, 294

Museum of Primitive Art, NY, 222

National Building Museum, 342

National Gallery of Art, Washington, DC, 137, 220, 230

Nix, W. Robert, Athens, GA, 166, 222, 257, 382

Oakes, Howie, Athens, GA, 348

O'Brien, Michael E., Seoul, Korea, 258

Oldenburg, Claes and Coosje van Bruggen, 383

Oliver, Teddy, Marietta, GA, 115

Phlegar, Julie Daniell, Slidell, LA, 163, 330, 367

Puskar, Marlee, Atlanta, GA, 48, 98, 157, 182

Ramsay, Ted, 55, 80, 83, 86, 88, 150, 155, 261, 282, 289, 295, 300, 305, 306, 307, 308, 310, 324, 325, 327, 329, 332, 335

Rives, Diane, Athens, GA, 5, 175, 334

Robinson, Virginia S., 290

Saga Prefecture, Kyushu Island, Japan, 139

Smith, 167

Stallworth, Lee, 224

Stueck, Lawrence, Athens, GA, 148, 338, 372

Swanson, Mary E., Nashua, NH, 231

Tanner, Jo Nan, Athens, GA, 349

Thomas, Barbara, Athens, GA, 36, 48, 68, 74, 84, 94, 96, 97, 104, 157, 169, 183, 190, 221, 327, 331, 346, 347, 348, 379, 381

Thompson, Jerry I., 328

Timothy Road Elementary School, Athens, GA, 21

University of Georgia, School of Art, 153

The University Museum, PA, 227

USSEA art collection of Dr. Anne Gregory, Los Angeles, CA, 33, 41, 45, 190, 265

Varon, Malcolm, NY, 227

Vroon, Joyce, Atlanta, GA, 6, 22, 34, 44, 45, 46, 48, 54, 58, 81, 82, 87, 88, 94, 95, 97, 98, 100, 101, 105, 106, 109, 116, 137, 149, 152, 154, 157, 158, 159, 161, 163, 164, 166, 167, 170, 171, 172, 173, 180, 181, 182, 184, 185, 186, 188, 189, 193, 197, 198, 200, 203, 205, 207, 208, 210, 211, 212, 225, 226, 254, 257, 258, 259, 265, 270, 276, 281, 283, 284, 304, 320, 339, 340, 353, 355, 371, 373, 374, 378, 380, 384, 386, 387, 389

Wachowiak, Frank, Athens, GA, 10, 13, 14, 19, 21, 23, 27, 29, 35, 47, 53, 55, 57, 62–63, 80, 83, 86, 88, 89, 114, 140, 142, 150, 155, 162, 168, 208, 222, 231, 232, 233, 238, 241, 254, 256, 257, 261, 262, 263, 267, 268, 269, 271, 272, 273, 276, 278, 279, 282, 286, 287, 289, 291, 292, 293, 295, 296, 299, 300, 302, 303, 305, 306, 307, 308, 310, 311, 312, 313, 324, 325, 326, 327, 331, 332, 333, 334, 335, 342, 343, 360, 363, 366, 382

Whipple, Susan, Medford, OR, 45, 190, 265

Winn Family, 213

Index

In this index, topics and related illustrations usually appear on the same page or within a range of pages. For this type of situation, page numbers are given in regular type. When an illustration on a particular topic appears elsewhere in the text, and not on the same page with its related text topic, the page number is given in italic type: *478*. When several listings are given for a topic, the main listing is underlined.

DATE DUE

AUG 2 6 2002			
AUG 3 0 2002			
1/31/03			
AG 30 '03			
JA 17 '04			
3 '05			
MR 13 '06			
5/31/11			

DEMCO 38-296